THE ORIGINS OF THE CIVIL RIGHTS MOVEMENT

Black Communities Organizing for Change

Aldon D. Morris

THE FREE PRESS

To the spirit of
W. E. B. DuBois, Martin Luther King, Jr.,
and freedom fighters throughout the world

The Free Press
A Division of Simon & Schuster Inc.
1230 Avenue of the Americas
New York, New York 10020

First Free Press Paperback Edition 1986

Printed in the United States of America

printing number

    25 27 29 30 28 26 24

Library of Congress Cataloging in Publication Data

Morris, Aldon D.
  The origins of the civil rights movement.

  Bibliography: p.
  Includes index.
    1. Afro-Americans—Civil rights. 2. Afro-Americans
—Southern States—History—20th century. 3. United
States—Race relations. 4. Southern States—Race
relations. I. Title.
E185.61.M845   1984   305.8'96073'075   84-10272
ISBN 0-02-922130-7 pbk.

CONTENTS

PREFACE

This book grew out of my life experiences as a black American and my scholarly interests as a sociologist. I spent my early years in the Mississippi Delta and moved to Chicago during my early adolescent years. Ella Baker, that great woman who has inspired so many people to struggle for human dignity and social justice, once told me that I had experienced a double dose of American racism, the Southern and Northern versions.

I vividly remember the South of the 1950s, where whites ruled supreme and blacks struggled under a system of oppression in many ways like that experienced by black South Africans today. The memory of the unpunished murder of young Emmett Till in 1955 makes my blood boil even now. My move to Chicago rudely awakened me to the reality that the North was no Promised Land but a bastion of racial segregation and discrimination. Social inequality numbs the minds and destroys the hopes of millions of Northern inner-city youths at very early ages. The brutal predawn murder of Black Panther leaders in their sleep by local and federal law officers in Chicago in 1968 showed the lengths to which this society will go to prevent black liberation.

The civil rights movement caught my interest on first acquaintance as a force I thought capable of transforming race relations in America. As a young adult, even as the dogs were lunging at demonstrators in Birmingham in 1963, I wondered about the origins, development, and personalities of this groundbreaking movement. That interest, coupled with the belief that racial and social oppression can be overthrown, culminated in the research and writing of this book.

In 1971 I began my professional training as a sociologist, which eventually led to graduate studies in sociology at the State University of New York at Stony Brook in 1974. The study of sociology provided an intellectual base on which to study social movements. In 1976 I began my research on the civil rights movement, which culminated in my doctoral dissertation and eventually this book.

PURPOSE AND SCOPE OF THE BOOK

The purpose of this book is to explain how this important movement took root and became a major force in American society. It seeks the origins of the civil rights movement by focusing on the crucial first ten years of the modern movement, 1953–1963. I made the choice to concentrate on that ten-year period in the hope that understanding a significant chunk of the movement in depth would be more productive than providing a comprehensive but weak analysis of all the explosive activities and complex movements that rocked America from the 1950s through the 1970s.

Restricting the analysis to a decade enabled me to give attention to many local organizations and movements largely ignored in most of the existing literature. I have provided not definitive histories of these diverse groups and organizations, but only an account and an analysis of the roles they played in the origins of the civil rights movement. I hope this book will generate additional research on these groups, especially regarding their efforts toward social change.

Another object of study for this book is the role of the black masses in the civil rights movement. Social scientists for too long have portrayed the masses as a flock of sheep reacting blindly to uncontrollable forces. Such a stereotype discounts the complex decision-making and actions undertaken by ordinary participants in the course of a social movement and robs the masses of the creativity and courage they often show. My research confirmed my appreciation of the creativity of the black masses by providing many concrete illustrations of this creativity in action.

ACKNOWLEDGMENTS

This book is even more a collective effort than most. My first debt is to the civil rights activists listed in the Appendix who agreed to participate in long interviews. These individuals searched their memories and collected papers to provide me with information as accurate as they could make it. Many of them even reviewed parts of the manuscript to make sure that I had presented their accounts as faithfully as possible. The response of these activists to the interviews reflects the maturity and sophistication they brought to the civil rights movement.

My academic debts are vast. Lewis A. Coser, a distinguished Professor of Sociology at Stony Brook, who served as my dissertation chairman, urged me to complete this work and made his wisdom available at every step of the research. Professor Charles Perrow, now at Yale, as a member of my dissertation committee constantly challenged my ideas in ways that generated new insights. Professors Paget Henry, Leslie Owens, and Fred Dube, also members of my committee, provided the dialogue crucial to any author.

My colleagues in the Center for Research on Social Organization at the University of Michigan read drafts of the manuscript and provided important criticisms that led me to refine and expand many of the ideas contained in this volume. My sincere thanks go to Professors William Gamson, Charles Tilly, Mayer Zald, Walter Allen, Mark Chesler, and Jeffery Paige. Professors William Wilson of the University of Chicago, Charles U. Smith of Florida A. & M., and Gary Marx of the Massachusetts Institute of Technology also provided critiques of the manuscript and helped guide me through the complex process of publication.

I also owe intellectual debts to Professors George Danns and Doug McAdam, both of whom were fellow graduate students at Stony Brook. My stimulating intellectual exchanges with them were all the more valuable because we were peers. My former teacher Richard Maxwell, Jr. of Olive Harvey College was instrumental in introducing me to the systematic study of black protest. I am sure they will see their imprint on the pages to follow. My wife, Kim Morris, read several drafts of the manuscript even as she worked and watched after our daughters, Kiana and Yondi. As she reads this book I am sure she will recognize many passages that were revised because she insisted that "these ideas are just not clear enough."

The following people played important roles either in the editing of this book or in the actual research process: Laura Wolff of The Free Press; Dr. Howard B. Gotlieb, Director of Special Collections at Boston University's Mugar Library; Conley Hughes of Boston University; Walter and Rose Davis of Tougaloo College; Philippa Jackson of the Smithsonian Institution; Arlene Mays, Martha Prescod Norman, Marsha Church, Cedric Herring, Melinda Hicks, Clarence Worsham, Mary Hartness, Janet Somers, and Sheila Wilder, all of the University of Michigan; and Valda Lovelace. I would also like to thank my mother, Mary Lyles, Freddie, Terry, Norm, Jerry, Gary, Olu, and Donnie for keeping the faith.

Finally, funds provided by the National Science Foundation and the Minority Fellowship Program (MFP) of the American Sociological Association made this research possible. Scholars associated with the MFP also provided intellectual support for this project.

INTRODUCTION

This book is about protest and conflict. It is a study of the first decade, ending in 1963, of the Southern civil rights movement. Black Americans, like oppressed groups elsewhere, have rarely accepted the subordinate position forced upon them by the larger white society. American racism and exploitation have therefore generated black protest. Social scientists have documented the rebellious spirit and acts of protest by blacks as they lay shackled in the holds of slave ships, labored in the fields of Southern landowners, and settled into the urban ghettos. At times the spirit of protest was expressed subtly in a black spiritual or a defiant glance. At other times protest burst forth in such organized and collective forms as the slave revolts, the Garvey movement, and riots. The organized and collective form of black protest is the subject of this book.

More specifically, the task here is to explore and analyze the origins and development of the "modern civil rights movement." That term refers to the black movement that emerged in the South during the 1950s, when large masses of black people became directly involved in economic boycotts, street marches, mass meetings, going to jail by the thousands, and a whole range of disruptive tactics commonly referred to as nonviolent direct action. The word that best expresses the spirit of this period is confrontation.

Certainly, any attempt to date a social movement is risky. My chosen starting point is June 1953. In that month the first major battle of the modern civil rights movement took place in Baton Rouge, Louisiana, where blacks successfully carried out a mass boycott against that city's segregated bus system. The authorities were forced to make concessions to the demands of the black masses. It will be argued later that the Baton Rouge protest represented a turning point in that the famous 1955–56 Montgomery bus boycott and similar confrontations immediately afterward were partly inspired by the Baton Rouge effort and to some extent modeled after it.

To contend that the 1953 Baton Rouge boycott was an important starting point is not to imply that the modern movement was unrelated to previous civil rights activities and protest movements. Organized protest against white domination has always been one of the cornerstones of the black experience. Most Americans have some knowledge of certain dramatic confrontations between blacks and whites. Yet the larger significance of black protest lies in the fact that it is forever present in some form. This persistent struggle has given rise to a protest tradition, which includes hundreds of slave revolts, the underground railroad, numerous protest organizations, the Garvey movement, and A. Philip Randolph's March on Washington Movement (MOWM). The tradition also encompasses bitter experiences and memories—lynch victims and murdered civil rights workers—that accompany oppressive social conditions.

The tradition of protest is transmitted across generations by older relatives, black educational institutions, churches, and protest organizations. Blacks interested in social change inevitably gravitate to this "protest community," where they hope to find solutions to a complex problem. Once the contact is made the newcomer becomes a link in the tradition. Thus the tradition is perpetually rejuvenated by new blood.

The modern civil rights movement fits solidly into this rich tradition of protest. Like the slave revolts, the Garvey movement, and the March on Washington Movement, it was highly organized.[1] Its significant use of the black religious community to accomplish political goals also linked the modern movement to the earlier mass movements, which also relied heavily on the church.[2] Finally, the modern movement was directly linked to the activism of the 1940s via civil rights organizations and activists who played important roles in both periods.

The March on Washington Movement, organized in 1941, was especially important as a forerunner to the modern civil rights movement. The MOWM demonstrated conclusively that masses of blacks could be organized for collective protest. During the MOWM, huge mass meetings and other forms of collective protest were organized across the country. Moreover, A. Philip Randolph, the leader of the MOWM, anticipated the upheavals of the 1950s and 1960s when in 1943 he explicitly called for mass nonviolent demonstrations against Jim Crow laws, to be modeled after Gandhi's passive resistance movement in India.[3] The threat of such demonstrations was enough to force Pres-

ident Roosevelt to issue executive orders forbidding racial discrimination in defense industries. The MOWM played a significant role in
inspiring the formation of the Congress of Racial Equality (CORE) in
1942 and thrust a cadre of nonviolent leaders such as James Farmer,
Bayard Rustin, and E. D. Nixon to the forefront of black protest. In the
early 1940s a nucleus of these activists became convinced that a black
nonviolent movement could be launched in the United States. They
would become key leaders of the modern movement.

The birth of the MOWM and CORE during the 1940s introduced
new methods of protest to the black community but did not supplant
the older NAACP and its legal approach. Rather, by the late 1940s there
was a real possibility that legal and mass-oriented approaches could
work simultaneously. That possibility came to fruition in the modern
civil rights movement, which incorporated not only CORE and the
mass-oriented leaders but also NAACP and the large number of activists associated with it.

The modern civil rights movement emerged in the South, where a
rich protest tradition was, and remains, firmly entrenched. Most slave
revolts occurred in the South, and the majority of Garvey's organizational branches were there.[4] Similarly, in 1918, just one year after the
NAACP began its organizing effort in the South, new members there
doubled the total membership of 1917.[5] The NAACP had been founded
in New York eight years earlier and had previously focused most of its
organizing activities on the North.

The modern civil rights movement broke from the protest tradition
of the past in at least two crucial ways. One, it was the first time that
large masses of blacks directly confronted and effectively disrupted the
normal functioning of groups and institutions thought to be responsible
for their oppression. The hallmark of the modern civil rights movement
is that these mass confrontations were widespread and sustained over
a long period of time in the face of heavy repression. Two, this was the
first time in American history that blacks adopted nonviolent tactics as
a mass technique for bringing about social change. For these reasons
the modern civil rights movement demands attention on its own terms.
Indeed, it will be years before the impact of the modern civil rights
movement on the preexisting protest tradition can be properly assessed.

THE APPROACH

Social movements can be studied from a variety of perspectives. Perspectives determine which questions are asked and significantly shape
the explanations that are thought to provide the key answers. A per-

spective is valuable if it provides answers to a set of core questions that enhance our basic understanding of an important phenomenon. Perspectives do not simply represent different opinions on a matter. Perspectives clash. The conclusions to which they ultimately lead are often contradictory. Perspectives may even differ over what are considered the essential elements of a phenomenon. Thus the question of which perspective is right—or more applicable to the problem at hand—inevitably arises. The value of a perspective can be judged by the quality of the insights it provides and the quality of the evidence assembled to support those insights.

In the present inquiry an indigenous perspective is used to study how the modern civil rights movement actually worked. The assumption is that mass protest is a product of the organizing efforts of activists functioning through a well-developed indigenous base. A well-developed indigenous base includes the institutions, organizations, leaders, communication networks, money, and organized masses within a dominated group. Such a base also encompasses cultural elements—music, oratory, and so on—of a dominated group that play a direct role in the organization and mobilization of protest. I argue here that it is within this indigenous base that the basic funding patterns, social resources, and organized masses are concentrated and activated for protest. A central concern of the indigenous perspective is to examine the ways in which organizers transform indigenous resources into power resources and marshals them in conflict situations to accomplish political ends. This approach to social movements will be demonstrated through an examination of the civil rights movement. Central issues addressed are: What were the basic social dynamics of the modern civil rights movement that made it a force to be reckoned with? Did the major events and confrontations of the movement arise from spontaneous explosions, or were they the products of skillfully organized efforts and preexisting institutions? How was the movement financed and sustained? What were the basic strategies and tactics of the movement? Were they used effectively against the opposition?

This book will demonstrate how blacks organized and sustained the movement. The spotlight will fall on the primary role that indigenous black institutions, organizations, leaders, and resources played in the rise and development of the movement. It will be argued that internal organization was the critical factor that enabled the movement to gather momentum and endure in the face of state power and widespread repression.

Most accounts of the civil rights movement make reference to the importance of the black church, but the central and overpowering role that the church played in this movement remains largely a story untold.

This book places the crucial connection between the indigenous church and the movement at center stage. Similarly, the commonly accepted assessment of Dr. Martin Luther King is that he was a great symbolic leader but possessed neither organizing ability nor a firm organizational base within the black community. Some even suggest that Dr. King was a media creation. These opinions will be tested by analyzing the Southern Christian Leadership Conference (SCLC) as an indigenous organization in its own right. Available evidence indicates that the SCLC remained at the organizational center of the movement because it had real power, and it was powerful because it functioned as the decentralized arm of the mass-based black church.

The NAACP and CORE played important roles in the movement. In examining the historical relationship of NAACP and CORE and with the black community we find that the importance of these two organizations stems from sources conventionally overlooked by scholars. Then, too, there were several predominantly white organizations closely allied with the movement: Highlander Folk School (HFS), the Southern Conference Educational Fund (SCEF), and the Fellowship of Reconciliation (FOR). The roles of these organizations will be clarified through an investigation of the important ties linking them to the movement's indigenous base.

In early 1960 the student sit-ins at lunch counters and the birth of the Student Non-Violent Coordinating Committee (SNCC) immediately brought the movement to a new level of intensity. Little is known about how the sit-ins actually operated. The commonly held view is that they were a spontaneous collegiate phenomenon, but evidence to the contrary will be presented in this study. The argument presented here is that the sit-ins spread rapidly thanks to indigenous leadership, organizations, and support. The birth of SNCC in 1960 created another source of power for the movement but fostered interorganizational tensions between the student and clergy wings of the movement. These tensions and the growing power of the movement will be brought into full view when the major confrontations at Albany, Georgia, in 1961 and Birmingham, Alabama, in 1963 are examined.

In short, this book will investigate how the modern civil rights movement unfolded over a ten-year period. The emphasis is on how a dominated group organized and propelled a powerful movement. The organizational forces—the church, SCLC, NAACP, CORE, SNCC, HFS, SCEF, and FOR—and the participants will be the primary objects of attention. The people of this movement energized it with music, trenchant sermons, and challenging oratory—all potent indigenous forces. My analysis will take these cultural factors into account in following the action of the movement. In addition, because the building process of an indigenous movement is heavily influenced by the opposition, the analysis will pay close attention to the white power structures of the South.

EVIDENCE

This study of the civil rights movement is based on several sources of data. Most of the analysis is supported by information from primary sources: formal interviews with leaders and participants in the movement and documents generated by movement participants. Secondary sources were used to complement the primary data.[6] A researcher is indeed fortunate to be in a position to collect information from actors who were directly involved in the drama.

1

DOMINATION, CHURCH, AND THE NAACP

THE TRIPARTITE SYSTEM OF RACIAL DOMINATION

By the 1950's Southern whites had established a comprehensive system of domination over blacks. This system of domination protected the privileges of white society and generated tremendous human suffering for blacks. In the cities and rural areas of the South, blacks were controlled economically, politically, and personally. Those three dimensions were combined in what can be called a "tripartite system of domination."

Economic oppression emerged in the fact that blacks were heavily concentrated in the lowest-paying and dirtiest jobs the cities had to offer. In a typical Southern city during the 1950s at least 75 percent of black men in the labor force were employed in unskilled jobs.[1] They were the janitors, porters, cooks, machine operators, and common laborers. By contrast, only about 25 percent of white males were employed in these menial occupations. In the typical Southern city approximately 50 percent of black women in the labor force were domestics, while slightly less than 1 percent of white women were employed as domestics. Another 20 percent of black women were lowly paid service workers, while less than 10 percent of white women were so employed. In 1950 social inequality in the work place meant that nonwhite families earned nationally only 54 percent of the median income of white families.[2]

1

The negative impact of racial inequality in the work place was more than financial. In factories and other places of employment, workers with authority over other workers enjoyed greater freedom, status, and deference. Being at the bottom of the work hierarchy, blacks were controlled in the work place by whites. Positions vested with authority—managerial and supervisory—were almost always filled by whites.

Whites had the jobs that required white shirts and neckties. Whites decided who would be promoted, fired, and made to work the hardest. While black men in greasy work clothes labored in these conditions, their mothers, wives, and sisters cleaned the houses of white women and prepared their meals. Blacks entered into these exploitative economic relationships because the alternative was starvation or at least unemployment, which was usually much higher than average in the black community.

Southern urban black communities of this period were oppressed politically because blacks were systematically excluded from the political process. As a general rule there were no black officials in city and state governments, because such measures as the poll tax, all-white primaries, the "grandfather clause," intimidation, and violence disfranchised blacks as a group. Law and order were usually maintained in the black community by white police forces.[3] It was common for law officials to use terror and brutality against blacks. Due process of law was virtually nonexistent because the courts were controlled by white judges and juries, which routinely decided in favor of whites. The white power structure made the decisions about how the public resources of the cities were to be divided. Blacks received far less than whites, because in practice blacks had few citizenship rights and were not members of the polity.

Compounding the economic and political oppression was the system of segregation that denied blacks personal freedoms routinely enjoyed by whites. Segregation was an arrangement that set blacks off from the rest of humanity and labeled them as an inferior race. Blacks were forced to use different toilets, drinking fountains, waiting rooms, parks, schools, and the like. These separate facilities forever reminded blacks of their low status by their wretched condition, which contrasted sharply with the well-kept facilities reserved for whites only. The "colored" and "white only" signs that dotted the buildings and public places of a typical Southern city expressed the reality of a social system committed to the subjugation of blacks and the denial of their human dignity and self-respect.

Segregation meant more than separation. To a considerable extent it determined behavior between the races. Blacks had to address whites in a tone that conveyed respect and use formal titles. Sexual relationships between black men and white women were viewed as the ultimate infraction against the system of segregation. Black males were therefore advised to stare downward when passing a white woman so that she would have no excuse to accuse him of rape and have his life snatched away. Indeed, segregation was a personal form of oppression that severely restricted the physical movement, behavioral choices, and experiences of the individual.

The tripartite system of racial domination—economic, political, and personal oppression—was backed by legislation and the iron fist of Southern governments. In the short run all members of the white group had a stake in racial domination, because they derived privileges from it. Poor and middle-class whites benefited because the segregated labor force prevented blacks from competing with them for better-paying jobs. The Southern white ruling class benefited because blacks supplied them with cheap labor and a weapon against the labor movement, the threat to use unemployed blacks as strikebreakers in labor disputes. Finally, most Southern whites benefited psychologically from the system's implicit assurance that no matter how poor or uneducated, they were always better than the niggers.

Meager incomes and the laws of segregation restricted city blacks to slum neighborhoods. In the black part of town housing was substandard, usually dilapidated, and extremely overcrowded.[4] The black children of the Southern ghetto received fewer years of formal schooling than white children, and what they did receive was usually of poorer quality. On the black side of town life expectancy was lower because of poor sanitary conditions and too little income to pay for essential medical services. Adverse social conditions also gave rise to a "black-against-black" crime problem, which flourished, in part, because its elimination was not a high priority of the usually all-white police forces.

Ironically, urban segregation in the South had some positive consequences. It facilitated the development of black institutions and the building of close-knit communities when blacks, irrespective of education and income, were forced to live in close proximity and frequent the same social institutions. Maids and janitors came into close contact with clergy, schoolteachers, lawyers, and doctors. In the typical Southern city, the black professional stratum constituted only about 3 percent of the black community, and its services had no market outside the black community. Skin color alone, not class background or gender, locked blacks inside their segregated communities. Thus segregation itself ensured that the diverse skills and talents of individuals at all income and educational levels were concentrated within the black community. Cooperation between the various black strata was an important collective resource for survival.

Segregation provided the constraining yet nurturing environment out of which a complex urban black society developed. The influx of migrants from rural areas intensified the process of institution-building. The heavy concentration of blacks in small areas in the cities engendered efficient communication networks. In cities, white domination was not as direct as on the plantations, because urbanization tended to foster impersonal, formal relationships between the races.[5] Within these compact segregated communities blacks began to sense their collective predicament as well as their collective strength. Growth in the black colleges and in the black church was especially pronounced.[6] It was the church more than any other institution that provided an escape from the harsh realities associated with domination. Inside its walls blacks were temporarily free to forget oppression while singing, listening, praying, and shouting. The church also provided an institutional setting where oppression could be openly discussed and resources could be developed to organize collective resistance. By the 1950s the tripartite system of domination was firmly entrenched in Southern cities, but in those cities were born the social forces that would challenge the very foundations of Jim Crow.

THE CHURCH

The black church functioned as the institutional center of the modern civil rights movement. Churches provided the movement with an organized mass base; a leadership of clergymen largely economically independent of the larger white society and skilled in the art of managing people and resources; an institutionalized financial base through which protest was financed; and meeting places where the masses planned tactics and strategies and collectively committed themselves to the struggle.

Successful social movements usually comprise people who are willing to make great sacrifices in a single-minded pursuit of their goals. The black church supplied the civil rights movement with a collective enthusiasm generated through a rich culture consisting of songs, testimonies, oratory, and prayers that spoke directly to the needs of an oppressed group. Many black churches preached that oppression is sinful and that God sanctions protest aimed at eradicating social evils. Besides, the church gave the civil rights movement continuity with its antecedents in the long-standing religious traditions of black people. Finally, the black church served as a relatively autonomous force in the movement, being an indigenous institution owned and controlled by blacks.

Scholars of the black church have consistently argued that it is the dominant institution within black society.[7] It has provided the organizational framework for most activities of the community—economic, political, and educational endeavors as well as religious ones. The black church was unique in that it was organized and developed by an oppressed group shut off from the institutional life of the larger society. Historically, the institutions of the larger society were of very little use to blacks. Blacks were never equal partners in those economic, political, and cultural institutions and in fact were systematically excluded from their decision-making processes. This institutional subordination naturally prevented blacks from identifying with the institutions of the larger society. In short, the larger society denied blacks the institutional access and outlets necessary to normal social existence.

The black church filled a large part of the institutional void by providing support and direction for the diverse activities of an oppressed group. It furnished outlets for social and artistic expression; a forum for the discussion of important issues; a social environment that developed, trained, and disciplined potential leaders from all walks of life; and meaningful symbols to engender hope, enthusiasm, and a resilient group spirit. The church was a place to observe, participate in, and experience the reality of owning and directing an institution free from the control of whites. The church was also an arena where group interests could be articulated and defended collectively. For all these reasons and a host of others, the black church has served as the organizational hub of black life.

The urban church, by virtue of its quality of religious services and potential for political action, developed into a more efficient organization than its rural counterpart. Even by the early 1930s urban churches had become significantly more powerful and resourceful than rural churches. Urban churches were better financed, more numerous, and larger in membership. Urban ministers usually received more formal education and earned higher salaries than their rural counterparts.[8] Stable leadership emerged as higher salaries led to a lower turnover rate among ministers, allowing them to become full-time pastors. The urban church was able to offer its congregations more activities and programs, which meant more committees and other formal bodies to run them, and greater organized cooperation within the church.

The great migration of blacks from rural to urban areas between 1910 and 1960 was responsible for the tremendous growth of the urban church throughout that period. By 1930 Southern cities had so many black churches that Mays and Nicholson, in their pioneering study of the black church, asked whether Negroes were overchurched. They found that in 1930 the Negroes of Atlanta constituted 33 percent of the total population but owned 57.5 percent of the churches; in Birmingham Negroes constituted 38 percent of the population while having 53 percent of the total churches; in New Orleans, the black population was 28 percent but owned 52 percent of the churches; and in Richmond blacks consistuted 29 percent of the population but owned 38 percent of the churches. They found similar ratios in Charleston, Richmond, and Memphis.[9]

Between 1940 and 1960 the black population in Birmingham and Montgomery, Alabama, increased by 84 and 40 percent, respectively. In Baton Rouge, Louisiana, the black population increased by 453 percent over the same period, while in Tallahassee, Florida, it increased by 145 percent.[10] Newly urbanized Southern blacks established close ties with the institution they knew best, the church. Numerous problems attended the major shift from rural to urban life, and the church facilitated the transition by offering valuable friendships and social networks through which the migrants could assimilate into urban life. Moreover, the Southern urban church was similar to its rural counterpart in that it provided an institutional alternative to, and an escape from, the racism and hostility of the larger society. Behind the church doors was a friendly and warm environment where black people could be temporarily at peace with themselves while displaying their talents and aspirations before an empathetic audience. For these reasons the urban church, like the rural church of the South, continued to function as the main community center. However, the great migration made it possible for the urban church to function on a scale unattainable in rural settings.

The urban churches of the South became organizations of considerable social power. The principal resource of the church was its organized mass base. The church not only organized the black masses but also commanded their allegiance. The fact that the church has been financially supported by its economically deprived parishioners clearly demonstrates that allegiance. Furthermore, the black community has always contributed the voluntary labor necessary to meet the church's considerable needs in its role as the main community center. W. E. B. DuBois, commenting on the large volume of church activity, stated, "so frequent are . . . church exercises that there are few Negro churches which are not open four to seven nights a week and sometimes one or two afternoons in addition."[11] These activities emerged from an elaborate organizational structure.

The typical church had a well-defined division of labor, with numerous standing committees and organized groups. Each group was task-oriented and coordinated its activities through authority structures. Individuals were held accountable for their assigned duties, and important conflicts were resolved by the minister, who usually exercised ultimate authority over the congregation. A strong work ethic existed in the church, where individuals and groups were routinely

singled out and applauded for their contributions. This practice promoted a strong group identification with the church as members were
made to feel important and respected, an experience denied to blacks
by the institutions of the larger society.

The black church is a complex organization but not a typical bureaucracy. Behavior within the church is organized, but much of it is
not highly formalized. The personality of the minister plays a central
role in structuring church activities. A striking feature of the church is
the considerable loyalty and commitment usually displayed by church
members toward the minister. The relationship between the minister
and the congregation is often one of charismatic leader to followers
rather than the formalized levels of command found in large corpora-
tions. In church people express their feelings and often mingle in informal groups long after service has ended. This fluid and informal
quality of the church has led some to view the church erroneously as
a nonorganization fueled by emotionalism.[12] Consistent with this view
is the notion that the church serves as a convenient safety valve for the
emotional release of dangerous tensions. While there is some truth to
this claim, it overlooks the extraordinary degree to which the church
is a sound mass-based organization through which diverse goals are
achieved.

The black minister presides over the church hierarchy. He is the
individual ultimately responsible for the overall functioning of the diverse committees and groups. In DuBois's words, "The preacher is sure
to be a man of executive ability, a leader of men, a shrewd and affable
president of a large and intricate corporation."[13] As a leader, the minister oversees the work force of the church and delegates authority
throughout its organizational structure. The minister, more than anyone else, determines the goals of the church and identifies the causes
to be supported by the congregation. The social power of the black minister stems from his personal persuasiveness and his considerable control over the collective resources of the church.

Charisma and the Black Church

Another source of the black minister's power is charisma. Max Weber,
the eminent sociologist of charismatic movements, argued that charismatic leadership arose outside of established organizations and group
norms.[14] But in the civil rights movements the process worked differently. The black church, a well-established institution, produced and
thrived on charismatic relationships between minister and followers.
Churches, especially the prestigious or leading ones, demanded min-

isters who could command the respect, support, and allegiance of congregations through their strong, magnetic personalities. Furthermore, the majority of black ministers claimed to have been "called" to the ministry directly by God or at least by God's son through such agencies as dreams, personal revelation, or divine inspiration. Once such a call was accepted, a minister continued—in his own perception and, usually, that of his congregation—to have a personal relationship with God. Clearly, the congregation's belief that such individuals enjoyed a direct pipeline to the Divine served to set them off from the rest of the population.

Charisma, however, is based not so much on the beliefs held by charismatic individuals or their followers as on performance. Experience is often crucial to performance, and most ministers who became charismatic civil rights leaders brought a great deal of experience into the movement. Most of them had grown up in the church and understood its inner workings. They knew that the highly successful minister developed a strong, magnetic personality capable of attracting and holding a following. Many of the ministers were college graduates with considerable training in theological studies. It cannot be overemphasized that much of these ministers' training occurred in black colleges and universities under the direction of leading black educators and theologians of the day. They were taught and counseled by such men as Dr. Benjamin Mays, C. D. Hubert, and S. A. Archer. The Reverend C. K. Steele, one of the early leaders of the movement, remarked: "These are strong men and you could hardly sit under them seriously and sincerely, without being affected."[15] He states further that these educators and theologians, who themselves had struggled to get an education, stressed such values as human dignity, personhood, manhood, and courage. These became core values of the civil rights movement.

During this period black universities and colleges were closely linked to the black church. Thus, a significant number of the leading professors were also ministers or closely attached to the ministerial profession. It was not unusual for the students to be required to attend daily or weekly chapel services, during which these influential cultural figures, expert in public speaking and the art of dramatic communication, attempted to imbue the students with certain values. In college as well as in the church, the future leaders of the movement were exposed to and taught the excitement and art of stimulating, persuading, and influencing crowds by individuals who had mastered the art of charisma.

The black church combines the mundane (finance of buildings, maintenance services, committee meetings, reports, choir rehearsals) and the charismatic (strong face-to-face personal relationships that foster allegiance, trust, and loyalty, and give rise to a shared symbolic world that provides an interpretation of earthly affairs and the anticipated after life). The charismatic element requires no allegiance to man, the government, the "city fathers," or traditional norms of behavior. For example, when Birmingham's blacks began to boycott buses, the Southern Conference Educational Fund reported:

> *The city's famous police commissioner, Eugene "Bull" Connor, issued a decree that no Negro minister should urge his people to stay off the buses. Mr. Shuttlesworth's response was typical: Only God can tell me what to say in the pulpit. And I'm going to tell my people to stay off those buses if I have to go to Kilby prison.*[16]

But, of course, allegiance was conferred by the congregation on the earthly but charismatic minister. Such ministers had to be aware of the power of charisma and prepared to use it. The Reverend C. T. Vivian, a key activist and minister, was asked whether ministers were aware of charisma as a resource. He replied, "Of course. After all, we were preachers . . . remember we're Baptist preachers. We know who controls meetings and things. We know what kind of people make things happen and what kind of people who just sit around and preside over something."[17] They therefore used their position, experience, and charisma to accomplish goals. The black Baptist church, in fact, encouraged the development of charisma through its ministerial recruiting procedures. The task of obtaining a pastorate confronted the ministerial candidate immediately upon finishing seminary training (or equivalent preparation). The first step in this occupational quest was usually to be invited to deliver a trial sermon to a congregation in need of a minister. The primary objectives of the candidate were to deliver a powerful sermon, to relate socially to the congregation members, and, above all, to impress them with his abilities. The Reverend Vivian explained that the black minister came up from the rank-and-file:

> *He had to be nominated to that post. He had to be voted in. He had to be made the pastor. Nobody sent him down. No bishop said here's who you're [the congregation] going to have whether you like it or not. That minister had to make it out of nothing, what we call the rough side of the mountain.*[18]

Vivian goes on to make the point that charisma is a central ingredient which heavily influences whether the candidate will be successful:

> *You don't make it simply by standing around and going yes, yes. Or by flashing your degree in front of people every fifteen minutes. They could care less. If you've got it, prove it. That's all folks are saying. "You know, don't tell me how many letters behind your name, just*

do it. We'll see what the letters mean." That's what folks say. "Can you really deal with us?" is what they're asking. "We have a bundle of needs and problems, and so on, out here. What you got to say to that? What can you do with it, and for it, in spite of it?" Lots of things you have to do as leaders in spite of all those problems. It takes charisma.[19]

A statement by Martin Luther King, Jr., regarding his trial sermon at Dexter Avenue Baptist Church is illuminating. He confesses that although he had preached many times in churches, "I was very conscious that this time I was on trial. How could I best impress the congregation? Since the membership was educated and intelligent, should I attempt to interest it with a display of scholarship? Or should I preach just as I had always done, depending finally on the inspiration of the spirit of God? I decided to follow the latter course."[20] It was the latter course that would allow him and the congregation the freedom to set in motion the dynamics of the charismatic relationship.

Students of charismatic leadership have persuasively argued that if individuals are to be recognized as charismatic leaders, they must personify, symbolize, and articulate the goals, aspirations, and strivings of the group they aspire to lead. The ministers who were to become the charismatic leaders of the movement occupied strategic community positions which enabled them to become extremely familiar with the needs and aspirations of blacks.

The black minister, because of his occupation, listened to and counseled people about their financial woes, family problems, and health problems, as well as problems stemming from discrimination, prejudice, and powerlessness. By the same token, the black preacher was the figure who witnessed the resiliency, pride, and dignity that resided in what Dr. W. E. B. DuBois had characterized as the "souls of black folk." The ministers listened to the educational and occupational aspirations of countless black children, along with the pleas of their parents that God and the white man give their offspring the chance to have it better than they had had. Part of the minister's job was to single out for praise those individuals in the congregation who landed impressive jobs, were admitted to colleges and universities, or made any other personal stride.

Thus the black ministers of the 1950s knew black people because they had shared their innermost secrets and turmoils. They were happy when blacks progressed, and, with their fellows, they recoiled in shock when a member of their race was tarred, feathered, and lynched while the white mob drank beer and assembled for "show time." The minister was firmly anchored in the center of the ebb and flow of the social and cultural forces of the black community.

Specifically, the words and actions of such leaders as Martin Luther King, Jr., Fred Shuttlesworth, and C. K. Steele seemed to radiate the qualities required to jar loose the tripartite system of domination that paralyzed the black community. Their displays of courage, dignity, integrity, and burning desire for freedom earned the approval of the black masses, because such values were deeply embedded in the social fabric of black society. Moreover, these ministers, with their oratorical talents and training, were able to instill in people a sense of mission and commitment to social change. The words they used were effective because they symbolized and simplified the complex yearnings of a dominated group. This is one of the reasons blacks in the movement showed little hesitation in accepting such personalities as their charismatic leaders.

The Collective Power of Churches

To some extent the large variety of churches represented social divisions within the black community. Conflict and competition among churches were not uncommon. At times conflict even arose between the minister and factions within a church, producing splinter groups. Yet the churches had many institutional commonalities. For one thing, they all had the responsibility of spiritually and emotionally soothing an oppressed group. Most of their congregations sang the same songs, were inspired by similar sermons, and recognized the importance of cooperation and of giving financially to their churches and other worthy causes. Therefore, it can be said that a common church culture existed in the black community. The church culture and even the churches themselves, however, could not provide the kind of social network that would be necessary to launch mass movements. That need was satisfied by formal and informal interaction among the clergymen who headed the various churches.

It was (and is) common for black ministers in a community and even in different communities to have personal relationships among themselves. They met at conventions, community gatherings, civic affairs, and the like. At times they exchanged pulpit duties and encouraged their choirs to sing at the churches of colleagues. Furthermore, black ministers in a community were linked formally by either a city ministerial alliance or an interdenominational alliance, through which they were able to debate and confer on issues important to the black community.[21]

Within the ministerial alliances were to be found ministers of the poor, the educated, the unemployed, professionals, laborers, housemaids—indeed, the entire spectrum of black society. If these ministers, through their informal and formal bodies, could be persuaded to support protest activity, each could then mobilize his own slice of the community. The National Baptist Convention, one such body, operates on the national level with a membership of more than 5 million.

Scholars of the church have consistently noted how rapidly and efficiently information is transmitted to the black community from the pulpit. This reliable channel for disseminating information greatly enhances the possibility for mass action. The minister can deliver any type of message to the congregation; his salary is paid by the church, which frees him from white economic pressures. Moreover, with their disciplined work forces churches are able to act collectively. Once a plan of action is agreed on by a number of congregations it can be implemented systematically. Thousands of dollars can be raised by a number of churches in a short time to finance a concerted plan.

The impressive social power generated when black churches act collectively has been appreciated by astute members of the white power structure. Whites have sometimes dealt with the black community by first gaining the cooperation of certain clergymen, who have helped them elicit favorable action from blacks through use of the church's influence. On the other hand, the same social power is essential to the furtherance of black interests, particularly through the organization of collective protest and political action. Several prominent scholars of the church noted this possibility even before the civil rights movement.[22] Gunnar Myrdal, for instance, perceptively wrote in 1944 that "potentially, the Negro church is undoubtedly a power institution. It has the Negro masses organized and, if the church bodies decided to do so, they could line the Negroes behind a program."[23]

In the chapters to follow it will be clear that a significant number of urban churches of the South and North acted collectively, and out of those efforts the first major battles of the modern civil rights movement emerged. However, another organization central to the black community kept the flames of protest alive long before the church became the vanguard. That organization was the NAACP.

THE NATIONAL ASSOCIATION
FOR THE ADVANCEMENT OF COLORED PEOPLE

Before the outbreak of the modern civil rights movement, the National Association for the Advancement of Colored People (NAACP) was clearly the dominant black protest organization. The NAACP, in contrast to the church, was organized specifically to fight for equal rights for black Americans. It was founded in 1909 and 1910 by a group of black and white intellectuals vehemently opposed to the racism that confronted the black community.[24] From the beginning the NAACP was interracial and Northern-based, with headquarters in New York City. The white founders were highly educated and distinguished within their professions or businesses. A number of them were wealthy philanthropists, and all were influential in the larger society.

The black founders were also highly educated professionals. Significant in uniting them was their displeasure over the accommodationist politics of Booker T. Washington. The black organizers of the NAACP maintained that aggressive action was required if blacks were to attain their full citizenship rights. The majority of the black founders came to the NAACP from the militant Niagra Movement, which had been organized several years earlier by W. E. B. DuBois and Monroe Trotter to fight for goals similar to those embraced by the NAACP.

The NAACP evolved as a bureaucratic organization.[25] It did not emerge within the black community, nor were the black masses involved in shaping the organization at the outset. The NAACP began as a small group of black and white intellectuals who intended to organize the black masses to struggle for their rights. With one important exception, all the top administrative positions of the NAACP—President, Chairman of the Executive Committee, Treasurer, Disbursing Treasurer, and Executive Secretary—were originally filled by whites. DuBois, who became the Director of Publicity and Research, was the only black highly placed within the administrative hierarchy.

Decision-making within the NAACP was highly centralized. Most plans of action had to be cleared through the hierarchy in New York. Within a short time detailed rules, regulations, and standard operating procedures were formulated to guide the activities of the NAACP and its branches.[26] Official policies were established by those at the top of the organization. The communication structure was formalized, and information flowed through the hierarchy via memoranda and other approved channels. Organizational protocol became an enduring feature of the NAACP.

The principal tactics through which the NAACP attempted to gain equality for blacks were persuasion and legal action. The early officials of the NAACP believed that much of American racism stemmed from the white man's ignorance of blacks. Early in the twentieth century, when the NAACP was founded, the belief that blacks were innately inferior was widespread. White newspapers and films promoted this view by portraying blacks in a demeaning light. NAACP officials attempted to enlighten white America through massive educational efforts aimed at depicting blacks in a realistic and nonstereotypical manner. NAACP founders, many of whom were versed in the arts and humanities, sought to change public opinion of blacks through press releases, speeches, lobbying, pamphlets, and Crisis, the official organ of the NAACP.[27] Much of this effort was undertaken by the black scholar W. E. B. DuBois, who directed the NAACP's Publicity and Research Department and founded Crisis. DuBois sought to counteract the negative image by conducting studies of blacks and publishing the works of gifted black poets, artists, and writers in Crisis. The NAACP's tactic of educational persuasion, well suited to the intellectual background of its founders, was based on the premise that white Americans would treat blacks as equals once they overcame their own ignorance.

Legal action became the main tactic of the NAACP. Its preeminence was reflected at the outset when Moorfield Storey, a distinguished Boston lawyer, became the NAACP's first president. Storey quickly established a Legal Committee headed by Arthur Spingarn and composed largely of distinguished white attorneys. The NAACP immediately began attacking the system of segregation and racial inequality in the courts. Within a short time the NAACP scored some impressive legal victories. For example, in 1915 the NAACP won a Supreme Court suit that invalidated the "grandfather clause," which made it illegal for most Southern blacks to vote, and in 1927 the organization won a Supreme Court case that began the important legal battle against the all-white primary. Its efforts also led to Supreme Court decisions requiring that blacks be admitted to white universities because they were superior to black universities.[28]

The early legal victories of the NAACP, coupled with educational persuasion, kept protest alive in the black community. Because of these successes the NAACP began spreading to cities outside the North. The organization of Southern branches did not get under way until eight years after the NAACP was organized, when James Weldon Johnson, a black man born and reared in the South, was hired by the NAACP as National Field Secretary and Organizer.[29] Johnson's persistent organizational efforts resulted in the creation of NAACP branches in all the Southern states by the end of 1918.[30] By 1919 Southern membership exceeded that of the North, 42,588 to 38,420.[31] The increasing importance of Southern branches was apparent by 1921, when NAACP officials agreed to hold the annual Conference in the Southern city of Atlanta.

From the very beginning, some Southern black NAACP leaders wanted to move faster than the national office,[32] which produced uneasiness and tensions between the Northern-based NAACP and its all-black Southern branches. However, racial oppression in the South was so deeply ingrained and powerful that in many places the NAACP was the only organized force pushing for change. Indeed, many of the legal cases originated in the South. They covered such varied aspects of oppression as political disfranchisement, segregated transportation, segregated education, lynchings, and so on. Southern whites immediately labeled the NAACP as an "outside agitator" seeking to "stir up trouble" between the races. Southern hostility toward the NAACP was formidable, because the economic and political life of the very people whom the NAACP attempted to organize was largely controlled by whites.

Out of necessity, the NAACP in the South was closely tied to the black church. The church, being independent of the white power structure, was often the only place where the NAACP could meet. Moreover, the NAACP in the South was largely financed through the church, and many of the local NAACP leaders were ministers.[33] Membership exposed these ministers to the workings of an organizational structure outside of the church. Many gained the experience of building NAACP chapters from the ground up and shaping them into organized bodies consonant with the bylaws and rules of national NAACP. They had to learn the NAACP's organizational procedures and protocol, then to make the political tradeoffs necessary to keep their local units in harmony with the national organization. Such activities enhanced the community status of local leaders by bringing them in contact with the famous lawyers and national leaders of NAACP. By the same token, the national NAACP had to cultivate working relationships with the Southern leaders because their local units were important sources of support for the national association.

Ministers were not the only community leaders brought together by the NAACP. Local lawyers, doctors, union organizers, and other professionals developed working relationships with each other by operating through the NAACP. Usually these leaders were already acquainted, and the presence of the NAACP further strengthened their ties.

For all the widespread sympathy and support it has enjoyed in the black community, the NAACP has never been able to organize a mass base. Its membership has seldom included more than 2 percent of the black population. White repression, the NAACP's bureaucratic structure, and the complexity of the legal procedures that absorbed its attention all discouraged mass participation. Individual involvement was often limited to making financial contributions and reporting incidents of racial injustice and discrimination to the local branch. Reports were passed along to the national office for decision on whether or not to litigate. These procedures discouraged mass participation. Local involvement was often confined to the actions of local leaders and a few litigants. Still, the black masses usually respected the NAACP as an organization fighting for their rights.

In summary, the NAACP became the dominant black protest organization for the first half of the twentieth century. Through agitation and legal action it presented an organized challenge to the rampant racism in America and to the racist regimes of the South in particular. The NAACP was particularly important in providing opportunities for local leaders to acquire organizing skills and develop networks through which resources could be pooled. The NAACP set the stage from which most of the leadership of the modern civil rights movement would emerge.

2

BEGINNINGS AND CONFRONTATIONS

THE BATON ROUGE BUS BOYCOTT

In Baton Rouge, the capital of Louisiana, the tripartite system of domination imposed on blacks was firmly in place in 1953. Under the Jim Crow system, every public bus had a "colored section" in the back and a "white section" in the front. If the white section filled up, blacks had to move farther toward the back, carrying with them the sign designating "colored." When blacks filled up the colored section, however, they had to stand even though seats in the white section were vacant. Most of the bus routes passed through the black community, which meant that the colored section was often full and the entire white section empty. In the heart of their own community, blacks had to stand over vacant seats designated for white passengers.

A Jim Crow bus was one of the few places in the South where blacks and whites were segregated under the same roof and in full view of each other. A segregated bus ride dramatized the painful humiliation of the Jim Crow system. White bus drivers often pulled away from a stop before blacks were seated, or even with a boarding black hanging half out of the bus. The Reverend T. J. Jemison, a black minister in Baton Rouge, recalls, "The Negro passenger had been molested and insulted and intimidated and all Negroes at that time were tired of segregation and mistreatment and injustice."[1] Furthermore, the Baton Rouge bus company was overwhelmingly financed by blacks. Their fares accounted for at least two-thirds of the bus company's revenue.[2] The practice of racial segregation on the bus was therefore an economically vulnerable enterprise.

17

In March of 1953 black leaders in Baton Rouge successfully peti-
tioned the City Council to pass an ordinance permitting blacks to be
seated on a first-come-first-served basis. The only stipulation was that
blacks had to sit from the rear to the front of the bus while whites sat
from the front to the rear. The ordinance did not require that any seats
be reserved for whites. When the ordinance went into effect on March
11 blacks began sitting in front seats previously reserved for white customers.

The bus drivers, all of whom were white, refused to accept Ordinance 222 and ordered blacks not to occupy front seats reserved for
whites. When the City Council and black leaders informed the drivers
that the new ordinance had to be obeyed, the drivers decided to go on
strike. They demanded that the four front seats be reserved for whites
and the four rear seats for blacks. As a result of the strike the Attorney
General ruled that Ordinance 222 was illegal because it conflicted with
Louisiana's segregation laws. When the buses began rolling after the
four-day strike, blacks found that drivers were continuing to insist that
they sit in the back.

The Mass Bus Boycott

In June 1953 the black community of Baton Rouge began a mass boycott
against the segregated buses.[3] The official leader of the boycott was the
Reverend T. J. Jemison, pastor of Mt. Zion Baptist, one of the largest
black churches in the city. When white drivers refused to allow blacks
to sit in the front of the bus, Jemison and Raymond Scott made a radio
appeal to blacks not to ride the buses. Reverend Jemison recounts that
the boycott was 100 percent effective: "Nobody rode the bus during
our strike. There were about eight people who didn't hear the call that
night [on the radio] and they rode to work. But by afternoon there was
nobody riding the bus. For ten days not a Negro rode the bus."[4] A New
York Times article in 1953 confirmed that at least 90 percent of the
black passengers refused to ride the buses during the boycott.[5]

The boycott galvanized the black community of Baton Rouge.
Nightly mass meetings were held throughout the seven days of the boycott. They attracted such large numbers that Jemison's church, with a
seating capacity of 1,000, proved to be too small. The meetings were
therefore held in the auditorium of the local segregated public school,
which normally seated about 1,200. On those hot June nights, 2,500 to
3,000 people would wedge themselves into the auditorium, and according to Jemison they stood around the walls, sat on window sills,
and occupied all available space. Bumper-to-bumper traffic en route to
the mass meetings tied up the town of Baton Rouge. Everyone was

aware that this was an important development. The scale and vigor of the nightly activity left an indelible impression on whites as well as blacks.

Officials of the movement closed down the community's saloons after 6:00 P.M. The drunks and winos of the black community were not allowed to do their customary drinking out on the streets. But, Jemison recalls, "they didn't seem to mind too much because their new role was to open up the car doors of movement participants as they arrived." Even they sensed that they were taking part in an important drama. The movement's leadership set up their own "police department," and city policemen remained outside the black community during the boycott. According to Jemison, the movement's "police department" did an effective job patrolling the community and providing him with bodyguards.

The refusal to ride buses, of course, confronted the protesters with the problem of how to eat and pay rent if they had no transportation to and from work. The black community laboriously worked out a "free car lift" to solve this problem. Personal cars were used to pick up the black work force on corners just as the buses had done. They would then proceed down the regular bus routes discharging passengers at their destinations. The car lift was highly organized, with a dispatch center and drivers stationed across the city prepared to swing into action when instructed. The passengers were not charged fares. If fares had been charged, the whole operation could have been shut down for functioning without taxi licenses. Movement strategists had to be aware of all the legal catches and skilled at avoiding them.

A mass movement such as the Baton Rouge boycott requires a high degree of planning and organization. Communication networks had to be activated, someone had to decide on the movement's meeting place, money had to be raised and strategies formulated. The Baton Rouge mass bus boycott suggests that movements are the products of organizing efforts and preexisting institutions. To understand the dynamics of the Baton Rouge movement a discussion of leadership, organization, and finance is necessary.

Leadership

The Reverend T. J. Jemison became the official leader and spokesman of the Baton Rouge movement. Reverend Jemison held a bachelor's and a master's degree from two black universities, Alabama State and Virginia Union, respectively. He had also done graduate work at New York University. As pastor of the largest and most respected church in the community, he was economically independent of the white community. This independence enabled Jemison to avoid many of the constraints facing the black leadership that functioned within the tripartite system of domination. Yet the severity of oppression of the black community made the masses distrustful of anyone claiming to be a leader. They knew that any leader would be subjected to pressure from whites to abandon the masses for personal gain. Jemison was not free from suspicion, but in several incidents prior to the boycott he had proved that his leadership was authentic.

One case involved the white owner of a candy store in the heart of the black community. When little black girls came in on their way to school to buy candy, the proprietor would take them behind a curtain and fondle them. No one would tackle this problem because the man was white. The owner was persuaded to close the store when Jemison threatened to have his business disrupted by some "young tough" blacks. In another incident, word circulated about a family comprising a mother, father, and nine children living in one 14-by-14-foot room. Jemison led a community effort to pool resources and buy the family a 60-by-90-foot lot on which a seven-room house was built. Jemison was relatively new in the community, and it was rumored that he had had the title to the property put in his name; after all, "people just don't do what he did." Immediately Jemison and his followers took out a full-page newspaper ad that showed the title in the family's name. Jemison later recalled that "from that point . . . they had confidence. There were other incidents, several of them. It was incidents like this that made people know that I was more or less for other people rather than for myself, and that I could be followed and that I could be trusted."

Jemison was also helped to become the leader of the Baton Rouge movement by his "newcomer" status. Contrary to popular belief among outsiders, a black community is usually well stocked with organized groups. This was true of Baton Rouge in the early 1950s. Many of its black inhabitants belonged to various churches, civic organizations, the NAACP, the Masons, lodges, and other groups. As in any organized social setting, various factions competed for cherished resources, prestige, and power. The longer a group or community leader has been in such a setting, the more likely he or she is to have made enemies or, more fundamentally, to be identified as representing a particular camp or special interest.

This is why the "newcomer" status was important for the Baton Rouge boycott leader. To cite Reverend Jemison:

I didn't have any conflict from others. And I was new in the community, more or less. I didn't come until 'forty-nine. So I didn't have the deep-seated problems with others, having been on this side or that

side. *I was a middle-of-the-road man. This is the same thing that happened in Montgomery. You had different ones there that had been
leaders in that community. But King had just come.*[6]

The lateness of Jemison's arrival thus enhanced his ability to unite the
diverse segments of the community for sustained protest.

Finally, Jemison became well integrated into community activities
and belonged to a number of organizations. As a minister he was clearly
connected to the black masses and the black clergy network that
stretched across Baton Rouge. This network gave him access to the
resources and organized work forces of the church community. In addition to managing his own large church congregation, Reverend Jemison belonged to the Baton Rouge Community Group, a local civic
organization. Significantly, he was a member of the local NAACP and
had previously served as its president. Most activities aimed at changing the racial status quo in Baton Rouge had been conducted by the
NAACP. One of the many contributions of the NAACP to the rise of
the modern civil rights movement was the training it provided to the
modern civil rights leaders, many of whom were high-ranking officers
of the NAACP.

Organization

The Baton Rouge boycott movement was mobilized and directed
through the local black churches and the United Defense League (UDL).
The local churches provided the institutional link to the masses. Jemison's large congregation immediately agreed to support the boycott.
Community support spread when Jemison called other ministers
throughout the city and asked that their congregations join the boycott.
It is not necessary for everyone to belong to a church for the entire
community to become unified for protest. Individuals who did not belong were sure to have relatives, friends, co-workers or neighbors who
did, and so the word got passed. Because churches were highly respected, any program initiated and backed by them had an excellent
chance to gain mass support. Black church congregations all over Baton Rouge rallied behind the boycott of 1953. The churches supplied
the manpower, finances, and communication networks that brought
about the indispensable mass participation.

The UDL was a unique organization formed in June 1953 to direct
the mass bus boycott. Churches were not ideal as the decision-making

center of a mass movement; they were too numerous and were preoccupied with too many other functions unrelated to protest. Besides, the church had no control over significant secular groups or formal ties to their leadership. It proved necessary to form an organization that was church-related but also included other important organized groups in the community. After its success in Baton Rouge, this procedure of forming a church-related organization became the fundamental organizing principle of many later movements. Jemison recalled: "We started an organization and we called it the United Defense League. And the reason we called it United Defense League, all of the other organizations within the community—there were about five or six—came together and united. They didn't lose their individual identity. But for the overall purpose of the whole community we formed what we call a United Defense League."[7] Thus the UDL became an organization of organizations.

Up to this point the boycott has been described as if it had one leader. That was not at all the case. The large number of ministers involved gave the movement a diverse leadership, because ministers were already leaders of their congregations. The UDL added to the leadership's depth by engaging the leadership skills of the entire community. It promoted creativity, discouraged jealousies and rivalries, eliminated needless duplication of effort, and maximized group cohesiveness. Measures to ensure solidarity were explicitly built into the UDL. Jemison explains:

> We brought all of them [leaders of the other community organizations] in, and recognized them as leaders, so that they would feel a part of the movement, and that it wasn't just my movement because there were many in the downtown power structure who would say to them that I was stealing their thunder, and they were all under me. But I tried to put them on the par, on the Board of Directors that would do the governing of this organization. And that was the one thing that kept us together. No matter how the power structure and splinter white groups tried to tear us apart, we were able to maintain a united front. . . . We were united.[8]

Clearly, then, the organization of organizations, the UDL, prevented the white power structure from exploiting schisms within the movement. Being separate from yet related to the mass-based black church, it joined with the churches to supply the comprehensive framework through which the Baton Rouge movement was organized and directed.

Finance

Social protest has to be financed. Investigation of how the Baton Rouge movement was financed leads directly to the black church. Just before the boycott Jemison's congregation had given him $650 to cover expenses for a business trip. The Sunday before the boycott Jemison informed the congregation that he was canceling the trip because of the pending boycott. He then told the church committee, "I want you to let me use this $650 as the first gift towards the boycott." An experienced official of the church, Jemison knew his personal example would communicate the seriousness of the boycott and the absolute necessity of financing it to the congregation and other churchmen of the city.

The Mt. Zion Baptist Church Committee set the financing process in motion by allowing the $650 to go toward the boycott. "That $650 inspired those in the church to give," Jemison says. "That Sunday morning our church gave $1,500." Jemison immediately approached the rest of Baton Rouge's church community: "I called around to churches that I had a chance to reach and told them what I was going to do, and that Sunday we took in somewhere—I think it was around about $3,800. That was how we started financing it."

Passing the hat became a regular feature of the nightly mass meetings. The mass meetings were the pulse and lifeline of the movement—its information center; the occasion for inspiration, rejuvenation, and commitment by means of rousing sermons and unifying black spirituals; the opportunity for planning and strategy sessions; and the financial center. The entire car lift, including maintenance and such equipment as tires and batteries, was financed by money raised at the church-based mass meetings. Jemison remembers: "At night we would have mass meetings. And the people would give money for the cars, but they would be giving it in just a mass rally. And we would pay for the gas that they were using. Monthly. Weekly. We wouldn't let anybody individually pay for anything."[9] Such financing enabled the movement to operate the car lift without a taxi license.

The movement's police department, which consisted of five body guards, was also financed with money collected at mass meetings, as were the countless ancillary goods and services required in any mass effort. In a summary of the movement's financial business, Jemison concluded: "The black citizens, mainly, and a few whites, contributed enough money to pay for all the tires, and batteries, and gas, and my bodyguards. And we owed nobody nothing. The black community paid for all that."[10] Hence, the churches were more than symbolic extensions of the movement. They became the bedrock through which movement funds were raised and other valuable resources activated. The procedure for collecting funds that was developed for the explicit purpose of indigenously supporting black protest in Baton Rouge was to endure throughout the modern civil rights movement.

Victory and Impact

The boycott differed from past protests in Baton Rouge, which had been initiated by the NAACP and had attempted to work through the courts. The Baton Rouge boycott was a mass, church-based, direct-action movement guided by a new organization of organizations. The boycott leaders formed the new organization after deciding that the NAACP was incapable of directing a mass protest. The main tactic of the movement—economic boycott—effectively disrupted the economy of the bus company, causing it to lose $1,600 a day.[11]

The demand of the black community was that blacks be allowed to occupy bus seats on a first-come-first-served basis, with no seats reserved for whites. To bring the effective mass bus boycott to a close the white power structure of Baton Rouge decided to work out a compromise with the movement leaders. The compromise stipulated that the two side front seats be reserved for whites while the long rear seat be reserved for blacks. All of the remaining seats were to be filled on a first-come-first-served basis.

On the sixth day of the boycott the Executive Council of the U.D.L. met and considered the compromise. Reverend Jemison urged that the compromise be accepted on a temporary basis and that the legality of bus segregation itself could be determined through the courts. There was heated debate over the compromise, although it was finally accepted by a 5-to-3 vote. The movement leaders took the proposal to a mass meeting attended by 8,000 blacks.[12] According to the State Times "a standing show of approval, or disapproval from the audience, at Jemison's request, showed a majority in favor of the group decision."[13] However, some movement leaders and many of the rank-and-file were dissatisfied with the compromise, arguing that the force of the mass movement was capable of ending bus segregation. The State Times reported the response at the mass meeting: "An echoing ovation of voices shouting 'stay off, stay off' rose up from the Memorial Stadium after Jemison's statement. . . . Other shouts of 'walk, walk' were heard throughout the audience, when Jemison said, 'But some of you good people have to work'."[14]

The boycott officially ended June 25, 1953, after Jemison informed the group that the free car lift would cease functioning. It appears that the Baton Rouge boycott could have functioned indefinitely, as did the subsequent Montgomery boycott, if the leaders had not accepted the compromise. In retrospect Reverend Jemison admitted, "My vision was not anywhere, at that particular time, other than to see that Negroes could sit down when they paid the same fare."[15]

The limited victory in Baton Rouge was easier than in some later movements, because the white power structure did not stand solidly behind the striking bus drivers. That does not diminish its importance as a major victory against the Jim Crow system in Baton Rouge. It was not simply a victory of a black middle class desiring integration. Most higher-income blacks could avoid the humiliation of the buses by driving private cars. A victory for the entire community, it was the first evidence that the system of racial segregation could be challenged by mass action.

The impact of the mass bus boycott went beyond Baton Rouge.[16] The news of it was disseminated through the black ministerial networks across the country. Jemison's access to those networks was solid. His father had been president of the 5-million-member National Baptist Congress for twelve years, and Jemison himself had been elected in 1953 as that body's National Secretary. In 1956, Rev. Jemison carried the blueprint of the Baton Rouge movement to the National Baptist Convention and made it available to activist clergy.[17] Martin Luther King, Jr., and Ralph Abernathy, both ministers in Montgomery, Alabama, were well aware of the Baton Rouge movement and consulted closely with Reverend Jemison when the famous Montgomery boycott was launched in 1955.[18] Similarly, the Reverend C. K. Steele, who became the leader of a mass bus boycott in Tallahassee, Florida, in 1956, was familiar with the Baton Rouge boycott and also consulted closely with Jemison.[19] The Reverend A. L. Davis of New Orleans, who led a protest against bus segregation in that city in 1957, was well aware of the earlier protest in Baton Rouge.[20] Small wonder that in organizational dynamics the later movements resembled the historic Baton Rouge movement, which provided a successful model.

The Baton Rouge boycott occurred before the famous 1954 school desegregation decision won by the NAACP and also predated the more celebrated 1955–56 Montgomery bus boycott. But it was the Baton Rouge movement, largely without assistance from outside elites, that opened the direct action phase of the modern civil rights movement. Its impact was temporarily overshadowed, however, by the 1954 Supreme Court decision in *Brown* v. *Board of Education of Topeka*, which thrust the NAACP into the limelight and crystallized the emerging massive resistance movement dedicated to systematically destroying the NAACP across the South.

CONFRONTATION: SOUTHERN WHITE POWER
STRUCTURE VERSUS THE NAACP

White Southerners looked with disfavor and contempt on the NAACP the moment it planted an organizational foot in the South in 1918. "After all," white Southerners argued, "we know what is best for the South in general and for our niggers in particular." Because the NAACP was based in the North, white Southerners immediately labeled it an outside agitator, out to destroy the "harmonious relations" that existed between the races. They even called this very American organization "Communist."

The endless court battles and agitation of the NAACP kept pressure on the Southern white power structures to abolish racial domination. It would be misleading to present the courtroom battles in a narrowly legal light. Their importance was more in demonstrating to Southern blacks and the NAACP that the Southern white power structure was vulnerable at some points. That vulnerability could be found in spite of the immense social, political, and economic efforts and terror tactics used by white Southerners to protect white dominance. As the conflict persisted, the NAACP continued to file suits and blacks kept attempting to enroll in all-white universities, vote, sit where they pleased on buses, and change the system of racial domination in general. Whenever the NAACP won a legal contest, it served to delegitimize the white racist system in the eyes of blacks. Beneath the white Southerner's rhetoric and name-calling lurked a genuine respect for, and fear of, their main adversary, the NAACP.

From 1918 to 1956 the NAACP grew and spread across the South despite many uncoordinated efforts to sabotage the organization. The growth of the NAACP in the face of violence and terror was an amazing feat. But a coordinated attack against the NAACP throughout the South began about 1950, became highly organized and effective from 1954 to 1958, and began to recede about 1959. A thorough documentation of this attack is necessary, because it will be argued that this attack contributed greatly to the emergence of the modern civil rights movement. It broke the hegemony of the NAACP and cleared the way for the use of other tactics in addition to the legalistic approach employed by the association. The result was a more favorable environment in which new mass movement organizations and tactics that directly confronted and challenged the Southern white power structure could emerge.

The white power structure of the South united to destroy the NAACP when the Association began to push for desegregation of public schools. In his study of the NAACP, Langston Hughes wrote: "In the summer of 1950 a National Conference in New York of lawyers associated with the NAACP decided to attempt a bold, all-out frontal attack upon ed-

ucational segregation."[21] The conference held many meetings and
brought together a few of the nation's leading sociologists, psycholo-
gists, and educators, who prepared the social and psychological arguments to be put before the court. This was indeed a serious effort on
the part of the NAACP. Between 1950 and 1952 lawyers filed five suits
in federal courts questioning the constitutionality of public school segregation. These suits were filed in South Carolina, Virginia, Kansas,
Delaware, and the District of Columbia.[22] The Kansas suit culminated
in the famous school desegregation decision rendered by the Supreme
Court in 1954.

The prospect of desegregating public schools was fundamentally ap-
palling to the average white Southerner. The thought of young "niggers" mixing in school with little white children jarred the sensibilities
of Southern whites, whether poor farmers or highly placed government
officials. Skirmishes between the Southern white power structure and
the NAACP over school desegregation from 1950 to 1954 usually followed this scenario: NAACP lawyers, along with parents and children,
filed their complaints with the local school boards, but nothing would
come of them. The NAACP attorneys then filed desegregation suits in
the federal district courts. The federal courts then ruled that Negro
schools had to be made equal to white schools, but segregation itself
was upheld as valid. The NAACP then appealed these cases to the U. S.
Supreme Court. All five cases reached the high court in 1952. At this
stage the best lawyers of the Southern white power structure and the
NAACP locked wits to determine the outcome of this fundamental challenge to segregation.

Prior to the 1954 decision, a number of white Southern officials had
already announced that if the decision went against them they would
not comply. Georgia's Governor Herman Talmadge "had been obsessed
with the possibility of such a decision from the Supreme Court for several years and had already expressed fierce opposition."[23] South Carolina's Governor James F. Byrnes warned even before the Supreme
Court hearings began: "Should the Supreme Court decide this case
against our position, we will face a serious problem. Of only one thing
can we be certain. South Carolina will not now, not for some years to
come, mix white and colored children in our schools."[24] Thus the white
power structure had already begun to stiffen against school desegregation before the 1954 decision was made.

The NAACP won the U. S. Supreme Court decision on May 17, 1954.
In the period immediately following the decision the Supreme Court,
Congress, and the executive branch of government made known their
positions regarding the desegregation of Southern schools. At best they
played a neutral to negative role in actually implementing the desegregation decision. The Eisenhower Administration never endorsed the

1954 decision. President Eisenhower played into the hands of Southern segregationists by calling for local and state action as opposed to federal action. He expressed a preference for the operation of intelligence and education rather than law and, by implication, power, politics and group interests, in human affairs. As late as 1957, after pro-segregation groups of the South had killed, maimed, and starved blacks and the few whites fighting for school integration, the President still appealed to the reason, education, and common sense of these groups. When the President was asked at a press conference on July 17, 1957, whether he would ever use troops to enforce a court integration order, he replied: "I can't imagine any set of circumstances that would ever induce me to send federal troops . . . into any area to enforce the orders of a federal court, because I believe that common sense of America will never require it."[25] So the celebrated five-star general, adept in conflict strategies and maneuvers, appealed to reason while the Southern white power structure engaged in warlike behavior to frustrate the law of the land. In essence, the executive branch of government encouraged Southern white defiance, intimidation, and violence by failing to take federal action to implement the 1954 decision. Indeed, the President came down squarely on the side of the Southern white power structure by calling for gradualism and upholding the right of individual states to work out desegregation plans.

Congress evaded the issue of school desegregation. Although a number of measures were proposed, not a single bill was passed in the Congress to facilitate school desegregation. Title III of the bill that became the Civil Rights Act of 1957 called for the "initiation of desegregation suits by the Department of Justice,"[26] but it was removed before the bill cleared Congress. A Gallup Poll on July 10, 1954, found that people outside the South overwhelmingly approved of the 1954 decision,[27] but such an indication of voter interest did not prompt Congress to take initiatives toward the implementation of school desegregation.

Like the President, the Supreme Court played into the hands of the Southern white power structure. In the original 1954 decision the court unanimously and unequivocally ruled against school segregation. Yet it left the door ajar for white resistance by stressing problems of implementation, citing a "great variety of local conditions." The Court did not decide on implementation procedures until May 1955, though it did invite submission of amicus curiae briefs from states regarding implementation. During the interim, members of the Southern white power structure, along with representatives from the President, began to plead for gradual implementation because of local diversity. The NAACP's official position was that desegregation should be ordered by a fixed date.

The position of the Southern white power structure prevailed in the implementation ruling of May 1955. In fact the wording of this ruling facilitated the emerging massive resistance movement: "Full implementation of these constitutional principles may require solution of varied local school problems. School authorities have the primary responsibility for elucidating, assessing, and solving these problems."[28] The court in effect gave the very groups that adamantly opposed school desegregation the responsibility to desegregate the schools. Beyond that, the high Court washed its hands of overseeing the matter: "Because of their proximity to local conditions and the possible need for further hearings, the courts which originally heard these cases can best perform the judicial appraisal. Accordingly, we believe it appropriate to remand the cases to these courts."[29] Predictably, white Southerners were relieved. The Court had decided that school desegregation was a Southern problem. Indeed, the President, Congress, and the Supreme Court had capitulated to the white Southern pressure and thereby abetted the terrorism and repression that was to be used against groups attempting to desegregate public schools.

After the national government steered clear of implementation, only three groups remained directly involved in the desegregation process: the white power structure as the opposer, local federal courts as arbitrators, and black citizens working with the NAACP as the initiators. The only organization left to fight against the strong white power structure, which could marshal all economic and political power at the state level against desegregation, was the NAACP.

In light of this circumstance, the significance of the coordinated attack waged against the NAACP becomes clear. As soon as the 1954 decision was handed down, the white South organized to fight its implementation. Racist groups (White Citizens' Councils, the American States Rights Association, the National Association for the Advancement of White People, the Ku Klux Klan, and others) organized for the express purpose of preventing school desegregation and Negro advancement in general.[30] These organizations did not operate separately or in total isolation from the respected power structure and officials of the South. With the same goals and considerable overlapping membership, they all engaged in repressive activities aimed at maintaining the racial status quo.[31] By the end of 1954 the organizational base and tactics of the resistance movement were firmly established. These groups openly decided that economic pressures, intimidation, and propaganda would be used. Violence and terror became an enduring part of the arsenal to keep black children out of white schools.

By 1955 the South had become an extremely dangerous place for blacks. In 1955 a number of hideous murders took place. One was the killing and removal of the testicles of a fourteen-year-old black boy named Emmett Till, who was visiting Mississippi from the North. Till was killed for allegedly whistling at a white woman. His Northern background had not prepared him to play the racial game of the South or to respond "correctly" to hostile whites when confronted. The Till murder was one of the more publicized acts of violence against blacks. But one notorious case, of course, cannot convey the magnitude and the impact of repression during this era, when many blacks were beaten, bombed, fired from jobs, or shot.[32]

Whites made it known to blacks that if they did not stay in their place, their livelihoods would disappear. This placed blacks in a near impossible situation: Desiring racial integration and the overthrow of racial domination, they had to act as if they accepted discrimination and racial segregation or lose their jobs. The first rule of survival was to avoid association with integration-minded people and organizations like the NAACP.

The acts of repression were not random. Many were committed against popular leaders affiliated with the NAACP. Before a school desegregation case could be opened, black parents had to sign school petitions. Those parents, who worked with NAACP, were often identified by whites and forced to withdraw their names or be fired from jobs and face the possibility of bodily harm to themselves or their children. Teachers belonging to the NAACP or who admitted that they would teach an integrated class were fired. Nevertheless, blacks and the NAACP continued to challenge local school boards to desegregate. Thus in 1955 "emergency conferences were called in Alabama, Florida, Georgia, North Carolina, Mississippi and Tennessee to acquaint leaders with the Supreme Court's May 31 decision", and numerous petitions were filed in at least seven Southern states.[33]

Official Attack on the NAACP, 1956–59

The year the white power structure of the South officially attempted to destroy the NAACP was 1956.[34] Its official attacks were spearheaded by the heads of state governments. Special sessions of the state legislatures were called, and plans to destroy the organization were formulated. In most Southern states it was decided that the NAACP should be forced to make available its membership lists. Charges that NAACP was communistic or subversive were used to justify this demand, and obscure legal precedents were cited to forestall legal recourse against such action. The intention was clear. If the NAACP yielded to this pressure and revealed its members' addresses, the members would suffer economic reprisals, violence, and other forms of repression. It was clear that the organization could be destroyed by exposing its members.

The NAACP, recognizing what the white power structure had in mind, refused to make membership lists available. Within a span of six months during 1956, the attorneys general of Louisiana, Alabama, and Texas obtained injunctions halting the operation of the NAACP within their states. In Virginia during the same year a special session of the state assembly met and passed seven laws designed specifically to prevent the NAACP from functioning. In Florida the legislature appropriated $50,000 to investigate the NAACP for communist involvement. In South Carolina a law that barred teachers from belonging to the NAACP went into effect. In Atlanta, Georgia, the NAACP's branch president was jailed for four hours until he agreed to submit all financial documents of the organization to representatives of the state legislature.

By the end of 1956 the official attack on the NAACP was well entrenched. Destroying the NAACP by enacting laws and obtaining injunctions against the organization was a brilliant strategy on the part of the Southern white power structure. Indeed, given the legalistic approach of the NAACP its leaders could not conceive of behaving unlawfully, even if the laws enacted against it were blatant displays of power by the enemy, justified only by self-interest, and even if such "unlawfulness" might prove the only way the organization could continue to function. For the NAACP to go outside the law would have required changing its basic operating methods and principles, which it was not prepared to do.

At the close of 1957 the Southern white power structure had stepped up its attack against the NAACP. Though under severe strain, the NAACP managed to win court rulings that allowed it to operate despite injunctions against it in Louisiana and Texas. But in Alabama it was outlawed and had to close down. In fact, Alabama became a model for the Southern power structure, and state after state attempted to follow its example.

In 1957 these states created more investigating committees and initiated more laws against the NAACP. Arkansas and Tennessee, where the NAACP was hotly pursuing school desegregation, entered the ranks of states officially seeking to outlaw the NAACP. By 1957 the NAACP was tied up in some form of litigation in the states of Louisiana, Texas, Virginia, Tennessee, Arkansas, Georgia, South Carolina, and Florida and was, of course, completely outlawed in Alabama.[35]

Here again, a one-dimensional focus on the legal troubles of the NAACP would be misleading. These attacks must be seen in the context of the violence, economic reprisals, and general repressive atmosphere plaguing the black community in this period. It must be remembered also that the Southern black community had been largely abandoned by all branches of the federal government. It is only in this light that we can begin to understand what it meant for NAACP officials to be dragged before investigating committees, to be arrested and thrown in jail, and to have their homes bombed. These were the leaders who spearheaded the resistance of the black community. White Southerners reasoned that if they controlled this group and their NAACP branches, they could shatter the critical thrust and momentum of the black community.

This was sound reasoning. Unlike the bulk of the black population, these leaders' fighting spirit, autonomy, and influence usually depended on their relative economic independence and their backing from the NAACP. Repressive acts were committed to serve as visible warnings to the black community. For example, a hearse was sent to the home of the black president of the Norfolk NAACP branch during his absence.[36]

In 1958 and 1959 the Southern white power structure kept the pressure on the NAACP. The NAACP *Annual Report* contains the following examples: John Patterson was elected Governor of Alabama in 1958 after campaigning on a "Kill the NAACP" platform; Mississippi attempted to intimidate Negro youth for their activity in the NAACP by subpoenaing them to appear before a grand jury in Jones County; and Mrs. L. C. Bates, head of the state NAACP in Arkansas, continued her militant activities even though the newspaper she and her husband owned, *The Arkansas State Press*, was about to go out of business because circulation and advertising revenues had fallen sharply in response to an anti-NAACP campaign.[37]

A similar picture emerges in 1959: Three NAACP leaders of Florida were cited for contempt of court when they refused to answer questions at a legislative inquiry session; in Arkansas the eighteen-year-old *Arkansas State Press*, owned by Mr. and Mrs. Bates, went out of business; an act was passed in Arkansas making it unlawful for any state agency to employ members of the NAACP. This act, along with another racial bill, resulted in the firing of seven principals and thirty-seven teachers by the Little Rock School Board. In Louisiana a state court enjoined the NAACP from doing business in that state.[38]

In spite of the pressure against the NAACP in 1958 and 1959, the Southern white power structure slowly began to lose the battle. By 1958 and 1959 the NAACP was able to obtain operating room by winning several key cases in the Supreme Court and lower federal courts. In 1958 the Supreme Court ruled that it was unconstitutional for the state of Alabama to require the surrender of NAACP membership lists.[39] Although Alabama refused to allow the NAACP to operate in the state for nine years, this ruling nonetheless signaled to other Southern states that similar action would be in direct conflict with the Supreme Court.

In January of 1958 a federal court in Virginia invalidated three damaging laws that the state had enacted against the NAACP in 1956.

The NAACP also began to win the battle because its leadership refused to be intimidated. They courageously took the punishment, and whenever they found an inch of legal leeway, they acted decisively. The NAACP *Annual Report* of 1959 stated: "During 1959 there was a noticeable easing of tension and friction growing out of the overt attacks upon the organization in the South."

An examination of NAACP's branches and membership between 1955 and 1959 reveals the devastating impact of the white power structure's coordinated attack on the organization. Local branches, the most basic units of the NAACP, initiated and organized protest activities in local communities and provided the national office with the bulk of its funds. As Myrdal wrote, "The branches are the lifeline of the Association, and the National office is constantly struggling to maintain them in vigor and to found new branches."[40]

During 1955–56 more than 60 percent of NAACP branches were located in fourteen Southern states and the District of Columbia. Because of the Southwide attack against the organization, by 1957 the South accounted for only 52 percent of the branches, and by 1958 the percentage had dropped to 50 percent. The official attack against NAACP, it should be remembered, began in 1956. It was during 1956 that injunctions preventing the NAACP from functioning were issued. From 1955 through 1957 the NAACP lost a total of 226 branches in the South. By 1958 these losses had increased to 246 branches.[41]

The same pattern was evident with regard to the NAACP's membership. In 1955 Southern states numbered 128,716 members, which represented 45 percent of the NAACP's total membership. By 1957 membership in the South dropped to 79,677, only 28 percent of the total.[42] Fortunately for the NAACP, the losses in the South were offset by gains made in the North and Midwest. In the Northeast there was a small but steady increase in branches beginning in 1955, and in 1959 branches in the Midwest increased from 139 to 161.[43]

The increase in branches and memberships in the North was the result of an intensive campaign. The NAACP decided that extraordinary efforts had to be made elsewhere in the nation to offset the losses in the South. Without such a successful effort the NAACP would have been in serious trouble. Even with increased support from the North, the attack hurt the NAACP financially. According to Hughes, the attack caused the NAACP to "spend thousands of dollars defending itself in court. The Southern states would like nothing better than to break the NAACP by forcing it to deplete its funds in numerous and costly court cases."[44] The NAACP *Annual Report* of 1957 stated:

At the year's end, the Association was involved in 25 suits in which its rights to function in the South was at issue. These suits were so complicated by legal maneuvers and collateral proceedings instigated by segregationists that they equaled several times that number in a normal law practice. Combatting these attacks has proven costly in time as well as in other resources.[45]

Two additional substantive points should be made regarding the whites' attack. First, it occurred at a moment when the NAACP stood a good chance of attracting a large following. The winning of the 1954 decision was the kind of victory the organization needed to rally the black masses behind its program; by appealing to blacks' widespread desire to enroll their children in the better-equipped white schools it reached into black homes and had meaning for people's personal lives. Thus the attack destroyed not only a great deal of what the NAACP was but also what it might have become.

Second, the attack on the NAACP left an organizational and protest vacuum in many Southern black communities. The NAACP was forced by law to close shop in many areas while at the same time it was losing branches in others because of intense terror and pressure. Once a branch was closed down by statute or by intimidation, blacks were deprived of an organization through which to address local grievances. This was an important role played by NAACP branches, even if their performance often was largely symbolic. In addition, many of the local branches were directly involved in seeking implementation of the 1954 decision. The extent of the organizational and protest vacuum created by the attack can be appreciated by considering that the NAACP was ripped from the social fabric of black society across the entire state of Alabama for nine years.

The outlawing of the NAACP in Alabama was important symbolically, for Birmingham was the site of NAACP's Southeastern Region headquarters. NAACP activities in Florida, Georgia, Mississippi, North Carolina, South Carolina, and Tennessee were generated and coordinated from this office. Its closing produced reverberations throughout the South and weakened public faith in the NAACP. People began to observe, "If they could close the NAACP in Alabama, they certainly are able to close it here." These perceptions and uncertainties regarding the efficacy of the NAACP widened the organizational and protest vacuum in Southern black communities at that crucial time when the possibility of public school desegregation had opened the prospect of massive recruitment of blacks. Communities confronted a choice: whether to submit to attack or reorganize and face the state power and terrorism head on. The NAACP furnished no immediate answers. It obeyed the anti-NAACP laws, closed down, and went to court to fight for the right to exist.

Bureaucratic Tactics Versus Mass-oriented Tactics

Ironically, the Southern white power structure's attack on the NAACP played an important role in the rise of the modern civil rights movement. To begin with, bureaucratic protest organizations of poor and dominated groups are not likely to initiate or direct a mass movement. They are unable to because their internal and external dynamics force them to march down a limiting institutional path. The critical choice of tactics and strategies immediately confronts a dominated group as it prepares to engage in social struggle for liberation. It is usually uncertain which tactics will be effective. Often this question can be resolved only through social experimentation.

It is precisely the problem of developing appropriate tactics that an established bureaucratic protest organization claims to have solved. If a bureaucratic organization is to maintain its privileged position, its leaders almost have to make this claim, because other tactics lie beyond their capabilities or are perceived as such. Alternative tactics therefore come to be viewed not as supplementary but as opposing, threatening, and incorrect. Alternative tactics may in fact be threatening to the bureaucratic organization if they reflect the desires of the dominated group. The established protest organization has much to lose if a significant segment of the dominated group supports alternative tactics, especially if that segment includes those who traditionally supported the bureaucratic organization.

Tactics of bureaucratic protest organizations are not usually designed to accommodate mass grassroots insurgency and the attendant uncertainty and experimentation.[46] The external environment—consisting of other *status quo*–oriented bureaucratic organizations such as courts and the media—forces the bureaucratic protest organization to formalize and stabilize its behavior. Organizational officials avoid uncertainty and seek a semblance of order and predictability so that they can smoothly and successfully pursue such goals as financial support, power, influence, and status.

From an internal standpoint the same quest for order and predictability characterizes the relationship between the bureaucratic center of the protest organization and its various units. Top officials in a protest organization must produce, if their organization is to continue to enjoy power, influence, and prestige. The professed goals of these organizations are usually stated in such grandiose terms as "bringing freedom" to the dominated group. Nevertheless, as with all bureaucratic organizations, business is conducted in terms of very specific goals (e.g. registering a stated number of voters, winning certain court decisions) achievable within specific time frames (year, fiscal period). It is as if the "freedom goal" can be parceled into manageable units of inputs and outputs that can be convincingly displayed in charts and graphs upon request. To accomplish these concrete goals, the organizational staff develops coherent and logical programs and methods.

Local units receive specific directives with respect to the implementation of the concrete goals. The procedures and progress of the local chapters or branches are monitored as closely as possible by bureaucratic officials. Significant deviations from tactics suitable to bureaucratic logic are discouraged, because such departures may be viewed as detrimental to "progress." Thus bureaucratic officials may apply pressure on local units to follow bureaucratically oriented strategies when these units show a desire to experiment with other methods or to define progress differently.

Since bureaucratic organizations are likely to aim at gradual and limited change for the dominated group, tensions may develop between those on the local level who become dissatisfied with the pace of change and the bureaucratic officials. Local groups may question the very validity of "progress" as defined by bureaucratic officials. When the tension and questioning become widespread within the dominated group, there will be fertile ground for the emergence of new protest organizations. The bureaucratic organization may be threatened, ironically at a time when it is experiencing success. It is during such times that the dominated group senses the possibility of greater social change and feels powerful. The possibility that new organizational forms will emerge among the dominated is further increased by the bureaucratic organization's reluctance to make any tactical changes itself during a period of relative success.

As shown in the preceding chapter, the NAACP of the 1950s clearly fits the bureaucratic model.[47] Its bureaucratic structure produced stability in the organization but also limited its tactics and strategies. As discussed earlier, the NAACP's operations on the national level, in every state, and in all branches were organized around the "lawyer approach," which produced primarily slow and limited changes for the black community. Wyatt Walker, a minister and former executive assistant to Dr. Martin Luther King, Jr., captures the essence of the problems with the legalistic approach: "You file one court case, you get one litigant, it takes from three to five years to get into the Supreme Court, and you spend at least a thousand dollars on the one case."[48]

Dr. Benjamin Mays, when he was president of Morehouse College and a member of the National Board of the NAACP, identified what set the NAACP apart from such later direct action organizations as the Southern Christian Leadership Conference (SCLC): There was "a fundamental difference between the NAACP and SCLC. The reason is that the NAACP was and is composed of lawyers and they don't march in the streets. They feel that the first thing you've got to do is to have the United States Supreme Court to declare this thing [racial segregation] illegal, and that's logical."[49] The winning of significant cases represented success for the NAACP as an organization. For the black community, however, such legal victories, while important in that they produced the perception that change was possible, at the same time required the expenditure of a great deal of energy and time for the sake of little relief from the yoke of domination. Indeed, in this context organizational success and group success can mean two entirely different things.

Lawyers were the principal status group in the NAACP on both national and local levels, but many of the local leaders came from other occupations, especially in the South, where a disproportionate number of black leaders were ministers. A study of Negro leadership in Little rock, Arkansas, found that 42 percent of the leaders were ministers.[50] Another study in New Orleans concluded that Negro ministers constitute the largest segment of the leadership class there.[51] It is important to remember that in the South the NAACP was closely linked to the black church. This was natural, given the tripartite system of domination, because the church was practically the only safe environment in which the NAACP could operate.

It is actually understating the case to say that a strong link existed between the church and the NAACP. Since ministers formed a preponderance of those at the head of the Southern NAACP branches and serving on their executive committees, it is much more accurate to say that in many cases the church ran the local Southern units, but within the constraints of the National office of the NAACP.

Organizational Shift in Black Protest

The ministers wanted to run the NAACP branches like a black church, where, as noted in Chapter One, the minister was all-powerful. The NAACP officials wanted them run according to their established organizational procedures. Additional strain resulted from the fact that the NAACP was based in the North. The decision-makers of the NAACP were physically removed from the Southern scene and therefore did not always have a grassroots sense of local white domination, yet they sent memos Southward explaining how Southern blacks could get free. Southern ministers knew the black rank-and-file much better and clearly understood the nature of domination that was peculiar to the South. Thus disagreements and tensions between these two sets of actors were inevitable.

The black minister and the black population of the South in general remained loyal to the NAACP despite the underlying strains. The Southern church and the Northern NAACP actually needed each other, because their combined resources were necessary for a sustained fight against white domination. Until 1955 the ministers and Southern blacks accepted the legal approach and centralized decision-making structures of the NAACP. However, following the mass bus boycotts of Baton Rouge (1953) and Montgomery (1955) and the all-out attack on the NAACP following the 1954 decision, the bureaucratic strategies of the NAACP came under intense scrutiny and criticism by blacks for the first time.

The mass movements of the mid-1950s generated lively debates about which strategies and tactics would work best. The Montgomery bus boycott, because it gained national attention, let the black population know that the tactics and strategies of the mass movement could be effective and could bring far faster results than the legalistic method of the NAACP. Once this alternative approach was firmly stamped in the consciousness of the social action–oriented black ministers, the underlying tension between them and the bureaucratic NAACP was exacerbated. Indeed, the restraining weight of the directives, bylaws, memos, and clearance procedures of the Northern-based NAACP officials on the Southern ministers seemed to grow heavier by leaps and bounds. The ministers saw this moment in history as a critical time when they and their churches could change the oppressive social system that choked Southern blacks at every turn.

When the NAACP came under fire in the South, the leading Southern ministers, not so much out of rational calculation as in response to the immediate pressing social reality, seized their opportunity and began organizing church-related direct action organizations. From then on the destiny of Southern blacks was no longer tied to the legal approach of the NAACP. No longer did it lie in the hands of whites in the judicial branch of the government. Their destiny was now in the hands of Southern blacks themselves—their institutions, their direct action organizations, and their leaders.

The Southwide attack on the NAACP prevented any significant showdown between the national headquarters and the Southern leaders by keeping black leaders and the black population loyal to the NAACP. At the same time, however, it created a protest vacuum, making room for ministers to create new church-related organizations designed to implement the mass movement approach. That is how, as emphasized previously, the Southern whites' attack greatly facilitated the emergence of new social protest organizations and promoted relatively smooth relations between those new organizations and the established NAACP. Thus the two approaches—legal action and mass protest—entered into a turbulent but workable marriage.

The Reverend Fred Shuttlesworth, one of the most courageous and outstanding leaders of the modern civil rights movement, recalls that he, as membership chairman of the Birmingham NAACP, was holding a meeting in 1956 when a representative of the Southern white power structure came and told him that the NAACP had been outlawed in Alabama. Becoming very pensive, he stated:

> And that man came to us with that sheet of paper that looked like it reached from his shoulders to the floor. And it looked like to me that that guy had the longest, shiniest pistol on his hip I had ever seen. . . . And I remember one guy went on TV from the state legislature and stated, "We got the old goose that laid the golden egg at last, the NAACP." I said to myself, "Yeah, you got the goose but I'm not sure that some of the eggs that she laid before you got her won't hatch out."[52]

The next chapter will examine those "eggs that hatched" and the tactics and strategies of social disruption that the new organizations implemented following the attack on the NAACP.

3

MOVEMENT CENTERS: MIA, ICC, AND ACMHR

The new form of mass protest launched in Baton Rouge in 1953 recurred in Montgomery, Tallahassee, and Birmingham in 1955 and 1956. This chapter will examine the structure of those local movements and their relationships with the black masses. The indigenous perspective on social movements stresses the important role of local protest groups in a major social movement. Instead of one homogeneous civil rights movement, there were dozens of local movements with their own organizations, activists, interorganizational relationships, boundaries, and funding bases. This fact tends to become obscured by the names of famous activists, organizations, and abstract concepts.

The concept "local movement center" is used here to characterize the diverse dynamics and confrontations of the civil rights movement. It requires a precise definition, because it is a central idea in this study and will be used extensively. A local movement center is a social organization within the community of a subordinate group, which mobilizes, organizes, and coordinates collective action aimed at attaining the common ends of that subordinate group. A movement center exists in a subordinate community when that community has developed an interrelated set of protest leaders, organizations, and followers who collectively define the common ends of the group, devise necessary tactics and strategies along with training for their implementation, and engage in actions designed to attain the goals of the group.

The local movement centers organized in Montgomery, Tallahassee, and Birmingham were among the first of the modern civil rights movement. This chapter focuses on the Montgomery Improvement Association (MIA), organized in December 1955; the Inter Civic Council (ICC) of Tallahassee, organized in May 1956; the Alabama Christian Movement for Human Rights (ACMHR) organized in Birmingham in June 1956; and the black communities they led through tumultuous conflicts.

By 1950 blacks constituted a significant percentage of the population in Montgomery (39 percent), Tallahassee (34) and Birmingham (41).[1] Before the opening of the twentieth century the picture was different. Indeed, as late as 1890 four out of five blacks still lived in rural areas.[2] This meant that large numbers of blacks fresh from the life of the plantation, with its direct surveillance and domination, in a relatively short time found themselves in urban settings and a capitalist economy that required them to become wage-earners. However, the tripartite system of domination followed blacks out of the rural cotton fields and rice and tobacco farms, into the factories, kitchens, hospitals, and mines of bustling urban centers.

An examination of the 1950 Census data reveals that approximately three-fourths of the black males employed in Montgomery (70.2 percent), Tallahassee (74.7), and Birmingham (81.8) were concentrated in the unskilled categories of laborers, service workers, and operatives. By contrast, only about one-fifth of white males employed in those cities (18.5, 14.6, and 24.6 percent, respectively) worked in those categories. The picture was similar for black women. In 1950 about three-fourths of employed black females in Montgomery, Tallahassee, and Birmingham (73.2, 70.7, and 74.1 percent) worked in private households and as service workers; less than one-tenth of the employed white women in these cities (8.6, 9.8, and 8.4 percent) were in these occupations.[3]

Thus there were no substantial black middle or upper classes in these Southern cities. A few blacks were in occupations usually thought of as middle-class jobs. The mean percentage of black males employed in the categories of "professional, technical, and kindred worker" and "managers, officials/proprietors except farm" for Montgomery, Tallahassee, and Birmingham was 3 percent, as against 12.3 percent for white males. These are the job categories that represent the underpinning of a solid middle class. But the notion of a "black middle class" has little meaning if it is not related to the larger class structure of American society. When we consider the place of black workers within the larger American capitalist system, we must question the concept of a black middle or upper class. In Montgomery, Tallahassee, and Birmingham in 1950 the majority of blacks classified as professionals were teachers and clergymen. These groups had influence and power in black classrooms and churches but little in the economic institutions where white managers and officials discriminated and controlled. The management and regulation of the labor force was considered "white folks' work." The black "middle and upper class" had little to say about such concerns. Thus blacks in the three cities, relegated to the bottom of the economic and political order, had a vested interest in changing the system of tripartite domination.

ORGANIZING THE ORGANIZED

Until the formation of the Montgomery Improvement Association, the Inter Civic Council, and the Alabama Christian Movement for Human Rights, the organized social and political forces in the black communities of Montgomery, Tallahassee, and Birmingham were divided. Writing of the Montgomery community, Dr. King describes a situation identical to that in Baton Rouge before the movement:

> First there was an appalling lack of unity among the leaders. Several civic groups existed, each at loggerheads with the other. There was the organization known as the Progressive Democrats headed by E. D. Nixon. There was the Citizens Committee headed by Rufus Lewis. There was the Women's Political Council headed by Mrs. Mary Fair Burks and Jo Ann Robinson. There was the NAACP headed by R. L. Matthews. Smaller groups further divided the Negro community.[4]

Similar organized schisms in the black community were identified in interviews with the Reverend C. K. Steele and the Reverend Daniel Speed of Tallahassee and the Reverend Fred Shuttlesworth of Birmingham.

Prior to the mass movements efforts had been made in these communities to unify the various organizations and groups, but without success. In Tallahassee representatives from the competing organizations had previously formed the Tallahassee Inter Civic League with the express purpose of ironing out differences and bringing about unity. According to Reverend Speed, "We had some other little organizations here in the city, and we had this Tallahassee Civic League for that purpose. Of course, somehow it just didn't seem to have worked out as strong as we had expected."[5] In Birmingham Reverend Shuttlesworth had become membership chairman of the NAACP, which put him in contact with organizations and civic leagues in the city. He tried to pull these community organizations together through the NAACP. Shuttlesworth stated that he wanted to show them "why they had the same needs and why everybody ought to work together. . . . I would draw on the fact that I knew people from different areas. . . . Now my purpose was to draw them all into NAACP."[6] The State of Alabama preempted that unification effort in Birmingham by outlawing the NAACP in June 1956. Dr. King wrote of a similar effort in Montgomery:

> *Many people sensed the effects of this crippling factionalism. Early in 1955 some influential leaders attempted to solve the problem by organizing a group which finally came to be known as the Citizens Coordinating Committee. I can remember the anticipation with which I attended the first meeting of this group, feeling that here the Negro community had an answer to a problem that had stood too long as a stumbling block to social progress. Soon, however, my hopes were shattered. Due to a lack of tenacity on the part of the leaders and of active interest on the part of the citizens in general, the Citizens Coordinating Committee finally dissolved. With the breakdown of this promising undertaking, it appeared that the tragic division in the Negro community could be cured only by some divine miracle.[7]*

The arrests of Rosa Parks in Montgomery and two college students in Tallahassee and the outlawing of the NAACP in Alabama created favorable social conditions for the organizational unification of these black communities. The MIA, ICC, and ACMHR were formed after local leaders decided that any successful protest movements would require a guiding organizational structure. The community groups and leaders who organized these movements immediately saw the need to create organizations that could cope with crises, direct mass insurgency, and unify the entire community. In fact many of the individuals who organized these mass movements came directly from the leadership of the established organizations that were previously locked in competition and conflict.

As movement organizations the MIA, ICC and ACMHR solved, to at least a workable extent, the problem of disunity. There are a number of factors which allowed them to accomplish the task. In chapter two it was noted that Reverend Jemison's newcomer status enabled him to become the leader of the protest movement in Baton Rouge because he was not identified as a member of the factional groups that divided the community. The ministers who became the leaders of the protest movements in Montgomery, Tallahassee, and Birmingham were also new to their respective communities: Dr. King, who became president of the MIA, had been in Montgomery for only two years; the Reverend C. K. Steele, president of the ICC, had been in Tallahassee for only four. The Reverend Fred Shuttlesworth, president of the ACMHR, was raised in Birmingham but left at an early age to seek work in Mobile in 1943, not returning to Birmingham until 1953. When the ACMHR was organized, Shuttlesworth had been in Birmingham for only three years.

Thus the newcomer status was apparently a determinant of who would become the leaders of the new mass movements.

The newcomer status was important in another respect. A common practice of the local white power structures in the 1950s was to co-opt and control black leaders by giving them personal rewards. This tactic gave whites a chance to gain some control over black ministers, who otherwise were economically independent of the white man. Here again, the newcomer status enabled ministers to be independent of the white power structure in actuality and in the eyes of the community. E. D. Nixon, who had organized the Black Brotherhood of Sleeping Car Porters Union in Montgomery and was a force in both the community and the bus boycott, makes this point when he explains why he backed Dr. King to become the leader of the boycott movement:

> Then the next thing, he had not been here long enough for the city fathers to put their hand on him. Usually, you come to town and you start wanting to do this and do that, and the city fathers get their hand on you probably and give you a suit of clothes or somethin' of that kind, and it ends up you're on their side. He wasn't the kind ever to accept it, even if they'd a tried it.[8]

On two counts, then, newcomer status provided the necessary latitude for these organizational presidents and their respective organizations to solidify the black community.

It was also observed in the preceding chapter that the various organizations in the black community of Baton Rouge were divided prior to the movement. The problem was solved there by forming an organization of organizations—the United Defense League—which unified the various groups by allowing the leaders of each organization to become leaders within the new organization and to serve on its board of directors. This approach allowed the entrenched organizations to coexist with the new one while simultaneously mobilizing their resources for protest. In Montgomery, Tallahassee, and Birmingham the same strategy was implemented to bring about organizational unity.

In Montgomery the MIA became the organization of organizations. E. D. Nixon, head of the Progressive Democrats, was elected to the MIA's negotiating and finance committees and became the MIA's first treasurer. Rufus Lewis, head of the Citizens Committee, was elected to the MIA's Committee of Negotiating and its Executive Board, and became the Chairman of the Transportation Committee. Mrs. Jo Ann Robinson, one of the leaders of the Women's Political Council, was elected to the Negotiating Committee and the Executive Board of the MIA. R. L. Matthews, who headed the local NAACP, was elected to the MIA's Executive Board. All the groups that King specified as having been at loggerheads before the movement were represented in significant positions in the new protest organization.

The ICC in Tallahassee followed a similar course. The NAACP, the Tallahassee Business League, and other black organizations existed before the movement. When it was decided that a mass bus boycott was needed, the leaders of these groups formed the Inter Civic Council, which included the existing organizations. The Reverend C. K. Steele, who was the president of the local NAACP and a member of the Civic League and the Inter Denominational Ministerial Alliance, was elected president of the ICC. With Steele as president of both the NAACP and the ICC, the efforts of these two groups became solidified. Reverend Speed, who had organized the business League, became chairman of the ICC's Transportation Committee. The leaders of other organized groups in Tallahassee also became leaders in the ICC. Thus the ICC became an organization of organizations. According to Rev. Speed: "When this thing occurred here in the city—the boycott movement—then we found out that this would be just right to bring together all the rest of the organizations that had been trying to work with us here in the city, trying to get things together."[9]

In Birmingham Shuttlesworth had a difficult time uniting the various black leaders behind the ACMHR. Support from a large segment of the black ministers was often sporadic and at times nonexistent. The reason was that the Reverend J. L. Ware, head of the local Baptist Ministers Conference, often opposed Shuttlesworth's direct action approach. Support from black lawyers was also sporadic, because they were accustomed to representing litigants who employed the traditional legal approach of the NAACP. For similar reasons some black professionals failed to embrace the program and policies of the ACMHR.[10] For movement centers to be classified as "organizations of organizations," however, it is not necessary for them to include all groups in their communities. It is necessary only that they include a significant number of such organizations. Most of the top officers in the ACMHR were ministers, which meant that their churches supported the organization. As a previous membership chairman of the NAACP, moreover, Shuttlesworth had developed ties with most of the civic organizations in Birmingham. Those ties enabled him to pull a number of leaders from those groups into the organization. George Walker, a civic leader, became a member of the ACMHR's security system with responsibility for guarding Shuttlesworth's home. Several former leaders of the outlawed NAACP became members of the ACMHR Board of Directors.[11] Thus the ACMHR could claim to be operating as an "organization of organizations."

The genius of these movement organizations—the United Defense League of Baton Rouge as well as the MIA, the ICC, and the ACMHR—

was their ability to unite community leaders by bringing them directly into leadership positions while simultaneously organizing the black masses. They were able to organize the black masses because they themselves were mass-based organizations that had grown directly out of a mass-based institution, the black church. It is almost inconceivable to picture an alternative route to mass mobilization in these complex black communities, with their deep social divisions and under a tripartite system of domination that controlled blacks and kept them powerless.

Social life, no matter how routine or novel, is woven around enduring historical practices and group structures. Thus on paper the new social movement organizations that guided the early mass movements were structured much like the NAACP branches with which their leaders were so familiar. And, to be sure, there were continuities of leadership and preestablished networks between the NAACP and the new organizations.

Nevertheless, the MIA, the ICC, and the ACMHR differed from the NAACP and previous protest activity in three important ways. The differences are to be found in (1) decision-making apparatus and procedures; (2) reliance on charisma, mass emotionalism, and mass enthusiasm; and (3) disruptive tactics by the masses. The last nationally influential Southern black leader before the modern civil rights movement was Booker T. Washington. Washington's death in 1915 signaled the end of an era. National black leadership shifted to leaders and organizations in the north. Men like W. E. B. DuBois, scholar and NAACP leader; Lester Granger of the Urban League; Charles Houston, a legal counsel of the NAACP; the union organizer A. Philip Randolph; and Walter White, Executive Director of the NAACP until his death in 1955, became the leaders and spokesmen for American blacks.

Southern black leaders began to regain leadership of the Southern blacks during the late 1950s as a result of mass movements, which called for local leadership. In the Southern-based MIA, ICC, and ACMHR, local black ministers and community leaders were in total control of the decision-making process. Decisions in the new organizations reflected input from community leaders and lay people through committees, executive boards, and mass meetings. However, in most instances the president of the organization held most of the power.

But it would be misleading to call these organizations one-man enterprises. Each had definite divisions of labor and clear lines of authority. Power was channeled through various organizational positions and personnel. Without such an arrangement, it is unlikely that the complicated business of managing mass movements could have been accomplished. The presidents of these organizations were nonetheless able to avoid organizational constraints characteristic of bureaucracy. They had the power to operate outside of procedures that hampered mass action. By directing the movement organizations in the way churches were run, the ministers and other movement leaders were able to act quickly and decisively. Obviously, such a decision-making process in these conflict situations often proved critical.

The MIA, ICC, and ACMHR operated in a context of charisma, mass emotionalism, and mass enthusiasm in consequence of being church-related protest organizations. The minister of the black church is often a charismatic personality and this certainly held true for the leaders of the MIA, ICC, and ACMHR. But that is only half of the story. The new movement organizations inherited the vibrant church culture, with its tradition of bringing whole congregations into community activities, a guarantee of mass participation. When the masses assembled at the meetings, everyone sang the black spirituals they knew so well. They all bowed their heads when the traditional prayers of the church were offered. When the leaders addressed the meetings their style of presentation was rooted in the tradition of the church sermon, which elicited the mass response of "amen." Indeed, mass participation at meetings was usually guaranteed because scripture reading, prayer, and hymns were built directly into the program. Commenting on the role of music and speeches at the MIA mass meeting, E. D. Nixon explained: "If you are going to continue to lead a group of people you are going to have to put something into the program that those people like. A whole lot of people came to the MIA meetings for no other reason than just to hear the music, some came to hear the folks who spoke."[12]

Dr. King was acutely aware of the role that church culture played in these protest organizations. In this regard he wrote:

> The opening hymn was the old familiar "Onward Christian Soldiers," and when that mammoth audience stood to sing, the voices outside (the church building could not accommodate the large gatherings) swelling the chorus in the church, there was a mighty ring like the glad echo of heaven itself. . . . The enthusiasm of these thousands of people swept everything along like an onrushing tidal wave.[13]

Lerone Bennett, an astute analyst of the black experience, has suggested another important role that church culture played in the Montgomery movement. In his view the church culture that permeated the meetings enabled the diverse groups (professors, porters, doctors, maids, laborers, housewives, even drunks) to abandon the claims of rank, class, and creed, while reaching out to each other in new hope and new faith. He further argues that "under the impact of the Old Negro Spirituals, of hand-clapping, shouting, 'testifying,' and 'amening,' personality shells dissolved and reintegrated themselves around a larger, more inclusive racial self."[14]

In short, the new protest organizations relied on much more than the dry organizational procedures associated with bureaucracy, where the memorandum and the Roberts Rules of Order predominate and which often favors only those skilled in the art of bureaucratic politics. To be sure, the new protest organizations attracted and held masses because the ordinary person felt "at home" in their meetings and actually played a participatory role. Thus the meetings stood in sharp contrast to the formal atmosphere that usually characterized the NAACP. Moreover, the charismatic clergy who led these organizations were comfortable with the cultural contexts of the meetings, which was not significantly different from the premovement environment they functioned in when church convened every Sunday morning.

Finally, in contrast to the legal approach of the NAACP, the MIA, ICC, and ACMHR relied on disruptive tactics. The principal methods of disruption employed by these new protest organizations were the economic boycott and direct action demonstrations. The legal method was included but with the explicit understanding that its role was to supplement direct action methods. Students of black protest have failed to pay sufficient attention to economic boycotts, even though much evidence indicates that blacks made extensive use of them. Meier and Rudwick reported that between 1900 and 1906 blacks in twenty-five Southern cities boycotted the Jim Crow streetcars. During one such boycott, a petition was circulated that stated, "Let us touch to the quick the white man's pocket. Tis there his conscience often lies."[15] In 1955–56, in Orangeburg, South Carolina, white businessmen began to use severe economic reprisals against blacks fighting for school desegregation. Blacks "replied with the only weapon known to them—the boycott." In that case both parties played economic politics. Summing up the famous Orangeburg boycott, Benjamin Muse wrote: "On the white side, one grocer went out of business, the laundry closed its pick-up station in the Negro section, and many merchants saw their sales dwindle. By the spring of 1956, the white business community was ready in effect to cry 'enough.'"[16] So the economic boycott has been a powerful weapon for blacks in conflict situations.

The modern civil rights movement and the modern direct action organizations grew directly out of bus boycotts. Boycotts brought widespread economic and social disruption to three capital cities, Baton Rouge, Montgomery, and Tallahassee. Buses became the first target of the movement because members of the black community had begun to see bus discrimination not as a private misery but as a public issue and a common enemy. It had become a widespread social grievance shared throughout the community.

For bus boycotts to be successful, masses of blacks had to participate and cooperate. When they did, economic and social disruption resulted. During the bus boycotts in Montgomery and Tallahassee the revenues of the bus companies plummetted, and the entire white business community was adversely affected. Once the mass boycotts were under way, they engendered violence or the threat of violence toward blacks by segments of the white community, and whites could not be sure that blacks would not retaliate with violence. Indeed, uncertainty is always introduced when a mass movement occurs in a community. All of a sudden social order becomes tenuous. The white business community suffered from that uncertainty. White men advised their wives not to shop too frequently downtown, because the "niggers were down there acting up and you can't be sure of what they might do next." The proprietors of segregated business concerns became jittery at the thought that their segregated enterprises could be subjected to a boycott target just as the buses had.

The disruptive qualities of the boycotts were evident throughout the community. The overwhelming majority of employed black females of these cities worked as domestics. Their job was to scrub floors, cook, clean, iron, and in general make life easier for white women. This was a valued economic arrangement whereby black women earned a small but important salary and white women were freed to tend to more "important" things of life. Once the boycotts were launched, the work relationship between the black domestic and her white employer became problematic. Ironically, the economic arrangement was disrupted whenever the opponents of the bus boycotts succeeded in obstructing the car lifts that boycotters had set up in Montgomery and Tallahassee, following the Baton Rouge example. The obvious problem was that such success prevented domestics from showing up for work. A less obvious problem, even more difficult, was the internal tension created between whites, as well as tensions between the white female employer and her domestic, when whites demanded that severe economic reprisals be used to break the backs of the protesters.

Preston Valien brought the situation to light in an interview with a Montgomery domestic who reported that her employer said to her: "I'm going to tell you this, Susie, because I know you can keep your mouth shut. In the White Citizens Council meeting, they discussed starving the maids for a month. They asked us to lay our maids off for a month, and they'll be glad to ride the buses again. If they do it, I still want you to come one day a week."[17] The domestic did not promise to alleviate any economic or social tensions when she replied, "Well, Mrs. Powell, I just won't come at all, and I sure won't starve. . . . So I'm not worried at all, cause I was eating before I started working for you."[18]

The modern civil rights movement thus stepped boldly forward brandishing the banner of economic boycott. The UDL, MIA, and the ICC were organized to direct mass bus boycotts. The ACMHR employed a small-scale bus boycott shortly after its inception and continued to fight for desegregration on the buses until it was finally accomplished in the early 1960s. The boycott technique became a spearhead of the civil rights movement precisely because it brought economic and social disruption to the Southern cities that specialized in backing the black community into the corners with the tripartite system of domination.

The economic boycott was a special form of a more general strategy that became known as direct action. During the civil rights movement direct action referred to a particular belief held by movement participants and to a whole battery of acts and techniques designed to cause disruption. In Montgomery, Tallahassee, and Birmingham large numbers of blacks came to believe that they could change their position in the society by directly and persistently engaging in aggressive protest activities. More specifically, they came to believe it was necessary to confront and attack the institutions and people standing as obstacles in their path to "freedom." The Reverend Fred Shuttlesworth's recollection of what he told the black masses who packed the church the night that the ACMHR was organized is characteristic of this aggressive thrust: "But I organized to fight segregation. I put this in their hearts and in their minds that night. Now when you organize to fight segregation, that means you can never be still. We gonna wipe it out, or it's gonna wipe us out. Somebody may have to die."[19] The historical record confirms that Shuttlesworth and his supporters kept the State of Alabama turbulently rocking with protest activity for more than twelve years.

The direct action orientation laid heavy stress on the "here and now." Movement participants and sympathizers believed that social change could be realized immediately if they forced the oppressors to yield by vigorously engaging in protest activities. The NAACP's time-consuming legal method, which challenged segregation through the courts, was superseded by mass direct action. Movement participants came to see themselves as efficacious agents of change, and they became convinced that it was they who had to act if change was to become a reality. A detailed examination of the movements in Montgomery, Tallahassee, and Birmingham reveals that it was effective mass organization that enabled these movement centers to challenge the racist regimes of the South.

MONTGOMERY

The Montgomery boycott was the watershed of the modern civil rights movement for several reasons. Even though it was the second mass bus boycott of the modern civil rights movement, among blacks and whites across the United States and the world Montgomery was thought to be the first. The Montgomery protest earned this recognition because it was launched on such a massive scale and lasted more than a year. Its contributions to the emerging civil rights movement were the MIA, the Reverend Martin Luther King, Jr., the nonviolent method, and success.

Mobilization

Mobilization occurred in Montgomery three days before the mass movement. On December 1, 1955, Mrs. Rosa Parks refused to give her bus seat to a white man in defiance of local segregation laws. Who was Rosa Parks? Most accounts, consistent with the view that social movements arise spontaneously, describe Mrs. Parks as a quiet, dignified older lady who, on that fateful day, spontaneously refused to move from her seat because she "had had enough" and was tired after a long, hard day at work. This account is as mistaken as it is popular. Mrs. Parks was deeply rooted in the black protest tradition. Indeed, in the 1940s Mrs. Parks had refused several times to comply with segregation rules on the buses. In the early 1940s Mrs. Parks was ejected from a bus for failing to comply. The very same bus driver who ejected her that time was the one who had her arrested on December 1, 1955. In Mrs. Parks's words, "My resistance to being mistreated on the buses and anywhere else was just a regular thing with me and not just that day."[20]

Mrs. Parks, like others steeped in the protest tradition, had a long history of involvement with protest organizations. She began serving as secretary for the local NAACP in 1943 and still held that post when arrested in 1955. In the late 1940s the Alabama State Conference of NAACP branches was organized, and Mrs. Parks served as the first secretary for this body. That position brought her into contact with such activists operating on the national level as Ella Baker, A. Philip Randolph, and Roy Wilkins. In the early 1940s Mrs. Parks organized the local NAACP Youth Council, which fizzled out after a few years. However, she and other local women reorganized the Council in 1954–55, with Mrs. Parks as its adult adviser. During the 1950s the youth in this organization attempted to borrow books from a white library. They also took rides and sat in the front seats of segregated buses, then returned to the Youth Council to discuss their acts of defiance with Mrs. Parks. Mrs. Parks had scheduled a NAACP Youth Council workshop to be held on December 4, 1955, but her arrest on December 1 canceled that function.[21]

Clearly, then, Mrs. Parks's arrest triggered the mass movement not only because she was a quiet, dignified woman of high morals but also because she was an integral member of those organizational forces capable of mobilizing a social movement. Importantly, Mrs. Parks was also anchored in the church community of Montgomery, where she belonged to the St. Paul AME Church and served as a stewardess.

The charismatic leader—Dr. Martin Luther King, Jr.—did not formulate the plan for a mass bus boycott in Montgomery. E. D. Nixon, a longtime resident of the city, who had only a grammar school education, and members of the Women's Political Council led by Jo Ann Robinson, an English teacher at Alabama State College, were the ones primarily responsible for planning the boycott. Mrs. Parks and Nixon had an organizational association of more than a decade's standing. During most of the years that Mrs. Parks worked as secretary for the local NAACP, Nixon served as its president. She traveled throughout the years with Nixon, assisting him in his work with various organizations. Nixon was an "organization man" in the full sense of the term. By 1955 he had headed the local Brotherhood of Sleeping Car Porters for more than fifteen years. He was also president of the Progressive Democrats, a local political organization.

In the black community E. D. Nixon was considered a militant and the person to see whenever blacks encountered trouble with whites or wanted to fight against racial domination. Three times in 1955, prior to Mrs. Parks's arrest, women had approached Nixon in reference to harsh treatment they had received on the buses. Nixon and other community leaders had discussed those incidents and even entertained the possibility of a bus boycott. It was decided, however, that those cases were not the ideal occasions for such an undertaking.

Nixon was informed shortly after Mrs. Parks's arrest. He immediately posted the bond and consulted with her, seeking her consent to the use of her case to challenge the Jim Crow laws on the buses. She agreed, and Nixon explains what happened next:

> I went home that night and took out a slide rule and a sheet of paper and I put Montgomery in the center of that sheet and I discovered that there wasn't a single spot in Montgomery a man couldn't walk to work if he really wanted to. I said it ain't no reason in the world why we should lose the boycott because people couldn't get to work.[22]

On the evening of Mrs. Parks's arrest a bus boycott was also being discussed and planned by a group of black women who belonged to the

Women's Political Council (WPC). The WPC was organized by professional black women of Montgomery in 1949 for the purpose of registering black women to vote.[23] Shortly after its inception it became a political force in Montgomery. Members of the WPC were especially prepared to play a leadership role in organizing the bus boycott because of their previous experience. For example, in 1954 the WPC and other community groups met twice with Montgomery's City Commission and discussed the grievances of the black community regarding segregated buses. They informed the Commission that blacks were dissatisfied with standing over empty bus seats, boarding the buses by the rear door after paying fares in the front, and bus stops twice as far apart in the black community as in white neighborhoods.[24] In response to these meetings the City Commission and representatives of the bus company acceded to the request that buses stop at every corner in the black community but refused to act on the other complaints.

The WPC was active on other fronts during the years preceding Mrs. Parks's arrest. In 1954 and 1955 the WPC and other community groups met with the City Commission and asked that black policemen be hired, that the situation of inadequate parks and playgrounds in the black community be changed, and that the horrible conditions on the buses be altered.[25] In May 1954 the City Commission hired four black policemen but refused to grant the other requests. Finally, on March 2, 1955, Claudette Colvin, a fifteen-year-old black, was arrested for refusing to relinquish her seat to a white person. She was found guilty of violating the bus segregation ordinance and assault and battery on the arresting officer. Members of the WPC were central in supporting Miss Colvin and even began formulating plans to boycott the Montgomery bus line. These plans were dropped after it was learned that Miss Colvin was expecting a child out of wedlock.[26]

A number of the women in the WPC had worked with both Mrs. Parks and E. D. Nixon several times. Members of this organization spoke with Nixon and agreed that a boycott should be initiated. These women immediately activated their organizational and personal networks and spread the word that a boycott was necessary to protest the arrest and challenge the Jim Crow bus laws. On the morning of December 2, Mrs. Robinson and Mrs. Mary Fair Burks of the WPC informed students and teachers at Alabama State College of the pending bus boycott. Mrs. Robinson composed a leaflet, which described the Parks incident and called for community action. Members of the WPC mobilized students and faculty, who immediately assisted them in mimeographing the leaflets and distributing them throughout the black community. Hence, the organizational forces of the black community that represented the protest tradition had begun to mobilize in support of one of their own, Mrs. Rosa Parks.

Meanwhile, on December 2 Nixon was busy compiling a list of ministers and asking them to support the boycott. When asked why he started with the ministers Nixon replied, "because they had their hands on the black masses." Some of the "progressive" ministers, including Ralph Abernathy and E. N. French, agreed that a boycott was needed. On Monday, December 5, Abernathy, French, and Nixon met and formulated the demands to be presented to the bus company. They decided that it was essential to form a new organization to lead the protest. Because all three were closely associated with the NAACP, Nixon was asked why they did not organize the boycott through the NAACP. Nixon stated that he explored the idea with the local NAACP, and

> . . . the man who was the president of NAACP at that time said, "Bro. Nixon, I'll have to wait until I talk to New York [NAACP headquarters] to find out what they think about it." I said, man, we ain't got time for that. He believed in doing everything by the book. And the book stated that you were suppose to notify New York before you take a step like that.[27]

Here is a concrete example of how a bureaucratized organization was inappropriate in the early mobilization stage of a mass protest. The group proceeded to form an "organization of organizations," and Abernathy named it the Montgomery Improvement Association.

Reverend Abernathy asked Nixon to become head of the new organization. Nixon, a shrewd analyst of the organizational nature of black society, decided that a black minister would be more appropriate. For a boycott to be successful, he knew, it was crucial that the churches be mobilized. He explained that a minister had to be chosen because "ministers will follow one another and then we wouldn't have to be fighting the churches to get something done."[28] A few months before Mrs. Parks's arrest, Nixon had heard Dr. King present a guest lecture for the NAACP. Nixon remembers that he was so impressed with King's speaking abilities that he told a friend who attended the lecture: "I don't know how I am going to do it but some day I am going to hang him to the stars. On December 5, 1955, I hung him there."[29] Nixon assisted in "hanging" King to the stars by supporting the decision that King become the head of the new organization. (Actually, it was Rufus Lewis, head of the Citizens Committee and a member of King's church, who nominated King for the presidency of the MIA on December 5, 1955. The nomination was seconded by Prince E. Conley.)

Thus the Montgomery movement contrasts sharply with the charismatic movement described by Max Weber, where the leader attracts a revolutionary following because of his extraordinary personality and compelling vision. In this instance the visions of an uncharismatic and largely uneducated pullman porter and members of the WPC and other community organizations were thrust into the hands of a charismatic minister who could play a key mobilizing role because he occupied a central position in the church.

Once the idea of the bus boycott was formulated, extensive organizing of the ministers continued, with Martin Luther King now directly involved. Dr. King wrote:

> With the sanction of Rev. H. H. Hubbard—president of the Baptist Ministerial Alliance—Abernathy and I began calling all of the Baptist ministers. Since most of the Methodist ministers were attending a denominational meeting in one of the local churches that afternoon, it was possible for Abernathy to get the announcement to all of them simultaneously.[30]

Before King and Abernathy began calling ministers, they obtained the support of the president of the Baptist Ministerial Alliance. The chance of getting support from ministers was greater if the head of the ministerial alliance gave his full support. The approach to the meeting of Methodist ministers demonstrates the interdenominational cooperation between church leaders and between their churches. Reverend Abernathy's organizational affiliation facilitated his mobilizing activities; he was pastor of the First Baptist Church and served as the secretary of the Baptist Ministerial Alliance. It is the presence of preexisting networks and groups that allows a movement to emerge.

When the first organizational meeting was held, E. D. Nixon, who had pressed the idea of a bus boycott, was out of town. King writes, "In his absence, we concluded that Rev. L. Roy Bennett—as president of the Inter Denominational Ministerial Alliance—was the logical person to take the chair."[31] Bennett was the "logical" person because of his important position as head of the organization that encompassed most ministers of Montgomery. These leaders knew that wide community support was needed for the planned boycott. The majority of Montgomery's black ministers on December 2, 1955, agreed to back the bus boycott. According to King:

> The ministers endorsed the plan with enthusiasm, and promised to go to their congregations on Sunday morning and drive home their approval of the projected one-day protest. This cooperation was significant, since virtually all of the influential Negro ministers of the city were present.[32]

Generally the mobilization techniques described here are quite similar to those employed at the beginning of the other three early mass movements of the modern civil rights period. They first took shape in

Baton Rouge in 1953 and emerged fully in the mid-1950s in Montgomery, Tallahassee, and Birmingham. In none of these cases did an angry or volatile mob gather and overpower the racist regimes of those Southern cities. On the contrary, it was the deliberate organizing efforts initiated by community leaders through mass-based organizations that made these movements possible.

Contributions of Montgomery

Social movement organizations are the vehicles of social movements. Before the Montgomery movement blacks had no mass-based movement organizations. The UDL of Baton Rouge had been successful, but that mass movement lasted only seven days and was practically invisible to the larger black community. The importance of the UDL lies in what it taught to a small but significant number of community leaders. Because it was led by a minister, news of its success and dynamics quickly traveled through ministerial circles. Therefore, it served as a protest model for those leaders rather than as a blueprint for the larger black population. A protest of the magnitude of Montgomery was required to provide the larger community with a blueprint.

Because of the visibility of the Montgomery movement, the MIA became known to blacks across the country. Black leaders, especially clergymen from across the South, visited Montgomery to gain a better understanding of the Montgomery Improvement Association. They attended its weekly mass meetings, sat in on some of its executive sessions, and observed its functioning. Those leaders came to understand the important political role that music and preaching played in organizing and removing fear from the masses. Knowledge about movement workshops, organization of effective committees, the raising of money, the tactics of the opposition, the connection between movement organizations and the masses, and the absolute necessity of church cooperation was disseminated. And, indeed, there was much to learn, for the MIA was a complex organization. It had sizable savings and checking accounts deposited in banks in at least nine states. This policy was initiated so that if any one bank froze its funds, its overall operation would not be seriously hampered.[33]

Because the Montgomery movement attracted widespread sympathy and media coverage from groups outside the South, the financial structure of the MIA was more complex than that of the UDL and most other direct action organizations of the period. That is, the MIA relied on both "inside" and "outside" money. Like the UDL, the Montgomery movement was initially organized and supported by donations collected at mass meetings.[34] This source of support remained central to the MIA throughout the bus boycott. However, large sums of money came from outside, especially the North. This has led some writers to conclude that the Montgomery effort was successful because of the money it received from Northern white liberals.

There are serious problems with this interpretation. For one thing, much of the "outside" money was raised by black churches, organizations, and individuals in the North.[35] Indeed, many Northern blacks identified with the movement because they had relatives in the South and because they had found racism, not the Promised Land, in the North. Northern blacks supported the movement also because the black church was a national institution through which Southern and Northern ministers stayed in close contact. The NAACP, which worked closely with the church, also provided important sources of Northern black financial support for the MIA. Shortly after the boycott was organized, NAACP branches and black churches throughout the country instituted a joint fundraising campaign. By May 1956 these organizations had sent the MIA more than four thousand dollars. Similarly, in 1956 the Brooklyn branch of the NAACP sent three thousand dollars, the Pittsburgh branch more than two thousand, and the national NAACP more than four thousand.[36] Throughout the boycott hundreds of NAACP branches sent money that had been collected at church mass meetings held within and outside the South. In this regard King wrote, "The largest response came from church groups—particularly, though by no means only, Negro churches."[37] This support link between Northern and Southern blacks is critically important and endured throughout the civil rights movement.

Northern white support of the MIA was also substantial. The money came from individuals and especially labor and peace organizations. For example, treasurer E. D. Nixon reported that when he met with the United Automobile Workers Union in Detroit they gave him $35,000.[38] Bayard Rustin, Executive Secretary of the War Resisters League, raised $5,000 for the MIA primarily through his contacts with labor and peace organizations.[39] So Northern white support was important, but it must be placed in perspective. Money from whites augmented the large sums systematically raised by local blacks of Montgomery and blacks throughout the country. In this regard, King wrote to Rustin: "If we can continue to get a reasonable sum of money from outside sources, I believe we will be able to raise enough in the local community to keep going indefinitely."[40] Money from blacks and whites outside Montgomery was so intertwined that a leader of Brooklyn's NAACP wrote King:

At present our Committee is raising money to buy a station wagon to send to Montgomery. Thousands of people, Negro and White, are working behind the lines to help you who are carrying on the fight on the front lines. All we ask is that you stand your ground, hold fast, and wait. . . . Help is on the way.[41]

Much of the money was spent on the sophisticated transportation system organized by the MIA. This system effectively transported black Montgomerites throughout the city for a year. At the outset black taxi companies provided transportation for the protestors, charging them the same fare they had paid on the buses. The police commissioner immediately halted this operation by making it illegal for taxi drivers to charge below a minimum fare of forty-five cents. Having anticipated this move, King and others devised an alternative system.

At that moment I remembered that some time previously, my good friend Rev. Theodore Jemison had led a bus boycott in Baton Rouge, Louisiana. Knowing that Jemison and his associates had set up an effective private carpool, I put in a long-distance call to ask him for suggestions for a similar pool in Montgomery. As I expected, his painstaking description of the Baton Rouge experience was invaluable.[42]

Thus the transportation system devised by the UDL provided the blueprint for the MIA. Within a matter of days the MIA had organized forty-eight dispatch and forty-two pickup stations. Black mail carriers played a key role in organizing this system, because they knew the layout of the city's streets.

The black church was central to the transportation system. According to King, "most of the dispatch stations were located at the Negro churches. These churches cooperated by opening their doors early each morning so that the waiting passengers could be seated, and many of them provided heat on cold mornings."[43] Summing up the effectiveness of the transportation system, King revealed that even the White Citizens' Council admitted that the car pool moved with "military precision."[44]

It cannot be overemphasized that out of Montgomery came the highly visible movement organization, the MIA. This organization and the dynamics it embraced were to be implemented across the South. Thus, Montgomery paved the way for the wide implementation of the basic organizational principle that originated with the UDL.

Martin Luther King, Jr., was another Montgomery contribution to the emerging civil rights movement.[45] King's charismatic qualities made him known, even among ministers, as the "preachers' preacher." He was the ideal preacher for a number of reasons. First, he was a superbly trained orator. While growing up, King participated in organized debates and oratorical competition, almost always winning the top prize.

His gift for oratory was nurtured by some of the greatest black orators of the twentieth century. The oratorical tradition runs deep in the black community and is riveted into the culture through the church. King clearly understood the social power of oratory and used it as a tool for agitating, organizing, fundraising, and articulating the desires of the black masses.

Second, King was highly educated, having received a doctorate in theology from a respected eastern university shortly after arriving in Montgomery. His educational attainments greatly helped his rise to leadership, because members of the black community had a deep respect for education. There had been a strong anti-intellectual tradition among some clergymen, though not all black ministers were uneducated. Indeed, the intellectual churches of the black community boasted a strong tradition of educated ministers. However, many ministers and congregations of the period before King's arrival were poorly educated because of the system of domination. Ministers of such churches often pushed an anti-intellectual line because they felt threatened by the educated. They based their right to interpret the earthly and heavenly affairs of humanity on having been "called" rather than schooled.

The ambivalent feelings within the black community about the idea of a "calling" emerged in anecdotes. Dr. B. J. Simms, a witty and educated black minister of Montgomery who served as Transportation Chairman of the MIA during the bus boycott, tells of a newly "called" black preacher who came before the elders of a church for employment. They queried the candidate as to why he was convinced that he had been called to preach. The man replied that he had been plowing in the fields in extremely hot temperatures. Then he glanced heavenward and saw the letters "GP" float across the sky. After that, he said, he knew that the letters meant God was calling him to "Go Preach." One of the elders, suspicious of the man's qualifications, gave him a piercing look and said, "Are you sure those letters didn't mean "Go Plow?"[46]

Uneducated ministers relied heavily on emotionally arousing techniques and parables to convey their tremendous store of informally acquired wisdom, nonsense, or both, rather than on carefully reasoned and logically sound arguments. Many of them knew the Bible only through memory because they could not read. They knew much about the sociology of groups through their pastoral duties, which required them to observe, manage, and organize actual groups. These ministers often warned their congregations to beware of the highly educated who bowed to science rather than to Almighty God. Yet blacks as a group cherished education because they viewed it as a way out of oppression. Consequently a latent tension existed between those members of the congregation who thirsted for education and the anti-intellectual position espoused by some clergymen.

Dr. King's ascent to the pulpit demonstrated that this strain was un-necessary and could be eliminated. Here was a highly educated min-ister who was at the same time an unmistakable product of the black church. One of King's talents was to use metaphors that communicated to the "cultured" and educated as well as the uneducated and down-trodden. He coherently wove together the profound utterances of ditch-diggers, great philosophers, college professors, and floor-scrubbing do-mestics with ease. To inspire the poor black masses and the educated through oratory King would tell the street sweeper to go out and sweep streets the way Michelangelo painted pictures or Beethoven composed music or Shakespeare wrote poetry. Moreover, King had the ability to convey in folksy language the commonalities that the contemporary black movement shared with great liberation movements of biblical times. That message was clearly felt among the masses: Protest was right and even divine, and Martin Luther King was the moral figure and prophet divinely inspired to lead the movement. The fact that the masses associated King with Jesus, Moses, and other biblical leaders strengthened King's charismatic appeal.

Thus his education and his many gifts—mastery of language, organ-izing skills, charisma—were central to King's appeal to black people. His presence generated pressure on the anti-intellectual clergymen to acquire relevant substantive information and impart it to their congre-gations. In other words, according to Dr. B. J. Simms, the congregations of such ministers began to demand more from their ministers.[47] When it came to protest, many of these ministers supported King of their own accord, because, being one of them, he spoke their language, and, per-haps more important, many of the congregations simply would have it no other way.

Finally, King was ideal because of the position his family occupied in the church hierarchy. His father was pastor of Ebenezer Baptist Church in Atlanta, one of the leading black Baptist churches in Amer-ica. This was important from both a political and a resource standpoint. Frazier referred to the Negro Church as a nation within a nation, which meant that the black church played an explicit political role in social affairs of blacks:

> As a result of the elimination of Negroes from the political life of the American community, the Negro Church became the arena of their political activities. The church was the main area of social life in which Negroes could aspire to become the leaders of men. . . . The church was the arena in which the struggle for power and the thirst for power could be satisfied.[48]

Frazier goes on to claim that church politics were "especially impor-tant to Negro men who had never been able to assert themselves and assume the dominant male role, even in family relations, as defined by American culture." Dr. King's father, the Reverend Martin Luther King, Sr., mastered the art of "preacher politics" and became an influential churchman.[49] To be an influential churchman meant having to operate on the national church level and to understand the politics of churches and ministers who interacted nationally. It is at this level that substantive church power was wielded and the political astuteness of a minister was put to test. Such was the vantage point from which "Daddy" King operated.

Martin Luther King, Jr., grew up in this political church environment and internalized its ways as he matured under his father's wing. King learned about the delicate art of negotiation, forming blocs, searching for consensus, and coordinating strong and talented men during his formative years. He learned to see the black church as an institutional whole with vast potentials. His environment gave him the critical church connections, alertness to church politics, and knowledge that would serve him throughout his career in the civil rights movement.

Successful politicians, whether in the church or in the electoral arena, quickly learn that resources are the backbone of any durable power arrangement. Large, successful churches like Ebenezer are a result of the generation and management of resources. Indeed, a substantial amount of the property owned by blacks is actually owned by churches, and churches have had close ties with black insurance companies, burial societies, and funeral homes. The successful church is in the business of managing resources. Again, King came from an environment where resource management was a virtue and a necessity, and he learned early how to collect and manage resources. To some extent this may account for his ability to build resource links among a number of organizations such as the NAACP, the Congress of Racial Equality, the Fellowship of Reconciliation, the Highlander Folk School, and the MIA. "Daddy" King's strategic position in the church hierarchy was a definite asset to his son's entry into the unfolding civil rights movement.

Dr. King quickly developed the kind of charismatic relationship with other ministers and the masses that was conducive to producing widespread social disruption. Many leaders interviewed for this study recalled that King could attract large segments of oppressed blacks from the poolrooms, city streets, and backwoods long enough for trained organizers to acquaint them with the workshops, demands, and strategies of the movement. Blacks would come from near and far to get a glimpse of King and to hear him speak. Once exposed to the organizational activities of the movement, the chance was greater that they too would soon be boycotting, contributing to the building of emergency transportation systems, singing movement songs, and creating political leverage by fostering social disruption. What resulted was the "collective power of masses." This power was highly visible. Widespread media coverage disseminated information about the drama across the country and the world. King, the charismatic figure, played a key role in bringing national and international attention to the movement, which generated pressure against the opposition.

The Montgomery movement introduced the nonviolent approach for social change to the black masses. Until this bus boycott, most blacks were unfamiliar with the techniques and principles of nonviolent direct action. The Montgomery movement served as a training ground where nonviolent direct action was systematically introduced and developed among the masses and the local leadership of the boycott.

A block of time was specifically set aside at the weekly mass meetings to train blacks in how to use nonviolence as a tool of social change.[50] That was how, in Montgomery, the "Nonviolent Workshop" was introduced to the civil rights movement. The workshops were often conducted by the Reverend Glenn Smiley and Bayard Rustin, both experts on nonviolent protest, having received extensive training through their long affiliations with pacifist organizations. During the workshops protesters participated in "socio-dramas" in which they were taught to respond creatively and nonviolently to the tense racial climate exacerbated by the boycott. At the workshops literature on nonviolent protest was distributed to the masses so that they could study the techniques at home.

The religious doctrines of the black church provided the ideological framework through which the doctrine of nonviolence was disseminated to black Montgomeryites.[51] For years blacks had been taught that Christian love conquered hate and that the individual should love everyone, including oppressors. King, Abernathy, and Smiley were familiar with the convergences between Christian theology and the philosophy of nonviolence, which they utilized when teaching nonviolence to the masses. In Montgomery blacks were systematically taught to engage in nonviolent protest aimed at bringing about social change. The organizational procedures developed in Montgomery were observed by black leaders (e.g. Steele and Shuttlesworth) across the country, who came to Montgomery to learn the details of the mass movement approach. They would use the same format in their own nonviolent movements.

Finally, Montgomery had a great impact on the black masses because it was successful. The collective power of the masses was generated from the instant that the entire black community boycotted Montgomery buses. Indeed, once the mass bus boycott was under way, the Mayor, the city commissioners, and officials of the bus company were forced to meet continuously with protest leaders to discuss grievances and demands. These meetings contrasted sharply with earlier sessions between black leaders and white authorities. The boycott made it clear that black demands could not be easily ignored, because the entire black community was mobilized in support of its leadership. Thus, from the very beginning Montgomery blacks were able to experience and define themselves as efficacious agents of social change.

Victory came to the Montgomery movement after an entire year of protest. On November 13, 1956, the United States Supreme Court ruled that Alabama's state and local laws requiring segregation on the buses were unconstitutional. Even though it was a Supreme Court ruling that made it possible to end the boycott, the black community of the United States knew that the disciplined and organized mass movement in Montgomery had created the pressure that contributed to the favorable court ruling. The victory was clear proof not only to Montgomery blacks but to blacks across the nation, protest organizations, opposition forces, and the general American population that power is created when masses act collectively. Before a movement starts, politically unconnected individuals of the dominated group are unaware of how to alter their position in the society. Once a movement is successful, the dominated come to know that there is power in organized collective action.

TALLAHASSEE

Tallahassee provided proof that the "collective power of masses" was indeed an authentic form of power. Tallahassee's mass bus boycott began just five months after the Montgomery movement started. In many respects Tallahassee stood in sharp contrast to Montgomery. First of all, it was a small city. According to the 1950 Census, it had 27,237 people residing within its standard metropolitan area. Of these, only 9,373 were nonwhite. The Reverend C. K. Steele referred to Tallahassee as a little, iron-tight town where "everybody knew everybody and white people had their friends, and the people they used to hold the community in check."[52] Speaking of a bus boycott, Steele stated, "I had no dream that it could happen in Tallahassee." The appearance of a movement in a small city would alert Southerners to the increasing power and pervasiveness of mass protest. Social disruption occurred in Tallahassee during May 1956. On a spring day two women students from Florida A. and M. College refused to give up their bus seats to whites. Organizational forces in the black community immediately began organizing a movement when the two students were arrested for their action. Steele was asked how much Montgomery had inspired the Tallahassee boycott. "Well, we had one, you must remember, in Baton Rouge," he answered. "I heard of it. I knew Rev. Jemison, had known his daddy. I knew about that."[53] This testimony places the origin of the modern civil rights movement in Baton Rouge. Steele acknowledged that Montgomery was also central, that he and others frequently visited that movement and learned its format for meetings, its procedures, and the nature of its demands.

As to the difference between Tallahassee and Montgomery, Steele states:

> It was Montgomery with the Ph.D.s as its leaders, and many of the Professors at Alabama State were involved. They had every kind of facility with which to operate, in a big manner, in a big way. They had attracted the attention of the whole world even people who were coming out from India, from everywhere.[54]

Whereas the Montgomery movement received important financial assistance from outside sources, the Tallahassee movement did not. In that regard the Tallahassee movement, like the one in Baton Rouge, was far more typical than the Montgomery movement. The civil rights movement did not emerge from the efforts of outside elites or ambitious participants who simply wanted to advance in the social structure. Rather, the overwhelming majority of the numerous local movements during that period were organized and financed by indigenous blacks.

A brief examination of the mobilization and organizational base of the Tallahassee mass bus boycott will uncover the logic of that movement. On May 27, 1956, two female students from Florida A. and M. College were arrested after refusing to move from seats in the "white section" of a local bus.[55] The student body at the all-black college took the first mass action. On May the 28 the students met and unanimously voted to stay off the buses for the remainder of the semester. The following day students monitored the buses passing through the campus and persuaded black passengers not to ride on them. The students had been successful in initiating the boycott, and within a short time word of the students' action had spread to the larger black community. The school semester would end in two weeks, however, and what would happen to the boycott after the students left was unclear. Black church leaders solved the problem by acting immediately.

On May 29 Reverend Steele—minister, community leader, and president of the local NAACP—along with Dr. James Hudson, president of the Inter-Denominational Alliance (a clergy organization comprising black ministers of all denominations) and former chaplain at the college, immediately arranged a meeting of community leaders to discuss the arrests. Again, it was established leadership closely tied to the mass-based church that spearheaded the movement after the students had acted. At that meeting a committee was formed to approach the city manager to ascertain whether members of the white power structure would desegregate the buses.

Anticipating a negative response, these church leaders, using their vast organizational contacts, called a mass meeting at the Bethel AME Church, which was strategically located in the center of the black community. The committee reported to the meeting that the city manager and the manager of the bus company maintained that bus desegregation was impossible. A motion passed that night to call an immediate boycott of the buses. At that moment Tallahassee's organization of organizations, the ICC, was formally organized. Ministers were elected to serve as president (C. K. Steele), vice president (K. S. Dupont), and secretary (M. C. Williams) of the new organization. Indeed, the ICC was modeled after the UDL and the MIA, having various committees and an organized church work force to accomplish its tasks.

Again, the Southwide attack against the NAACP played a role in the formation of the new protest organizations in Tallahassee. Reverend Steele, as president of the local NAACP, was asked why the boycott was not organized through that organization. He replied: "We would have fought this thing under the NAACP. But there were people who said they've outlawed it in Montgomery, the NAACP. They're going to outlaw it here, and it was for that reason that we formed another organization in Tallahassee, other than fighting it under NAACP."[56] Historical events prevent us from knowing whether a mass direct action movement could have been organized through the NAACP in Tallahassee. What is clear, however, is that the attack against the NAACP caused the local black leadership and black institutions of Tallahassee to become the agents of social change in the community.

In Tallahassee, an effective transportation system was organized by the Transportation Committee, chaired by Reverend Speed. Steele recalled:

> That committee's job was to see to it that people got to and from wherever they wanted to go. They proceeded to set up the following system; that anybody who would drive were to go to various of our own filling stations authorized to give them two dollars' worth of gas, and when they ran out they could come back for more. We designated various places in town where people could assemble to be picked up to go to work or what have you.[57]

Within a couple of days no blacks in Tallahassee rode the buses. The new transportation system enabled them to continue working and moving about the city.

The financial base of this movement was also rooted in the black church. In Reverend Speed's words:

The bulk of the money came from the black people in the community, from church to church. The various churches would take up a collection, and they would bring it over if they weren't at the mass meeting at that particular time. They would bring that money from those churches to the mass meeting. Every church at that particular time where we were holding the meetings were the largest churches we had here. They would be overrun.[58]

Thus, the money for the movement was collected through the church community.

An effective boycott in Tallahassee required the total mobilization of the black community. As in Montgomery, long-term mass mobilization was attained through the churches and especially the grassroots mass meetings. Reverend Steele recalls that "we held two mass meetings a week," but since "no church in town could accommodate the people we finally had to have two a night on either side of town. About three of us would visit at each one of those meetings and talk."[59] Moreover, to ensure solidarity the mass meetings rotated from church to church. Pointing out the utility of rotating the mass meetings, Reverend Speed informs that "when we would go to those various churches at various times in the community, we would pull all the people from the North side to the South, and all the people from the South to the North all the time."[60] This method allowed community people to exchange ideas and resources. The method of rotating the mass meetings between churches had been adopted earlier in Montgomery. The mass movement in Tallahassee, then, was not spontaneous; it grew out of the deliberate efforts of organizers, who mobilized the community through preexisting organizations coordinated by the ICC.

The Tallahassee movement provided a training ground for the further development of the nonviolent strategy. As was shown earlier, local movements were connected rather than isolated. These connections become evident when one investigates how the philosophy and tactics of nonviolence spread throughout the South. Nonviolence was first introduced to the black masses in Montgomery. Indeed, as a disciplined form of mass struggle it was systematically taught to blacks by experts at each mass meeting of the MIA. These experts formed a "nonviolent team," including Reverend Abernathy and the Reverend Glenn Smiley of the Fellowship of Reconciliation.

Part of their mission was to visit other "trouble spots" in the South and teach nonviolence. At the outset of the Tallahassee movement the nonviolent team was dispatched there to teach the new method. For many local movements the possibility of violence was strong, because they faced opposition forces accustomed to its use or making threats of its use. Yet blacks for the most part remained nonviolent. How was this accomplished in Tallahassee, where the Ku Klux Klan, the White Citizens' Council, and other racist groups made it known that they were prepared for violence?

Reverend Speed was asked whether the Tallahassee leadership had problems keeping the masses nonviolent. He replied:

> Not a lot, because we had some experts in nonviolent training here at all times. One person in particular was Dr. Glenn Smiley. Glenn was the active chairman for the committee of the nonviolent group that talked to all of the various assemblies. When he didn't do it himself, somebody out of his committee would be there to talk with them. . . . The various leaders in the churches and other persons would in turn talk to their memberships. Consequently, it had a tendency to always keep a kind of a shadow of direction over the people.[61]

Speaking about one of the tense moments in Tallahassee, Reverend Steele explained: "Something was going to happen, because it had come to a breaking point. They may have had a riot, a race riot. I don't know what would have happened in Tallahassee had we not had the background of this philosophy of love and nonviolence actually demonstrated in Montgomery."[62] Blacks did not struggle nonviolently because they were peaceful by nature. Rather, nonviolence became a disciplined form of mass struggle because it was systematically developed through the organized structures of the movement.

As for results, the mass boycott put the buses out of business in the black community of Tallahassee. Considering that it was concurrent with the boycott in Montgomery, in which the issues were being deliberated by the Supreme Court, the Tallahassee leaders decided to continue the boycott until that ruling was made. When the Supreme Court ruled against bus segregation in Montgomery, blacks in Tallahassee resumed riding buses, with desegregated seating. Even after the ruling, however, blacks often encountered difficulties when they attempted to use the front seats. Periodically the boycott was reinstituted until bus desegregation was achieved for good, two years after the start of the boycott.

The wider significance of the Tallahassee victory was in demonstrating that the black masses could be organized for protest in small Southern cities. It was becoming clear that the power of social disruption would be not a transitory oddity but an enduring social reality. By January 7, 1957, the Southern Regional Council (SRC) in a press release "disclosed that 21 Southern cities had ended compulsory segregation on local buses without difficulty." The SRC went on to state: "In every case the desegregation took place without court action—usually by a change of policy on the part of the transit company involved. The change caused no incidents of violence or organized protest."[63] In these cities, then, the *potential* for mass action was sufficient to cause elements of the white power structures to capitulate. The Tallahassee struggle signaled to the unfolding civil rights movement that Montgomery was no accident and that massive social disruption was an effective weapon that could be used across the entire South. Indeed, many more bus protests would be conducted, especially in the deep South. Tallahassee played a significant part in establishing the lines along which many of these battles would be fought.

BIRMINGHAM

By Southern standards Birmingham was a large city. Its population exceeded 300,000, and the black population alone was nearly 150,000. The tripartite system of racial domination was firmly entrenched and buttressed by violence. Indeed, Birmingham became known as "Bombingham" because of the bombs that frequently exploded in the black community. By 1956 the NAACP had built a strong organization in Alabama, with fifty-eight branches and a membership of more than 14,000.[64] Moreover, Birmingham was the site of the NAACP's Southeastern headquarters, which coordinated the association's activities in seven Southern states. Following the 1954 Supreme Court school decision, the NAACP was vigorously pursuing desegregation of the public schools. On June 1, 1956, the white power structures in Alabama struck a vital blow to this effort by outlawing the NAACP throughout the state.

The outlawing of the NAACP in Alabama triggered the direct action movement in Birmingham. New protest machinery was developed to replace the NAACP. The Birmingham movement's contribution to the unfolding civil rights struggle was thus in demonstrating that direct action movements could be organized to confront issues other than bus segregation. The Montgomery and Tallahassee movements were organized around acts of defiance (women riders ejected from buses and arrested), which required immediate mobilization of the black community for an effective fight against this specific pattern of domination. Although the outlawing of the NAACP presented the black community with a difficult situation, it was by no means immediately clear what the appropriate response should be or whether any response was necessary.

Reverend Shuttlesworth, minister of Birmingham's Bethel Baptist Church and former membership chairman of the outlawed NAACP, decided it was time to organize a direct action movement in Birmingham. Indeed, it was clear that masses of blacks could be mobilized for social change, for at that very moment blacks were boycotting buses in Montgomery and Tallahassee. Shuttlesworth had observed these movements closely and had visited Montgomery the night its movement was organized. With support from several ministers and community people, Shuttlesworth called a mass meeting to discuss an alternative to the NAACP.

At that meeting the ACMHR was organized. Like the UDL, the MIA, and the ICC, this was a church-related organization with the top leadership positions held by ministers. Also like those organizations, the ACMHR held rotating mass meetings at various churches every Monday night. Shuttlesworth recalls that "when things were really hot, we would hold mass meetings every night."[65] The mass meetings were packed with community folk who came out to fight against domination and participate in the fervent religious culture that undergirded the movement.

Once again, the Birmingham movement was financed largely by the indigenous community. A Southern Conference Educational Fund publication issued about 1959 reported that "since June, 1956, a total of $50,000 has been raised and spent by the ACMHR, most of it on court litigation. Most of this has been contributed by the Negroes of Birmingham, many of whom make scarcely enough to live on."[66] Writing about ACMHR finances somewhat later, Shuttlesworth explained:

I doubt very much if we have gotten over $8,000 from outside of Birmingham in the three years in which the Movement has been organized. Our major weekly source of income is derived through weekly contributions at mass meetings. In addition, we receive some donations, and some income from honorariums I receive for various speaking engagements throughout the country and contributions which are made at these meetings to be given to ACMHR (for all of which we are exceedingly grateful).[67]

When interviewed for this study, Shuttlesworth further clarified the financial structure of the ACMHR: "Our money came from mass meetings. We collected it at the different churches. That was the chief basis of our funding. We didn't get a lot of money from outside. At the first meeting of the ACMHR, we raised $400. We could usually raise $200–300 a night."[68] In short, it was the Birmingham black community that financed efforts aimed at its own liberation.

The grievances, demands, and activities of the ACMHR clearly reveal the character of this new organization. Its first act was to request the hiring of black policemen to patrol black communities. When the white power structure denied that request, the ACMHR filed a lawsuit against Birmingham's Personnel Board to open all civil service examinations to blacks. The Personnel Board responded by removing the "white only" restriction from all jobs and allowing blacks to take the examination, but none were hired. As in Tallahassee, the leaders of the ACMHR decided to ride the Birmingham buses on a desegregated basis immediately after the Supreme Court ruling was handed down in the Montgomery case. Two hundred fifty members of the organization announced that they would ride the buses on December 26, 1956. Violence, Birmingham style, reared its ugly head on Christmas night, 1956. While the city's marquee proclaimed peace unto mankind, Shuttlesworth's home was bombed and the bed in which he slept was shattered. Somehow Shuttlesworth emerged from the wreckage unharmed. A voice louder than any of the other vociferous individuals that had gathered around the bombed house exclaimed, "God saved the Reverend to lead the movement." One of the mottoes of the ACMHR was that you had to keep pushing, testing, and learning. On December 26, 1956, the group of 250 rode the Birmingham bus in mass violation of the local law. Twenty-one were arrested, and the ACMHR immediately filed suit in federal court.

Six months later Shuttlesworth, his wife, and several others attempted to desegregate the Birmingham railroad station. They were forced to flee when they were met by a white mob intent on killing them. Three months later Reverend Shuttlesworth, his wife, and another minister attempted to enroll their children in an all-white school. A mob beat Reverend Shuttlesworth with chains while Mrs. Shuttlesworth was stabbed in the hip, and one of their children sustained a foot injury. In response, the ACMHR filed suit against the board of education. That same month another bomb was tossed into Shuttlesworth's church. By this time, however, the ACMHR had established a security system whereby guards patrolled its president's church and home. A guard threw the bomb out of the sanctuary, but it exploded on impact, damaging part of the church. Three months later members of the ACMHR again attempted to ride a segregated bus. They, along with Shuttlesworth, who was not one of the riders this time, were thrown into jail for violating segregation ordinances. The night of the trial "an orderly crowd of 5,000 Negroes gathered on the Courthouse lawn in non-violent protest against the arrest."[69] All the defendants were convicted but released on bond. The ACMHR responded by filing another injunctive action against the city and the bus company.

Thus, the ACMHR attacked the tripartite system of domination along several fronts: the right to have black police patrol black communities; discrimination in hiring; bus and train segregation; disfranchisement at the polls; segregation of public schools; and segregation at swimming pools, libraries, and retail stores. In Shuttlesworth's words, "I was trying to tear the system down. Out to kill segregation before it killed us."[70] The ongoing mobilization of a large segment of Birmingham's black community through the churches was the backbone of ACMHR's efforts. It was such mobilization that made it possible for five thousand people to protest in an orderly manner on the lawn of the courthouse at an agreed time. The presence of the nonviolent team, which had gathered experience in Montgomery and Tallahassee, was the principal factor that prevented blacks from engaging in violence, an ever present threat in this tense racial atmosphere. Indigenous resources enabled the ACMHR to file lawsuits frequently and confront the white power structure continuously. Shuttlesworth recalls that "the people had so little but did so much to carry on the cause."[71] To be sure, the Birmingham movement was propelled by an organization of organizations and was church-based, but personality factors were central in developing this multipurpose mass movement.

The Reverend Fred Shuttlesworth, president of the ACMHR, personified the spirit of the new direct action era even more than King or Steele. For Shuttlesworth and his supporters were involved in the tedious business of organizing a movement without benefit of a dramatic precipitating event like the ones in Montgomery and Tallahassee. The first grievances of the ACMHR make this clear. The absence of black police was certainly a grievance to which blacks could respond, but it was not a pressing grievance like bus segregation. Most blacks were so oppressed that the idea of having black policemen had never occurred to them. The prospect of hiring black policemen had not been widely discussed in Birmingham's black community, although an interracial committee had pursued the issue since 1952 with no success.[72] Thus Shuttlesworth shocked most of his fellows when he made the request for black policemen. Many considered him a crazy fool or even an opportunist for voicing such a demand. Furthermore, the black community could not boycott the police force the way they could bus companies. The ACMHR therefore applied the legal strategy in attacking this particular grievance in late 1956. In fact, the ACMHR effectively combined the legal approach pioneered by the NAACP and direct action tactics.[73] It was the direct action approach that distinguished the ACMHR from previous struggles in Birmingham.

Because Shuttlesworth was organizing a movement without the benefit of a precipitating outrage, such as the arrest of Rosa Parks, he was forced to make direct action popular by his personal acts and courage. Dr. King and Reverend Steele were not placed in this predicament; their leadership evolved from dramatic situations conducive to mobilizing direct action movements. But history and the social forces of the day could not have produced a leader more ideal for the Birmingham role than Shuttlesworth. On the other side of the fence, history and the social forces of the day provided an ideal white commissioner, who, in his every act, personified and embodied the fighting spirit of the white segregationist. This "redneck" Commissioner of Public Safety, Eugene "Bull" Connor, locked horns with Shuttlesworth in a classic battle that continued for almost a decade. It must be said that from the beginning history was partial to the "Bull," for at his disposal were a large police force, vicious attack dogs, electric cattle prods, the White Citizens' Council, the Ku Klux Klan, and the established institutions of Southern white society. At Shuttlesworth's feet lay the arduous tasks of mobilizing the black community through the ACMHR and staging confrontations with the white power structure.

Yet Shuttlesworth, standing in the center of his group and propelled by their institutions and desires, somehow lived up to what his group later viewed as the historical demands of the movement. He became a public and charismatic figure by continuously defying the white power structure. In connection with his role, Shuttlesworth has stated: "I always believed that the minister is God's first line soldier. . . . I always believe that a preacher ought to be able to speak out and say what thus say the Lord and then he ought to be acting out thus said the Lord. . . . I should say I'm a battlefield type general like Patton, I guess."[74] To build a movement, the people out front had to show no fear. Shuttlesworth was the epitome of courage. In his own words: "I tried to get killed in Birmingham. I literally believe that he that lose his life shall find it. He who lose it for my sake (meaning God) shall find it. I literally believe that. And I believe that if I lose my life, it was the struggle of living."[75]

Shuttlesworth was known throughout movement circles as having no fear. The Reverend Glenn Smiley, who on occasions worked with Shuttlesworth, remarked:

> Once he told me, after he had been chain whipped by going into a white group that chased him and whipped him with a chain, that "it doesn't make any difference. I'm afraid of neither man nor devil." And I said, "Fred, don't ever ask me to go with you on a project because if you're not afraid on occasions, and there's plenty to be afraid of here, I don't want to be around you.". . . Now Martin [King] and these other guys just wouldn't allow their fears to govern their actions. Now this is courage. This is bravery. Not Shuttlesworth. I think Shuttlesworth, his bravery is in defiance of possible consequences. But that's the way he is. He is a strong-willed, strong character person, and directed.[76]

This was the kind of personality around which a direct action movement was built in Birmingham. Shuttlesworth's colleague in Tallahassee, the Reverend C. K. Steele, seemed to have summed it up:

See, nothing was happening in Birmingham, but they had outlawed the NAACP in Birmingham, and so Fred said, "We've got to do something." And all of the bigwigs said, "Now Fred's going crazy, he's trying to whip him up some, you know." But Fred persisted. Because he persisted, he finally got it off the ground. I expect that the Birmingham movement remained strong longer than almost any movement in the South that I know of.[77]

Birmingham demonstrated that movements could be deliberately organized to accomplish long-term goals. Birmingham created a model for many subsequent consciously constructed movements, not the least of which was Birmingham in 1963.

CENTRALITY OF MOVEMENT CENTERS

The three movements discussed in this chapter, along with the one in Baton Rouge, gave rise to the first "local movement centers" of the civil rights movement. The early centers stimulated the organization of similar centers in numerous cities of the South during the late 1950s.

The existence of movement centers in the black communities of Montgomery, Tallahassee, and Birmingham in the late 1950s was the new reality that distinguished them from the period preceeding the mass movements. Studies of protest activities in these communities conducted in the late 1950s provide evidence that they had developed movement centers. For example, in a study of the Tallahassee black community during the late 1950s, Lewis Killian and Charles Smith found that the leaders of the 1956 bus boycott replaced the conservative pre-boycott leaders. They point out that in the late 1950s:

. . . these "new" leaders have sought to keep the Negro community of Tallahassee militant and dynamic by continuing weekly meetings of the ICC, the organization formed to promote the bus boycott, conducting institutes on nonviolence, taking preliminary steps toward school integration, working to get more Negroes registered and voting, and making many local and nonlocal public appearances in connection with the uplift of Negroes.[78]

Thus a genuine movement center developed out of the 1956 boycott movement. In another study the same authors conclude that "it was not until the formation of the Negro Inter-Civic Council that any organization embarked on a program of action either for or against any form of segregation in Tallahassee."[79]

Similarly, Jacquelyne Clarke, in her pioneering study of the MIA and the ACMHR during the late 1950s, argued that "they represent the strongest and most publicized forces working for civil rights within their own communities, where they appear to have appealed more to the masses of Negroes than has any other organization with a similar purpose (e.g. the NAACP)."[80] Moreover, consistent with the argument of the present study, Clarke argued that these "Negro civil rights leaders and the masses of Negroes have developed increasing organizational strength and unity to achieve full citizenship rights" and that these organizations were the "most significant of the contemporary civil rights 'grass roots' organizations of American Negroes anywhere since 1954."[81] Clarke provides evidence that the movement centers in Montgomery and Birmingham were church-based because more than 98 percent of their members were also church members.[82] Further, it is clear from Clarke's study that the people who were active in these centers had come to embrace new tactics in addition to the NAACP's legal approach, as more than 80 percent of them preferred nonviolent techniques, including "mass meetings, boycotts or protests and other nonviolent techniques, and legal means."[83] It is important to point out here that as late as 1959 these centers still had significant followings. Writing of the weekly mass meetings in Birmingham at that time, Clarke notes that "mass meeting attendance averages anywhere between 500 and 600 persons, increasing in time of crises."[84] Clarke estimated the attendance at a mass meeting in Montgomery in April 1959 at 350.[85]

Data from these early studies and the present one clearly demonstrate that the centers discussed in this chapter did in fact exist and meet the basic criteria for the definition of movement centers discussed earlier. In my view scholars of the civil rights movement have consistently reached erroneous conclusions about the origins of the civil rights movement because they have dismissed these centers as weak and incapable of generating mass collective action.[86] Piven and Cloward, in their important study of poor people's movements, go even farther by arguing that the early confrontations of the modern civil rights movement were spontaneous and successful because these activists did not engage in the counterproductive process of organization-building.[87] In their view, the process of organization-building is the very activity that smothers movements and robs them of their underlying force of mass defiance and spontaneity. The concept "movement center" suggests that an alternative view best fits the data regarding the civil rights movement: Movement centers provided the organizational framework out of which the modern civil rights movement emerged, and it was organization-building that produced these centers.

If movement centers were important to the emergence of the civil rights movement, then the question arises as to why contemporary scholars have largely dismissed them. The most feasible explanation seems to be related to the nature of movement centers themselves. Movement centers and the collective action they generate rarely develop in a benign environment. Rather, they must contend with a number of problems, including repression, fear among members of the subordinate group, difficulties associated with devising effective strategies and tactics, and meager financial resources. Thus movement centers will experience both "hot" and "cold" periods. In the early studies of protest activities in the cities discussed here, researchers have pointed to the real problems these centers faced.[88] Later studies have tended to dismiss these centers because they focused on the problems they faced rather than on their wider significance, organizational strength, and capabilities.

There is another important reason why scholars have dismissed these centers. It is often a wise strategy on the part of activists in movement centers to give the impression that their organization-building activities are helter-skelter and spontaneous.[89] Publicity about an effective, coordinated movement center can draw the opposition's attention to the center and invite repressive actions against it. Besides, spontaneous mass activities are less open to charges of conspiracy by the authorities. Smith and Killian found evidence backing this argument in the case of the Tallahassee movement center during the mass bus boycott. They point out that in September 1956 "the City Court subpoenaed all the records of the ICC, demanding transportation schedules, minutes of meetings, membership lists, finances, etc."[90] As pointed out earlier, authorities in Alabama and elsewhere had effectively used this tactic in their attack against the highly structured NAACP. The ICC responded differently; it produced no records of any consequence.[91] Smith and Killian point out:

> During the summer months [of 1956] the ICC discontinued reading financial reports, etc., in public for two reasons: one, both white reporters and other unidentified white persons were permitted at the open mass meetings; and two, the ICC felt it was getting an unfair press. . . . The minutes were kept in such a way as not to endanger personalities in the bus protest.[92]

Therefore it is of strategic importance for activists in movement centers to project a spontaneous image, enabling authorities to label them as ungrounded, impulsive, and nonrepresentative. Social scientists whose accounts emphasize disorganization and spontaneity miss the mark by mistaking an image, projected to and taken up by repressive authorities, for the reality.

Finally, implicit in the work of a number of civil rights movements scholars, including Piven and Cloward and Anthony Oberschall, is the assumption that subordinate groups are usually without organizational resources and skills.[93] This assumption discourages researchers from closely scrutinizing the important roles that organization-building and skilled activists play in producing collective action. Such assumptions leave the central role of movement centers largely undiscovered.

This chapter has analyzed the early mass movements of the civil rights movement and the movement centers that developed to direct them. The central argument, to be developed further in later chapters, is that these centers existed during the late 1950s and provided the organizational framework that enabled significant collective action to "explode" in the early 1960s. But in order for collective action to spread throughout the South, movement centers had to be developed in numerous locales, and their activities had to be loosely coordinated. The Southern Christian Leadership Conference (SCLC) was formed to accomplish precisely these goals. The next chapter will explore that Southern black indigenous organization.

THE SCLC: THE DECENTRALIZED POLITICAL ARM OF THE BLACK CHURCH

Thus when judging the SCLC, one must place above all else its most magnificent accomplishment: the creation of a disciplined mass movement of Southern blacks. . . . There has been nothing in the annals of American social struggle to equal this phenomenon, and there probably never will be again.
—Bayard Rustin[1]

To this point the first important struggles of the modern civil rights movement have come under study. The present chapter will consider how the dynamics of those struggles were developed in multiple communities, creating a nexus of local movement centers capable of sustaining a Southwide movement. The contention here is that the Southern Christian Leadership Conference was the force that developed the infrastructure of the civil rights movement and that it functioned as the decentralized arm of the black church.

Scholars of social movements have been concerned with the important issue of how movements become forces in a society. Some theorists suggest that movements gather their strength by breaking from existing social structures, while others take the opposing view that movements draw their strength from preexisting organizations and social networks. In the case of the civil rights struggle, the preexisting black church provided the early movement with the social resources that made it a dynamic force, in particular leadership, institutionalized charisma, finances, an organized following, and an ideological framework through which passive attitudes were transformed into a collective consciousness supportive of collective action.

But a new political dimension was needed to mobilize those church resources on a wide scale and commit them to the active pursuit of social change. The SCLC, because it was a church-based movement organization, supplied the political dimension that pulled churches directly into the movement and made it a dynamic force. Before examining how that happened, a succinct history of the early SCLC will be helpful.

Several historical phenomena were critical to the emergence of the SCLC. The most important was the rapid urbanization of blacks, which transformed them into modern wage-earners. The two world wars, the cold war, the anticolonial struggles in African countries, and the U.S. Supreme Court school desegregation decision of 1954 were also important for their impact on the collective psyche of blacks. The values and rhetoric arising from these important events converged on the black consciousness, intensifying black people's thirst for freedom.[2]

The rural setting was hardly ideal for organized, sustained collective action by blacks.[3] In the rural milieu blacks experienced grinding poverty that closely tied them to the land and to the white man. Whites usually arranged the economy so that blacks always owed them money and were forever dependent on them for food and shelter. Outnumbered, defenseless, and with no hope of protection from the law, blacks usually avoided overt conflict with whites simply to stay alive. On the rural plantations, furthermore, blacks seldom experienced themselves as a tightly knit, cohesive group, because they were widely dispersed across the countryside. The sociologist E. Franklin Frazier described rural black communities as follows:

> The cabins are scattered in the open country so that the development of village communities has been impossible. Consequently, communication between rural families as well as the development of rural institutions has been limited by the wide dispersion of the population.[4]

Frazier's point is instructive. The rural setting gave blacks no opportunities to congregate regularly in large numbers and experience themselves as a distinct group possessing social power. This absence of group consciousness and solidarity discouraged the emergence of collective black protest.

Finally, white Southerners relied heavily on the methods of terror to keep blacks oppressed.[5] Personal domination was severest in the countryside, where the oppressor knew the oppressed personally and the two groups were constantly engaged in face-to-face encounters. In those encounters whites, in their every act, impressed upon blacks the reality of their subordinate position. Blacks who "got out of line" were subjected to tongue-lashings; those who "went too far" were visited by white sheriffs and adventure-seekers by night. Whites often had black informers strategically placed to relay information about any behavior that appeared rebellious. In all, rural control was the most direct form of personal domination that riveted blacks into "their place."

Black migration to Southern and Northern cities in the first half of the twentieth century had a profound impact on the group structure of black society. During that period Southern cities experienced tremendous growth and industrialization, thanks in significant part to the migration of rural blacks. Census figures on black population for 1900 and 1940, for example, show the growth in these cities: New Orleans from 77,714 to 149,034; Memphis from 49,910 to 121,498; Birmingham from 16,575 to 108,938; and Atlanta from 35,729 to 104,533.[6] These figures document a trend that swept across large and small cities of the South. Blacks were swiftly becoming urbanized.

The sociological importance of black urbanization in the Southern cities was substantial. First, rural blacks were transformed from tenant farmers and sharecroppers into unskilled industrial workers and domestics. Now employers no longer "owned" blacks but simply employed them as menial labor for a fixed number of hours. In the urban factories and other industrial concerns the white man still ruled supreme, but these new wage workers were exposed to different experiences in the urban work place. For the first time they were introduced to the discriminatory labor movement and its fight to create unions. They learned also of the daring and successful attempts of one of their own in the railroad industry—A. Philip Randolph—to create unions for blacks. The newly urbanized blacks were introduced to a world where organized struggle was evident. Black workers, concentrated in unskilled jobs and in the most unhealthy locations at the factories, developed a group identity around their shared situation in the work place. Although money was scarce and unemployment high, blacks also fared slightly better economically in the cities than they had on the farms.[7]

Second, black urbanization created densely populated black communities. Economically poor and socially oppressed, such communities nevertheless afforded blacks opportunities to interact freely among themselves. It was clear now that a distinct entity, the "black community," existed. The heavy concentration of blacks in a relatively small space contributed to both a sense of community and institution-building.[8]

As pointed out in Chapter One, the black church in the Southern cities experienced a tremendous growth in membership. Urbanized blacks found they no longer belonged to small, poorly financed rural churches where the pastors held a second job to survive. They were now in congregations whose memberships ranged from the hundreds to the thousands. On the urban scene the minister devoted full time to church matters and belonged to ministerial alliances that encouraged community service. In those large churches, small individual offerings added up to sizable group collections, and the singing voices now joined together in large, complex choirs. Black churches were fast becoming organizations of social power.

Indeed, by all accounts blacks were becoming an urbanized group. Sprinkled throughout the neighborhoods were telephones and television sets. In the cities communication flowed via telephone and the "grapevine," which worked more efficiently in heavily populated city blocks than over lonely country roads. The tripartite system of domination was firmly entrenched in these urban settings, but blacks proceeded to build powerful organizations and to experience themselves as a potent group. It was the social and institutional soil from which the SCLC would emerge.

People's symbolic worlds play an important role in their political affairs. During the two world wars enthusiasm for the ideology of democracy reached a crescendo in America. Black and white soldiers died in the name of democracy and for its ideals. For democracy's sake—so they were led to believe—ordinary citizens suspended their preoccupation with deep internal problems and became patriotic so that equality and freedom could be extended across the globe. After the world wars, black Americans expected the government to deliver democracy in the Harlems and Montgomerys of America. It never happened, and blacks began to understand the nature of the society they were up against. Black soldiers returning from the wars began urging their relatives and friends not to accept domination. In many instances black soldiers disobeyed the policy of bus segregation and refused to give up their seats to whites long before Rosa Parks "sat" her way into history. On November 27, 1953, forty-eight black soldiers in Columbia, South Carolina, were arrested and fined a total of $1,573 because one of them refused to move from a bus seat he occupied next to a white girl. The November 28, 1953, *New York Times* reported the white girl's testimony in court that "she asked the Negro soldier to move when he sat by her. He refused."[9] Thus, the two world wars created an ideological atmosphere that intensified the desires of blacks for freedom and democracy. Coupled with the overt protest acts and agitation of black soldiers, this atmosphere and its watchwords went far in symbolically preparing blacks as a group for organized protest.

A substantial number of informed blacks understood the meaning of the international politics produced by the cold war of the 1950s. They made use of it by articulating to the American government and blacks the inherent hypocrisy of pursuing democracy abroad while upholding racial domination at home. Again, the cold war atmosphere kept criticism of American society alive in the black consciousness.

Similarly, some black leaders took note of the struggles to overthrow colonialism in Africa. They described to American blacks the successful and momentous struggles that Africans were waging against their oppressors. Informed American blacks felt strong sympathy for the African liberation movements, carried on by other oppressed people who were also black. Symbolically, American blacks were being pulled into the orbit of a world that included the protest tradition and struggles of oppressed people around the globe. From hindsight it is clear that the time was fast approaching for American blacks to step onto the world stage by directly confronting their oppressors.

Finally, the symbolic world of blacks was ignited with hope after the favorable Supreme Court decision of 1954. Dr. Benjamin Mays, a scholar of the black experience who worked closely with the NAACP, has stated, "we all underestimated the impact of the 1954 decision . . . people literally got out and danced in the streets. . . . The Negro was jubilant."[10] The 1954 decision was important for allowing many blacks to think for the first time about the possibility of social change. However, a legal ruling such as the 1954 decision does not a movement make. Dr. Mays pointed out that blacks "thought that the decision was going to make them free. They didn't realize that every case had to be his own. . . . The 1954 decision was based upon clients. A lawyer got to have a client."[11] Dr. Mays clearly saw the limitations of the 1954 case even before the decision was rendered. In an article in *New South* he maintained that even if the decision was favorable it would apply directly only to the five cases before the Court; the problem of residential segregation would remain, and blacks would probably have a tendency to withdraw pressure once they had gained the legal right to attend nonsegregated schools.[12] Mays later concluded that another type of movement, in addition to the NAACP, was needed to bring about desegregation.[13] Yet the 1954 decision did demonstrate that organized pressure could have a positive impact on the federal government.

In examining the formation of the SCLC, which stimulated the appearance of new local movements and coordinated those already under way, a guiding assumption will be that the civil rights movement was *not* simply a by-product of urbanization and economic modernization.[14] To insist that it was such a by-product is consistent with the view that social movements are spontaneous outbursts of mass defiance in response to rapid social change and community breakdown. Analysis of the SCLC will make it plain that the civil rights movement grew out of the conscious and deliberate efforts of organizers who understood the organizational nature and capacity of black society. Economic modernization and urbanization were necessary, but not sufficient, causes of the civil rights movement.

FORMATION OF THE SCLC

By 1957 local movements were under way in a number of Southern cities. They were often vigorous movements that engaged in nonviolent confrontations. In early January 1956, for example, seventy-two blacks, mostly students from Xavier University in New Orleans, were held in jail for defying segregation on a city bus. The local movement center in New Orleans was led by the Reverend A. L. Davis. Davis was ideal for mobilizing protest, because he headed the New Orleans Interdenominational Ministerial Alliance. In March 1956, at a mass meeting called by the alliance and attended by five thousand blacks, Davis urged blacks to "rise up and let White Citizens' Councils know the time is out for segregation".[15] After continuous protest action, New Orleans buses were finally integrated in the summer of 1958.

The New Orleans struggle typifies the local protest movements prevalent in the South during the middle and late 1950s. Many of the confrontations were not directed by visible movement organizations, nor did the protesters receive notoriety for their unprecedented efforts. But the clergy and the black church were at the center of the conflicts. Movement participants were meeting on a systematic basis, planning strategy, collecting funds, encouraging protest, and confronting local white power structures. For their efforts, many were paid off with bombed homes, burnt crosses, threats, and beatings. Nevertheless, as shown in the previous chapters, the local movements endured. They did so because they were organized and rooted in community institutions.

The organizers of the various local movements usually maintained informal contact between localities and sporadically provided mutual support. At mass meetings of the New Orleans groups in 1956, $3,000 was collected for the MIA to assist the Montgomery movement.[16] A "talking relationship" existed among many local movement leaders throughout the South before the formation of SCLC. Such informal contact existed among Dr. King of Montgomery, the Reverend Joseph Lowery of Mobile, and Reverend Shuttlesworth of Birmingham. The three Alabama leaders would meet to discuss their local movements and to coordinate activities on a state level, previously the task of the outlawed NAACP. The Alabama group discussed formalizing contact among the various movements. Lowery, leader of the emerging movement center in Mobile and president of the Mobile Interdenominational Ministerial Alliance, has recalled that in the informal meeting before the SCLC was organized, "we saw this need to get together and then we just talked about how we ought to broaden it to include Steele, Jemison, and the other guys."[17]

In the meantime Bayard Rustin, Ella Baker, and the white attorney Stanley Levison, all living in New York, were continuously analyzing and supporting the local movements. During the Montgomery bus boycott Levison, Rustin, and Baker formed an organization in New York called "In Friendship." Its purpose was to assist movements in the South financially and to inform the nation about racial injustice.[18] A. Philip Randolph was closely associated with "In Friendship" and gave his support. Then, according to Reverend Steele, who at the time was deeply involved in the Tallahassee bus boycott, "I was called one night . . . and asked if I would call a meeting of the Southern leaders who were involved in these various tension points in the South. . . . I discovered later, I think, that that person was Bayard Rustin."[19]

Ella Baker, one of the most significant and unheralded leaders of the civil rights movement, adds: "The idea [SCLC] grew out of our [Baker's, with Rustin and Levison] discussions . . . the suggestion was made that there needed to be an organization."[20] Finally, Stanley Levison pointed to the collective effort that gave rise to the SCLC:

> It would be very difficult to single out one individual as the originator of the SCLC idea. Many discussions by Dr. King and other leaders such as Fred Shuttlesworth, C. K. Steele, Ralph Abernathy, Mrs. King and with Northern figures who were consultants such as A. Philip Randolph, Bayard Rustin, Ella Baker, and myself were held. In brief, it arose out of a great deal of collective discussion, and if there was one individual who clarified and organized the discussion it was unquestionably Dr. King.[21]

After the call from Rustin, Reverends Steele, King, Shuttlesworth, and Jemison issued a call to black churchmen and leaders across the South urging them to meet at the Reverend M. L. King, Sr's, Atlanta church early in January 1957 to form an organization to coordinate the local protest movements. As a result black leaders representing eleven Southern states converged on the historic Ebenezer Baptist Church in Atlanta.

It is no surprise that nearly all the participants were black.[22] Glenn Smiley, a white friend and colleague of Dr. King and Rustin, has recalled: "Bayard Rustin had called together a group of labor leaders, churchmen, and so on, a select group. They were all black. I was not invited to the meeting and they set up the SCLC."[23] From the outset the black leaders established a pattern whereby white groups could contribute to the movement through their organizational, individual, and group channels rather than occupying leadership roles in the SCLC. From its inception the SCLC was led by indigenous black leaders.

The first meeting of what was to become the SCLC was held in Atlanta on January 10 and 11, 1957. The title of this meeting, "Southern Negro Leaders Conference on Transportation and Integration," highlights the role the bus grievances played as a central organizing focus for the local movements and for the conference. Indeed, the discussions of the meeting centered on the dynamics and outcomes of the mass bus boycotts. Seven working papers, written in advance by Bayard Rustin, attempted to distill the importance of the local movements and were used to focus the discussions and chart a course for the new organization.[24]

The first working paper addressed the role of the bus grievance in the protest movement. It pointed out, "The people *knew* that in bus segregation they have a just *grievance*. No one had to arouse their social anger."[25] It was recognized that a preexisting shared grievance facilitated rapid mobilization. The working paper further argued: "These protests are directly related to *economic survival*, since the masses of people use buses to reach their work. The people are therefore interested in what happens in buses."[26] Rustin's insight suggested that grievances vital to the masses were the ones that triggered organized collective action.

The working papers made it clear that the local protest movements broke from the legal strategies of the past and initiated the new period of mass confrontation. Working paper no. 7 acknowledged the break:

> We must recognize in this new period that direct action is our most potent political weapon. We must understand that our refusal to accept Jim Crow in specific areas challenges the entire social, political and economic order that has kept us second class citizens since 1876.[27]

The method of nonviolent direct action was stressed. It was contended that "nonviolence . . . makes humble folk noble and turns fear into courage."[28] The working papers also insisted that nonviolent direct action was a tactic that immediately thrust power into the hands of every individual desiring to strike out directly against oppression. The tactic of direct action was conducive to mass protest. Moreover, it allowed the very bodies of blacks to become potential power instruments in the sense that ordinary people could organize together in masses and boycott, crowd the jails, march, and nonviolently create the crisis of social disruption. Indeed, throughout the turbulent protest years that followed, the familiar question asked of activists was, "Have you put your body on the line for the struggle?" The battle had shifted from the courtrooms to the seats of power in local communities.

The institutional base of the local movements was the next issue addressed by the working papers, which disclosed what the conference participants already knew: The protest movements grew out of an in-

stitutional base and culture rather than erupting spontaneously. Statement five of working paper no. 1 unequivocally stated, "The campaign
is *based on the most stable social institution in Negro culture—the
church.*"[29] This document summarized the important role of the church
in producing *community sharing* through mass meetings, collective giving of economical assistance and other contributions, and a *community
spirit* that generated enthusiasm and promoted group pride.[30] The
working paper argued that these dynamics were generated in normal
community functioning even before the boycotts. Yet it was maintained
that during the direct action movements, it was the church that harnessed these dynamics and gave them the form and momentum necessary for the effective organization of car pools, mass meetings, and
organized protest.

The working papers also stressed that the white power structure
was not homogeneous. In working paper no. 4, entitled "The Relationship of Community Economic Power Groups to the Struggle," Rustin
wrote:

> *The bus protest has clearly revealed certain economic facts. (1) The
> Negro's dollar is a factor in the economic organization of the com-
> munity, (2) his refusal to ride had a catastrophic effect on the econom-
> ics of the bus companies, and (3) the unintended but nonetheless direct
> effect of the protest on downtown merchants is real, indeed.*[31]

These statements document the fact that these conference participants
were being exposed to how economics could be used in terms of strategy. Indeed, the bus protest taught these leaders that the white community was not a monolithic entity but a heterogeneous one with an
array of interests. They came to learn that the basic concern of the
business community was money, while other groups, such as elected
political leaders, were preoccupied with political power. The conference participants were thus beginning to realize that the movement had
a greater chance of success if it could divide the white community along
the lines of its diverse interests. Later chapters will show that this insight was put to use, especially in Birmingham in 1963.

In short, the documents of the first organizational meeting of the
SCLC stated that (1) the church had functioned effectively as the institutional base of protest movements; (2) aggressive nonviolent action by
blacks was necessary if the system of segregation was to be overthrown;
(3) an organized mass force was needed to supplement the activities of
the NAACP, which was under fierce attack throughout the South; and
(4) movements could be generated, coordinated, and sustained by activist clergy and organized black masses working in concert.

The working papers also contained definite plans to be implemented by the new organization. Foremost among them were the propositions that additional bus protest movements had to be initiated and developed; new protest movements focusing on voting, but modeled after the bus movements, had to be organized; and there was a pressing need to create an organization to unify the Southern movements. Thus the conferees made plans to attend subsequent meetings, a number of which followed in various Southern cities. After those meetings terminated, the group that began as the "Southern Negro Leaders Conference on Transportation and Non-Violent Integration" transformed itself into the "Southern Leaders Conference" and finally the Southern Christian Leadership Conference. The Reverend T. J. Jemison, a founding member of the SCLC, vividly points out why the name "Southern Christian Leadership" was adopted:

> Since the NAACP was like waving a red flag in front of some Southern whites, we decided that we needed an organization that would do the same thing and yet be called a Christian organization. . . . We said Southern Christian Leadership Conference, so they would say, well, that's Baptist preachers so they didn't fear us, but they didn't bother us. . . . The Negro minister only lost his place in the sun with whites when he started leading boycotts, and trying to tear down their social structure.[32]

We turn now to this new organization, the SCLC.

STRUCTURE: POLITICAL ARM OF THE CHURCH

Ministers who were in the process of leading local movements became leaders of the SCLC. Indeed, the criteria for leadership in SCLC proved to be movement experience and stature. After the initial organizing meetings of the SCLC, nine men emerged as its leadership: the Reverend Dr. Martin Luther King, Jr., leader of the Montgomery bus boycott, president; the Reverend C. K. Steele, leader of the Tallahassee bus boycott, first vice-president; the Reverend A. L. Davis, leader in the bus protest of New Orleans, second vice-president; the Reverend Samuel Williams, leader in efforts to desegregate Atlanta buses, third vice-president; the Reverend T. J. Jemison, leader of first mass bus boycott in Baton Rouge in 1953, secretary; the Reverend Fred Shuttlesworth, leader of the mass direct action movement in Birmingham, corresponding secretary; the Reverend Ralph Abernathy, a leader in the Montgomery bus boycott and confidant of Dr. King, treasurer; the Reverend Kelly Miller Smith, local NAACP President and activist of Nashville, chaplain; and Lawrence Reddick, a scholar at Alabama State College and an activist of the Montgomery bus boycott, SCLC historian.

All but Reddick were clergymen. They were all educated, having completed their undergraduate training in black institutions. They were all males. Except for Reverends Williams and Davis, they were all young, averaging approximately thirty years of age. They were all black and Southerners.

An examination of the Executive Board, which included the officers listed above, is instructive. What is striking is that of the sixteen remaining board members, thirteen were clergymen. Among the other three were a dentist, a pharmacist, and an attorney. All of the board members were black, and they came from eleven Southern states. The geographical residency of the board members highlights the fact that in the beginning the SCLC was first and foremost a Southern organization. The early SCLC needed board members from across the South so that access to many Southern communities could be ensured. The majority of the board members were direct action–oriented people. Many had been key organizers in the various bus movements of the day. Others were directly involved with direct action projects or had been in the past.

The Southern Christian Leadership Conference did not emerge out of a vacuum. It was closely related to two enduring institutions of the black community—the NAACP and the church—and it was rooted in the black protest tradition. At the time of the SCLC's formation at least five of its Executive Officers were either current or former local NAACP presidents; another had been a local membership chairman; still another was a member of the local NAACP's Executive Committee; and the remaining two officers were also active in the NAACP.

The SCLC was a church-related protest organization. The overwhelming majority of the SCLC's original leadership were ministers. The original SCLC had thirty-six formal leadership positions, including the Executive Staff, Administrative Committee, and Executive Board. Only four of the thirty-six were filled by nonclergymen. Most of the SCLC's decisions, therefore, were made by activist clergymen. Indeed, the important decisions of the early SCLC were made by the Administrative Committee, comprising thirteen individuals, eleven of whom were ministers.

Thus, the SCLC was anchored in the church and probably could not have been otherwise. For it was these activist ministers who became the leaders and symbols of the mass bus boycotts, controlled the resource-filled churches of the black masses, had economic independence and flexible schedules, were members of ministerial alliances that spoke the same spiritual and financial language whether in Brooklyn or Birmingham, and who came to understand that there is power harnessed in an organized group. So central was the church to the SCLC that Reverend Lowery, one of its original founders, stated: "[The SCLC] was really the black church, that's what it was. It was the black church coming alive. It was the black church coming together across denominational and geographical lines."[33]

Not only was the SCLC tied to the NAACP and the church, but it was also rooted in the black protest tradition. The SCLC leaders, educated in black colleges, had learned about the great black protest leaders of the past—Denmark Vesey, Nat Turner, Sojourner Truth, Frederick Douglass, Booker T. Washington, Harriet Tubman, and W. E. B. DuBois—and about the protest tradition they spearheaded. The accomplishments and sacrifices of these historical warriors inspired the leaders of the SCLC. Shuttlesworth recalls:

> And of course, we based [the SCLC] on everything that happened in the past—Frederick Douglass, slaves, and Marcus Garvey; everybody who struggled for freedom and who were caught up in the same web. And we were giving it an upward thrust. Not that we sat down and said, "Now let's give the movement an upward thrust." No, we were meeting and matching our moment in history. That is what we sought. This was the need we saw.[34]

Shortly after Dr. King was assassinated, his friend and colleague the Reverend Ralph Abernathy wrote King a letter to be delivered to him in heaven. In this letter Abernathy wrote:

> It wouldn't be a surprise to me, Martin, if God didn't have a special affair just to introduce his special activist black son to so many others like you that have gone on ahead. . . . Martin, find Frederick Douglass, that great and marvelous human personality who lived in even more difficult times than we live today. Check with Nat Turner, and Marcus Garvey, for they, too, are heroes in our crusade. . . . And don't forget Malcolm X. Look for Malcolm X, Martin . . . he was concerned about the welfare of his people.[35]

These activists were rooted in and conscious of a protest tradition.

AFFILIATE STRUCTURE

To understand the SCLC one must abandon the idea that it was one formal movement organization located in Atlanta. Another erroneous assumption often found in studies of the civil rights movement is that the SCLC was not a real organization at all, but simply the shadow of Dr. King.[36] This assumption is usually asserted without any in-depth analysis of the SCLC's affiliates. The SCLC's Southwide affiliate structure, in fact, was one of the central factors responsible for its power. A prime reason why SCLC affiliates' structures had power lies in the fact that they were often mass-based.

The view that the SCLC had a mass base during this period departs from previous research. Oberschall, relying on data presented by J. J. Clarke in her early study of the MIA and the ACMHR, concludes that these organizations "were heavily middle class in membership."[37] However, Clarke's findings suggest something very different from this conclusion. Clarke found that 49.6 percent of the members of the ACMHR and 44.7 percent of MIA's membership were in unskilled or semiskilled occupations.[38] She further found that the mean annual family income of the ACMHR membership was $3,715 and the corresponding mean for MIA was $3,094. Clarke also studied the Tuskegee Civic Association during this period and found that the mean family income of its members was $7,477.[39] This sharp difference in family income can be attributed to the fact that the majority of blacks in Tuskegee historically have been highly educated and have held jobs at Tuskegee Institute. Pointing to the mass base of the MIA and the ACMHR, Clarke wrote that "the membership of the MIA is drawn from all the Negro social strata within Montgomery, but the largest number of members are middle-aged females and elderly men from the lower strata. Roughly the same membership characteristics prevail in ACMHR."[40]

Clarke also pointed out that the MIA and ACMHR use of sermons, prayer meetings, or devotional periods is an adequate way to attract the lower-class elements of the Negro communities, and "In Montgomery and Birmingham, the decisions seem to be to attract the lower class elements; this is, after all, where the masses of Negroes are to be found."[41] SCLC movement centers across the South operated largely in the same manner as the MIA and the ACMHR. In this regard, Dr. Simpkins of the UCMI claimed that at least 90 percent of the black communities in which they worked supported them. According to Simpkins, "they [black masses] felt very much a part of it, not only in Shrevesport, but the whole area, I mean, the whole North Louisiana area."[42]

Piven and Cloward have promoted the view that the SCLC did not have a mass base. Relying on a brief article written by Kenneth Clarke,[43] Piven and Cloward maintain that SCLC was "amorphous and symbolic" so that the large numbers of people drawn to its demonstration were not members."[44] What they overlook is that the SCLC functioned as the decentralized arm of the mass-based black church. That mass base was built into the very structure of the SCLC.

The SCLC was not an individual-membership organization. Only other organizations, such as churches or civic leagues, could become its affiliates. Here we see the impact of the MIA and the other local "organizations of organizations," which had demonstrated that community resources could be mobilized by uniting the various community organizations. Indeed, it was known that the Montgomery boycott had endured more than a year because the Women's Political Council, the Progressive Democrats, the NAACP, the Citizens Coordinating Committee, and dozens of churches coordinated by the MIA provided it with the necessary organizational networks and resources. The founders of the SCLC reasoned that it would organize a large Southwide mass movement if it were able to mobilize and coordinate community organizations across the South. The SCLC was to be a Southwide organization of organizations.

Although the SCLC was officially incorporated to function in sixteen Southern states, it was clear from the beginning that the black community outside the South had an important role to play. Thus, the SCLC bylaws stated, "the magnitude of the problem calls for the maximum commitment of resources of all institutions in Negro life, North and South."[45] In later discussions the central role played by Northern blacks in the SCLC and the Southern civil right movement will be demonstrated. Suffice it here to say that the SCLC relied on their support from its inception. To gain the support of the national black community it was decided that the SCLC affiliate structure would comprise community organizations whose aims and methods were closely akin to those of the SCLC. Community organizations became affiliates of the SCLC by paying a twenty-five-dollar fee and signing a charter committing them to organize their communities to engage in direct action protests.

It was the local movements that created the need for the SCLC. Local movement centers already in existence provided the SCLC with its initial affiliated structure. Thus, the MIA, the ICC, the ACMHR, the Mobile Civil Association (MCA), and similar organizations became the early affiliates. Moreover, ministers from across the South who attended the SCLC's organizing meetings were encouraged to affiliate their churches. The action of the Reverend Kelly Smith, local president of the Nashville NAACP, typifies the response of many of these ministers:

> After the [SCLC organizing] meeting and after the discussion that we had and all that, it became clear to me that we needed something in addition to NAACP. So I came back and I called some people together and formed what we named the Nashville Christian Leadership Council in order to address the same kind of issues that the SCLC would be addressing.[46]

Some of these ministers formed new direct action organizations, while others affiliated their churches with the SCLC.

Indeed, during the late 1950s the SCLC held numerous meetings across the South where various community groups, including some nonreligious organizations such as Black Masons, lodges, and labor organizations, became affiliates. But it was the churches and church-related organizations, including Interdenominational Ministerial Alliances and local Baptist Conferences, that constituted the bulk of SCLC affiliates.[47] The churches and related organizations constituted the crucial internal organization enabling the SCLC to mobilize community resources. They were so central that SCLC leaders called them the "invisible hand of God." Thus Dr. King was not merely a symbolic leader created by the mass media. His power, like that of other important leaders, stemmed from the fact that he and his colleagues were able to mobilize a variety of resources through community organizations.

It is useful, therefore, to think of the SCLC of that period as the decentralized political arm of the black church. The SCLC's leaders did not attempt to centralize the activities of its affiliates, because it was felt that centralization would stifle local protest. Rather, the role of the SCLC's affiliates was to organize local movements and address grievances salient in local communities. Speaking of local leaders, the Reverend Wyatt Walker, who affiliated his Gillfield Baptist Church of Petersburg, Virginia, with the SCLC, explained that "they knew their communities better than anyone else could ever know them."[48] Reflecting local diversity, some affiliates organized around bus boycotts; others focused on voting drives; still others concerned themselves with school integration. The role of the SCLC was to coordinate and strengthen these efforts by linking the various leaders so that they could share resources and experiences. Finally, affiliation meant that local groups were organizationally linked to a charismatic leader, Martin Luther King, Jr.

THE SCLC AND CHARISMA

At the heart of the SCLC's organizational structure was a charismatic center. As in the black church that spawned it, institutionalized charisma was an important resource of the SCLC. It cannot be overemphasized that the SCLC's power grew out of a dynamic combination of organizational strength and charisma. Without the church base, it is unlikely that King would have become a great organizer and symbol of an effective mass movement. Being at the center of a church base allowed King to use his charisma as a mobilizing force. In the church community it is customary for black churches to conduct revival services once a year. The purposes of a revival are to convert new souls for Christ, increase church membership, and raise money for the host church. Seldom will the church's pastor preside at the revival. The common practice is to invite a renowned and often charismatic minister from outside to present a series of sermons. The renowned charismatic minister was important for the revival, because his presence attracted large numbers of people who provided the needed resources.

Most of the community meetings and rallies sponsored by the SCLC and its affiliates resembled the revival. Dr. Martin Luther King became the centerpiece of these gatherings, because his presence attracted people and resources. The leaders and organizers who worked closely with King agreed that his presence mobilized and attracted resources. Reverend Walker, who became Executive Director of the SCLC in 1960, maintained that when local groups needed to raise money or were engaged in difficult struggles,

> . . . they wanted Martin and Ralph [Abernathy] to come. 'Cause they knew they could get the folk; you can't do anything without folk. And, Martin and Ralph could get up the folk. . . . Charisma plays a great role. Martin Luther King's great leadership came from the fact that he was able to get more warm bodies in the street at one time than anybody else we've ever seen in American history. That's what gave him his tremendous influence and power.[49]

Ella Baker, the SCLC's first Associate Director, its second Executive Director, and a critic of charismatic leadership in general and of Dr. King's in particular, admits: "The charismatic figure has value certainly—because it's like having a basis for calling people together. They responded to his call. People will come."[50] The Reverend James Lawson, who organized in numerous communities with King, arrived at a similar conclusion:

> It was the nature of the struggle at that time, that [King] was the single overwhelming symbol of the agitation and of the struggle. . . . He gave the black community an advantage the black community has never had, and has not had since his death. Namely, that any time King went to a community, immediately the focus of the nation was on that community. And the people were prepared to start coming, and they may not have come otherwise. Many of them didn't. He had the eyes of the world on where he went. And in the black community it never had that kind of person.[51]

Finally, Reverend Smith of Nashville noted that any activity associated with King drew large numbers of people and generated interest because

"Martin's name was magic."[52] Thus, a movement organization with a charismatic leader rooted in a mass-based institution is more likely to mobilize masses of people than a movement organization without such a leader. Charismatic leaders of this type play a crucial role in the mobilization process and the building of an internal organization.

POWER AND DECISION–MAKING

In addition to charismatic authority, King had organizational power. As president, King had the ultimate power in the SCLC. King's former officers and colleagues unequivocally state that the power of the SCLC resided in the man they affectionately refer to as "Martin." The Reverend C. K. Steele declared that "Dr. King was the last word on everything. I don't remember any time that Dr. King made a proposal that we did not accept."[53] Reverend Lowery, the current SCLC president, stated that the power in SCLC has "always resided in the president." In response to the question, "Are you saying that the power resided in King?" he replied, "Exactly."[54] The Reverend Fred Shuttlesworth, one of the most influential figures in the SCLC from its beginning, agreed. Ella Baker pointed out that the power in the SCLC was supposed to reside in the board, but it resided in the person who had the greatest contact with the outside world, and "Martin became the great person out there."[55] Finally, Mrs. Diane Nash Bevel, who came to the SCLC about 1961 after becoming an important leader in the Student Nonviolent Coordinating Committee (SNCC), said:

> I remember being very impressed by the fact that Martin clearly had veto power. I guess I didn't always like that, because I was more oriented to the SNCC style decision-making, which was more oriented in terms of a majority . . . the staff [of SCLC] really hammered out and made decisions, but in the final analysis, Martin had veto power."[56]

Thus, most of those in a position to know agreed that the ultimate power in the SCLC resided in King.

Yet it would be misleading to view the SCLC simply as an extension of King's personality. SCLC officials were usually strong public personalities who led movements and collectively shaped the new organization. According to Shuttlesworth, the SCLC's officials debated policy issues and stated their disagreements forthrightly. However, he quickly added: "We recognized that we had to exist as an organization and once the disagreements were stated we proceeded as a united team."[57]

The SCLC's decision-making process consisted of accepting suggestions from staff, then giving final responsibility to specialized committees. This does not erase the fact that SCLC officials believed that only one individual—Dr. King—should be the leader. The SCLC was not a one-man enterprise but an organization that attracted and utilized some of the best black and white minds in America. In another context, Lerone Bennett makes a similar point: "What is important is that King, like Franklin Delano Roosevelt, demonstrated in Montgomery and later a rare talent for attracting and using the skills and ideas of brilliant aides and administrators."[58] Those who misunderstand this point are likely to attribute superhuman qualities to King instead of analyzing the organizational machinery, skilled staff and consultants, masses possessing talents and resources, and creative collective ideas, all of which were the real substance upon which King's leadership was based.

THE SCLC AND THE LOCAL COMMUNITY

The newly organized local movements evolved in conflict-ridden settings. Black protest groups were up against an opposition that included white terrorist organizations, the courts, Southern governments, and police departments that deployed attack dogs, high-powered rifles, and policemen who were not reluctant to use intimidation and violence against people they referred to as "niggers." The dangers encountered by protest groups often went unchecked in the late 1950s because the Eisenhower Administration, reluctant to intervene, was promoting the politically expedient line that Southern problems had to be worked out by Southerners. That left black protestors in local communities to confront a vicious opposition largely alone. The moment Reverend Abernathy reflected on this situation, his jovial mood turned into melancholy. He characterized those early protestors as the ones who traveled "out there on that lonely road."[59]

The formation of the SCLC made a great contribution to the local struggles by creating deep social bonds among these "lonely protestors." At early SCLC meetings and conventions it was important for protest leaders to engage in meaningful face-to-face social interactions. Abernathy, as he recalls those early meetings, quickly recaptures his joviality and states:

> But, every now and then you get together with members of the household of faith, and you get a sort of camaraderie. You get strengthened, backed, and supported because you see a Kelly Miller Smith from Nashville and C. K. Steele from Tallahassee and T. J. Jemison. We shared at our conventions.[60]

Abernathy explained that during these meetings an hour was set aside for mutual sharing, when participants would give reports from the field. Aaron Henry, an SCLC board member from Clarksdale, Mississippi, told of difficulties resulting from his affiliation with the movement, while others experiencing similar problems across the South listened. According to Abernathy, problems that seemed insurmountable to one's local movement were placed in perspective through comparisons with problems of other movements.[61] Face-to-face interactions among local protest groups diminished the opposition's effectiveness by minimizing the potency of its tactics.

The formation of the SCLC also contributed to local struggles by strengthening their internal organization. Jemison stated that the Baton Rouge movement was helped by joining the SCLC: "People would feel that you [the local SCLC leader] were tied to the whole thing, so they didn't mind following their leadership locally because you were one of the ones that was leading it all over the South."[62] It was very important politically for local black communities to be linked symbolically and organizationally to the larger movement. When asked, "What did it mean to be affiliated with SCLC?" the Reverend C. T. Vivian, a local leader in Nashville during the late 1950s, responded:

> If you ask it that way, it meant Martin Luther King. It also meant a central focus. It meant that there was something outside of ourselves which gave one a certain sense of security. Though you didn't know what it was . . . it meant that you had a national symbol. It meant you had a spokesman. That you had forces outside yourself working. It also meant you had a success in Montgomery.[63]

In Shreveport, Louisiana, C. O. Simpkins, a dentist who became a local SCLC leader and affiliated his direct action organization with the SCLC in 1957, said the affiliation meant "that you would enlarge your contacts and knowledge of what was going on, and we would get support on a national level for our efforts."[64] Reverend Shuttlesworth, when asked what effect the early SCLC meetings had on local movement bases, answered: "In one word, elevating and lifting, because it's always lifting and moving to know that something that is moving has just come to your area. I think that people were inspired to ask for more, seek more, and try to get more."[65] Every local SCLC leader interviewed for this study stressed the importance of the support and national context the SCLC provided for their local movements. In Reverend Lowery's words, affiliating with the SCLC helped,

> . . . 'cause it gave you a national backing. This is very significant— and the white folks in the community knew that when you spoke, you

didn't just speak for yourself, that you had some supporters around the South and around the country.[66]

Finally, the SCLC played a direct role in producing among local community people the mental attitudes conducive to protest. The SCLC promoted "consciousness raising" by engaging in the politics of agitation and refocusing black religion. Indeed, SCLC officials brought direct action workshops, voting clinics, and mass rallies to many local communities across the South. Community leaders, students, and young people usually attended the daytime meetings and workshops, because they had flexible schedules. It was at night that the adults came out to hear the singing and oratory about this desired thing called "freedom." According to Steele, at the nighttime meetings, "people filled up the auditorium."[67] The Reverend Kelly Smith recalled:

The meetings always had mass meetings attached to them that people came out to hear and just to be spurred on . . . and to be reminded of what needs to be done and how badly we're being treated, and how we can do things to overcome. That was in the public meetings—that was done.[68]

In some periods members of an oppressed group who appear docile are rapidly transformed into active protesters. While the transformation process is crucial to understanding a protest movement, it remains largely unexplained. Some light can be shed on how this mental transformation occurred in the civil rights movement. The point is that people's attitudes are heavily shaped by the institutions with which they are closely affiliated. This is especially true of such institutions as schools and churches, whose primary purpose is to interpret social reality and make moral pronouncements regarding the "right" relationship for people with the world around them. These institutions provide the cultural content that molds and shapes individual attitudes. Therefore, fairly rapid transformation of those attitudes may be accomplished by refocusing the cultural content of the institutions engaged in defining social reality. Changing attitudes by refocusing the cultural content of institutions can be much more effective than changing the attitudes of separate individuals, because institutional refocusing enables organizers to reach large numbers of people simultaneously.

The mass-based black church played the leading role in interpreting reality and providing moral standards for blacks. The effects of refocusing the cultural context of the church would have to be great, because it significantly shaped the attitudes of a large number of black people.

For the first half of the twentieth century most black churches taught that the meek would inherit the earth; that God would judge the oppressor according to his wicked deeds; that God loved the dispossessed and would provide them with just rewards after they had fought the long Christian fight; and that a good Christian was more concerned with perfecting his or her spiritual life rather than with material wellbeing. These messages were expressed through elaborate and eloquent rituals of song, prayers, and sermons. It was a religion of containment, the opiate of the masses, a religion that soothed the pains of economic, political, and social exploitation.[69]

The mass meetings that the SCLC and its affiliates held in oppressed communities resembled revivals. It was Dr. King, the renowned charismatic minister, who attracted large numbers of people and resources to these gatherings. But, a new message crept into the "revival" and began refocusing the cultural content of a significant number of churches. King carried the new message:

> But a religion true to its nature must also be concerned about man's social conditions. . . . Any religion that professes to be concerned with the souls of men and is not concerned with the slums that damn them, the economic conditions that strangle them, and the social conditions that cripple them is a dry-as-dust religion.[70]

A refocusing of the cultural content of the church was required to operationalize King's view of religion. This "militant" view of religion has always existed in the black church, as the fact that such leaders of slave revolts as Nat Turner and Denmark Vesey adopted it attests. This view of religion guided the efforts of Frederick Douglass and Harriet Tubman as they fought the slave regime and transported slaves through the underground railroad. This religious view became institutionalized through songs, sermons, and the literature of the church. Dr. Benjamin Mays, an authority on black religion and a minister who taught King and many other civil rights leaders the militant view of religion, maintains that "the Negro was selective in his preaching. He usually selected Biblical passages which emphasized that all men are children of God." Mays pointed out that such a position suggests equal treatment and social equality. Thus Mays concluded that black ministers "preached a revolution but in disguise."[71] In addition, the view of religion as a dynamic force for social change was a cornerstone of the "social gospel" movement. A significant portion of the SCLC's leadership was familiar with the main doctrines of the "social gospel" movement, and King studied them while in graduate school.[72] Even though this view of religion was institutionalized, it was not usually the aspect emphasized. However, refocusing black religion was made easier for King and his counterparts because they were activating a religious view latent in the church rather than creating it from a vacuum.

The SCLC represented the emergence of an organized force across the South, dedicated to refocusing the cultural content of the religion of the black masses. This discussion has focused on Dr. King because he was regarded as the master of this refocusing process, but he is also important for having served as a model for activist clergymen across the South. King was able to succeed in "refocusing" black religion because by any criterion he was a Christian minister, and the masses regarded him as that. It would surely have been difficult for an "outsider" to tamper with the sacred religious beliefs and practices of a people. King's power was enhanced by his image among blacks as a respectable man, the "Reverend Doctor King," who practiced what he preached. In Reverend Walker's words, King was a hero who would go to jail, confront redneck racists, and speak boldly before them without hating them and taking a club to them, or trying to shoot back.[73] Finally, King's oratorical abilities aided him in refocusing the cultural content of black religion. Septima Clark, a great grassroots organizer of the period, said of King: "As he talked about Moses, and leading the people out, and getting the people into the place where the Red Sea would cover them, he would just make you see them. You believed it."[74] Mrs. Clark maintained that King's speeches made people feel that if they worked hard enough, they really could make justice roll down like water, and righteousness like a mighty stream.

The Reverend Daniel Speed of Tallahassee explained that King wore many oratorical hats and had the ability to reach any audience. To church people he would preach protest by citing relevant scriptures from the Bible. To a highly learned audience he would preach protest by engaging in precise historical and philosophical discourses. Speed recalled an interesting incident where King spoke to an audience in Tallahassee with some white racist reporters in attendance. Speed emphasized that these reporters were "diehard" racists. King began to preach forcefully about oppression, effects of segregation, justice and righteousness, and then, Speed exclaimed:

I saw that lady get up and whoop and scream. I'm talking about a white woman. [A reporter?] Yes. A reporter. She forgot her job. I personally had to get her. She said, "I'm sorry." I remember hearing Reverend Steele saying, "No, don't feel sorry, just let it come."[75]

Thus, by giving contemporary relevance to familiar biblical struggles through spellbinding oratory and by defining such religious heroes as Jesus and Moses as revolutionaries, King had begun to refocus the content of black religion.

The issue, of course, is whether this refocusing process actually worked. There is evidence that it did. For instance, in assessing Dr. King's role in the Albany, Georgia, movement, the attorney C. B. King maintains that Dr. King

> . . . was a catalyst for mass involvement because he made a very sig-
> nificant difference in terms of how the masses of people were willing
> to interpret this opiate. King served up religion in a rather unique
> fashion as a militant force for the first time. King was using religion
> as a key to inspire a perception which moved the masses in what could
> be conservatively considered the direction of revolution.[76]

Yet it was not an easy task. For example, Reverend Shuttlesworth required members of his church to register and vote. He explained that when he asked deacons to register, they immediately fell to their knees and uttered long prayers. They were substituting the opiate for direct action. Shuttlesworth, practicing the militant religion, demanded they stop wearing out the knees of their pants and personally took them to register.[77] In short, during the late 1950s the SCLC leadership began preparing members of the black community to participate in protest activities by systematically introducing them to direct action workshops, movement literature, and a familiar religious doctrine that had been significantly altered to encourage protest. In this context a "good Christian" was one who actually sought to change "sinful" social conditions.

This chapter has investigated the formation, structure, and purpose of the Southern Christian Leadership Conference. It was argued that the SCLC during the late 1950s and early 1960s crystallized and strengthened the internal organization of the movement because it functioned as the decentralized political arm of the black church. The black church provided the SCLC with leadership, institutionalized charisma, a mass base, and other social resources. It was shown also that the formation of the SCLC organizationally linked the various local movements that emerged across the South during the late 1950s into a Southwide organization of organizations. Moreover, the formation of the SCLC marked the period when members of the black community were being prepared to engage in nonviolent civil disobedience by the newly established direct action organizations and churches. The preparation involved refocusing the religion of the black masses in such a way that protest against oppressive conditions was encouraged. The next chapter will explore the further development of these dynamics.

5

THE SCLC's CRUSADE FOR CITIZENSHIP

Movement centers mobilize, organize, and coordinate collective action. They are dynamic forms of social organization within which activists prepare communities for collective action and actually initiate struggles against the power-holders to bring about social change. These struggles often pursue limited goals perceived as attainable and positive steps toward realizing ultimate goals. Analysts and participants often measure the success or failure of a movement by the attainment of its announced limited goals. Use of that criterion ignores the overall benefits such efforts may have for the infrastructure of a movement.

A case in point is the SCLC's Crusade for Citizenship program, which unsuccessfully attempted to enfranchise Southern blacks in the late 1950s. Even though that limited goal was not accomplished in the appointed time, the effort itself actually strengthened and multiplied the developing movement centers, creating greater power for the larger movement.

FROM BUS BOYCOTTS TO THE BALLOT

The bus protests clearly demonstrated that Southern blacks could be organized to engage in large mass movements. Whether mass movements could be organized around grievances other than bus segregation was debated at length during the meeting from which the SCLC was eventually organized. After distilling what were considered the basic factors giving rise to the mass bus boycotts, SCLC working paper no. 1 concluded that "when a group of people have developed them in one area (e.g. public transportation), these qualities can be transferred to any other constructive one through *education by action*, the final quality."[1] The SCLC leaders argued that political disfranchisement was an important part of the oppression of Southern blacks and urged that collective action aimed at seizing the vote was "the next stop for mass action in the struggle for equality.[2]

Dr. King and others argued that winning the vote was critical. The achievement of such other goals as school integration, decent housing, job opportunities, and integrated public transportation was closely tied to the Negro masses' having the right to vote.[3] The SCLC leadership reasoned that movements could be organized around voting for two reasons: (1) Extraneous issues such as "race-mixing" and the separate-but-equal doctrine were irrelevant to the vote, and (2) no vast legal machinery stood between blacks and the vote, as with school integration. It was also maintained that industrialization made it necessary to seize the vote:

> [I]ndustrialization of the South now emerges as a new factor, effecting the political structure of the South. The one party system is breaking up. Republicanism is coming South with new industrialization. This before long may lead to a two party South, competing for Negro votes. Negro voting in such a situation can also hasten the decline of the one party system which has been able to exist primarily because of the Negro's enforced economic and social position.[4]

Finally, the civil rights bill that eventually became the 1957 Civil Rights Act was being considered by Congress at the time of the SCLC'S formation. The bill, which contained measures to protect the voting rights of all citizens and to establish a Commission on Civil Rights and a Civil Rights Division in the Department of Justice, helped persuade the SCLC to concentrate on gaining the ballot. It was thought that if blacks gained the right to vote through a mass movement they could influence the legislative branch of the federal government, which had not passed civil rights legislation in more than 80 years. Working paper no. 2 concluded: "In any event, the time has come to broaden the struggle for Negroes to register and to vote, for the simple reason that until this happens, we can not really influence the legislative branch of the government."[5]

Thus one of the important decisions to emerge from the SCLC's initial meeting was that new mass movements would be organized around gaining the franchise. The effort was called the "Crusade for Citizenship Program," and its aim was to double the black vote in the South for the 1958 and 1960 elections. The strategy was to build a Southwide mass movement around the vote modeled after the bus boycotts. The bus boycotts had shown the power of mass collective action, and activists knew that attempts to gain the franchise would fail if they were not backed by a mass movement. It was the responsibility of the central office in Atlanta to perform the day-to-day coordination of the new movements. The quality of the staff and administrative machinery of the central office was important to this ambitious project.

PERSONNEL AND ADMINISTRATION

Ella Baker was the central figure in the SCLC Atlanta headquarters during the late 1950s.[6] To understand the functioning of SCLC headquarters, some background on Baker is essential. The granddaughter of a proud, rebellious slave minister, Ella Baker was born in the South in 1903 and received her undergraduate degree from Shaw University in Raleigh, North Carolina, where she was valedictorian of her class. In 1927 Baker moved to New York City and discovered a political environment that stood in sharp contrast to the conservative background of her youth. Baker found that New York, especially Harlem, was a reservoir of challenging new social and political ideas. She frequented New York's Washington Square Park because it reminded her of the Southern landscape of her youth. But this park had a different atmosphere. It exposed her to heated debates over fundamental ideas such as the relative merits of communism, socialism, and capitalism. These stimulating ideas drew Baker into the overall political and cultural ferment of the city. She began a long involvement with social change organizations.

In 1932 Baker worked with a black writer for the *Pittsburgh Courier*, George Schuyler. Together they developed the Young Negro Cooperative League, and Baker traveled through the Eastern states organizing groups to promote the consumer cooperative concept. Through that experience she learned how organizations worked and made important contacts. During 1941 and 1942 Baker served as the National Field Secretary for the NAACP, which required her to travel through the South and conduct membership campaigns and develop NAACP branches. In those two years she attended 362 meetings and traveled 16,244 miles for the NAACP. In 1943 Baker became the Director of Branches for the NAACP and in that year alone attended 157 meetings and traveled 10,244 miles, conducting membership campaigns in Birmingham, Mobile, and Tampa.[7]

In 1946 Baker left the NAACP, having learned a great deal about the structure of Southern black communities, including details about local organizations, leadership, and literacy rates. The NAACP experience had also afforded her the opportunity to make numerous personal contacts throughout black neighborhoods of the South. Between leaving the national NAACP and organizing the SCLC's headquarters, Baker held positions in the New York YMCA and later became president of the New York branch of the NAACP. Baker thus brought to the SCLC valuable organizational experience and a wide array of community knowledge and contacts.

Most accounts of the SCLC mistakenly identify Baker as the organization's first Executive Director.[8] She was the SCLC's first Associate Director, and the Reverend John Tilley became the first Executive Director in May 1958. Reverend Tilley was chosen because he had recently directed a successful voting drive in Baltimore, and SCLC officials believed he would be ideal to administer the "Crusade for Citizenship" movement. The fact that Tilley was a minister also weighed heavily in the decision to hire him as Executive Director.[9] When the SCLC's Executive Board met on November 5, 1957, and established the criteria for hiring an Executive Director, Dr. King maintained that the director did not necessarily have to be a minister. Still, the clergymen on the board thought that Tilley, being a minister as well as an experienced hand at voting rights campaigns, would fit in well with the SCLC's church-based leadership in addition to having the organizational skills required to launch the Crusade.

Before Tilley arrived it was Baker who established the SCLC's central office. She operated the mimeograph machines, wrote much of the early correspondence, and performed what James Forman called the "detailed and tiresome work of administration."[10] Baker had administrative skills, but her genius was her ability to organize and inspire people to seek change. However, Baker's definite views about social movements caused tensions in the new organization, because they differed from the views of the ministers.

Here was a woman, twenty-five years older than most of the SCLC's leadership, who possessed a solid organizational background, entering an organization controlled by black ministers. During that era men in general, and many black ministers in particular, were condescending toward women and could not envision them as full-fledged leaders. This stance of the ministers was bound to generate friction with Baker, who was self-directed and did not feel that women should automatically defer to men. Other fundamental differences also set Baker apart from the SCLC's clergy leadership.

Baker brought a distinct concept of leadership and organization to the SCLC. She believed that movement organizations should not be built around a leader or even a few leaders. She argued that for people's movements to be effective, participants must encourage and build local leadership among the masses:

Instead of "the leader"—a person who was supposed to be a magic man—you would develop individuals who were bound together by a concept that benefited larger numbers of individuals and provided an opportunity for them to grow into being responsible for carrying on the program.[11]

In particular, Baker felt that the civil rights movement was unduly structured around Dr. King, which prevented potential leadership from women, young people, and other members of the community from developing. From her perspective, movements and their organizations should be built around "group-centered leadership." This approach, she argued, allowed movements to be democratic and minimized struggles aimed at acquiring "personal leadership."[12]

The SCLC's executive officers were local leaders, but they viewed King as the central leader of the SCLC and the movement. A minister's background taught him that a leader was required if large-scale human efforts were to be coordinated and centrally directed. In Reverend Shuttlesworth's words, "We recognize that there can't be but one leader at one time. You know, one leader of a whole movement."[13] Hence the ministers thought a charismatic leader was a necessary ingredient that sparked movements into motion, while Baker contended that movements fail to develop or fizzle because the "prophetic leader turns out to have heavy feet of clay."[14] Baker's view that King was too concerned with his own leadership therefore generated tension between the SCLC's leadership and the central office and would later become the basis of the conflict between the SCLC and the black student movement of the early 1960s.

Baker also differed over the type of organizational structure that should be established at SCLC headquarters. Drawing from her NAACP experiences, she emphasized that the SCLC should have clearly defined personnel practices that outlined the tasks and obligations of the staff. In her view these "office rules" should be binding on both the employer and employee. In contrast to the ministers, Baker emphasized the need for a minimal degree of formal organization. As will be seen later, these disagreements affected the outcome of the Crusade.

STRATEGY OF THE CRUSADE FOR CITIZENSHIP PROGRAM

During the late 1950s the overwhelming majority of Southern blacks were not registered to vote. Black disfranchisement was a deliberate design of powerful Southern whites implemented through a battery of tactics to prevent blacks from voting. Among these were the all-white primaries, literacy tests, the grandfather clause, poll tax, economic reprisals, and outright violence. For example in 1955 the Reverend George Lee, a black minister in Mississippi, and Gus Courts registered to vote. Speaking before a Senate subcommittee in 1957, Mr. Courts stated:

> *Two hours before he (the Rev. George W. Lee) was killed, he called me over to his store and he showed me a letter that . . . was sticking in his screen door, and it said:*
> *"Preacher, instead of you preaching the Gospel, what you say you were called to do, you are preaching to Negroes here in Humphreys County to register and vote. You had better do what you claim that you were called to do, that is, preach the Gospel."*
> *On May 7, 1955, he (Rev. Lee) was driving home in his car from town. Someone drove up beside him in a car and shot him through the window with a shotgun. The blast tore off all the side of his face.*[15]

The following morning Mr. Courts was visited by a member of the White Citizens' Council, who told him he would suffer the same fate if he did not remove his name from the register. Courts testified, "I told him I would do just like Reverend Lee; I'd as soon die a free man than live a coward. I was not going to take my name off the register."[16]

These examples demonstrate the resistance blacks faced when attempting to vote, and it was especially fierce in areas where blacks outnumbered whites. All segments of white society, including legislators and members of the White Citizens' Councils and the Ku Klux Klan, united to prevent blacks from voting. Other barriers standing between blacks and the ballot were fear and ignorance. Reverend Lee and Mr. Courts were not typical; the majority of blacks feared voting because it could get them killed or fired. Indeed, most blacks were so systematically excluded from the political process that a tacit understanding emerged that voting was white folks' business. Because only a few had ever voted, blacks did not know how to operate voting machines, did not know the qualifications required to register, and could be easily manipulated or misdirected by white registrars.

The Crusade for Citizenship thus had substantial barriers to overcome in its efforts to enfranchise Southern blacks. White resistance and black fear made a lethal combination. The idea that urbanization created a "New Negro" eager to change his status in American society is not borne out by the evidence, yet the "New Negro" thesis has been advanced as an explanation for the emergence of the civil rights movement by a number of activists and some social scientists. Dr. King did so in a speech in 1956:

> *The tension which we are witnessing in race relations in the South today is to be explained in part by the revolutionary change in the Negro's evaluation of himself. . . . You cannot understand the bus protest in Montgomery without understanding that there is a New Negro in the South.*[17]

The evidence indicates that King and other activists themselves barely believed the "New Negro" thesis and that the day-to-day reality of organizing taught them quite differently. In December 1958 the SCLC's Executive Director wrote that the SCLC had created the machinery for "penetrating each community, reaching the man on the streets, bringing him a simple, practical way of life which will help him to break through the oppressive system of discrimination and oppression, change his surroundings, and his oppressors and make a new person."[18] This document suggests that during the late 1950s the SCLC was attempting the difficult task of producing the "New Negro" through its organizational efforts. Furthermore, in an SCLC document as late as February 1959 we find this:

> *Many Negroes of the South have developed, not simply an indifference or apathy toward voting, but a strong fear and a deep antipathy toward having anything to do with politics. These fears and misconceptions of the Negro in regards to politics, must be overcome . . . his thought patterns must be changed by an effective crusade to inform, impress and recondition his thinking and feeling.*[19]

Thus a goal of the Crusade was to create the "New Negro" through workshops, mass rallies, and movement literature. Activists used the "New Negro" thesis as an ideological byword and a self-fulfilling prophecy with which to challenge blacks to take on the responsibilities of fighting for their rights.

The goal of the Crusade was to enfranchise Southern blacks by organizing a mass-based political movement for the explicit purpose of acquiring the vote. There had been vote drives in the South prior to this effort, but the SCLC was the first organization to attempt to acquire the vote through a Southwide mass movement. The SCLC leaders believed that the only force capable of liberating blacks was the blacks themselves rather than the courts, Congress, or the executive branch of government. Actions by those external groups were thought to be effective only in the context of a mass movement. Thus, documents generated during the planning of the Crusade proclaimed that the "Negro must be the primary force in determining his own destiny"[20] and that the black community of the South had the responsibility to confront its problems directly—"since the largest segment of the Negro population lives in the South, the problem must be solved in the South or it cannot be solved anywhere."[21] SCLC officials also maintained that Southern black leaders had to function as the vanguard of the movement, because "the national psychology and the maintenance of the dignity of the Negro masses of the South, requires that the campaign for registering and voting be led by Southern leaders."[22]

The SCLC's intent, then, was to acquire the vote by generating an independent source of power. This intent is evident in the SCLC's discussions of the weak 1957 Civil Rights Act, which passed after Senator Strom Thurmond of South Carolina had filibustered for a record-breaking twenty-four hours, eighteen minutes and after heated discussions in Congress. SCLC leaders argued that the effectiveness of the act depended on "whether these rights and benefits are the result of sporadic and individual action or whether they are the result of a mass movement in the South."[23] After the reading of a report by the American Jewish Congress, which concluded that the Senate would take considerable time approving the new appointee to the Commission on Civil Rights and that this would function as a dampener on the 1957 act, SCLC officials responded:

> Obviously this delay would be less likely if there was now a mass movement throughout the South on voting comparable in vitality and determination to Montgomery in the bus situation. The very demands of such a people's movement would necessitate the immediate appointment of the Commission.[24]

The 1957 act established the commission for only two years, after which Congress would decide whether to extend it or make it permanent. Again the report by the American Jewish Congress warned that the U.S. Congress in 1959 might not extend the commission. SCLC officials responded:

> The answer to what happens in 1959 can be determined conclusively in the meantime. If a south-wide movement on voting has emerged with a dynamic program, the likelihood is that the legislators will have no choice but to accommodate to it and extend the Commission and perhaps give it more power. If on the other hand no such mass movement has developed and no crisis has occurred, all the begging and "political" action cannot insure that the Commission can be extended to say nothing of giving it greater power.[25]

SCLC leaders realized that building a mass movement around voting would require detailed planning and coordination. For example, when outlining the program, they wrote:

This action would involve the selection of a date on which in each city, carefully trained groups of individuals would march in a procession to the registration offices, and, in a nonviolent spirit, insist upon being registered. Acting with firmness and determination they would remain in the office even if arrest is the consequence.[26]

In essence, the plan was to build a mass movement around the vote by mobilizing the masses through existing community organizations, especially the church. The SCLC was attempting to unify existing organizations across the South for mass protest by using the model recently provided by local movements. Again, planning and organization were considered essential—"the community should be organized down to the shortest street and the smallest church, or club."[27]

Within this larger strategy were plans designed to overcome the fear and ignorance the black masses had of voting. Thus the movement was to be "educational in the sense that it would have to establish means through which Negro masses could be aroused and made aware of the importance of the vote."[28] This "consciousness raising" was to be accomplished through workshops, mass rallies, and politically relevant sermons presented to church congregations. To overcome ignorance the plan called for distributing voting clinics, experts, and voting machines throughout Southern black communities. To overcome repression and intimidation, it was decided that the SCLC would "carefully and vigorously utilize the Federal Civil Rights Act of 1957,"[29] which gave the Justice Department limited powers to intervene in voting cases when local whites interfered with the rights of blacks to vote. The SCLC was to provide trained personnel to assist local people in filing complaints with the Justice Department. Finally, the Atlanta headquarters was to publicize the vote grievance through radio, television, and the press. It was hoped that publicity would arouse the American public and generate moral, financial, and political support for the movement. Thus, the strategy of the Crusade was to build a highly organized mass movement which would seize the franchise for Southern blacks. How the plan tallied with what actually happened is the subject of the next section.

THE VOTING MOVEMENT

The Crusade began officially on February 12, 1958, when the SCLC held simultaneous mass meetings in twenty-two Southern cities. The meetings dramatically announced that the voting movement was under way. The first money to finance the project was collected. During the meetings SCLC leadership from across the South exchanged pulpits to promote the idea that resources had to be shared on a Southwide basis and to demonstrate that success resulted from planning and coordination. The SCLC's first newsletter reported that although the mass meetings occurred "on the coldest night in 50 years," more than thirteen thousand persons "were inspired and informed at these meetings."[30]

Following the February 12 meetings the SCLC began implementing its Crusade for Citizenship program. Its basic approach was to organize the movement by mobilizing the masses through preexisting political organizations and churches, coordinated by the SCLC. By the late 1950s civic leagues specifically organized to register blacks to vote existed in numerous Southern communities. It was this network of political organizations that the SCLC attempted to coordinate.[31] Before the SCLC's effort of coordination, these organizations usually operated in isolation. It was not unusual for a city to have several civic leagues, and a state often had as many as twenty. In early 1958 the SCLC approached these organizations and encouraged them to create citywide, countywide, and statewide voter registration committees capable of coordinating the various vote drives. The SCLC informed these groups that it could provide them with resources (e.g. personnel trained in mass organizing and versed in the particulars of the 1957 Civil Rights Act, literature explaining the mechanics of voting and providing statistics on eligible voters, and workshops) to facilitate mass mobilization.

A second approach was to politicize the churches by persuading them to affiliate with the SCLC and become directly involved in the voting movement. The SCLC leaders believed "if every Negro church or even the majority of them in the South' were active members of the Southern Leadership Conference, the increase in registered voters would be phenomenal."[32] From minutes of the National Baptist Conventions and other ministerial records, Tilley compiled a list of ministers' conferences in all Southern cities with populations of 25,000 or more. He selected key ministers in each of the cities and sent them information with an appeal for assistance in getting the local churches to become affiliates. Tilley's message to churches across the South was that they had a responsibility to change the material life of the oppressed. He wrote: "As Christian Leaders, charged with the responsibility of helping to bring abundant life to our constituencies and others, we can find no more direct and quick route to full citizenship than the full and proper use of the ballot."[33] This is an example of the SCLCs attempt to refocus the cultural content of the church and encourage it to become directly involved in politics. To accomplish these ends Reverend Tilley and Ella Baker worked in local communities and provided literature requesting churches to organize social action committees, set up voter clinics, and affiliate with the SCLC.

In short, during the late 1950s the SCLC attempted to organize movements around the vote by consolidating the efforts of organizations through citywide and countywide committees, which would serve as local organizations of organizations while the SCLC played the same role on a regional level. As the SCLC's leadership calculated:

> These committees would include the churches, social, civic, fraternal, labor and other organizations of the community. These committees would be responsible for the setting of quota, time schedules, voting clinics, and thus setting into motion all groups in this one central direction.[34]

In many cases the preexisting organizations actually formed these umbrella committees, and a significant number of churches became directly involved in the movement to acquire the vote.

During 1958 and 1959 civic organizations and churches reported that organized operations were in place to register voters. For example, in Shreveport Dr. Simpkins, president of the local SCLC affiliate, reported:

> There are some 15–20 churches that now have special registration committees which are available each Sunday to give instructions to prospective voters after services. The United Christian Movement, Inc., is holding voting clinics every Monday night; has secured the use of a voting machine for instruction and is publishing a monthly mimeographed news letter.[35]

In Baton Rouge Reverend Jemison reported, "Eighteen (18) social and civic clubs have accepted the responsibility of providing the manpower to do the house-to-house canvassing. . . . the registration lists are being checked weekly and weekly classes are being held in several churches."[36] Similar coordinating committees were organized in Montgomery, Birmingham, Chattanooga, Memphis, Atlanta, and Columbia.

Cross-fertilization of ideas and resources occurred between Southern communities involved in the voting movement and the SCLC's central office. Speaking of the City-wide Registration Committee of Birmingham, Ella Baker wrote that the SCLC had "supplied several thousand pieces of mimeographed material from our office."[37] Baker and Tilley shuttled between communities conducting direct action workshops and compiling complaints of repression against potential voters, which they sent to the Justice Department. Reverend Tilley spoke to numerous church groups and rallies, assuring them that God was interested in civil rights. Pointing to the importance of these meetings Rufus Lewis, Chairman of the Montgomery Committee, wrote:

[T]hese meetings have been helpful in showing first, what things are being done in other states; and how successful they are in solving their problems; second, in developing good working relationships with other groups; third in helping each other to see the vast extent of the whole problem.[38]

The Crusade played an important role in acquainting the masses all over the South with the SCLC's "direct action" approach, introduced earlier in Baton Rouge, Montgomery, and other cities. Whenever local churches or organizations affiliated with the SCLC, members of the community were exposed to an organized group identified with the new approach. That community was now under the wing of an identifiable organization, which conducted nonviolent direct action workshops; disseminated Dr. King's *Stride Toward Freedom*, a book describing the dynamics of the Montgomery bus boycott; and urged blacks to change their status in American society by building mass movements.

While the Crusade was contributing to the crucial but slow process of building local movement centers, between 1958 and 1960 it did not accomplish its objective of doubling the number of black voters by building a Southwide mass movement with the strength and efficacy of the Montgomery bus boycott. Factors both external and internal to the movement were responsible for that failure.

The chief external factor was white resistance. When confronted by blacks seeking to vote, Southern whites marshaled all their repressive power, which included economic reprisals, gerrymandering, delay tactics by white registrars, and legal maneuvers to neutralize the monitoring power of the Civil Rights Commission. Such measures effectively limited the impact of the Crusade. For example, in Louisiana, where the SCLC came close to creating a mass movement, Dr. Simpkins recalls, "When blacks went to register they were cut off the welfare rolls. . . . We had people who actually had difficulty selling their crops and things because they did go register."[39] Baker, who spent five months in Shreveport in 1959, wrote of the delaying tactics:

A city-wide voter-registrator drive was organized and launched, and was highlighted by a special demonstration on March 19th. On this date, 250 persons crowded the Caddo Parish Courthouse in an attempt to register. Only 46 persons were interviewed that day, and only 15 registered.[40]

The SCLC attempted to counter the repression by preparing case-by-case complaints for the Civil Rights Commission. But again, the white power structure responded. Baker wrote that "the July 13th hearing of the Civil Rights Commission on denial of voting rights was, as you know, blocked by injunctive procedures by the state of Louisiana."[41]

Most Southern states in the 1950s required that eligible voters pass a literacy test before registering. The measure was largely used to disfranchise blacks, as the white registrars enforced the requirement stringently for blacks and leniently or not at all for white registrants. Most blacks could not pass the test because they were illiterate. The white power structure devised other methods to disfranchise educated blacks as well. In Tuskegee, Alabama, where many blacks were well educated, the Tuskegee Civic Association joined the statewide voting committee and hotly pursued the franchise. The white power structure responded by implementing a massive gerrymandering plan. One writer described the measure as follows: "The Alabama legislature unanimously altered the city boundaries in 1957, putting all but four or five Negro voters outside the city, and changing the city map from a 4-sided to a 28-sided figure resembling a paralytic sea horse."[42] In short, local Southern white power structures unleashed a barrage of repressive tactics, effectively curtailing the impact of the SCLC's Crusade.

Problems internal to the voting movement were also evident. First of all, the SCLC Executive Director, Reverend Tilley, lasted one year. Tilley, like most of the SCLC's leadership, was tied to the church; while serving as Executive Director he also pastored a church in Baltimore. The two responsibilities forced Tilley to travel constantly between Atlanta and Baltimore, and to countless communities. At times his absence during critical periods generated friction between the SCLC and local communities. On April 15, 1959, Reverend Tilley terminated his service without having accomplished the goals of the Crusade.

Ella Baker became acting Executive Director. She shared the original notion that the Crusade should be a mass movement. In a memorandum of October 23, 1959, she wrote:

> The word Crusade connotes for me a vigorous movement, with high purpose and involving masses of people. In search for action that might help develop for SCLC more of the obvious characteristic of a crusade, a line of thinking was developed which I submit for your consideration. . . . [T]o play a unique role in the South, SCLC must offer, basically, a different "brand of goods" that fills unmet needs of the people. At the same time, it must provide for a sense of achievement and recognition for many people, particularly local leadership.[43]

Yet the classic problems that develop between charismatic leadership and administrators surfaced when Baker became Executive Director. She continued her fight to get the SCLC to install established personnel practices and stock the office with the necessary operating equipment, but to little avail.

King and other SCLC leaders often failed to respond to such requests, even though the changes were needed to increase efficiency. The SCLC leadership's attitude toward formal organization grew out of the charismatic and fluid personal relationships characteristic of the black church. Ministers often carried the same style into their direct action organizations, showing little regard for formal, bureaucratized behavior. For example, most ministers made appointments but were quite casual about keeping them on time. Reverend Lowery describes how he and Fred Shuttlesworth would attend scheduled meetings in Montgomery:

> I was driving from Mobile, Fred was driving from Birmingham, we'd get to the meeting before Ralph and Martin. They lived in Montgomery. We'd wait on them. It's true that they were always late. Always. Most intentionally. [Why intentionally?] Oh, you know, late entrance, dramatic. Plus it's just that old line Baptist tradition. Start late. Colored folks start late—Well, I say that in kindness, you know, in fun. But they did.[44]

Reverend Shuttlesworth commented on the same issue:

> Martin never considered time to be a virtue. It was a rarity, being on time. . . . You could telephone him, and he ought to be out here before the cameras. He was the kind of man that anybody on the street, who did not have anything to say, could stop him and talk to him. In a march, that's a great characteristic. Except that when you are marching, got to meet a deadline, might not be so great.[45]

According to Baker, the charismatic leaders arrived at the office late but expected the staff to work enthusiastically for long extra hours. From her perspective, it was work that should have been done earlier.

> But, I didn't think it was fair, for the men to assume that they could demand of, say the young lady who was the secretary, who had a family, that she would stay there all hours, anytime they wanted her to. The unfortunate thing is that our ministers—most of them—are spoiled by the idea that they own the cards. And I mean, if they came in late—it's natural. "Well, they are busy." . . . I have no respect for that.[46]

The inattention to the SCLC's central office meant that at times local communities received valuable information after a vote drive ended because the necessary resources had not been in place earlier. Moreover, closer monitoring of the central office might have revealed that additional staff was needed and that Reverend Tilley needed a leave of absence from his church while serving as Executive Director. The impact of the Crusade appears to have been less than hoped because steps were not taken to increase the efficiency of the central office.

The problem of fear and ignorance among the masses about voting was not overcome by the Crusade. Dr. Simpkins pointed to the difficulty of persuading people "even to think about voter registration."[47] When people were won over, they had to pass the literacy test. The voting clinics and other measures were not able to prepare large groups to pass the test. Baker proposed a possible solution to the literacy problem—citizenship classes to teach the masses basic writing and reading skills. Baker's work in the community had shown her that the talent and resources for such a project already existed. She wrote:

> It was not my idea that S.C.L.C. should conduct classes, but that we could interest such groups as the Women's Baptist Convention, the National Council of Negro Women, and national college sororities in such projects. . . . On the other hand, the literacy project could provide a "respectable" channel for helping the cause without too close identification with more militant aspects of the struggle. The literacy project could well serve as the basis for calling a Southwide meeting of women, as we proposed before.[48]

The SCLC would discover in 1961 that citizenship schools were quite effective in overcoming the literacy problem, but in the late 1950s Baker's suggestion was not implemented.

It is difficult to assess why the SCLC leadership failed to implement some of the important ideas advanced by Baker. It appears that sexism and Baker's nonclergy status minimized her impact on the SCLC. Baker, being a woman and having worked with women's groups across the South, recognized that women had enormous contributions to make to the movement. She began pushing the SCLC to involve both women and young people at all levels of the organization. In a 1959 report she wrote that "the participation of women and youth in the southern civil rights struggle must be promoted."[49] Writing in the SCLC's newsletter, Baker indicates how limited the use of women in the young organization was: "Mrs. Katie Whickham, one of the two women of S.C.L.C.'s Executive Board, became the first female member to attend a meeting when she participated in the December 10, 1958, session in Atlanta."[50] In a memo to King she shows her interest in combating sexism: "You will also note that Mrs. Katie E. Whickham was elected Assistant Secretary to become the first woman officer of the SCLC. This is in keeping with the expressed need to involve more women in the movement."[51] Thus in the late 1950s Ella Baker took a strong position against subservient roles for women in social change movements, anticipating the centrality of women's issues in movements of the 1960s and 1970s.

Baker's role as Director was restricted also because the SCLC's leadership viewed her as a lame duck executive. The SCLC leadership never accepted Baker as Executive Director; from the very beginning King had wanted Bayard Rustin to set up the central office. Rustin was not hired because it was feared that his homosexuality would cause unnecessary problems. Baker received the job only after Tilley proved unsatisfactory, and even then SCLC leaders appointed her only as acting Director. The Reverend Wyatt Walker, who succeeded Baker, recalls, "When John Tilley left it was within 90 days of his leaving or less [that] they knew they were going to hire me if they could get me, and Ella was just a holding action."[52]

Finally, the fact that Baker held a different conception of leadership from the ministers' contributed to her isolation in the organization. Baker focused most of her attention on developing local leadership rather than the SCLC center. This went against the desires of the SCLC leadership, who felt that the movement could not be developed without a strong church organization, enhanced by a charismatic leader. Reverend Walker put it best when he stated that Baker "could not fit into the mold of a preacher organization. It just went against the grain of the kind of person she is and was."[53] The tension between the SCLC and its central office contributed to diminishing the impact of the Citizenship program.

The SCLC's inability effectively to coordinate and determine the strategy of the various groups involved with the movement was a central internal problem of the Crusade. In this regard King wrote in 1959 that "there has never been any genuine cooperation and coordination between national and local organizations working to increase the vote."[54] The SCLC discovered that it was difficult to coordinate the activities of preexisting organizations and persuade them to supplement the legal approach with direct action. Furthermore, the preexisting groups often approached the SCLC with apprehension because it was new and advocated a new plan of attack. It appears too that neither Tilley nor Baker had been concerned with making the SCLC, as an organization, highly visible. King wrote of the organization's invisibility in 1959: "There can be no gainsaying of the fact that the SCLC has not been publicized through the press or otherwise. The aim and purposes of the Conference have not gotten over to a large number of people North and South."[55]

This problem was compounded by the fact that some preexisting organizations, especially the NAACP, perceived the SCLC as a threat. According to SCLC documents, the NAACP circulated information in 1959 that the program of the SCLC had folded. The SCLC's leadership saw this action as an attempt by the NAACP to drive the Crusade out of existence. King moved swiftly to take the momentum out of NAACP's maneuvers by recommending to the committee on the SCLC's Future Programs:

> In order to attempt once more to coordinate the activities of the NAACP and the SCLC in the vote drive, and clear up what appears to be seeds of dissension being sown by persons in the top echelon in the NAACP, the president, accompanied by one person from the official family of SCLC, should immediately have a conference with Roy Wilkins and other NAACP staff members whose presence Mr. Wilkins may deem necessary.[56]

In addition, King asked that press releases be sent out immediately to counteract these false ideas. In another attempt to save the organization, King recommended that an informative newsletter be mailed to at least five thousand persons. He advised drawing the mailing list "from minutes of church groups, thus covering a large number of ministers, the MIA files, select groups from In Friendship and persons who wrote to the president during his illness. This newsletter should clearly express the aims and purposes of the conference, its past accomplishments and future proposals."[57] In short, the NAACP did not always welcome the SCLC, and tensions were frequently present between the two. Organizational conflict and the difficulties of coordinating the program with preexisting organizations were other factors minimizing the results of the Crusade for Citizenship program.

FINANCE

The following investigation of the SCLC's financial base centers on the period between 1957 and 1960, key years of the Crusade for Citizenship program.[58] That was the period when the infrastructure of local movement centers, the vehicles of collective action, were being established.

To understand the SCLC's financial base, it is crucial to distinguish between the financing of local movements and that of the central office. In earlier chapters we have seen that local movements were usually financed by local blacks. The SCLC's funding policies required that local movements fund their own activities but not those of the central office. On the other hand, the central office was responsible for providing the local movements with the services of experts on nonviolence, charismatic leaders, and a host of other resources needed for confronting the power structure in the interest of the movement's goals.

The central office had expenses distinct from those of the local movements, so the SCLC developed a policy that "all national fund-raising will be conducted by the central office."[59] The SCLC leadership decided that it would raise the monies to fund the central office by canvassing churches, trade unions, and foundations of the North and South.

There is evidence (which will be discussed shortly) to suggest that during the early years of the SCLC most of the money used to finance its central office came from the black religious community, principally outside of the South. The method of fundraising during those crucial years when the movement centers were being developed followed a distinct pattern. Most funds were raised at mass church rallies, which resembled revival meetings, often with Dr. King as the main speaker.[60] The SCLC leadership organized the rallies through their clergy contacts. In most cases they would ask the president of the ministerial alliance in a Northern city to secure the support of a number of local churches. Once that was accomplished, local ministers had their organized church work forces look after the innumerable details. After large contributions were collected, King delivered his address, in which he described the conditions of Southern blacks, their local movements, and the responsibilities of Northern blacks to support the protest efforts of their Southern brothers and sisters. Fundraising through mass church rallies was implemented in the South as well, and smaller contributions from nonreligious black organizations and from white individuals were other sources of SCLC funding during its early years. A look at the finances of the Crusade for Citizenship Program will show how the funding operation worked.

SCLC leaders decided that an initial budget of $200,000 was needed to fund the Crusade adequately. SCLC documents reveal, however, that from 1957 to 1960 the SCLC raised about $50,000 annually. About 65 percent of this amount was spent on salaries, rent, and travel, and the remainder went into the program itself. Three points should be made about the SCLC's finances during that period: (1) Most of the money came from outside the South; (2) it came largely from organizations rather than individuals; and (3) the money came primarily from black religious organizations across the nation, but principally the North. Affiliate fees of twenty-five dollars coming largely from Southern churches constituted the second largest source of money, but this source generated far less than the rallies.

Detailed financial data on the organization covering a four-month period in 1959 provide some information on the sources of SCLC finances. Seventy-eight percent of the $11,500 collected in the four months came from non-Southern states; 93 percent of it came from organizations rather than individuals. Eighty percent of the organizations contributing were black religious organizations. Most of the remaining 20 percent of the organizations were largely black, comprising fraternal orders, unions, and social clubs. Individual contributions, which constituted 7 percent of the finances during the four months, came largely from Northern whites.[61] These data, covering a four-month period, are not sufficient to prove that the same composition of sources of the SCLC's income held true for the whole 1957–60 period. But additional information from organizational documents and letters suggests that the SCLC did raise the bulk of its income from black church-oriented mass meetings outside the South in those years.

The SCLC perfected a standard practice of raising money through church rallies. A letter from King in 1959 points to this method:

> Most of my speaking is in the interest of raising funds for this conference. One of the methods that I have used in the past few months is that of selecting cities across the country and asking the ministerial groups to come together and sponsor a city-wide meeting at which time I speak, and funds are raised through the churches and other organizations for the work of the Southern Christian Leadership Conference.[62]

Abernathy, the financial secretary-treasurer of the SCLC at the time, highlighted the predominance of this method in his 1959 financial report: "Small individual contributions are still coming into the office from individuals and groups across the country, but the vast amount of our funds are raised through mass meetings in which our president, Dr. Martin Luther King, Jr., serves as the speaker."[63] King's ability to raise money was remarkable. He was also president of the MIA at the same time and supported that organization by the same method. According to Coretta King, within the span of a year (1957–58) "King traveled 780,000 miles and delivered two hundred and eight speeches."[64] King's heavy financial responsibilities were clearly expressed in a letter he wrote after returning from India, where he had discussed nonviolent civil disobedience with former strategists of the Gandhi movement:

> I also came back and discovered that the funds for both of the organizations which I am heading have gotten pretty low. This meant getting out on the road immediately to bring some finances in. With all these things rolling before me like a mighty flood, I just haven't had time to sit down and write an article.[65]

The financial picture of the organization during the late 1950s suggests that SCLC leaders were able to convince many blacks that "the magnitude of the problem calls for the maximum commitment of resources of all institutions in Negro life, North and South."[66]

In summary, during the late 1950s the SCLC attempted to enfranchise blacks through building a mass movement. It was partially successful, as movement-related activity around the vote did occur in many cities. Yet in no way did a coordinated Southwide mass movement develop. White resistance certainly played a part, it is hardly the whole explanation, for resistance not only was expected but was the very reason the SCLC attempted to build a mass movement. The mass movement was supposed to generate an independent source of power within the black community to overcome resistance. It appears that factors internal to the black community and the SCLC were at the center of this specific failure. But the failure cannot be attributed entirely to an underdeveloped central office. In my view, the primary reason for failure is to be found in Southern black communities, because in the middle to late 1950s the internal organization—movement centers—of the civil rights movement had not yet developed to a point where a Southwide mass movement could be generated and sustained. Thus the real value of the SCLC's Crusade during this period lies in the fact that movement participants associated with the project were developing a viable internal organization—financial base, workshops on nonviolent confrontation, refocusing of the cultural content of the black church, direct action leaders, and church-related protest organizations—specifically geared for nonviolent confrontations. Finally, the activities of the early SCLC were partially shaped and constrained by other civil rights organizations in the field. The next chapter is devoted to a discussion of the interactions among the SCLC, the NAACP, and CORE.

6

ORGANIZATIONAL RELATIONSHIPS: THE SCLC, THE NAACP, AND CORE

SCLC–NAACP

The SCLC and the NAACP were closely linked. Indeed, most of SCLC founders were members of the NAACP, and many were current or former NAACP leaders at the time of the SCLC's formation. So closely linked were the two organizations that it was common for a community leader to function as president of both the local NAACP branch and the local SCLC affiliate. Moreover, the mass movements led by the SCLC founders did not arise outside of the NAACP's influence. The NAACP often provided substantial sums of money for the expensive legal cost of these movements, and in many cases it was NAACP lawyers who defended movement participants in court. Many NAACP branches sent money directly to the headquarters of these movements to help finance their overall efforts. Thus the NAACP, as a preexisting national organization with branches throughout the South, served as a vital resource for the mass movements. But even though NAACP officials assisted the direct action movements, many of them thought it unwise to form a new protest organization for the explicit purpose of organizing direct action.

NAACP officials and many members generally believed that the NAACP was *the* organization through which to free blacks. Indeed, James Weldon Johnson, the NAACP's first black Executive Secretary, wrote in 1934 that in order for blacks to be liberated they should pool their resources and protest into a single unit, which he referred to as a central machine. "I believe we have that machine at hand," he wrote, "in the National Association for the Advancement of Colored People. I believe we could get the desired results by making that organization the nucleus, the synthesis, the clearinghouse, of our forces."[1] The idea that the NAACP was the only proper vehicle to achieve racial equality was widespread throughout the organization in the late 1950s. James Farmer, a founder of CORE, who served as the National Program Director of the NAACP from 1959 through 1961, recalled the thinking of that period:

> The NAACP staff, bureaucracy . . . and it was a heavy bureaucracy there . . . most of the persons had been there for many, many years and they had been conditioned to perceive the NAACP as being the civil rights organization. And all others were viewed as interlopers. So they viewed the SCLC as a potential rival . . . as an interloper. And felt it was not needed because they [NAACP] were doing what needed to be done.[2]

So top NAACP officials did not welcome the formation of the SCLC. Reverend Lowery recalls one occasion as SCLC was being organized:

> We met with strong opposition from the NAACP. Well, the thing got so bad, that Martin, Ralph and I went to New York and had a meeting with Roy Wilkins [then NAACP Executive Secretary], John Morsell [then Assistant to the Executive Secretary], and Gloster Current [then Director of Branches]. [We] met half the day and night. Roy was very sophisticated, you know. He wouldn't dare show any antipathy. John Morsell was a little bit more matter-of-fact, but Gloster was the hatchet man. Gloster said, "To tell you the truth, gentlemen, at the end of the bus boycott, you all should have disbanded everything, and been back in NAACP."[3]

Lowery concluded that Gloster Current's view reflected the official NAACP position when Wilkins "didn't say 'Amen,' neither did he say 'Nay.' " This resentment toward the SCLC was reflected in an editorial in the *Pittsburgh Courier*, a prominent black newspaper:

> Another Civil Rights organization would seem to be one thing that colored America does not need, and yet representatives from 12 states and the District of Columbia meeting in Montgomery, Alabama, answering the call of Dr. Martin Luther King, have set up the Southern Christian Leadership Conference. . . . Are the organizers of the Southern Christian Leadership Conference implying by their action that the NAACP is no longer capable of doing what it has been doing for decades because it is now under attack in several Southern

*states? . . . What sound reason is there for having two organizations
with the same goal when one has been doing such an effective job?*[4]

The reluctance of NAACP officials to endorse the SCLC became evident when King asked a number of prominent Americans to join the
SCLC's National Advisory Committee. Those who accepted were not
expected to do extensive work, but their names were needed to add
prestige and legitimacy to the young SCLC. Ralph Bunche and Herbert
Lehman, both highly visible board members of the NAACP, refused to
join the SCLC's Advisory Committee on the grounds of their affiliation
with the NAACP. Lehman sent a $250 check with his letter of refusal
to show his personal interest in the work of the SCLC.[5] Clearly, the
NAACP was attempting to protect its organizational monopoly over
black protest. The NAACP leadership's fears about the rise of the SCLC
were not unfounded. The emergence of the SCLC represented a threat
to the NAACP's local leadership, its financial base, and its patiently
cultivated strategy of working within the law. To add to the NAACP's
fears, the SCLC was being organized at precisely the time when the
NAACP was losing strength in the South as the result of attacks by the
Southern white power structure.

The formation of the SCLC threatened to drain away some of the
NAACP's local leadership because, as Reverend Lawson has noted,
"most of the people who began to surround King and saw him as the
symbol of what we hoped for and wanted to happen, would have been
people who, for lack of any other tool, would have been in the NAACP
just as common procedure."[6] With the rise of the SCLC it was unclear
whether the leaders on whom the NAACP had relied in the past would
shift their allegiance to the new organization. It would be difficult to
find people in the South willing to take on the harassment and sacrifices that association with the NAACP would automatically entail at a
time when the NAACP was being treated as a radical organization by
the white power structure. James Farmer indicated that a problem
would remain even if leaders stayed with the NAACP, "because if
church members, ministers, and others became active in SCLC they
might become less active in the NAACP branches."[7]

The SCLC was a threat to the NAACP's financial base because much
of that base was anchored in the church. Any NAACP leader who gravitated to the SCLC represented not only a loss of leadership but, in most
cases, the loss of a minister in control of a congregation, hence the loss
in turn of the substantial financial support forthcoming to the NAACP
from that congregation. In 1947 the NAACP created a Church Department for the express purposes of coordinating activities between
churches and the NAACP and acquiring NAACP memberships and fi-

nancial support from the church. Ten years later, when the SCLC was being organized, the NAACP's Church Department began an aggressive campaign to win and consolidate Southern church support. To this end local NAACP branches established church committees and conducted ministers' workshops. The NAACP annual report for 1957 contains this comment:

> The branch church committees, it was learned, have been invaluable sources for securing memberships, mobilizing the support of local church leadership and giving concrete expression to the social concern of church groups by involving them in the struggle for equality on the community level.[8]

James Farmer, who worked in the NAACP during the late 1950s, was in a good position to observe how the NAACP and the SCLC drew from the same financial base in the South. He says the NAACP felt financially threatened because the SCLC's "base was the Baptist church in the South . . . and that black Baptist church was . . . one source of funds which the NAACP branches traditionally tapped. So SCLC was viewed as a threat in that sense. Because the money which went to SCLC might have gone to the NAACP had SCLC not been around."[9] The SCLC was in a better position to capitalize on the NAACP's church base by virtue of being a church organization with clergy leadership and being indigenous to the South.

Finally, the SCLC's strategy of nonviolent direct action by the masses was threatening to the NAACP's legal approach because of its mass appeal and wider effectiveness, as demonstrated by the Montgomery bus boycott and similar confrontations. The lack of a mass base has always been a problem for the NAACP. During the 1950s NAACP membership comprised less than 1 percent of the total black population, and the legal method itself served as one barrier to mass involvement. Dr. King was well aware that the NAACP's legal approach discouraged mass participation when he wrote, "when legal contests were the sole form of activity . . . the ordinary Negro was involved as a passive spectator. His interests were stirred, but his energies were unemployed."[10] James Farmer, hired in 1959 by the NAACP precisely for the purpose of reviving local activity, found that the NAACP chapters "didn't seem to be doing much except raising funds, raising the freedom budget each year. And many of the chapter branches had become essentially collection agencies."[11]

On the other hand, the SCLC's approach depended directly on mass involvement. Reverend Lawson accurately characterized this important difference between the two organizations' approaches:

The point of the whole problem is that when people are suffering they don't want rhetoric and processes which seem to go slowly. . . . Many people, when they are suffering and they see their people suffering, they want direct participation. They want to be able to say, what I'm doing here gives me power and is going to help us change this business. . . . That's one of the great successes when you do something like a school boycott . . . or an economic boycott. Because here I am, mad already, with the racism I see, and now you tell me, okay . . . here's a chance for us to do something. So you stay out of that store until they do XYZ. . . . Just stay out of that store. So you put into the hands of all kinds of ordinary people a positive alternative to powerlessness and frustration. That's one of the great things about direct action.[12]

The SCLC's strategy advocated a new method of mass protest. The mass movements that gave rise to the SCLC stood as proof that masses could be organized for collective protest through the churches. Thus the SCLC was capable of mobilizing a mass base, which the NAACP had never been able to do.

Shortly after the Montgomery bus boycott the effects of the direct action strategy began to be felt within the NAACP. The new approach was especially appealing to the young adults and teenagers associated with the NAACP Youth Councils. The NAACP was not a monolithic organization; it housed a range of protest leaders, some of them cautious, others aggressive, and a few militant. The diverse leadership clustered in the NAACP generated differences between NAACP chapters on the local level. Some NAACP members were dissatisfied with the pace of change resulting from the legal approach and felt that their branches functioned primarily as collection agencies for the national office rather than as effective social change organizations. Members of the young, aggressive wing of the NAACP often served as adult advisers to NAACP Youth Councils. A disproportionate number of these advisers were women: Rosa Parks, Daisy Bates, Clara Luper, and Vera Pigee. Men like Floyd McKissick, Hosea Williams, and Ronald Walters also served as leaders of NAACP Youth Councils. These were the NAACP leaders who were impressed by the direct action strategies used in the Montgomery bus boycott, and they were not hesitant in adopting and implementing these strategies. The aggressive wing of the NAACP had always existed, but it was given new life after the mass movements began to be organized. Indeed, in the late 1950s numerous NAACP Youth Councils were reorganized after disappearing early in the decade for lack of support, and many of them began functioning as direct action organizations.

Some of the Youth Councils became involved in highly organized direct action projects, such as sit-ins, in the late 1950s. In 1957 the Oklahoma City NAACP Youth Council, headed by Mrs. Clara Luper, began formulating plans to sit-in at local stores with segregated dining facilities. Mrs. Luper wrote that "for eighteen months, the members of the NAACP Youth council had been studying non-violence as a way of overcoming injustices."[13] She pointed out that the group followed what it called Martin Luther King's nonviolent plan, which specified seven steps of action:

> [R]esist the evil of segregation in a passive, non-violent way. . . . mobilize for an all out fight for first class citizenship. [T]he church must be awakened to its responsibility. Religion is the chief avenue to the minds and the souls of the masses. [C]ontinue our struggles in the courts, and above all things, we must remember to support the National Association for the Advancement of Colored People. [A]t the same time we must support other organizations that are molding public opinion.[14]

Dr. Benjamin Mays, who worked on NAACP membership drives, clearly captured the impact of the aggressive wing of the NAACP: "You must remember that the local chapter was bringing pressure upon the NAACP to get out and do the kind of thing that Martin Luther and his group were doing because they're [SCLC] getting the prestige and they are being called the movement that is struggling for the masses."[15] The wing of the NAACP that Luper's group represented had obviously begun to emphasize the direct action method symbolized by King, E. D. Nixon, and thousands of nonviolent protestors rather than the legal method symbolized by such personalities as Thurgood Marshall and Roy Wilkins.

The discussion so far has shown how the emergence of the SCLC threatened the NAACP's leadership structure, financial base, legal strategy, and monopolistic status as the black civil rights organization. These were the underlying organizational reasons why the NAACP did not welcome the presence of the SCLC. In many instances members of the NAACP responded by spreading negative information about the SCLC in the community, as they did in the vote drive. In some situations the national NAACP attempted to prevent local chapters from engaging in direct action. Lawson, who assisted in training Luper's group to conduct sit-ins in 1957, recalls the NAACP's response: "The NAACP opposed [sit-ins]. The parent body, the branch body, chastised the school teacher [Luper] who was responsible for it, chastised them, told them to desist."[16] Specific strategies were pursued by the SCLC to overcome the attacks by the NAACP and promote cooperation between the two organizations. Because most SCLC leaders were either former or current leaders of the NAACP, they were able to understand its attitude toward the SCLC. That understanding was an important aid to SCLC leaders in formulating effective strategies of cooperation.

First, the SCLC's leadership seized every opportunity to praise the NAACP as an organization both privately and publicly and to plead for continuing support of it. On May 17, 1957, a number of organizations, including the SCLC and the NAACP, conducted a Prayer Pilgrimage on Washington, D.C., that attracted 25,000 people. King told the gathering:

> We have won marvelous victories through the work of the NAACP. We have been able to do some of the most amazing things of this generation, and I come this afternoon with nothing but praise for this great organization. Although they outlawed the NAACP in Alabama and other states, the fact still remains that this organization has done more to achieve Civil Rights for Negroes than any other organization we can point to.[17]

King expressed the same sentiment to Thurgood Marshall privately: "NO sane, objective, intelligent individual can deprecate the work of the NAACP."[18] It was common for SCLC leaders to back their words of respect by taking out life memberships in the NAACP. King and the MIA each took out a life membership at a cost of $500 each. King then persuaded his church to take out a life membership and promised NAACP officials that he would urge other Montgomery churches to do likewise. The intention was plainly to promote harmonious relations with the NAACP.

Second, the SCLC pursued strategies aimed at convincing the NAACP that the SCLC's presence would not erode NAACP membership or weaken its financial base. SCLC leaders constantly reminded the NAACP that the SCLC was not seeking individual members or chapters but affiliates that were preexisting organizations, hence was no threat to draw away NAACP members. For the NAACP's benefit many of the SCLC's printed materials proclaimed in bold print, "SCLC DOES NOT establish local units nor solicit individual membership."[19]

To avoid conflicts over funding, the SCLC and the NAACP developed a strategy of raising money jointly and dividing it. Evidence of this strategy is clear in Ella Baker's report to the SCLC in 1959:

> In order to generate real interest throughout the state in the fund raising aspects of the Columbia meeting, it seems highly desirable to follow something of the pattern that was used in the promotion of the Norfolk meeting. As you know, the NAACP and S.C.L.C. shared in proceeds from the Norfolk Mass Meeting.[20]

This was an ideal strategy from which the SCLC gained use of the NAACP's networks for organizing fundraising rallies and the NAACP gained the presence of the charismatic figure. During the late 1950s and early 1960s King played an important role in NAACP fundraising activities. It is safe to say that during this period King spoke for the NAACP more than for any other organization. He spoke for local NAACP branches across the country during their membership drives, often delivered the main address at NAACP annual conventions, and, in 1957, became a member of the National Advisory Committee for the NAACP Freedom Fund Campaign.[21] The importance of King's presence at NAACP fundraising events is evident in a letter from the Executive Secretary of the Detroit NAACP branch, written when he learned that King could not attend the branch's 1958 Freedom Fund Campaign:

> In view of your public acclaim and the unusually valuable position you now hold, I hope that you will be ever mindful that a helping hand from you is ten, twenty-five, one hundred times more productive than that of countless other friends whose resources and influence can never quite measure up to their interest in this work.[22]

In short, the financial strategy devised by the SCLC and the NAACP benefited them both and minimized the potential for a destructive conflict between two organizations whose personnel and funding bases were so intertwined.

Finally, the SCLC mitigated the NAACP's fears that direct action would replace the legal strategy. The SCLC emphasized that a division of labor was sorely needed in the movement, and the NAACP was superbly qualified for the legal role, leaving the SCLC to specialize in direct action at the community level. This effort took some force out of the NAACP's complaint that SCLC leaders were opportunists seeking to establish an organization while NAACP was under heavy attack in the South. SCLC officials reached to the heart of the matter by arguing: "A strong mass organization indigenous to the South is the greatest assurance for restoring the legal and emotional atmosphere in which the NAACP can again fully operate in the South."[23] The SCLC further pointed out that its approach complemented the legal strategies of the NAACP: Because "it is on the community level that court decision must be implemented," the SCLC's direct action approach was designed to make sure that the NAACP's legal victories were actually enforced. King often assured top NAACP legal experts, "you continue winning the legal victories for us and we will work passionately and unrelentingly to implement these victories on the local level through nonviolent means."[24]

Although the SCLC emphasized the necessity of an organizational division of labor, it still had to assert itself strongly as a new force capable of transforming the racial caste system of the South. But its assertiveness had to be established while maintaining a harmonious relationship with the NAACP. It did so by challenging NAACP to accept direct action as a useful approach. At the Prayer Pilgrimage of 1957, where the NAACP's highest officials gathered, King, after praising the accomplishments of the NAACP, warned: "We must also avoid the temptation of being victimized with a psychology of victors. We have won marvelous victories through the work of NAACP. . . . Certainly this is marvelous. We must not, however, remain satisfied with a court victory over our white brothers."[25]

In conclusion, the SCLC deployed a complex array of arguments to decrease NAACP animosity toward the new civil rights organization. Such defenses were necessitated by the fact that the two organizations overlapped in fundamental ways. Although tensions and conflicts remained between the NAACP and the SCLC, those specific strategies promoted cooperation and prevented the two organizations from engaging in destructive interorganizational rivalry.

SCLC–CORE–NAACP

The Congress of Racial Equality (CORE) also had an important role in the modern civil rights movement, and the interorganizational relationship that developed among CORE, the NAACP, and the SCLC calls for analysis.

In the 1950s CORE had no mass base in the South or the North. Before the late 1950s CORE had a national office consisting of one paid official and a number of small local Northern chapters. The chapters usually included five or six dedicated activists who periodically demonstrated against racial discrimination. Masses were not involved in the demonstrations. Rather, in attorney Stanley Levison's apt words, CORE activities were carried out in a "witness fashion by small groups."[26]

In the South during the early and mid-1950s CORE was unknown to the black masses; in fact, it was no better known to middle-income Southern blacks than to the poor and unemployed. CORE's first full-time field secretary, who was educated and had been a superintendent of public schools in South Carolina, acknowledged that before being hired by CORE in 1957, he "had never heard about it." This Southern black man, James McCain, who for years had been fighting for racial equality, went on to say: "At that time [1957] no. I didn't know anything about any other organizations. The only thing we knew about was the National Association, NAACP."[27] The reasons blacks had not heard of CORE are obvious. First, CORE was a Northern organization founded in Chicago in 1942. Most of its members were pacifist graduate students at the University of Chicago. One of its principal founders was James Farmer, a black man trained as a minister who had never pastored a church. The organization from the start was interracial, with whites far outnumbering blacks. That by itself is a strong indication that CORE was organized to function in the North, for something bordering on a revolution would have to occur in the South before interracial protest groups could function.[28] After its emergence, CORE's small groups sporadically attacked racism in a few Northern cities, at times with success. Yet CORE, the organization, was unknown to Southern blacks.

CORE was an intellectually oriented organization, concerned as much with broad philosophical issues as with racial equality. CORE members usually came from pacifist backgrounds or had adopted pacifist ideals and principles. The overriding goal of CORE members was to demonstrate that large social problems could be solved through nonviolent means. Gordon Carey, the second full-time field secretary hired by CORE, makes this point clearly:

> Most of the people involved in CORE in the early days were there because they saw a means of working out their own political and social ideologies. It was not a struggle for freedom. They looked upon what they were doing as working on huge social problems. Now, that's a very impersonal theoretical kind of thing. . . . The idea was that you came into CORE or you were in CORE and you believed in nonviolent direct action. That's really what you believed in.[29]

James Farmer, who became CORE's National Director in 1961, emphasized:

> CORE, you must remember, from its early days was a means-oriented organization. It was oriented toward the techniques of nonviolent direct action. That was perhaps more important in the minds of many of the persons there than the ends which were being sought . . . it was means, finding some way to use nonviolence to show the world that nonviolence can solve racial problems.[30]

Farmer also maintained that CORE usually attracted middle-class white intellectuals, because they were interested in finding alternatives to violence in resolving social conflict. He added that very few blacks had the interest, desire, or background required in CORE. James Robinson, national Executive Director of CORE until 1961, agreed that CORE members were "Looking for a method, developing a method, popularizing a method. . . . CORE used nonviolence as a tactic, but I think a lot of the people including myself, thought of nonviolence as a value in and of itself."[31] In the middle and late 1950s the primary goals of Southern blacks were to desegregate buses, public schools, and voting booths; to prevent lynchings and beatings; and to overthrow racial domination. For CORE, on the other hand, the most important endeavor was to locate a set of social problems appropriate to its goal of demonstrating that a particular method could work. Although not necessarily incompatible, the two sets of goals were not the same.

Prior to the Southern mass movements of the 1950s CORE had concluded that the South was an impossible place to prove the efficacy of the nonviolent method. According to Farmer, the South was considered a "never-never land" by CORE's staff.[32] When masses of blacks began protesting nonviolently in the south, CORE became interested. As James Robinson recalls, the Montgomery movement demonstrated that something could be done in the South and "that there were people who would follow and take action in the South."[33]

CORE's staff explored ways to enter the South. Before 1957 CORE had no chapters in the South and had not succeeded in proving the efficacy of nonviolent protest on a large scale. In fact, CORE had a difficult time finding a favorable testing ground for the method of nonviolence. Carey shows the essence of the problem:

> Now, where can you apply that? Well, you can't apply it in the international scene, you can't apply it in the labor relations very much. Hell, they've been doing that in unions long before CORE was ever heard of, you know, with sit-down strikes and all this sort of thing. So a good place in which to practice your ideologies, so to speak, would be in race relations. And that's what really happened, I think.[34]

If one wanted to apply the method of nonviolence to problems of race relations during the late 1950s, the South was indeed the place that presented the challenge.

However, the CORE of the mid-1950s had greater problems than finding a testing ground for its method. With few resources and no national image, it was an organization more in spirit and commitment than in reality. CORE's Executive Secretary decided that the organization should enter the South in quest of organizational stability, national stature, and the development of a method.

CORE and the South

In 1957 CORE made its first attempt to establish a base in the South. Because CORE was largely led by middle-class white intellectuals during the late 1950s, it entered the South with a paternalistic attitude about how poor blacks should fight for liberation. James Farmer recalls:

> *My friends in CORE at that time did view CORE as being their property. . . . It was paternalistic, very paternalistic. . . . They viewed the black brother as the junior partner in the alliance, not quite of age. So, thus they viewed themselves as senior partners, obviously. . . . CORE was a small organization that was standing outside of the ghetto, the minority community, working in its behalf.*[35]

Farmer maintained that CORE leaders resisted having meetings in the black community because they favored taking blacks outside the ghetto into integrated situations. To illustrate CORE's paternalism, Farmer told of a time he proposed that CORE hold a rally in Representative Adam Clayton Powell's church in Harlem. Marvin Rich, a long-time activist with CORE who became Community Relations Director in 1959, opposed the rally, whereupon Farmer exploded. He argued: " 'This will tie in the black community.' [Marvin Rich's] argument was, 'We're not interested in the whole black community.' [Is that right?] Yes. 'We're only interested in the activists in the black community.' "[36]

Floyd McKissick, a black attorney from North Carolina who had participated in CORE's 1947 "Journey of Reconciliation" project, an attempt to integrate buses in the border states, and who became its National Chairman in 1964 and its National Director in 1966, agreed that most whites in CORE were not directly concerned with "the causes of freedom of black people." He added: "Now certainly, they did not appreciate blacks who asserted themselves. And some particular people who asserted themselves as I did."[37] Gordon Carey, the white field secretary, also agreed that CORE in the early days of the movement was paternalistic. The whites in CORE were not affected by problems that confronted blacks, he observed, so they were unable to view the situation from the vantage point of blacks.[38] This is not to say that CORE did not work tenaciously to bring about black liberation. It does mean, however, that the effective implementation of nonviolent strategies was as important a goal to CORE as black liberation.

Finally, Jim McCain, CORE's first full-time field secretary, immediately encountered problems with CORE's Executive Secretary over how blacks should struggle for freedom. McCain says he thought the quickest route to black liberation was acquiring the vote: "I felt that voter registration was one of the main thrusts with the blacks in the South, because we . . . had been disenfranchised."[39] From CORE's viewpoint, a protest centered on voting was not direct action. CORE officials explained to McCain that CORE was a direct action organization, and in voting protests "you don't picket." McCain replied, "Don't tell me you don't picket for the vote." He pointed out to the Executive Secretary that before CORE entered the South blacks were picketing for the vote in "Williamsburgh County and several counties." McCain explained to Robinson, who was issuing directives from CORE's headquarters in New York: "Plenty of black people down here don't feel like doing what you have in mind."[40] They knew that "some white people might come in and knock you off the stool" while you sat in. "James Robinson and I differed on that," McClain relates. "And so I told him, 'okay you're the boss. I'm working for you. I'll try to do it your way.' "[41]

Evidence about CORE's paternalism has been presented because it had a fundamental bearing on the organizational activity and the interorganizational relationships CORE established in the movement. It also has a direct bearing on one major thesis of this book: Because the SCLC functioned as the decentralized arm of the black church and its leadership was all black, it did not have to devote important resources, time, and energy to in-house racial bickering. By 1964 so much racial fighting had occurred in CORE that Farmer concluded: "There are many Negroes who will not work with an interracial organization because of their suspicion of whites. . . . White liberals must be willing to work in roles of secondary leadership and as technicians."[42]

Social movements and their organizations are rooted in the social structures they seek to change. Racism, sexism, and classism will therefore be found in American movements, because they are deeply rooted in American society. Social movements display existing social contradictions when they are pushed to the foreground by activists constrained by them. Often those who gain power in social change groups do not realize that the dynamics of a movement may eventually call their own privileges and leadership positions into question. Thus, even though the SCLC did not suffer from racial bickering, it did have to deal with problems and conflicts generated by sexism.

We are now in a position to analyze CORE's relations with the NAACP and the SCLC. CORE's entrance into the South in 1957 was facilitated by the organizational attack that white Southerners leveled against the NAACP, which again suggests that that attack is central to understanding the origins of the modern civil rights movement. CORE's initial entrance into the South was effected through one man, James McCain. Mr. McCain obtained his bachelor's degree from Morris College, a black institution in his hometown of Sumter, South Carolina, and did graduate work at Temple University in Philadelphia. After completing his education he returned to Sumter and taught at Morris College for more than a decade. In the meantime, when NAACP came to South Carolina, he became one of the youngest members on the State Board and the first president of its Sumter branch. He remained the president of the local NAACP for ten years and was re-elected after two years off the job.

After a successful stay at Morris College, where he was promoted to dean and served in that capacity about seven years, McCain accepted a job as supervising principal of a school district in Marion, South Carolina. After five productive years there he received a shock. "Because of my connection with NAACP, I was fired."[43] He was accused of having written an NAACP petition back in 1954, when the school desegregation case was being decided.

"Black parents in Mullens wrote a letter to the School Board, asking them if the Supreme Court decision was favorable on the school desegregation decision, would they start making plans now to admit black children to all white schools," McCain recalls.[44] Although he did not write the petition, he continues, "I was told if I would recant and apologize that most likely I could keep my job. But I refused to do it because I didn't have anything to do with it. So my contract was terminated."[45]

Following his dismissal, McCain was hired as a high school principal in Clarendon County, South Carolina. After one year, a reporter from Charleston asked McCain if he would teach white students if the school was forced to integrate. "I told him I was certified to teach, and it wasn't on my certificate, black or white. Any child that would come to school had a right to be taught by all of us."[46] McCain then uttered words that are quite revealing:

> So then he asked me the $64 question. He asked me whether I was a member of NAACP. And I told him, "yes." And in less than ten days I got a letter from the School Board that my contract was expired. [So in those days the question as to whether you were a NAACP member ·was a $64 question?] That's it exactly—most likely your job in the public school system depended upon your denying it or not getting a job.[47]

This is an individual account, but it portrays an environment created to destroy the NAACP and its protest activities. It also shows how the attack freed NAACP activists, making it possible for them to join direct action organizations.

After being fired, McCain became Assistant Director for South Carolina Council of Human Relations. He held that job for two years, long enough for him to meet a visiting woman CORE member, who sent his name to the Executive Secretary of CORE. In the meantime she told

McCain he probably could get a job in CORE, because the "movement was heating up" and "CORE wanted to have a national image." From then on McCain was linked with the organization that he "had never heard about."[48]

After the Montgomery bus boycott CORE's Executive Secretary decided that the organization could become important in the movement if it could find a competent black organizer capable of building CORE chapters in the South. McCain was ideal for CORE, because he had stature in the black community and he knew that community. His education enabled him to speak CORE's language and write solid field reports, and he had acquired organizing experience while holding offices in the NAACP and a black college. McCain was popular with young people in South Carolina, having worked with them at both the college and the high school levels. CORE was particularly interested in a link with Southern young people, because it believed that the young were better suited to do CORE-type work. Finally, the organizational experience and contacts McCain had amassed as local president and State Board member of the NAACP were invaluable for his new post. Indeed, the early CORE activity of South Carolina would be closely tied to NAACP groups.

By October 1958, a year after McCain was hired by CORE, he had established seven CORE groups spanning the State of South Carolina. Unwittingly, he was developing a base through which the Carolina sit-ins of 1960 would spread. In many respects CORE chapters in the late 1950s resembled NAACP chapters, and most of their early work centered on voter registration. This reflects the reality that protest organizations entering new situations must adapt to the social context they seek to change. But it also meant that tensions would persist between blacks on the local level and whites who represented CORE at the national level because of differences over approaches and goals.

Funding Base

Up to 1960 the relationship CORE established with the SCLC and the NAACP was largely one of cooperation. The fact that CORE had no mass black base and had funding sources distinct from those of the SCLC and the NAACP made cooperation possible. According to James Robinson, CORE's Executive Secretary during the late 1950s, "SCLC was more important in the South than CORE ever was, because it had a predominantly black base. Through the churches it had a mass base, which CORE never really had."[49] The fact that CORE was a secular organization removed it even farther from the black church base.

Farmer has noted: "CORE was a secular organization. It was non-religious. In fact, when we set it up, I insisted that CORE not be a religious organization."[50] Farmer had reasoned that a secular social change organization could best serve his goal of creating a mass movement in the North.

Having no mass base, CORE depended largely on funds from middle-class whites living in Northern and Western states. Small proportions of the funds came from the top level of the white working class and from a few wealthy individuals, who also resided predominantly in Northern and Western states. A small amount of CORE's funds did come as a result of mail appeals from what are known as the border states.[51]

To understand important aspects of modern social movements, an organizational perspective is valuable. Leaders in pacifist organizations, such as George Houser of the Fellowship of Reconciliation, who already possessed valuable information (e.g. addresses, phone numbers, size of contributions), including mailing lists, made it possible for CORE to locate some of its original financial contributors. Once these supporters were located, CORE began to build its own lists, which it then had to share with other related organizations.[52] In the early years of the movement CORE had no basic conflict with either the SCLC or the NAACP, because its money did not come from the South or from black churches. In fundamental ways, however, the financial development necessary for CORE to become a national organization depended on the activities of the Southern church-based mass movements.

Before the Montgomery bus boycott CORE barely raised the funds to pay its one full-time employee, its Executive Secretary. Following the Montgomery movement CORE changed this situation by "exploiting the headline-making development in the Southern black protest movements."[53] For example, in 1956–57 CORE sent forty thousand copies of King's pamphlet on the Montgomery movement with its mail appeals. Meier and Rudwick found this strategy to have been so successful that "the number of individual contributors nearly doubled between 1954 and 1957."[54]

The SCLC, and Dr. King in particular, played a key financial role in CORE's expansion between 1957 and 1959. For example, CORE was involved with a school integration project in Nashville. Anna Holden, Chairman of the Nashville CORE, wrote a lengthy pamphlet entitled *A First Step Toward School Integration*, in which she described the integration project and the central role that CORE played in it. Dr. King wrote the foreword to the pamphlet and signed a CORE appeal letter for funds. Both of these items received large circulation thanks to King's assistance, enabling CORE to double its list of contributors.[55]

King joined CORE's Advisory Committee in 1957. This meant his name could be added to the letterhead on CORE's correspondence and financial appeals. James Robinson explained that it was extremely important to have respected individuals on CORE's letterhead so that, "when appeals went out across the country, recipients could look down through the list, and see that there were prominent people who supported the organization."[56] CORE needed prominent people on its letterhead who were clearly not communists to defuse accusations that the organization was communistic, while soliciting financial support from contributors who were usually, according to Robinson, slightly left of center politically.[57]

Marvin Rich, whose duties included fundraising and public relations, said that as soon as he became Community Relations Director of CORE in 1959, he "helped to increase the size of the Advisory Committee. Not simply increase the size but add key people to it to be helpful in our relations with other organizations and with the public generally. . . . These are people who gave us entry into various segments of society."[58] An organizational perspective here is again important. In order for CORE to expand and acquire national status, it needed respectable names on its letterhead to facilitate fruitful connections with other organizations. Marvin Rich explained that his job in CORE was "to enhance the prestige and influence of CORE both within the civil rights movement and in the larger community." He was equipped to accomplish this because "I also knew how other organizations worked and therefore I was able to interpret CORE to a wider audience."[59] King's name, along with such others as the famous writer Lillian Smith, the protest leader and union organizer A. Philip Randolph, and the peace organizer A. J. Muste, made CORE's organizational task easier.

Finally, King was important to CORE's finances in another respect. On a number of occasions potential donors approached CORE to say that they wanted to make substantial contributions to the organization, but with the stipulation that CORE demonstrate that King had an interest in the organization and approved of its work. CORE officials wrote King asking him to convince such individuals that CORE was deserving. In reference to a potential donor, Robinson asked King to write a brief note explaining that "you serve on the CORE Advisory Committee, have confidence in the organization, and that a substantial contribution would be much appreciated."[60] King wrote the potential donor strongly praising the organization and its work. Thus, mass movements of the South and King's influence were critical to CORE's finances and expansion between the years 1955 and 1960. Indeed, King's view of the movement usually enabled him to rise above narrow organizational interests and support all civil rights organizations fighting for black liberation. James Robinson provided insight into this aspect of King by recalling a television interview that included both King and a representative of CORE:

> I shall never forget watching that program, and over and over and again our field secretary mentioned CORE. King, who talked quite a bit, never once mentioned the SCLC. He was not an empire builder, as Wilkins to some extent was, and as I to some extent was with CORE. He was interested in the movement and the organization was just a means of pushing the movement. He always struck me as having extraordinarily little ego. He didn't need to have, because he was so superior.[61]

CORE and the Black Church

Turning from money to action, we find that the black church played an important role in CORE's protest activities in the South. Black ministers were essential to McCain's early organizing. He recalls: "I knew quite a few of the ministers because every place I went as a field secretary, the first person I most likely talked with was a minister who was a member of SCLC."[62] McCain did more than talk with ministers in his initial organizing in South Carolina in 1958. Indeed, in Clarendon County, Sumter, Spartanburg, and Greenville the chairmen of the local CORE groups were ministers.[63] On August 1, 1958, Gordon Carey, who was white, joined McCain as a full-time field secretary for CORE and helped organize local CORE groups in the South. In 1958, while organizing in Virginia, they persuaded the Reverend Wyatt Walker to become the State Director of Virginia CORE while at the same time heading the local SCLC and NAACP groups. In 1959 the two field secretaries traveled to Tallahassee, and with the assistance of Reverend Steele they established an affiliate there. Contrary to claims that outside elites (e.g. organizations, resource groups, and individuals) create movements by themselves, the data here clearly demonstrate that blacks possessed the key resources CORE, an "outside" organization, needed to become a solid organization with a national constituency. In a 1960 CORE document referred to as CORE's "Contact List," intended to "include all local CORE officers and other key people in local groups," we find that black ministers in Tallahassee, Florida; Charleston, Florence, Clarendon County, Greenville, Rock Hill, Spartanburg, and Sumter, South Carolina; Norfolk, Virginia; and Charleston, West Virginia, held important leadership positions in CORE chapters.[64] The bulk of CORE Southern chapters were situated in those cities, and activist ministers were central to their activities.

Thus, CORE's activities in the South during the late 1950s was linked with and facilitated by black indigenous institutions, especially the churches and local NAACP chapters. It was the expertise and contacts of black leaders like McCain and the ministers that enabled CORE to be linked with the movement. CORE's expansion and building of a national image was so dependent on these groups that often CORE watched helplessly while the NAACP received the credit for activities CORE had initiated, because the local CORE leader was also an NAACP president and a black minister.

Besides, much of CORE's early Southern work resembled that being performed by the NAACP and the SCLC (e.g. voter registration activities carried out by black groups as opposed to "direct action" performed by interracial teams), because it had to be adapted to the Southern black base and the patterns of Southern race relations before it could acquire distinctiveness. The Southern brand of racism prevented close interactions between blacks and whites, and this included protest groups. Hence CORE, with important assistance from black organizations and activists, emerged as an organizational actor in the Southern movement and carved out a central niche for itself in the social conflict, which was to become more intense and pervasive. In the process CORE contributed to the building of movement centers during the late 1950s. It was another force, along with the SCLC and the direct action wing of the NAACP, that had begun to prepare the Southern black community for nonviolent confrontation with white racists.

The next chapter will analyze the relationship of the indigenous base of the movement with another set of concerned institutions, which I have termed "halfway houses."

7

MOVEMENT HALFWAY HOUSES

Mrs. Septima Poinsette Clark was born in Charleston, South Carolina, on May 3, 1898, approximately thirty-three years after her people had emerged from slavery. She acquired her education in segregated schools. Determined to be an educator, Mrs. Clark began teaching in Southern public schools in 1916. Because she never accepted the role imposed on her race, Mrs. Clark began working with the NAACP in 1918. When she had taught in the public schools for forty years, school officials asked her if she was a member of the NAACP. In her biographical sketch she wrote: "In 1956 I refused to disown the NAACP and lost my job as a public school teacher in South Carolina, as a result of my membership and inter-racial activities."[1] She searched for work across the state, only to discover that all employment doors were closed to her. She then went to work for the Highlander Folk School, high on a scenic mountain in Monteagle, Tennessee. Mrs. Clark had entered a movement halfway house.

A movement halfway house is an established group or organization that is only partially integrated into the larger society because its participants are actively involved in efforts to bring about a desired change in society. The American Friends Service Committee, the Fellowship of Reconciliation, the War Resisters League, and the Highlander Folk School are examples of modern American movement halfway houses. What is distinctive about movement halfway houses is their relative isolation from the larger society and the absence of a mass base. This generally means that such groups are unable to bring about wide-scale change or disseminate their views to large audiences. Nevertheless, in their pursuit of change movement halfway houses develop a battery of social change resources such as skilled activists, tactical knowledge, media contacts, workshops, knowledge of past movements, and a vision of a future society. What they lack is broad support and a visible platform.

An emerging mass movement provides an ideal setting for movement halfway houses to gain access to large audiences, especially if the movement's philosophy and programs are consonant with the goals and principles pursued by the halfway house. Indeed, an emerging movement can provide new avenues for movement halfway houses to agitate for change, expand, and acquire additional influence and resources. By the same token, preexisting movement halfway houses are valuable to emerging movements because they can provide additional resources (training in tactics, skilled activists, and the like) to augment those of the movement's indigenous base. Such resources assist the movement in rapidly developing the internal organization necessary to engage in sustained collective action. The optimal conditions exist for such mutual sharing when the goals of the movement and the halfway houses are similar.

Several preexisting movement halfway houses assisted the emerging civil rights movement in a number of important ways. For example, halfway houses assisted in disseminating the tactic of nonviolent direct action, developing mass education programs and publicizing local movements. This chapter will investigate the role that three central movement halfway houses—the Highlander Folk School (HFS), the Fellowship of Reconciliation (FOR), and the Southern Conference Educational Fund (SCEF)—played in the origins of the Southern civil rights movement. It should be said emphatically at the outset that other movement halfway houses—the Southern Regional Council, the American Friends Service Committee, the War Resisters League, and others—also were important to the movement. The three chosen for attention here clearly highlight the relationships that *can* exist between social movements and movement halfway houses and *did* exist in the case of the civil rights movement.

The HFS, FOR, and SCEF shared similar properties as preexisting movement halfway houses. They were all small and predominantly white, had limited resources and no mass base, and were relatively isolated from the larger society because of their social change goals; they all pursued goals related to those of the emerging civil rights movement. Finally, they all had specific resources of value to the movement, and the movement provided them all with the opportunity to pursue their goals on a much larger scale.

The focus on halfway houses of the civil rights movement also reveals the organized efforts that certain courageous and committed white people gave to the civil rights movement. Mrs. Anne Braden, a former field secretary of the SCEF, expressed it best when she said that as whites they worked

> ... on the theory that this was just as much in the interests of white Southerners as it was the blacks. In other words, that it wasn't a matter of white people helping the black people sort of get free, but that this was the key to freedom for whites too. And that the white people in the South had to see that.[2]

We turn now to the important roles that each of the three halfway houses played in the civil rights movement.

Highlander Folk School

The HFS played three important roles in the civil rights movement. First, before and during the movement the HFS assisted in pulling together black leadership. Second, as an institution it provided a visible and successful model of a future integrated society. Finally, the HFS developed a successful mass education program that was later transferred to the SCLC, along with three trained staff members. That program was revolutionary from an educational, political, and social standpoint and was directly involved in the mobilization of the civil rights movement.

The Highlander Folk School was organized and directed by a remarkable man, Myles Horton.[3] Horton, born in 1905, came from a poor white working-class family in the small town of Savannah, Tennessee. According to Horton, "I was poor, we were sharecroppers, we worked in factories. I had to leave home when I was fourteen to go to school, and start earning my own living—we lived in the country and we didn't have a school. . . . I was the first person in my family ever to go to college."[4] Poor Southern whites of Appalachia had begun to suffer accutely by the 1920s, already experiencing the economic and social impact of the Great Depression that wrecked the national economy during the 1930s. In the late 1920s and early 1930s Horton began searching for effective solutions to the problems of these oppressed mountain people.

After working closely with mountain people in Ozone, Tennessee, during his senior year at Cumberland University in Lebanon, Tennessee, Horton searched for answers at Union Theological Seminary in New York. There Horton met a great theoretician of the social gospel, Dr. Reinhold Niebuhr, who influenced him and encouraged him to think about "the idea of a school in the mountains for mountain people."[5] By then Horton had become an avid reader, and after absorbing the works of John Dewey, Edward Lindeman, and Joseph Hart, he was convinced that adult education could be used as a potent agent of social change. In 1930 Horton left New York to study for a year with Robert E. Park, a pioneering sociologist at the University of Chicago.

While in Chicago Horton learned that folk schools had existed in Denmark since 1864. Late in 1931 he traveled to Denmark, studied those schools, and interviewed the older folk school directors. Horton returned to the mountains of Tennessee in 1932 with definite ideas about how to organize an effective folk school. He decided against modeling the HFS after existing institutions because, after reading numerous books and visiting various schools, Horton "found that they were all too opinionated and doctrinaire, academic . . . but primarily they did not deal with the problems of people. They only dealt with some conception of what education is, and imposed it on people."[6] Rejecting these "models," Horton located himself and the HFS among the oppressed mountain people and began studying the problems of their everyday lives.

The basic philosophy of Highlander was the idea that oppressed people know the answers to their own problems and the "teacher's job is to get them talking about those problems, to raise and sharpen questions, and to trust people to come up with the answers."[7] Horton stressed, however, that the answers to problems of the oppressed lie in the experiences and imagination of the group rather than individuals. He argued that the oppressed seldom discover these answers, because they do not engage in group analysis. In his words:

> They've got much of the knowledge as a group. Not as individuals, but the group as a whole has much of the knowledge that they need to know to solve their problems. If they only knew how to analyze what their experiences were, what they know, and generalize them . . . they would begin to draw on their own resources.[8]

Horton insisted that the way to bring about change for the oppressed was by a process of education through actual experiences. Highlander's philosophical outlook was derived from religious principles and Marxism. Yet Horton persistently held that theoretical and academic approaches were of no value if they did not grapple with practical problems. Highlander's staff operated under the following assumptions: (1) Education through experience was a potent social change force. (2) The solutions to oppression were rooted in the experiences and communities of the oppressed. (3) People and their situations would inform Highlander's educational programs. (4) The task of changing society rested on the shoulders of the oppressed. In this way, Horton, points out, "we stay with the people, we have ideas, we have philosophy, we have theories, but we always stay where the people are. [And] try to give a little leadership, help develop leadership among the people, whatever stage of development they're at a given time."[9] Over the years Horton and Highlander "stayed with the people," both geographically and educationally.

Highlander attempted to assist the oppressed in overcoming their problems by training potential leaders. It was too small, and its resources were too meager, to train more than just the potential leaders. Potential leaders from local communities dealing with the same problems were identified, brought to Highlander, and taught to analyze their situation in a group context. Then the leaders were taught how to go back and take other community people through the same process. Horton contended that it was crucial to train leaders to introduce the process to the community.

> *If you don't do that, they inevitably go back with these ideas, get up with all these solutions and people say what they do to anybody that comes up with solutions: "Go ahead and do it. Fine, go ahead and do it." . . . We debunk the leadership role of going back and telling people and providing the thinking for them. We aren't into that. We're into people who can help other people develop and provide educational leadership and ideas, but at the same time, bring people along.*[10]

From the beginning Horton envisioned HFS as an integrated institution, a rarity in the South of the 1930s. Horton's persistant attempts to attract blacks to Highlander usually went unrewarded. Blacks who attended Highlander were taking a great risk, because such participation would at best cause them to lose jobs and, at worst, their lives. Chances of being discovered were fairly good, because the HFS was often under surveillance. It was constantly accused of being a communist training ground. Yet during the early 1930s, a few black leaders, such as Professor Herman Davis of Knoxville College and the black sociologist Charles Johnson of Fisk, took a chance and visited the HFS.

When efforts to unionize workers became widespread in the South, the HFS found itself directly involved in the conflict and conducted numerous workshops for labor groups. Highlander's staff also assisted workers on the picket lines, taught them protest music, and performed many other services for the labor movement. Horton maintains that the labor movement showed many Southerners that poor blacks and poor whites had common economic interests. Hence the question of racial oppression immediately confronted the labor movement. For example, during the late 1930s some workers who had attended the HFS attempted unsuccessfully to organize the all-black labor force of a pickle factory into a CIO union. Horton asked his friend E. D. Nixon—the man who would later play a prominent part in organizing the Montgomery bus boycott—to organize the black workers.

The majority of working-class white Southerners upheld segregation in the belief that blacks were inferior and segregation was their "way of life." Even common class interests were not enough to dissuade them. Horton found, as he worked with labor unions, that racial segregation "just kept blocking everything." Horton had wanted HFS to be integrated because it was the "right thing to do," but, he now discovered, "We weren't hitting that problem head on programmatically, but later as we worked in the labor unions . . . we had to deal with it head on."[11]

"In 1940, Highlander informed all the unions that it served in the South that the school would no longer hold worker's education programs for unions that discriminated against blacks." One scholar of the HFS states that the position taken by Highlander

> . . . first paid off four years later when Paul Christopher, regional CIO director and a member of Highlander's board, organized a workshop for the United Auto Workers. It was attended by forty union members, black and white, from every corner of the South. The workers attended classroom sessions on collective bargaining, the economics of the auto and aircraft industry and the UAW's postwar plans; while there, they also organized a cooperative food store. After this, Highlander began urging other unions to join the pioneering UAW. Support was soon developed from the Tennessee Industrial Union Council and the Southern Farmer's Union. Others followed.[12]

Horton's treasured dream of Highlander as an integrated institution was finally materializing. In the 1940s Highlander began pulling Southern black and white leaders together and encouraging them to struggle against domination.

Highlander's staff believed that oppressed people remain dominated because they are unaware of isolated individual efforts made by some of their members to overthrow domination. Thus Highlander's role has been to send its staff to oppressed communities and bring the potential leaders together so they can exchange information and build group resources. Earlier HFS had brought together leaders of coal miners, labor organizers, and leaders of educational institutions. People interested in solving the same problems attended the workshop uniquely organized for them. Highlander developed techniques that enabled every potential leader to participate by speaking up and sharing his or her respective knowledge. Horton found it important to develop these sharing techniques, because otherwise the "talkers" would monopolize the discussion.

Once solutions emerged in workshops, Highlander's staff turned to questions of action. They informed the potential leaders:

> The way to use this information is not to say that we have learned a lot, and isn't it wonderful and great to have been at Highlander? Unlike people in school, there's no exams to put it down and then you're through with it. You're here to act on it. It was education for action. . . . Now, how you going to act on this? Let's just plan what you're going to do when you go back. Let's start talking about how you're going to use this new insight and understanding you've got. . . . So they begin to formulate their actions so when they leave, they're geared to action. They got plans they're going to carry out when they get back. . . . Then we say, now when are you going to do this? You get time in that.[13]

One's "diploma" from HFS was the action performed upon return to the local community.

Beginning in the mid-1940s, Horton and Highlander's staff brought together blacks and whites at the school specifically to confront the problem of segregation and to discuss the United Nations, world problems, local problems, school problems, and community organization. As time passed, individuals who wanted to meet on an interracial basis and discuss racial problems would hear about Highlander and find their way there, often bringing others with similar concerns. During the 1940s and 1950s HFS attracted a particular segment of the black population. As Horton stated, "What you had to do in the pre–civil rights period was to find black people who for the most part were in situations where they weren't too dependent on white people. Otherwise, they would lose their jobs for coming."[14] For that reason HFS attracted black ministers, funeral home directors, beauticians, people in unions, and independent small farmers.

Horton discovered that black beauticians were quite important in the pre–civil rights period:

> A black beautician, unlike a white beautician, was at that time a person of some status in the community. They were entrepreneurs, they were small businesswomen, you know, respected, they were usually better educated than other people, and most of all they were independent. They were independent of white control. Just by sheer accident, I noticed that some of the people that came to Highlander were beauticians, and I followed up that lead and used to run beautician's workshops at Highlander, just for beauticians.[15]

Horton explained that people thought his main consideration when he organized beautician workshops was vocational. "They thought that I was bringing these beauticians together to talk about straightening hair or whatever the hell they do." But, he continued, "I was just using them because they were community leaders and they were independent. . . . We used to use beauticians' shops all over the South to distribute Highlander literature on integration."[16]

During the 1940s and 1950s independent blacks, including E. D. Nixon, Shuttlesworth, Reverend Vivian, Septima Clark, Esau Jenkins, and others, visited the integrated school surrounded by poor mountain people. Significantly, Rosa Parks attended Highlander workshops just four months before she "sat" into history. A number of black leaders met each other for the first time at HFS and began relationships that would prove important during the movement. Highlander's message to these leaders was that the dominated themselves had to bring about social change, or none would result. Horton would inform the community leaders that they "couldn't wait for some government edict or some Messiah, it had to be done by the people. And that was a message that wasn't too well received." The reason:

> Both blacks and whites thought somehow somebody would do this big thing. They wouldn't have to do it. They couldn't do it, they didn't know how to start it. Somebody was going to do it for them. . . . Blacks would quite often say to me, "It isn't right that we have to struggle, we have to stick our necks out, that we have to take chances. We didn't ask for this. The people who are doing this to us should have to change, and they should be the ones that do this."[17]

Horton had heard these same pleas from the mountain people. While understanding their perspective, he put forth another view:

> I'd always agree that [the dominators] should [change], that the blacks weren't responsible for their plight, they were victims, and you should never blame the victims, but I said, "You know, now that that's agreed on, let's talk about the reality." The reality was [Southern whites] aren't going to change, the realities are they never will, and there's nothing in history to suggest that they will, so the right thing is not going to be done . . . so if that's not going to be done, black people are going to have to force the white people to respect them . . . the burden and the responsibility is on the whites, but the burden of change is on the blacks.[18]

In this way HSF pulled together many of the individuals who became civil rights leaders and prodded them to become activists.

In the early 1950s black students came to Highlander, many of them children of economically independent adults who had attended the school. Of the rest, a significant portion had heard of Highlander by word of mouth or directly from Horton, who frequently spoke at black colleges about Highlander and its programs. Young blacks often thought their parents and Horton were kidding, because the idea of an integrated school up on a mountain, surrounded by blue lakes, sounded like a fairy tale. They had been taught that failure to keep a distance from whites and respond to them with "yes, sir" rather than "yes" could be fatal. They had heard adults speaking softly of how fourteen-year-old Emmett Till was killed in 1955 for allegedly whistling at a white woman. To these young people the existence of a place like HFS seemed unreal.

Gradually young blacks took the trek up the winding mountain and discovered that Highlander was, indeed, a reality. Many of them were attending college, where they were immersed in academic theories. Highlander's workshops looked to them like the ideal setting in which to expound academic theories. Horton informed them that, on the contrary, Highlander's workshops were designed to deal with concrete community problems. Horton's admonitions upset parents and students, so he decided in 1953 to create the "Annual Highlander Folk School College Workshops." The students accepted the idea and began to attend the annual workshops organized specifically for them. As a result, Highlander was also bringing young black leadership together. Many future sit-in leaders, such as Marion Barry, the present Mayor of Washington, D.C., James Bevel, Diane Nash, John Lewis, and Bernard Lafayette, were visitors to Highlander.

At the college workshop of April 1959 a number of issues were discussed. Resolutions were made regarding "campus censorship; integration of college faculties and student bodies; exchange opportunities between Negro and white colleges; treatment of the 'minority' student Negro or white as the case may be; and fraternity exclusion."[19] The Reverend James Bevel, a young student at the time, spoke of a 1959 workshop he attended at Highlander:

That's when I first met Mrs. Septima Clark, Myles Horton, and I guess for the first time in my life, I was introduced to a man who reminded me of Socrates. Myles was a guy who'd ask questions about your assumptions. He would challenge you on your inferior feelings. He sort of decrudded Negroes from being Negroes and making them think of themselves as men and women. His psyche didn't agree with a "nigger" being a "nigger." So that's not a game with him. He has arrived at a self-respect and self-appreciation of mankind. He, in that sense, is not a liberal, he's an enlightened man. When you come upon it, and

*you assume that you're a Negro, and you assume that white folks are
oppressing you, he would tear your assumptions up. He, like, destroyed all the false assumptions of the oppressor and made us deal
with the fact that we were cowards and that we were lying, and were
not serious about being who we said we were.*[20]

Bevel's conception of Highlander and its staff during the late 1950s was
shared by the other activists interviewed for this study who had visited
Highlander.

Being an integrated institution, HFS provided its participants with
a microcosm of an integrated society and facilitated interpersonal relationships of social equality through the use of music, poetry, song,
and dance. The staff recognized the centrality of human feelings in social life and in social action designed to change society. At HFS one
found well-equipped, expertly staffed departments of drama and music,
as well as the academic subjects. Zilphia Horton, director of the music
department, traveled through oppressed communities singing and rec-
ording the songs and experiences of indigenous people. She visited
picket lines of workers during the 1930s and 1940s and observed the
solidifying role that music played in protest activities. Those songs were
meticulously recorded and stored away in Highlander's music files.
Myles Horton had discovered in 1931, while studying the Denmark folk
schools, that the successful ones had been "emotionally charged."

Emotions and the lessons of racism usually determined the behavior
of the newly integrated recruits who nervously entered Highlander for
the first time. The staff members were trained to make these recruits
comfortable by engaging them in music, song, and dance before entering the workshops. The immediate task was to create a new social definition of the situation. That is, blacks had to be convinced that they
could trust whites at Highlander and that interracial encounters would
not cause them to be thrown into a river for failing to arrive at the
"true" definition of the situation. Horton related:

*And as you know, black people can't be very easily fooled. And it
doesn't do any good to talk. We never spent any time stating what we
believed, and how we felt, or anything like that. We wouldn't expect
you to believe it. We just went ahead and ran our program and everybody was accepted as an equal and treated as an equal, and they got
the message.*[21]

Because Highlander practiced what it preached, blacks and whites
came away thinking maybe this "integration thing" was possible. Horton and Septima Clark pointed out that Rosa Parks, four months before
the Montgomery boycott, came to the conclusion that here were at least

a few whites who could be trusted. Septima Clark recalls Parks's visit to Highlander:

> *Rosa Parks was afraid for white people to know that she was as militant as she was. She didn't want to speak before the whites that she met up there, because she was afraid they would take it back to the whites in Montgomery. After she talked it out in that workshop that morning and she went back home, then she decided that, "I'm not going to move out of that seat."*[22]

The myth that Rosa Parks was simply a tired old lady who decided on a particular day not to give her seat to a white man falls by the wayside in the face of the evidence of her long involvement in the movement.

Also in the late 1950s, Reverend Shuttlesworth's children attended workshops at HFS. Mrs. Clark tells what happened on their trip back to the Birmingham movement center:

> *Riding back through one of those towns [Gadsden, Alabama], they sat in the front seat, and they arrested those children. Fred came up there in the middle of the night, about 2 o'clock in the morning, without a gun or anything, he walked through there, and went in to that little town—He got his children out. I say that man had a lot of guts.*[23]

HFS and Citizenship Schools

The citizenship schools were probably the most profound contribution of all those made to the emerging civil rights movement by movement halfway houses, and Highlander made that contribution. During the 1940s and early 1950s Esau Jenkins, a black community leader of Johns Island, South Carolina, spent long hours trying to formulate methods by which his people could overthrow the yoke of domination. One day Jenkins hit upon what he considered "the solution." He reasoned that blacks were oppressed because they had no political power, so the vote was the key to freedom. He was overwhelmed by the idea that the main obstacle standing between blacks on Johns Island and the vote was their inability to read or write.

The "white man" required blacks to read and interpret complicated sections of the Constitution of South Carolina before they were allowed to vote. The "white man" had the system of domination structured so that blacks were systematically excluded from the opportunities to learn to read and write. Jenkins decided that he would teach them. He drove busloads of blacks to their work places in Charleston from Johns Island.

Jenkins, who himself had little formal education, set up a school on the bus and began teaching blacks how to read the South Carolina Constitution. For thirty minutes each working day, the blacks who rode Jenkins's bus struggled with complicated sentences that included such words as "miscegenation," "larceny," and "patriotism." That remarkable effort, however, resulted in the addition of very few blacks to the voting rolls; it did not yield the sort of political power that Jenkins had envisioned. The efforts of one man could not wipe out the massive black illiteracy that had existed for centuries. The collective efforts and resources of countless people were needed to attack the problem effectively.

Jenkins's friend, Septima Clark, who had taught in the public schools on Johns Island and who was also affiliated with Highlander, asked Jenkins to accompany her to its workshops. After much persuasion Jenkins agreed to participate in a workshop on the United Nations. At the end of the session the participants were asked, "What are you going to do for the United Nations?" Mrs. Clark recalls Jenkins's response: "I don't want to do a thing for the United Nations. I want to do something for Johns Island. I want black people of Johns Island to learn to read and write, so they can register to vote. This is the kind of thing, and if you can help me, I can get them together."[24] Jenkins explained that a building, books, and transportation were needed to make such an effort fruitful. Horton remembers Jenkins as a brilliant man who knew exactly "what he wanted to do, and he also knew what he wanted us to do." Indeed, "He knew we were into education and he thought we might be able to figure this thing out." So it was decided to organize schools for teaching blacks on Johns Island to read and write so they could seize political power.

Clark, Horton, and Jenkins spent several months on Johns Island formulating an educational program that was to become extremely successful. Their first step was an investigation to discover why other educational methods had failed. Horton and his team found that educational programs existing on Johns Island had money.

> They had money from the state fund, the federal fund for literacy training for black people, but they couldn't get any black people to take the training. It wasn't lack of money. They had teachers who hadn't had a class in two years, just getting on the payroll for doing nothing. The black people who were teachers couldn't find anybody to teach.[25]

Then it was discovered that mature people who labored in the fields and headed large families had been made to sit at little school desks designed for children. Children of the community joked about the men who sat at those desks, referring to them as "Daddy Long-Legs." The adults were also being taught as children,

> . . . step-by-step; a-b-c-d; "the ball is red"; "New York is a big city." They were being asked to delay reading sentences useful to them until they could read sentences of dubious value to children. It seemed very far from the Constitution. The few who had enrolled just stopped going to classes.[26]

Horton, who understood the culture of the poor and the working class, was appalled at his group's discoveries. It was decided that an effective educational program would have to honor the life-style and self-worth of the people on Johns Island. It would have to discard the paraphernalia of grade schools. Horton decided that intimate knowledge of the people was required before an authentic program could be instituted. He moved to Johns Island and lived there for several months. Horton recalls that once he was situated,

> . . . I would just sit and watch them. Go fishing with them, work with them and sit in homes with them. You began to see how they live. Get a feel on it. Got to internalize it. How do you treat this person with respect? How do you honor their dignity? Somehow it was just intuitive. You wouldn't make a survey to find out. You have to get closer to it than that.[27]

After the "field work" had been completed, Horton, Clark, and Jenkins met to formulate the guidelines for the program.

It was agreed that the program would not be limited to voter registration training. It would be built around " 'big ideas,' 'adult ideas,' ideas worthy of a good, strong, intelligent people."[28] They believed that blacks on Johns Island would learn to read and write if they came to view voting, writing, and reading as an obligation and a political responsibility. They began to find ways to convince blacks that they owed it to their grandchildren and the community to learn to read, write, vote, and change society. Horton explained:

> We decided we'd pitch it on a basis of them becoming full citizens and taking their place in society and demanding their rights and being real men and women in their own right. Putting into practice all these religious things they talked about, and the humanitarian things they talked about, and doing something about it. They owed it to the future generations.[29]

In other words, the citizenship schools were designed for goals similar to those of the emerging civil rights movement. Horton's group turned to practical matters once the guiding principles of its novel educational approach were cemented into place.

The first practical decision was to use a nonteacher, because anyone trained as a teacher would probably revert to traditional schoolroom methods. Horton persuaded a black beautician, Bernice Robinson, to become the first citizenship teacher. Classes would be held in the back room of Jenkins's small co-op store two nights a week for two hours, covering a three-month period. Benches, pencils, paper, and a stove were placed in the room, and explicit instructions were given to keep the environment simple. The adult students were told that they could come and go as they pleased and if they wished they could sew, knit, chew tobacco, or use snuff while learning to read and write. The idea was to maintain a "homey" environment and at all costs to avoid intimidating the students. Finally, Robinson was instructed to "keep the ideas big."

By this time Clark had joined the staff at Highlander on a full-time basis as Director of Education after being fired from teaching in the public schools for her NAACP activities. While Robinson taught on the Island, Clark refined the educational program. She reports: "In '56 and '57 night after night I sat down and wrote out a citizenship education program which would help illiterates to learn to read and write, so they could register to vote."[30] Clark became the theoretician of the citizenship school, while Robinson creatively taught adults the difficult task of reading and writing.

The method employed in the school followed Highlander's axiom that the oppressed had to be educated through their own concrete experiences. Robinson began a class by asking the participants what they wished to learn. Many of the students wanted to learn to write their names in their Bibles, others wanted to write to their sons in the military, and some wanted to make out money orders. Robinson laboriously worked through these formidable tasks. At times the students were instructed to visit the employment office and return with the name of the supervisor, the hours the office was open, and information about how they could apply for work. Clark recounts:

> When they came back the next night, they'd bring us this information. Then we had dry cleaners' bags. We wrote the information on dry cleaners' bags and hung it on a broomstick. They learned to read those things that were said to them. That's one way of teaching the reading.[31]

Many ingenious methods were used. People were taught to write words they had sung for years. Newspapers were brought in, and words taken from them were woven into new paragraphs.

As soon as the students learned to read and write simple ideas, Robinson challenged them with the "big ideas." After the first group had successfully mastered the basic tasks, Robinson asked Horton to send over the Declaration of Human Rights of the United Nations. Horton, a little bewildered by the request, sent over a copy. A few days later he discovered that "Bernice was absolutely right. She wanted to treat these people as world citizens and adults, and let them learn something important. They would struggle to learn that. Damned if they didn't learn to read that and to copy it instead of, 'Mary did this and that.' "[32] Horton went on to say that Mrs. Robinson "was getting them to work. It was perfect. These people felt important. They were important. They weren't treated like kids. They were treated like adults. They were into adult stuff. We found that big words were no harder to learn than little words. If they wanted to learn them, they'd learn them."[33] They were reading the South Carolina Constitution, smoothly pronouncing such words as "miscegenation," and becoming familiar with other big words they had never heard.

The motivational level of the students was remarkable. The original school was held during the winter months. The students came out at night in the cold weather after a long, hard day of work, and more chores confronted them after classes. Yet the size of the class increased rather than decreased. A trip to City Hall, where the students attempted to register to vote after three months of preparation, constituted the "final exam." One study found:

> At the end of three months and thirty-six classes in all, the first fourteen students took the voting test. Eight of them were registered. And before the first citizenship school ended its size had more than doubled from fourteen to thirty-seven, just opposite of the "regular" reading school.[34]

Shortly after the first citizenship school, blacks on the Sea Islands of South Carolina began to make it known that they too wanted citizenship schools. These requests came despite the fact that the school had received no publicity or promotion. At that point two important decisions were made. First, only black people would be allowed to teach in the citizenship schools. According to Horton, whites would have taken them over by force of habit, being so accustomed to dominating, and blacks often labored under the misconception that whites were superior.

Second, it was decided that instructors recruited for these schools would be "nonteachers," that is, people not trained as public school teachers. The recruiting process for citizenship school teachers was straightforward. Any local black person who could read and write was eligible, and formal education of any kind was not required. The requirement was simply that a person be black, able to read and write, and able to recruit students. Finally, prospective teachers were required to attend citizenship schools already functioning to receive their on-the-job training. The salary of the teacher was set at $30 a month, or $1.25 an hour. Horton remarked, "No big pay was in it. Just minimum expenses. So we didn't get anyone who wanted a job. We only got people who wanted to help their people. That eliminated a lot of people."[35] Shortly after the first school had been completed, several other schools got under way.

Requests to open more schools began reaching Robinson rapidly. The original school had been financed with a small grant awarded to Highlander by the Schwartzhaupt Foundation. Once the schools began multiplying, Highlander received several hundred dollars from the Field Foundation to meet the additional costs. The schools then spread all across the Sea Islands. According to Clark, "They were being taught in kitchens and outside under trees in the people's yards."[36] And, of course, they were being taught in that "interesting sociological setting," the black beauty parlors. With tobacco between their teeth, sewing bags on their arms, and high levels of determination, blacks assembled by their dry cleaners' bags and broomsticks and began the arduous task of learning to read and write.

The job of training citizenship teachers became too big for Robinson to do alone, so the citizenship training center was moved to Highlander. Clark and Robinson established a procedure whereby future citizenship teachers came to the mountain and received their training in just five days. After hearing tape recordings of successful teaching sessions and receiving directives from Robinson and Clark, the citizenship teachers were prepared to return to their communities and establish schools. Schools were established across South Carolina and spread to Savannah, Georgia. During the late 1950s Hosea Williams, who was to become a prominent leader of the SCLC, began establishing citizenship schools in his native state of Georgia. Within three years the schools were spreading elsewhere across the South. The responsibilities of the training center at Highlander began expanding drastically. Horton recalls: "It was getting so big that at Highlander, it was beginning to be a bigger program than all the rest of Highlander put together."[37] Because Highlander's function as an institution was to develop programs, not to administer them, Horton became alarmed:

We weren't interested in administering a running program, we were just interested in developing it. . . . By that time, it was getting pretty important and we decided we had to cut loose from it, because it was swamping Highlander. We wanted to get out of it and let other people run it.[38]

Highlander's staff mimeographed statements to the effect that the citizenship program was available to any organization that could administer the citizenship schools. During 1959 and 1960 a few NAACP chapters and church groups took over a fraction of the administrative load, but the main operation remained at Highlander.

The link between Highlander and the SCLC was important during the late 1950s and for the decade to follow. In the 1950s Hosea Williams served as vice president of the local NAACP in Savannah, but after the Montgomery bus boycott he began to identify with Dr. King and to adopt his emphasis on direct action tactics and community organizing. The citizenship schools became the vehicle through which Williams moved away from the NAACP's courtroom orientation and into direct action. Williams recalls:

But that was a way to get into that community, man, basically for me, because—you know, you go in and say, "I'm going to set up an NAACP chapter," them white folks go crazy. You go in there and say, "We're going to set up adult citizenship schools to teach these niggers how to read and write so they can drive you white folks' trucks better. . . . "But that was a camouflage for us, who was really in the know.[39]

The citizenship schools would serve a number of political, educational, and social purposes for the SCLC and the emerging movement, and eventually the SCLC would take over the program. The continuing link between the citizenship schools and the mobilization of the civil rights movement will be discussed further in later chapters.

The SCLC and Highlander

During the late 1950s Martin Luther King, Jr., maintained direct contact with Highlander. He and Horton were friends and consulted frequently about their respective concerns. On Labor Day weekend of 1957 Horton invited "friends of Highlander" to visit the folk school and discuss ways in which HFS could enhance its contribution to the struggle of the South.[40] At the time Highlander was being labeled as a communist training ground. Dr. King attended the meeting, as did an undercover agent sent by Marvin Griffin, the Governor of Georgia. The agent took a photograph of Horton, Aubrey Williams, Rosa Parks, John

Thompson, Dr. King, and Abner Berry, who had neglected to tell any-one that he was a columnist for the *Daily Worker*. Governor Griffin later had 250,000 copies of the photograph sent all over the South. Accord-ing to one account, "Shortly, billboards using the photo started ap-pearing across the South, claiming in huge lettering that King attended a Communist Training Center."[41]

In 1959 the State of Tennessee labeled HFS a subversive organiza-tion. When the charge could not be substantiated Highlander was raided on July 31, 1959. Horton wrote to King that on that date "Mrs. Septima Clark . . . and three volunteer workers were arrested and jailed on trumped-up charges; Mrs. Clark of possessing whiskey and others of drunkenness."[42] A number of buildings at HFS were then padlocked by the state. The state prepared to prosecute those arrested to the fullest extent of the law and sought to close Highlander permanently. Horton asked King if he could use his name on a statement of Highlander. King replied: "You definitely have my permission to use my signature on the statement which you have prepared concerning Highlander Folk School. . . . We are all in this struggle together, caught up in an ines-capable network of mutuality."[43] That is to say, this movement halfway house and the SCLC were connected. Of course, Septima Clark had already experienced this kind of harassment while in the NAACP. In her biographical sketch she wrote: "I was arrested for allegedly pos-sessing whiskey (which was found by the courts to be untrue, and the case dismissed). This attack was made on me, I feel, to scare me, the only Negro resident in Monteagle, Tennessee, so I would leave. I stayed."[44] Black women were at the center of the civil rights movement. The SCLC's Executive Director, Ella Baker, who maintained contact with HFS during the late 1950s, understood the potency of the citizen-ship schools. Indeed, Baker continuously pushed the SCLC and King to take an interest in the citizenship schools. In her Executive Direc-tor's Report of 1959 she wrote:

> *Because of the potential value of an adult education movement to the Negro's drive for first-class citizenship, the director has attempted to find out what is happening in this field and how it can be related to the program of SCLC. To this end, the Labor Day Weekend was spent at Highlander Folk School in Monteagle, Tennessee. A primary pur-pose of this trip was to meet and talk with Mrs. Septima Clark, edu-cation director there.*[45]

In the same document Baker explained the details of the citizenship movement to the SCLC leaders and requested that she be "authorized to explore this field further."[46]

Finally, several of the college professors who served in 1959 as consultants to the student workshops at Highlander were members of the Nashville Christian Leadership Council and colleagues of the Reverend Kelly Miller Smith. Highlander, as we shall see later, continued to play a central role in the emerging civil rights movement. Therefore HFS was and is a classic movement halfway house. Its unpretentious former director summed it up best:

> But it's so misleading, you know, to interpret that the name Highlander was instrumental in starting the civil rights movement. Movements are not started by educational institutions, I don't care how good they are. We might have been pretty good, at least the enemies thought so. But not that good, you know.[47]

THE FELLOWSHIP OF RECONCILIATION

The Fellowship of Reconciliation (FOR) was organized in England in 1914. In 1915 the organization was established in the United States and quickly became the central pacifist organization in America. Many of the great architects of nonviolent protest in the United States—among them A. J. Muste, Bayard Rustin, A. Philip Randolph, James Farmer, Glenn Smiley, and James Lawson—received training from FOR. According to Glenn Smiley, FOR's former national field secretary, "The major goals of FOR were to eliminate war and the occasions of war, and to change the attitudes that dominant social groups held toward minority groups and other less powerful groups."[48] The people who gravitated to FOR were dissatisfied with many aspects of the American society and actively sought to change them through nonviolent protest.

FOR was important to the civil rights movement in five ways: (1) FOR was instrumental in the organization and development of CORE. (2) FOR was a vehicle through which the method and history of nonviolent protest was introduced to Southern black communities and the emerging leadership of the civil rights movement. (3) FOR provided the Montgomery bus boycott movement and the MIA with an "intelligence service," which gathered information from white opposition groups. (4) FOR made available to the civil rights movement two of its well-trained staff members and continued to pay their salaries. (5) FOR provided the emerging movement with important literature and films. Such actions confirmed FOR as a halfway house in the civil rights movement.

FOR gave rise to CORE. In the late 1930s and early 1940s FOR members were organized into "cells" or "peace teams,"[49] each having its own focus and responsibilities. CORE emerged in 1942 from a FOR race relations cell on the campus of the University of Chicago. In its early days CORE served as one of the vehicles through which the pacifists of FOR introduced the tradition of nonviolent protest to a small number of black and white leaders. The formation of CORE brought black FOR activists like Howard Thurman, then Dean of the Howard University chapel, James Farmer, Bayard Rustin, and Joe Guinn into close contact. The black union leader A. Philip Randolph was also closely associated with this group. Randolph, who was familiar with nonviolent protest in India as well as America, was influential in persuading E. D. Nixon and Mrs. Daisy Bates to explore nonviolent protest.

Thus CORE and FOR were closely intertwined during the 1940s and 1950s. The two pacifist organizations kept the tradition of nonviolent protest action alive within the circles of a few black American leaders.

Chapter Three discussed how the nonviolent method of protest was systematically introduced to the black community. It was a difficult task, because blacks, like other Americans, were not naturally inclined toward nonviolent action. "Nonviolence as a way of life was just as foreign to blacks as flying a space capsule would be to a roach," Hosea Williams has said. Indeed, members of black churches and even their ministers did not practice nonviolence as a way of life. Converting the ministers and leaders of the movement to a nonviolent approach was usually no less difficult than convincing the rank-and-file. Williams continued his thought:

> I'm not ashamed to say that I've never believed in nonviolence as a philosophy of life. And I don't know nobody else who did but Martin Luther King, Jr. Andy [Young] jumped on me one day, physically— knew he couldn't whip me—and if you think Ralph [Abernathy] is non-violent, back him up—I don't believe I ever met but one man in my life that believed in nonviolence, accepted it totally as a philosophy, and that was Martin Luther King, Jr.[50]

Williams was speaking of a general reality: Nonviolence was practically unheard-of in Southern black communities before the civil rights movement.

The question, then, is: How did Southern black Americans suddenly become nonviolent when the civil rights movement unfolded? The answer, of course, is that they did not. Rather, through continuous non-violent workshops and constant appeals to the nonviolent tradition rooted in the black church and in the life of Jesus, blacks were persuaded to accept nonviolence as a tactic to reach a specified goal. It was a remarkable feat, and FOR had an important hand in the process.

Until the Montgomery movement nonviolent protest methods had

never been used in America on a mass scale by any of the pacifist organizations, including FOR. According to Glenn Smiley, FOR "has always been an intellectual movement . . . which is accounted for by the
fact that the majority of its members are students, college professors,
clergymen or their counterparts—housewives, women professionals,
etcetera."[51] FOR's basic method of spreading nonviolent tactics, therefore, was through intellectual and philosophical discussions. They
worked on the theory that the "confrontation of ideas is productive."[52]
FOR, along with CORE, also had amassed some practical knowledge
regarding nonviolent direct action and had compiled a practical but
limited protest record. By assembling together in small interracial
groups, they had protested discrimination in Northern restaurants,
theaters, parks, and swimming pools.

Therefore, when the Montgomery bus boycott unfolded before the
American public under a banner of nonviolence, FOR became interested. Within two months FOR dispatched its national field secretary,
Reverend Smiley, to Montgomery to assist the movement's leadership
in disseminating the techniques of nonviolent protest to the local black
and white communities. Bayard Rustin was also sent to Montgomery
to assist King in organizing the boycott. Rustin had previously worked
with FOR for twelve years, serving first as a field secretary and later
as Race Relations Secretary, and he had helped FOR organize CORE.
At the time he worked in Montgomery, Rustin was Executive Secretary
of the War Resisters League, another movement halfway house closely
associated with FOR. Both Rustin and Smiley were skilled colleagues
who shared similar movement halfway house experiences, and both
were equipped with a theoretical and practical understanding of nonviolent direct action. Thus their roles in the Montgomery movement
were complementary.

Smiley began assisting in training Montgomery blacks in the methods of nonviolent protest action in February 1956. In 1935 Richard
Gregg's *The Power of Nonviolence* had become required reading for
pacifists like Smiley and Rustin. In a chapter on training, Gregg wrote:
"It is not necessary always for the rank and file to read about the subject [nonviolence]. But the leaders must understand it and the rank and
file must trust the leaders and learn from them what to do and not to
do."[53]

However, Dr. King, Rev. Abernathy, and many of the Montgomery
leaders knew little of nonviolence. Smiley's role was to teach them both
the methods and philosophy of nonviolence.

Gregg pointed out that it is essential for the leaders to understand
the nonviolent approach. Smiley recalls his effort in this regard: "The
role that I played . . . with Martin was one in which I literally lived with
him hours and hours and hours at a time, and he pumped me about

what nonviolence was."[54] Reverend Abernathy provided corroboration: "FOR played a very vital role in my pilgrimage and Dr. King's pilgrimage to nonviolence and helping us to understand nonviolence from a philosophical base, and by conducting workshops for the leadership of the movement."[55] Smiley did not always find it easy going:

> When I was pressing the importance of the tactic, he [King] said, "But Glenn, I'm not really interested in tactic although I realize that it cannot be separated from principle. But what I'm really interested in, can I apply nonviolence to my own heart?" That was the debate that he and I had over a period of, I would say, almost a year.[56]

This was the period when King actually accepted nonviolence as a way of life and became a symbol of nonviolence to blacks and to the world, as his very life personified the approach.

Yet King could not disseminate the precepts and training of nonviolence singlehanded. FOR's secretary, Smiley, was to be of considerable assistance, especially because, in addition to his knowledge of nonviolence, he was a minister and a Southerner. He knew the language of Southerners and was comfortable in the black churches where the mass meetings were held. Moreover, blacks quickly accepted him as a man of the struggle rather than as a "white man." Smiley has told of attending many of the MIA's mass meetings after arriving in Montgomery. His responsibility was to speak fifteen minutes at the meetings, explaining the principles and techniques of nonviolence and persuading blacks that it was the method they should pursue.

It is important to understand that Reverend Smiley was not simply an individual discussing nonviolence in these meetings but an organization man trained and employed by the FOR. In Smiley's words, his job was "to carry the mail of the organization and that mail was the method of nonviolence." Smiley explained to movement participants that the principal exponent of nonviolence in the modern world was Mahatma Gandhi, "but it goes back to the sixteenth century." He made use of the black church setting by emphasizing that nonviolence was the approach and teachings of Our Lord. Then he instructed the protesters who were being terrorized by the Klan, the White Citizens' Councils, and the local sheriffs: "If you are struck on one cheek, this does not mean that you are to turn the other cheek and allow yourself to be beaten into a bloody pulp, but you turn the other cheek, as Jesus would say—in effect, He is saying do not be caught in the trap of violence but try another way."[57]

Smiley was delivering lectures he had presented hundreds of times as an FOR representative. The difference now was that he spoke in the context of a mass movement in crowded black churches, where audi-

ences shouted "amens" rather than the "I understand" response of the
more "intellectual" audiences to which he was accustomed. Smiley's
imagination and training allowed him to make the fine adjustments required to be effective with this audience. Because he often conveyed
his message through timely anecdotes, he came to be known, along with
Abernathy as one of the great storytellers of the movement. When Smiley finished his discourse on nonviolence, King usually addressed the
crowd. He would assure his listeners that nonviolence was not a weak
method and that "through nonviolent resistance the Negro will be able
to rise to the noble height of opposing the unjust system while loving
the perpetrators of the system."[58] Through the tradition of the black
church and one of its greatest ministers, and through the efforts of
Glenn Smiley of FOR, a new "nonviolent black" was created for protest
purposes. It was a difficult task requiring intense preparation.

After the mass movement that generated tremendous pressure, the
Supreme Court on November 12, 1956, ruled that segregation on Montgomery's buses was unconstitutional. After the decision King and his
colleagues "went to work to prepare the people for integrated buses.
In mass meeting after mass meeting we stressed nonviolence."[59] Smiley recalled a nonviolent workshop held at one of these meetings: "It
was the biggest nonviolent workshop, I guess, in history because it involved about five thousand people and people had said that you cannot
hold a workshop with five thousand people."[60] They did; in fact, they
were held on four consecutive days before the buses were desegregated
in Montgomery. Smiley and others created hypothetical situations
where they placed a number of chairs on a platform to simulate a bus.
People took various roles, such as the white racist rider who objected
to having a black sit by him. King wrote:

> Sometimes the person playing a white man put so much zeal into his
> performance that he had to be gently reproved from the sidelines.
> Often a Negro forgot his nonviolent role and struck back with vigor;
> whenever this happened we worked to rechannel his words and deeds
> in a nonviolent direction.[61]

It took time to create the nonviolent protester.

Prior to desegregating the buses, MIA leaders visited schools and
colleges and urged blacks to remain nonviolent. "We also distributed
throughout the city a mimeographed list of 'Suggestions for Integrating
Buses,' " King recalled. "In preparing this text we had the assistance
of the Rev. Glenn Smiley."[62] Two days before Montgomery desegregated its buses, Smiley met with seventy sympathetic whites and conducted the same nonviolent workshops with them that had been held
in the mass meetings. As those whites were trained to help integrate

buses nonviolently, proof was provided to other whites that peaceful integration was possible. On December 21, 1956, blacks of Montgomery rode on buses side by side with whites. King remarked, "Glenn Smiley sat next to me. So I rode the first integrated bus in Montgomery with a white minister, and a native Southerner, as my seatmate."[63]

FOR contributed to the civil rights movement by supplying the MIA with intelligence information. An understanding existed between Smiley and King that Smiley would visit the white community and convert as many white Southerners as possible to the viewpoint and goals of the MIA. "My role in Montgomery was to visit the white community leadership to try to provide an open and above-board intelligence for the Montgomery Improvement Association," Smiley explains. He would report back: "This is what they planned to do to the degree that I had been able to find out."[64] Smiley occasionally attended meetings of the Ku Klux Klan and the White Citizens' Council and fed information back to the MIA regarding the strength and plans of those groups. He says his Southern background enabled him to "understand more of the situation and secondly, if necessary, I could lapse into the vernacular. And for the purposes of getting into the white community . . . this was important because they looked with suspicion upon Yankees."[65] It is difficult to assess the effect of Smiley's intelligence work on the success of the MIA and the Montgomery movement. To be sure, any organization will benefit tactically if its intelligence work enables it to anticipate the moves and plans of its opponents.

James Lawson and FOR

The Reverend James Lawson arrived in Nashville in 1957 as a Southern field secretary of FOR. Lawson was a product of the black church, pacifist organizations, CORE, and the NAACP. The twenty-seven-year-old Lawson had been hoping for a nonviolent black mass movement since the early 1950s. In the fall of 1956 he went to Montgomery and met King, who was impressed with Lawson's understanding and experience in nonviolent protest action. King urged Lawson to come south and get involved in the movement. FOR appointed Lawson as a Southern field secretary and dispatched him to Nashville. Thus by 1957 FOR was supporting two staff members who were key figures in the unfolding movement.

FOR's influence on Reverend Lawson went deep. Lawson's father was a Methodist minister, so Lawson grew up in the church and learned of the nonviolent teaching of Jesus very early. He was unaware, however, of the existence of a pacifist wing in the Christian Church. In his words:

*I really began to meet that wing when I joined the FOR as a college
freshman. Then I became aware of a whole library of literature. Then
I heard lectures by A. J. Muste and Bayard Rustin. I joined, I began
to get the monthly magazine, to see their bibliographies, and then I
began to read into those bibliographies and began to get some of those
books, and studied them.*[66]

Lawson studied nonviolent movements that had taken place in France,
Denmark, and Norway. He learned how a nonviolent Protestant pastor
in France organized "cells" and developed an underground movement
to help Jews escape from Nazism. This shows how movement halfway
houses often function as repositories for the history and knowledge of
earlier social movements and make those resources available to contemporary activists.

Lawson's previous training had also been influenced by FOR. Like
most black ministers, he had learned the art of public speaking and of
organizing social groups from the church. Lawson's skills were strongly
buttressed by his FOR activities:

*Even as a freshman I was participating in workshops, doing some of
the lecturing, speaking, helping to organize students for FOR. And at
different times in college the FOR asked me to organize student meetings. They sent me to speak to college campuses, to speak and defend
the pacifist point of view. And then church groups learned of my concerns and interests and ability [and] invited me into campuses to debate military officers, to debate professors. . . . When I moved into the
Southeast, even Southern Methodists knew who I was. I knew many
people already by that time in the Southeast, from national meetings
and regional meetings of all kinds. I guess part of the answer has to
be that yes, FOR was part of my nurturing process, and it remained
so.*[67]

By the time Lawson arrived in Nashville in 1957, he had amassed experiences similar to those of other pacifists. Like Bayard Rustin, he had
served a prison term for refusing to serve in the armed forces. Like
James Farmer, Glenn Smiley, and many other pacifists, Lawson had
participated in various forms of direct action such as sit-ins. Thus James
Lawson entered the early civil rights movement at Nashville as a black
minister and as a trained pacifist of FOR.

The critical training and organizing role Lawson played in the
SCLC's affiliate, the Nashville Christian Leadership Council, will be
analyzed in the next chapter. Suffice it at this point to say that his background was a key to his success in that setting. Yet Lawson's contribution to the civil rights movement was wide-ranging and reached far

beyond Nashville. In this regard, Smiley and King reached an agreement that Smiley would "travel through the South and find black leaders who were similarly inclined and try to draw them together, try to impart what little knowledge I had of nonviolence to see if there was the possibility of a movement. This we did accomplish."[68] The individuals primarily responsible for this task were Reverends Smiley and Abernathy. Lawson joined them in 1958. It should be remembered that by 1957 mass movements were in progress in a number of Southern cities, and there was a strong possibility that violence might occur in those movements at any moment. This was especially true of the Birmingham movement, where "Bull" Connor and his police force constantly menaced the movement and the fearless Reverend Shuttlesworth.

FOR's task was to visit the ongoing mass movements and to train the leadership and the rank-and-file to bring about social change without violently tearing the community apart. In most cases it appears that such leaders as Shuttlesworth, Speed, and Dr. C. O. Simpkins rejected nonviolence as a way of life but agreed to use it as a tactic. Reverend Speed, who was Transportation Chairman of the Tallahassee movement, spoke of the importance of the nonviolence training:

> Man, if it hadn't been for [Smiley] I reckon we would have had a "can opening" [violent confrontation] here. I got hot with these folks [Southern white racists] one time. . . . I told [Smiley] I'll accept the nonviolence to a certain extent. . . . To me and probably a few of the rest of them like me, it has a limited function. Now I wasn't mean or nothing. . . . I said this, "I could take it until you strike my son or my wife. I don't know what I'd do if you slapped me. I think I'd slap you back. . . . I could take it, but don't hit my wife or children. . . . Don't mess with them." . . . I remember one time a man tried his best to make me commit myself to say that I wouldn't hit back, I wouldn't retaliate or nothing. I say, "Man, no way. No way for me to tell you that. If I told you that, I'd be lying." If that man slaps my wife, I'll break his neck. The only way I wouldn't do it would be because I couldn't get to him. He [nonviolent trainer] said, "Well, you pray." I said, "well, I am praying. Christ doesn't take everything."[69]

Reverend Shuttlesworth agreed that FOR had an important part in keeping the Birmingham movement relatively peaceful. Then he disclosed that "I and others who might not have believed, accepted nonviolence as a principal tactic, anyway. We knew we couldn't fight the white man with guns and bombs and so forth."[70] Keeping movements nonviolent in the South during the late 1950s was a difficult task. King realized this when he wrote, "Realism impels me to admit that many

Negroes will find it difficult to follow the path of nonviolence."[71] "Difficult" was putting it mildly. In late 1958 Smiley wrote King: "My analysis of the situation at Birmingham remains substantially the same, that [it] is one [with] great danger [and] some personality difficulties that make for increased problems."[72] On October 27, 1958, police burst into Reverend Shuttlesworth's home, where an Executive Board meeting of the ACMHR was in progress, and arrested all of the ministers present. A mass meeting was held that night to discuss how the movement would respond to the incident. On October 30, 1958, Rev. Lawson wrote to King: "The disturbing features of the mass meeting were indicators that ministers were unprepared to deal with the situation in the spirit of Christian nonviolence. Not explicit so much as evident in comments on strategy."[73] Lawson told King he was afraid that violence would erupt in Birmingham. He concluded, "Glenn Smiley and the FOR should get to Birmingham right away if the movement breaks over the weekend."[74] This shows how the black church, the movement organizations, the movement halfway houses, and black leaders all made crucial efforts to prevent the early civil rights movement from becoming a violent struggle.

Reverend Lawson constantly traveled across the South to confer with black movement leaders and to conduct workshops in their communities. Lawson also performed these functions in areas where no movement had been organized. This was necessary to the accomplishment of one aspect of his and Smiley's task: to create the will to resist. Finally, Lawson and Smiley were instrumental in pulling together the black leadership of the emerging movement. In that sense FOR was similar to Highlander. When Smiley, Lawson, or Abernathy visited a community, he brought names, addresses, and phone numbers of other leaders and movements. They explained to these groups how a particular tactic might be relevant and how it had worked in other areas. These reports had a solidifying effect on movement leadership across the South and supplied it with valuable information.

Movement literature was important to the civil rights movement, and FOR produced several pieces of literature of consequence. Immediately following the Montgomery bus boycott, FOR secured a grant of $5,000 and used it to publish a comic book about the dynamics of the Montgomery movement. This comic book, entitled *Martin Luther King and the Montgomery Story*, was prepared in close consultation with King. The original intention was to disseminate knowledge about nonviolent protest to the semiliterate. It was thought that this particular medium would be effective because comic books were so well established among the target population. Unintentionally, the ten-cent comic book was written in a way to appeal mainly to the literate. Smiley recalled:

It was not used popularly as we had thought it would be, but it was largely used—the biggest buyer were sociology classes from the universities. . . . We've had sociology departments from I don't know how many universities, that would order a thousand copies or a hundred copies and say we use it as an illustration of modern means of propaganda.[75]

According to one writer, within the next two or three years 200,000 copies of the comic book were sold, "seeding the ground for nonviolence."[76] Moreover, the comic book was read by one of the black college students who sat in at Greensboro, North Carolina, and sparked the famous sit-in movement of 1960.[77]

FOR also made a film of the Montgomery movement while it was in progress. The film, called *Walk to Freedom*, depicted blacks of Montgomery walking to work rather than riding segregated buses. It was shown in many local movement centers throughout the South. Finally, FOR produced a four-page leaflet written by Smiley, "How to Practice Nonviolence." According to Smiley, it was widely circulated through Southern black communities and was effective because he had "based it on scripture aimed specifically at the church audience—the black church audience."[78] Experts on nonviolence such as Lawson, Smiley and Abernathy, carried these leaflets and other literature on nonviolence with them when they visited communities across the South.

King became a member of FOR in 1958, signed a number of its financial appeals, spoke at some of its conferences, and regarded it as an important link in the movement. In sum, FOR became a movement halfway house *par excellence*. Smiley tells why:

The Fellowship of Reconciliation was the only organization that did not come with a ready-made program and said "this is what you ought to do. . . . And this is what I think,"—that gave us tremendous advantages, in the closeness with which we could get to the leadership . . . the only thing that we would carry as the mail of the organization would be the method.[79]

THE SOUTHERN CONFERENCE
EDUCATIONAL FUND

The Southern Conference Education Fund (SCEF) was important to the development of the Student Nonviolent Coordinating Committee and was linked with the emerging civil rights movement during the late 1950s. In that period the SCEF's presence and activities suggested that an integrated society was possible. The SCEF also provided media coverage for certain local movements and made small but important financial contributions to them. The SCEF was established in 1942 as the tax-exempt educational wing of the Southern Conference for Human Welfare (SCHW).

The SCEF's role in the civil rights movement cannot be understood without examining its parent organization, the Southern Conference for Human Welfare, founded in Birmingham, Alabama, in 1938. The SCHW was organized by liberal Southerners who believed that President Roosevelt's New Deal measures were capable of bringing a new industrial order and prosperity to the South. The organization was the result of these Southerners' conviction that the "New South" would emerge only through organized efforts aimed at eliminating the region's poverty, labor problems, racism, segregation, and disfranchisement.

A wide range of liberal Southerners, including labor leaders, educators, politicians, socialists, women, and youth groups, attended the SCHW's first convention in 1938. The gathering at Birmingham was clearly interracial. The black college presidents F. D. Patterson of Tuskegee, Rufus Clement of Atlanta University, and Benjamin Mays of Morehouse had agreed to attend. Such black educators as Mary McLeod Bethune of Bethune-Cookman College; Forrester Washington, a social worker at Atlanta University; and a Fisk sociologist, Charles Johnson, were delegates. Representatives of numerous black organizations also came to the convention. Myles Horton's observation that racial segregation blocks progress in all Southern interracial activities was borne out at this convention.

Rev. Abernathy has said that the 1963 movement in Birmingham "worked on 'Bull' Connor and changed him from a bull into a steer."[80] In 1938, however, Eugene "Bull" Connor was far from being a steer. Participants at the interracial conference were in violation of the segregation laws: "Although Negroes and whites ate and slept separately, they mingled freely during the convention's opening session."[81] Connor stopped this "interracial mixing" by ordering the police to enforce the city's segregation statute. From that day on, "for the remainder of the convention, Negroes and whites sat on opposite sides of the Municipal Auditorium."[82]

The initial goals of the SCHW centered on labor and race issues. Regional wage differentials and wage differentials between racial groups were criticized. The SCHW argued against economic reprisals that prevented workers from organizing unions and fought for the extension of the franchise to all qualified citizens. In order to extend the franchise to poor whites and blacks, the SCHW vowed to have poll taxes abolished. The organization took a stand against the lynching of blacks and supported state and federal antilynching statutes. Those were the kinds of issues that concerned the organization until its demise.

The SCHW began and ended as an interracial organization. Anne Braden, who is white and who later became a field secretary for the SCEF, has remarked that whenever Southern whites and blacks organized to overcome specific problems, they discovered that they had a mutual oppressor. It was in the ruling class's interest, she said, to prevent blacks and whites from making connections. Thus the interracial composition of the SCHW broadened some of its members' perceptions about the larger society. For example, at the SCHW's founding convention the black sociologist Charles Johnson

> . . . exorted the Conference's Negro members to become conversant with the broad range of Southern problems instead of concentrating on the race question. Negroes can never be presumed to speak wisely . . . unless they are known to be acquainted with the total structure of southern life and the confusing interrelationship of all its problems.[83]

The organization's leadership and financial supporters, however, were largely middle-class and white, while workers and blacks made up the rank-and-file. The narrow leadership base was probably responsible for steering the bulk of the organization's efforts into electoral politics rather than into direct attempts to transform the South. Organizational resources were used to support candidates who advocated liberal policies in labor and race issues. Furthermore, the organization suffered early from poor financial management and internal disputes, exacerbated by the SCHW's attempts to coordinate a wide array of diverse groups.

Finally, the organization's internal growth and expansion were hindered from the outset by charges that the SCHW was a communist front. Any Southern organization of that period that attempted to alter the region's racial and economic structure was inevitably branded as communist. This was especially true of an interracial organization such as the SCHW, where black participation remained strong, although not at the leadership level. Thus, the SCHW was under constant surveillance by Southern U.S. Senators and Representatives and local authorities. Anne Braden explained how charges of communism and terror against the organization came about:

> The facts of life are that this society that we happen to live in was built on slavery basically—and the slavery of blacks. This is built into the very structure of it. Therefore, it's just natural that when black people move to change this, it shakes up the whole society, you see. It's like the foundation stone of the building shifts, and the whole

structure shakes . . . that ought to be very obvious, but sometimes it isn't. But once people understand that, they understand a lot of other things too.[84]

Because of internal and external pressures, the SCHW ceased its operations in the late fall of 1948, ten years after it was organized.

The SCEF, the tax-exempt arm of the SCHW, survived, along with the organization's paper, the *Southern Patriot*, and two top officials. James Dombrowski, former Executive Secretary of the SCHW, became the SCEF Executive Secretary in 1947. It was Dombrowski who transferred the highly successful *Southern Patriot* to the SCEF. Aubrey Williams, an influential figure in the SCHW from its inception and a supporter of Dombrowski, also moved to the SCEF.

The SCHW had been a multipurpose membership organization with branches across the South. Dombrowski and Williams decided that the SCEF, in contrast, would be a nonmembership organization with only one goal: to assist blacks in overthrowing all forms of racial segregation in the South. The SCEF Board remained interracial, with Dr. Benjamin Mays and E. D. Nixon among its black members. The SCEF's two executives and the Board decided that educational and persuasive techniques would be the principal methods used by the organization to fight racial injustice. Consequently SCEF activities in many ways paralleled those of the NAACP.

In 1947 the material in the *Southern Patriot* ceased to focus on electoral politics and began to consist largely of articles documenting the negative effects of job discrimination, segregated education, segregated hospitals, and lack of the franchise on the Negro. The paper argued that racial segregation also had crippling effects on whites and prevented Southern institutions from functioning democratically. The *Southern Patriot* was read by significant numbers of Southern and Northern whites and high-income blacks.[85]

In the early 1950s the SCEF became involved in the school desegregation issue. The NAACP, blacks, and a few sympathetic whites began anticipating a favorable Supreme Court decision for school desegregation as early as 1952. At that time the SCEF arranged conferences and workshops in Atlanta, Houston, Richmond, and other cities to discuss the school issue and prepare people to give the "proper" response to the decision once it was handed down. In localities where "race mixing" was relatively safe, the conferences were interracial.

For its efforts, the organization received similar treatment from white Southerners as did the NAACP. In 1954 the U.S. Senate's Internal Security Subcommittee, chaired by Senator Eastland of Mississippi, charged that the SCEF was a subversive organization and subpoenaed its entire leadership, demanding it turn over its membership lists. Eastland prepared a report calling the SCEF the main voice of communism in the South. According to Braden, the staff learned to use these attacks to the SCEF's advantage when defining and defending itself to the press and supporters:

> One way of dealing with that attack was [Dombrowski] sent letters to a lot of people—black and white—which said in effect—"We're inviting you to join the board of SCEF, to spit in the eye of Senator Eastland." He said all these things, and you know a lot of people did. It was sort of an act in a way, of saying no to Senator Eastland.[86]

Throughout the early and mid-1950s the SCEF, with few resources, continued to fight for the abolition of legal segregation and against those groups attempting to drive it out of existence by labeling it as subversive.

The emergence of the mass movement in the South during the 1950s immediately attracted the interest of the SCEF. In 1957 Dombrowski hired Ann and Carl Braden as field secretaries and looked around for money with which to pay their salaries. The SCEF's only income came from individuals, because the foundations usually supported "safer" organizations like the Southern Regional Council. But over the years the SCEF had accumulated a revenue fund of $15,000 in the expectation that the government would at some point impose a large tax against the organization. This fund was used to hire the Bradens in 1957 at a joint salary of $4,000.

Carl and Anne Braden were both radical newspaper people. Mrs. Braden had grown up in white middle-class Mississippi and Alabama, where racial domination was considered part of the natural order. After college she worked as a reporter in Alabama covering the "police courts in the small town of Anniston and courthouse in Birmingham."[87] These experiences sharply drove home the reality that blacks were oppressed and that the system of domination perverted the personalities of whites. Carl Braden was a product of the white working class of Louisville, Kentucky, and had firsthand experience in unions and labor organizing. By twenty-five he was editor of the Kentucky edition of the *Cincinnati Enquirer*, a job that radicalized him. When the two met and married, Carl was working for the *Louisville Times*. Movement halfway houses are often such small organizations that details of biography and personality are indispensable to an understanding of them.

Before coming to the SCEF, the Bradens purchased a house for a black family in a white section of Louisville, Kentucky in the mid-1950s. Within two years the house had been bombed, Carl Braden had spent seven months in jail, and both parties to the purchase had been subjected to terrorism. The SCEF stayed abreast of this ordeal and supported the Bradens. It was shortly after this experience that the Bradens were hired by the SCEF as field secretaries. According to Mrs. Braden, when they first arrived on the job, they found "a small operation, very much under attack, very beleaguered, but it was like a voice crying in the wilderness in the South . . . in those days. And visible, partly visible because of the attacks against it."[88] The hiring of the Bradens increased the full-time staff to three individuals.

The Bradens' first task was to visit the Southern movements of the late 1950s and to support them. They were assigned also to locate sympathetic whites in the communities they visited and encourage them to support the black movements.

At mass meetings the Bradens informed blacks that some Southern whites identified with their struggle and would willingly support and speak out on behalf of the movement. For some whites, they said, an integrated society was a desired goal. The Bradens emphasized the connection between black oppression and that of lower-class and working-class whites: Labor problems, economic subjugation, segregation laws, and the denial of the vote all represented forms of oppression imposed on both groups by powerful Southern whites.

The SCEF also made practical contributions to the emerging movement. Carl Braden, as editor of the *Southern Patriot*, turned it into a "movement paper" and used it to publicize local movements and their leaders, usually ignored by the press. When Shuttlesworth was asked about the SCEF's role in Birmingham, he said:

> Well, it helped us in the first place by white folks identifying with black folks. . . . The other way, which I think historians have overlooked, if it had not been for Carl and Anne Braden, I'm sure I would have been dead already. We couldn't get the news out many times.[89]

Anne Braden commented in the same vein:

> The thing that we were able to do was set up a whole communications network. You know, of getting the word out about what was happening, because the South wasn't in the headlines yet, at that point. You had to let people know, it saved lives. We were able to get news out about what was happening. That was one thing that was valuable to the Birmingham movement that SCEF was doing.[90]

Beside filling subscriptions to the *Southern Patriot*, the SCEF staff would distribute the papers at various meetings free of charge.

The SCEF also assisted the emerging movement financially through the newspaper. The January 1957 issue contained the following:

M. C. Williams, D.D.S., Executive Secretary of the Inter-Civic Council of Tallahassee, Florida, has asked us to thank the many friends of the SCEF who contributed to the special New Year's gift to the ICC of $1567.80, to help with the campaign to establish integrated buses.[91]

There were also advertisements in behalf of local movements:[92]

FUNDS NEEDED

THE MANY ACTIVITIES OF THE ALABAMA CHRISTIAN MOVEMENT FOR HUMAN RIGHTS, PLUS THE COST OF A MULTITUDE OF COURT ACTIONS, REQUIRE THE OUTLAY OF LARGE SUMS OF MONEY. PERSONS WISHING TO HELP SHOULD SEND FUNDS TO THE REV. FRED SHUTTLESWORTH, CHAIRMAN, 3191 29TH AVENUE, NORTH BIRMINGHAM.

Finally, a prime task of the SCEF was to persuade Southern whites to join the movement. Dombrowski decided in 1947 that the chief goal of the SCEF was to fight segregation, because the liberation of whites required the overthrow of racial domination. Anne Braden recalls that the organization attempted to reach the white working class, but the Klan and White Citizens' Councils had far more success with that group: "The kind of people we were basically reaching were white ministers, white teachers, white college professors, professional people, and eventually white students."[93] Yet the SCEF did manage to articulate an analysis and a social vision that challenged those of the Ku Klux Klan, the White Citizens' Councils, and the Southern white power structure. Blacks in the movement were undoubtedly inspired by the SCEF's alternative views and support.

The SCLC and the SCEF

The SCLC, as we have seen, had ties with the SCEF. In fact, Reverends Shuttlesworth and Steele, both SCLC leaders, became Board members in the late 1950s, and Shuttlesworth became the SCEF's President in 1963. Publicly King and Abernathy kept their distance from the SCEF to avoid being labeled as communists. Dr. King did on occasion meet with the SCEF, however, to work out lines of cooperation. Anne Braden adds that King "Took a stand supporting my husband when he went to jail as a result of the charges by the House Un-American Activities Committee. . . . It got him a lot of attack. He had no reason in the world to do it . . . people don't know that about him and don't want to deal with it now."[94]

In 1960, a year that will come under scrutiny in a later chapter, the SCEF went on to become an important movement halfway house associated with the Student Nonviolent Coordinating Committee (SNCC).

This chapter has focused on the contributions that three movement halfway houses made to the emerging civil rights movement of the 1950s. It has demonstrated how these groups strengthened the base of the movement by providing it with important resources. The next chapter traces the continuing development of local movement centers, which were to provide the internal organization through which the civil rights movement grew into a national force.

INTERNAL ORGANIZATION AND DIRECT ACTION

The pioneering movements in Baton Rouge, Montgomery, Tallahassee, and Birmingham, which set the modern civil rights movement in motion, have been described and analyzed. This chapter will examine other movements to show how they were further developed by the SCLC in the late 1950s. Specifically, the movement centers in Nashville, Tennessee; Petersburg, Virginia; and Shreveport, Louisiana, organized and developed by local SCLC affiliates, are studied for what their experience reveals about the evolution of the civil rights movement. That subject will lead as well to an analysis of the sit-ins that occurred from 1957 through 1960, setting the stage for the massive student sit-in movement of 1960.

THE NASHVILLE MOVEMENT

The black community of Nashville in the late 1950s and early 1960s was central to the civil rights movement. In fact, Nashville produced a disproportionate number of leaders in the 1960 student movement (e.g. John Lewis, Diane Nash Bevel, James Bevel, Marion Barry, Cordell Reagon, Bernard Lafayette, and Matthew Jones), who were key actors in both the Student Nonviolent Coordinating Committee (SNCC) and the SCLC. Why did Nashville produce these leaders and the disciplined mass movements they organized?[1] The perspective developed in this book can account for the disproportionate number of SNCC's early leaders from Nashville. It was argued in Chapter Four that movement centers define the common ends of a dominated group, devise appropriate tactics and strategies to reach those ends, and train people to implement those tactics and strategies when they initiate collective action. As will be demonstrated shortly, the movement center established in Nashville in the late 1950s was the organizational framework in which college students in Nashville received the training and preparation that enabled them to fill a disproportionate number of SNCC's early leadership positions by reason of their superior skills and background. The Nashville Christian Leadership Council (NCLC), an affiliate of SCLC, was the driving force that developed the Nashville movement.

The NCLC was rooted in the black church and college communities of Nashville. It was organized in January 1958 by the Reverend Kelly Miller Smith, a scholarly young minister who had participated in the SCLC's founding meetings and had been in Nashville for seven years. When Reverend Smith became president of the NCLC, he was already president of the local NAACP. He continued in both posts for a number of years. He recalls that the NCLC "began as a movement of ministers, then it expanded to include lay people, nonclergy."[2]

In 1958 and 1959 the NCLC grew into a major movement center. Reverend Smith was a charismatic personality around whom activist ministers and students assembled. John Lewis, a student at the American Baptist Theological Seminary in Nashville during the late 1950s who later became chairman of SNCC, has described Reverend Smith's style:

> *First Baptist Church . . . became a rallying point, it became the meeting place, it became the place where students, young people, community leaders, could meet and discuss, debate and argue about what the city should become. . . . Kelly's church became a sort of haven where people could come on a Sunday evening at 6 o'clock and discuss social action, debate the question of segregation and social discrimination. And on Sunday morning at 11 o'clock, we'd go to his church. And he would preach what I like to call not just—well, he didn't talk a great deal about, you know, pie in the sky when you die, and all of that. And he didn't talk about hell. But his gospel, his message had some social relevance. He was concerned about the way people were living and being treated in Nashville. Not just on Sunday morning at 11 o'clock, but on Monday morning, and throughout the week. And so his ministry at the church and his leadership in the community went hand in hand. He had a tremendous influence over almost everything that was taking place in the city of Nashville, in the black community.[3]*

Reverend Smith taught homiletics at the Baptist Theological Semi-nary. Students in his classes included James Bevel, John Lewis, the Rev-erend C. T. Vivian, and Bernard Lafayette. All of these men went on to prominence in the leadership of SNCC and the entire civil rights movement. The Reverend James Bevel stated:

> When you're a young preacher, Kelly Miller Smith was a natural to be the idol of young preachers. . . . He was down to earth, he was young and he was logically clear. He never did come to the end of his sermons whooping and screaming. He came to logical rational cres-cendos, based on logic, something like King. . . . He was like a new breed of preachers . . . they would inspire social action rather than shouting to go to heaven after you die. So that's a whole new ethos, you see.[4]

An important group within the NCLC was the Projects Committee chaired by the Reverend James Lawson, another scholarly young min-ister. Lawson, who had studied the entire world history of nonviolent social action, was a theological student at Vanderbilt University during the late 1950s. Because of his experience, Reverend Smith appointed Lawson to the chair of the Projects Committee with the explicit mission to train people in nonviolent direct action. In 1958–59 Lawson held weekly workshops in various black churches of Nashville, at which members of the black community were trained in the techniques of nonviolent direct action.

The proximity of four black institutions of higher learning in Nash-ville—Fisk University, Tennessee State College, American Baptist The-ological Seminary, and Meharry Medical School—made it an ideal city for the recruitment and training of students to participate in the emerg-ing civil rights movement. Sprinkled throughout these colleges and uni-versities in the late 1950s were students angry at the domination they and their people suffered in every area of life. Future movement lead-ers, including Diane Nash and Marion Barry at Fisk University, sat in their dorms wondering how they could change society.

At the time Lawson, working through the Projects Committee of the NCLC, was already training small numbers of community people. Then, Reverend Smith recounts, James Lawson came to him and "told me that some college students wanted to know if they could participate. We had begun having workshops. He said, 'Can they participate?' I said, 'Yeah, why not?' "[5] In 1959, therefore, a cadre of students from the various black colleges in Nashville began attending nonviolent workshops, and all of them refer to Lawson as one of their mentors. Among other things, they learned about the experiences of one of their fellow students, the Reverend C. T. Vivian. Between 1945 and 1947 Vivian and a black chemist, Benjamin Alexander, along with a small interracial group, had conducted nonviolent demonstrations at segregated restaurants, hotels, and lunch counters in Peoria, Illinois. The participants were associated with the West Bluff Christian Church in Peoria, pastored by the Reverend Barton Hunter. The group used sit-ins and other related nonviolent techniques and learned how to deal creatively with irate and recalcitrant proprietors. After more than a year of demonstrations the owner of Bishop Restaurant desegregated its facilities because it had been losing customers. More establishments in Peoria where demonstrations were conducted desegregated their facilities within a relatively short time after Bishop.[6] Exposed to the experiences of activists like Vivian, participants in the Nashville workshop learned to protect themselves in the midst of violence and to be creative in difficult situations.

Finally, Diane Nash Bevel relates, the workshops were geared "towards sit-ins and nonviolent action at the department stores in Nashville, a couple of large department stores that had eating facilities."[7] Indeed, in late 1959 Jim Lawson's workshop students conducted "test sit-ins" at large department stores in Nashville. The so-called spontaneous, student-initiated sit-in movement of 1960 was developing.

The NCLC was an important movement center built around the SCLC chaplain, the Reverend Kelly Miller Smith, but it was much more than one man. It formed committees with specific assignments to accomplish movement tasks, and it put down roots deep within the community. Like most other local movements, it was financed by the black community. Reverend Smith said this about finances: "We raised our funds through contributions from churches, organizations, individuals, and through special efforts. [Would you say the bulk of these funds came from black people?] Oh, Yes, yes. Oh, yes, beyond a doubt."[8] During the late 1950s members of the NCLC held systematic discussions on ways to overthrow the system of racial domination. Questions pertaining to tactics and grievances were debated. For example, the Reverend Andrew White, an officer of the NCLC, raised the issue of economic exploitation. Reverend Smith remembers that White

... *was insistent that the economic issue was what we should zero in on first. We did not disagree with the fact that that was most important, but our view was that sit-ins would lend themselves to kind of a public presentation of the issue. Kind of a dramatizing of the issue that would be better than any procedures of which we were aware when dealing with economics.*[9]

In short, during the late 1950s members of the NCLC were preparing the black community for protest by training future leaders in the philosophy and tactics of nonviolent direct action, by refocusing the cultural content of a number of churches in such a way that oppressive conditions were defined as sinful, by debating grievances of critical importance to the community, and by teaching indigenous people that it was absolutely essential for them to finance efforts of protest.

THE LOUISIANA AND TEXAS MOVEMENT

The United Christian Movement, Inc. (UCMI) was organized in Shreveport, Louisiana, in late 1956 as a movement of ministers. In March 1956 the Attorney General of Louisiana took the NAACP to court with the demand that the organization submit its membership lists to the state. NAACP officials refused, prompting the State of Louisiana to slap a "temporary injunction restraining the NAACP from holding meetings or otherwise operating in that state."[10] The NAACP's *Annual Report* documents that economic pressures and other forms of intimidation were carried out against NAACP members in Louisiana.[11]

The UCMI was organized by ministers in the wake of these repressive actions. Dr. C. O. Simpkins tells that it was "organized to fill the void of NAACP,"[12] further evidence that the Southern attack against the NAACP was central to the rise of the modern civil rights movement. The 1954 Supreme Court decision had awakened the perception among blacks that change was possible, but it was the attack on the NAACP that created social conditions favorable to the emergence of direct action. Some people of the black community in Louisiana thought that other people besides the ministers should be organized. Dr. Simpkins recalls: "We started to form another organization and then there were some ministers who invited us to be a part of the United Christian Movement."[13] Simpkins and others joined the UCMI, and "some of the ministers dropped out when things got a little hot."[14] Dr. Simpkins, a dentist, became president of the UCMI. The majority of the UCMI leadership positions, however, were filled by ministers. On the letterhead of a February 12, 1960, correspondence, six out of eight of the UCMI executive officers listed were ministers. The exceptions were Dr. Simpkins, who was president, and Madeline Brewer, general secretary. Out of the twenty-six Board members of the UCMI, twenty were ministers. The chairman of the Board was the Reverend J. R. Retledge.

It is important to note that each of these ministers represented a congregation. One prominent writer on the movement has advanced the opinion that black ministers became involved in the movement because they wanted a place in the limelight like Dr. King.[15] A conclusion

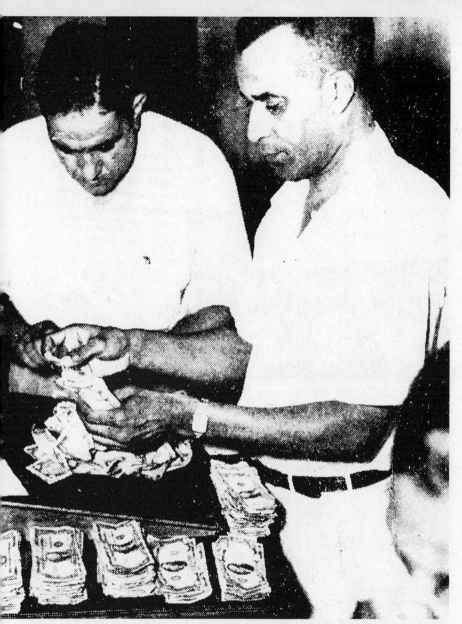

The pioneering 1953 Baton Rouge bus boycott was financed by the black community. Above, two members of the United Defense League counting over $1,500 donated by blacks at a nightly mass meeting to finance the movement. (*Morning Advocate*, June 21, 1953)

The black church functioned as the institutional center of the Movement, providing meeting places and a financial base.

Reverend C. K. Steele presiding over strategy meeting of the original Executive Board of the Inter-Civic Council during the Tallahassee bus boycott of 1956. (Courtesy of Rev. Henry Steele and Bethel Baptist Church)

The black church community in other areas of the country provided key financial support to the Southern Movement. As seen here in 1956, Rev. C. K. Steel receives from the Second Baptist Church of Los Angeles a $500 check sent by Dr. J. Raymond Henderson. (Photo provided by Rev. Henry Steele)

NAACP, the dominant black protest organization for the first half of the
entieth century, emphasized legal action, but also provided important oppor-
ities for local leaders to acquire organizing skills.

As president of the Montgomery NAACP during the 1940s and 50s, and a key
organizer of the Montgomery bus boycott, E.D. Nixon provided a visible model of
successful protest, a source of inspiration and practical guidance to the entire
Civil Rights Movement. (AP/Wide World Photos)

The young fought for freedom.
Removing chairs did not prevent
Lana Pogue from waiting to be
served at an all-white lunch
counter in Oklahoma City. This
sit-in was one of several nonviolent protests planned and
initiated by the NAACP Youth
Council of Oklahoma City.
(Clara Luper, *Behold the Walls*)

The SCLC and the ACMHR, one of its major affiliates, often held meetings in churches during the late 1950s. Their meetings and protest activities developed the mass base of support, as well as many Movement leaders, which made the Birmingham confrontation possible. (Photo by Elaine Tomlin)

SCLC leaders Reverends Ralph Abernathy, Wyatt T. Walker, Martin Luther King, Jr., Fred Shuttlesworth, and James Lawson with student sit-in leaders at 1960 Shaw University conference, from which SNCC emerged. (Photo by Don Uhrbrock, Life Magazine, © 1968 Don Uhrbrock)

The February 1, 1960 sit-in at Woolworth Store in Greensboro, North Carolina, often described as a spontaneous protest of four college students which sparked the sit-in movement. In fact, these students had all been members of an NAACP Youth Council and were familiar with the Durham sit-ins and others of the late 1950s. (UPI Telephoto)

SNCC staff members initiating a sit-in at Dobbs House in Atlanta during the early 1960s. SNCC focused much of its efforts on activating and organizing high school and college students, as well as the larger black community. (Danny Lyons/Magnum Photo)

The Highlander Folk School was a Movement halfway house, an institution removed from the larger society which served the Movement by developing resources for social change, skilled activists, tactical knowledge, and media contacts. HFS helped pull together black leadership, provided a successful model of an integrated society, and developed a successful mass education program later transferred to SCLC.

Rosa Parks attending Highlander workshop prior to being arrested in Montgomery. Septima Clark is second left. (Archives of the Highlander Research and Education Center)

Bernice Robinson teaching one of the first citizenship education classes in the Sea Islands in the late 1950s. (Archives of the Highlander Research and Education Center)

Women like Septima Clark, Rosa Parks, and Ella Baker played pivotal roles in the Movement.

Ella Baker, one of the founders of the SCLC and SNCC. (Photo © Diana J Davies)

Rosa Parks (right) at Highlander with Septima Clark, Director of Education at the Highlander Folk School and creator of the Citizenship School Movement, one of the key organizing bases for SCLC and the Civil Rights Movement. (Archives of the Highlander Research and Education Center)

In Birmingham, known as the racist capital of the South, business leaders capitulated to SCLC demands—despite the opposition of the political leaders—in order to stem the disruption caused by the mass demonstrations and economic boycott.

The power of organized collective action stood fast even against Sheriff "Bull" Connor's dogs and hoses. (AP/Wide World Photos)

King and Abernathy defying state injunction against demonstration in Birmingham by leading march on Good Friday, 1963. (AP/ Wide World Photos)

that such leaders are political entrepreneurs seeking individual gains must result from a superficial analysis. Among the hundreds of ministers who participated in the movement, the overwhelming majority knew that they could not become "another Dr. King." The black church community had been at the center of the mass movements in Baton Rouge in 1953 and in Montgomery in 1955. The ministers who became involved did so because as church leaders they held most of the institutional power of the black community. Rather than seeking to become another King, they were busy building the organizational base of the organization King headed, the SCLC. Such facts lead to the conclusion expressed by Dr. Lowery: With respect to social protest, many of the "black churches of the 1950s were coming alive."[16] Dr. Simpkins pointed out that before the formation of the UCMI, teachers and any others in the pay of state or parish (county) governments, if they involved themselves in protest or the NAACP, "were fired from their particular positions." For that reason, the UCMI "was set up with the ministers because they could not be really touched. So, it started mostly with ministers."[17]

The UCMI's headquarters were in Shreveport, but its organizing activities reached far beyond that city. It concentrated its organizing activities in Northern Louisiana and Northwest Texas as well as Shreveport. According to Dr. Simpkins, "we were very effective in Louisiana and Texas."[18] The UCMI was especially active in Marshall, Texas, where Dr. Simpkins had prior connections with two institutions, Bishop College and Wiley College, respectively. Dr. Simpkins had earned his undergraduate degree from Wiley, and his father was a graduate of Bishop.[19] In the late 1950s Simpkins and other UCMI activists worked closely with student groups at these two institutions and often involved them in demonstrations. Students from Marshall were instrumental in organizing a March 19, 1959, demonstration in Shreveport,[20] discussed in Chapter Five, as well as some of the activities the UCMI initiated in such Northern Louisiana parishes as Minden, Mansfield, and Monroe.

The UCMI leaders developed its activities beyond Shreveport for strategic reasons, as Dr. Simpkins, explained: "Our whole effort wasn't just one thing. We believed in diversification. As soon as we had one action moving, we'd start on something else. You've got to keep them off balance."[21] Thus, in some areas the UCMI attacked bus segregation while simultaneously attacking political disfranchisement in others. In later chapters it will be shown that the UCMI, along with its associated student groups at Bishop and Wiley, had an important hand in initiating sit-ins in Marshall, Texas, in early 1960.

The UCMI staff kept the organization loosely structured to avoid the problems its predecessor, the NAACP, had encountered. Dr. Simpkins, who knew the inner workings of the NAACP, having been on its state board before the injunction, said the UMCI

> . . . had to improvise as we went along. We had to change our structure, and being too organized was what got you in trouble. We were organized to the point where we were able to get people together . . . things were so fluid you had to change your whole structure to deal with the situation. A case in point was the NAACP when they were outlawed in the State of Louisiana. The minutes were very accurate, in fact, so accurate, that they were able to pinpoint the whole activity. If they weren't quite as accurate, they wouldn't have been able to go into court and get the type of injunction against them that they did. So sometimes it doesn't pay to have too good records, to be too structured.[22]

It was argued in Chapter Three that activists in movement centers may project a spontaneous image to turn away the repressive activities of authorities. Here again we find this strategy used by UCMI activists.

The fluidity of the UCMI served it well. When UCMI officials organized its bus desegregation project, they knew that a number of the people participating in the activities of the UCMI were police informers. President Simpkins publicly announced, "We just can't ride the buses because Shreveport has too many policemen."[23] The informers alerted the police that blacks had decided not to ride the buses. The same night, following the meeting, Simpkins privately told approximately a dozen members of the organization to meet him at the office at four in the morning.

> We decided to ride those buses that Sunday. And we organized. We had our photographers there and we had our attorneys standing by. We had people who were sitting in the rear of the bus just to be observers, just to observe what was going one. And we rode the buses Sunday, almost all day.[24]

Members of the UCMI employed this strategy successfully a number of times. Their position was that once they knew who the informers were, "Don't let them out, don't hate them, 'cause all they would do is replace him with another. You know this one, so keep the one you've got."[25] In the late 1950s UCMI officials frequently announced plans to integrate libraries or the movies on a particular day, intending all the while not to show up.

Simpkins maintained that those maneuvers had a devastating effect on the morale of the police and the "stool pigeons." "They lost confidence in their own people, who were informing on us. . . . So we were organizing the way we could move at a moment's notice and could change a whole thing. . . . I think that was our saving grace."[26]

The UCMI created its own "intelligence department," Simpkins said.

> *Like we knew . . . things on the police. Their girlfriends. We knew their sexual habits. We knew their weaknesses; just like they studied us, we studied them. We had a file on them. . . . We knew exactly what they were doing. We knew who the chief of police's girlfriend was. We knew everything. And we studied them. We had to follow them.*[27]

A favorite technique of the authorities was to identify protestors so that they could be physically assaulted or denounced to their employers and fired. By collecting information on the authorities, Simpkins recalls, members of the UCMI were able to forestall those consequences by threatening to divulge what they knew about the authorities. "They'd back off with that."[28]

So the movement center in Shreveport did not arise out of "unorganized spontaneity," nor were outside elites crucial. The members of the UCMI received no outside funding or trained "movement entrepreneurs." Many of the activities of the UCMI could be carried out without large sums of money; when money was needed, blacks dug down into their pockets to support the Louisiana and Texas movements.

Let us examine the UCMI financial situation, which Dr. Simpkins describes elegantly:

> *We didn't have the largest amount of money. We didn't need it. We didn't have a lot of funds, 'cause you've got to account for them. We didn't ask people to give a lot of money because we didn't want your money. You keep it yourself. 'Cause if we need it, we'll ask you for it. We asked for just what we needed. We would account for everything. Our people put their money into it. If you believe in something you put your own money into it. That's what we did. So there were some rallies for money, but not a lot. [When you say our people supported it, do you mean members of the organization?] Members of the organization themselves. The ministers themselves. They reached in their own pockets and pulled out their money. When we do that, you're going to have no trouble in other people putting theirs in. People will come to you and want to give you something. 'Cause they realize you're putting your life on the line, you're putting yourself up, so there's no funny business. And you got good support.*[29]

Simpkins, remembering the violence and economic pressures black activists had experienced because of NAACP activities, related how people were protected in the UCMI:

> Why expose them to that for a few dollars? And if you can talk to their ministers, the ministers can preach to them. They know the message. When the old slave sings about "There's a great day coming"—the old spirituals—the message is in there, and the ministers gave a certain sermon. [The people] knew what was going on. They put extra money in the collection plate. You couldn't trace that. But he knew where it was coming from. He could give it, you see. Why expose people to be damaged or hurt when you didn't have to?[30]

Simpkins maintained that the UCMI did not hold large numbers of large mass meetings and related demonstrations, because the likelihood of being bombed was considerable. The plans, finances, and strategies of the Louisiana/Texas movement were organized through the churches and the UCMI, which was a church-related direct action organization. The church culture was also important: Key messages pertaining to strategy and finance were communicated through the familiar black spirituals and religious sermons. The development and use of these organizational and cultural factors enabled the protestors to confront the problem of white domination directly.

The UCMI developed a procedure that enabled it to organize across income lines, thanks largely to ministers who represented various strata of black society. In addition, the UCMI developed a philosophy and practice that encompassed the entire black community. The soft-spoken dentist explained:

> In civil rights you didn't have to shape up to what we were selling. We worked with you, with what you had. When you've got an organization, you've got to structure them. That's no organization to me. You work with what you've got and let each person play a role that they can play. And you don't castigate anyone. . . . Too often we have a picture of a person being a certain way—"you've got to be this way to be with the organization. You've got to do this for us." I think in civil rights or any organizations, let people be as they are. Let them be in their natural habitat. Enhance him and kind of guide them to be constructive for you.[31]

Dr. Simpkins provided marvelous examples of how use was made of cowards, teachers, and local drunkards. A well-known drunk in Shreveport was affectionately referred to as "Papa Tight." Simpkins related:

*Anything you want to know in that area, you see Papa Tight. So we
didn't criticize him. We actually worked with him, and he got some
respectability 'cause he could get people out to vote. . . . So why replace him with someone who was more elegant and more of a Christian? He did a good job and he felt proud of himself.*[32]

Simpkins pointed out that teachers and others dependent on the white
power structure could not be overtly identified with the movement, for
"they'd lose their jobs. You've got to realize this. Don't make them lose
their jobs because you can't feed them."[33] Hence teachers were called
upon to supply the movement with stencils, pencils, paper, and money.
At times professional blacks placed garbage barrels at designated places
for movement activists to pick up. Inside the garbage containers were
the names of prominent blacks who wanted to support the movement
in any way they could. Members of the UCMI secretly made contact
with those named and put to use whatever services and resources they
could provide. The UCMI, then, operated under the assumption that
all strata of black society would support the movement if they were
creatively sought out in their natural habitats, because they all had a
vested interest in the movement. According to Simpkins, all strata of
black society actually did support the movement in Louisiana.

Finally, the UCMI worked hand in hand with students through its
Youth Department. Before the student sit-ins, the young people held
meetings. "A lot of times they met right with us," Simpkins says. "There
was no separation. They felt a part of what we were doing, and we
tried to coordinate the activities."[34] In a 1959 issue of a SCLC newsletter, Ella Baker, in her "Salute to Youth" column, stated: "We com-
mend: The United Youth Council of Shreveport as the largest and most
active youth group in the deep South struggle for Freedom."[35] The future sit-in protests were incubating here. As a principal SCLC affiliate
in the late 1950s the UCMI was engaging in direct action and building
in Northern Louisiana and parts of Texas the internal organization necessary for initiating and sustaining large volumes of collective action.

THE VIRGINIA MOVEMENT

By 1958 SCLC movement centers were being organized across the state
of Virginia. The Reverend Wyatt Walker of Petersburg and activist
clergy across the state were at the core of this massive organizing effort. Indeed, Reverend Walker's Petersburg Improvement Association
(PIA) became the model for direct action movements across the state.
Walker, who was president of the PIA, described himself as follows:

An organization man. . . . It just happened to be that the Lord blessed me with the administrative skills and the characteristics of a son of a bitch who didn't care about being loved to get it done—I didn't give a damn about whether people liked me, but I knew I could do the job.[36]

Walker had been associated with the SCLC from its beginning and held a number of leadership positions in protest organizations. In the late 1950s Walker was a Board member of the SCLC, president of the Petersburg local NAACP, and state director of CORE. Marvin Rich of CORE praised leaders like Reverend Walker for their ability to "take one hat one day, and put on another the next day."[37] Walker identified the main ingredients of the Virginia movement as (1) church leadership that was (2) committed to nonviolence and (3) functioned under the umbrella of Martin Luther King.[38]

The Gillfield Baptist Church of Petersburg, Virginia, where Reverend Walker was pastor, "became the headquarters and the focal point for organizing demonstrations" in the state of Virginia.[39] In October 1958 the SCLC held workshops and a mass meeting in Norfolk, which attracted four thousand people and raised $2,500. The meeting was so successful that Reverend Hamilton, an activist minister,

. . . sent out letters to several ministers and others interested, inviting them to meet in Richmond October 31 in the office of the NAACP, to consider the feasibility of forming an organization on the state level that would have objectives similar to those of the Southern Christian Leadership Conference, or serve as a branch of the Southern Christian Leadership Conference. Such an organization would supplement the work of the NAACP.[40]

Some clergy leaders of the NAACP were reluctant to take this kind of action, but others were not. In the latter part of 1958 the more enthusiastic ministers, many of whom were NAACP leaders, began to form what eventually became the Virginia State Unit of the Southern Christian Leadership Conference. A solid state structure of SCLC affiliates was organized across Virginia by the time Reverend Walker left Petersburg in 1960 to become the SCLC Executive Director.

Reverend Walker's Gillfield Baptist Church became the center of this large network of SCLC affiliates. In 1958, under Governor Lindsay Almond's "massive resistance" scheme, public education officials in Virginia decided to close the public schools rather than integrate them. At that time Jim McCain and Gordon Carey of CORE were traveling through Virginia seeking to organize CORE chapters. They met with Reverend Walker, and out of the meeting came the idea to conduct a mass march on Richmond, which would protest the closing of public schools to avoid desegregation. The march was set for January 1, 1959, with Walker as its coordinator. CORE agreed to underwrite the initial expenses and to assign Carey to assist behind the scenes. The goal was to mobilize a large number of people to march to the State Capitol in Richmond to voice their protest. Understanding the mobilization effort in Virginia, is important, because the mobilization of the famous civil rights marches of the 1960s was carried out in a similar manner.

Being a minister, Walker knew that black people could be mobilized through churches. It is the black preacher who meets systematically, every week, with the movement troops, he reasoned, so in order to mobilize blacks you must work through the "Revs." Walker's first step was to write asking Dr. King to endorse the march: "What we really need now, Mike, is your support. We need a letter from you similar to the one enclosed, to be sent to every minister in the state. Your support means a lot to me and to the success of this movement."[41]

The enclosed letter, the appeal to Virginia's ministers, proclaimed: "Today is a day for great men, great ideas and great movements." It continued: "Virginia . . . has the opportunity to give direction and destiny to our troubled South. As Virginia goes, so goes the South, perhaps America and the world." Then Walker, who wrote the appeal, gave political content to Christianity: "Christian Democracy is at stake."[42] Walker's appeal ended with this specific request:

> *My Brethren in Christ. . . . As ministers and leaders of our people, we have an obligation to Jesus and His quest to elevate each human personality, to rally the community in support of this project. We ask but little of you. We ask only that each church in the state of Virginia send at least two bus loads of people to petition the Governor on Emancipation Day for the opening of schools in compliance with the Supreme Court Decision of 1954. We, as leaders, must do much more in this struggle for first-class citizenship. . . . Let it be your personal responsibility to send at least 50 persons to Richmond from your church community on that day. Let us make this small sacrifice as a symbol of our faith in Christ and his way.[43]*

King sent this letter along to the ministers, adding his own encouragement: "My prayers and good wishes are with you in this great undertaking. If my health permits, it may be that I shall join you on this great day." As it turned out, King did not recover from stab wounds in time to attend, and January 1, 1959, was a day of heavy snow in Richmond. Walker later wrote King: "There was moments on January 1, when I wished that I had never heard of a Pilgrimage of Prayer for public schools." But this was followed by a note of excitement: "You can imagine my shock and surprise at 2:10 when I took a peek into the main auditorium of the Mosque and saw more than 1500 people. With the promise of bad weather we had expected no more than 500. I was really 'shook.' "[44]

The mosque was seventeen blocks from Richmond's Capitol building. Reverend Walker had decided that if a hundred ministers marched that distance in the rain, it would be a significant demonstration. His description resumes:

> *Two blocks from the Mosque it happened all over again. When I looked back across a small park that adjoins the Mosque I saw a number behind me that 'no man could number.' We began singing, at this point, the great hymns of the church and Negro spirituals. It was in these moments that I felt keenest the solidarity of our struggle in the South. For twelve or thirteen blocks, men, women, and children; the halt and the lame; the young and the aged; orderly, and with dignity, making a nonviolent protest against the evil of closed schools in our Commonwealth. It was really a sight to behold.*[45]

When Walker learned that King could not attend the demonstration, he had asked King to tape a message in advance for the occasion. The tape arrived at 9 o'clock the morning of the demonstration. Reverend Walker's letter made mention of the tape: "You could not have spoken more directly to the situation if you had been here yourself." He added, "I am now convinced 'that God knows what He is about.' "[46] The choice of words is interesting, for as the civil rights movement unfolded, the role of the church came to be known as the "hand of God." Reverend Walker concluded the historic demonstration with the familiar:

> *Walk together Children,*
> *Don't you get weary,*
> *There's a great camp meeting in the*
> *Promised Land.*

The march had such an effect on the people in the Virginia SCLC unit that they conducted similar marches to Richmond on each New Year's Day throughout the early 1960s.

In June 1959 Reverend Walker prepared a petition for presentation to the local City Council, urging that public library facilities in Petersburg be desegregated. Walker placed this heading on the petition: "By the Branch president of the NAACP, the Rev. Wyatt Tee Walker." He then received a surprise:

> *The NAACP of which I was the branch president cut and pulled the rug out from underneath me the morning that I was to go down to*

the City Council. . . . The NAACP lawyer of Petersburg and of the state Legal Staff . . . told me that he had talked with the boys in Richmond and they had decided I should not go down.[47]

Walker was obliged to call the City Council clerk's office with the information that the NAACP people were not coming after all. Word circulated through the streets, barbershops, and work places that Reverend Walker had sold out. "The word was that they thought that I was one black man that the white folks couldn't get to, but they had gotten to me too."[48] Many in the "rank-and-file" apparently desired a faster pace of social change than some of their "leaders."

The act of nonsupport by the NAACP forced Walker to find a way to restore his credibility in the movement community. In his words:

So my credibility was at stake and I immediately organized the Petersburg Improvement Association . . . and I just made an umbrella group for anybody who wanted to belong, anybody and any organization could belong. And I made the NAACP, since I was its president, I made it a part of that umbrella and CORE a part of the umbrella and any church and whoever.[49]

Thus one of the many counterparts of the Montgomery Improvement Association—the Peterburg Improvement Association—formally emerged.

Young blacks across the State of Virginia attended the churches of the SCLC's affiliates. Many of the ministers there preached that oppressive social conditions right here on this earth are sinful and a stench in the nostrils of God. Future sit-in protesters were among those who often attended churches espousing what the Reverend James Bevel called the "new ethos." Some were acquainted with activitists who were leaders of movement centers. For example, during the late 1950s Charles Sherrod, who would later become a high-ranking leader in SNCC, was closely acquainted with Wyatt Walker.

The three movement centers in Nashville, Shreveport, and Petersburg represent a trend that was developing during the late 1950s. It is a trend inadequately analyzed by civil rights scholars who view the period between the mass bus boycotts of the mid-1950s and the 1960 sit-ins as relatively quiescent. Analyses based on this position either imply or state outright that the heavy volume of protest beginning in early 1960 was independent of the movement centers of the late 1950s.[50] The present analysis suggests that during the "quiescent" period organizations appropriately designed to facilitate collective action were established. Those organizations operated in a fluid but organized manner as they mobilized and prepared the masses to engage in direct action. My analysis also stresses that previously established movement centers were directly involved in the planning and execution of the early 1960 sit-ins. A demonstration of this thesis will be the objective of later chapters.

ROOTS OF A TACTICAL INNOVATION: SIT-INS

During the late 1950s activists associated with direct action organizations began experimenting with the sit-in tactic. The 1960 student sit-in movement followed naturally from the early efforts to mobilize for nonviolent direct action that took place in black communities across the South. Analysis of sit-ins of the late 1950s will reveal the basic components of the internal organization that was necessary for the emergence of the massive sit-ins of 1960.

In earlier chapters it was demonstrated that the NAACP Youth Councils, CORE chapters, and the SCLC affiliates were the main forces organizing the black community to engage in nonviolent protest. It was emphasized that these groups were closely tied to the black church base. The adult advisers of the NAACP Youth Councils were often women, who supervised the activities of fifteen to twenty young people, but it was not unusual to find men functioning as advisers also. Some of the Youth Councils felt a kinship with the direct action movement and were not rigidly locked into the legal approach of the NAACP.

The Southern CORE chapters, operating primarily in South Carolina and several border states, were organized by James McCain and Gordon Carey, were headed largely by local ministers, and had a disproportionate number of young people as members. These groups were preparing the way for the massive sit-ins of 1960 by conducting sit-ins between 1957 and 1960 at segregated facilities, including lunch counters.

Early Sit-ins: Forerunners

On February 1, 1960, four black college students initiated a sit-in at the segregated lunch counter of the local Woolworth store in Greensboro, North Carolina. That day has come to be known as the opening of the sit-in movement. Civil rights activists, however, had conducted sit-ins between 1957 and 1960 in at least sixteen cities: St. Louis, Missouri; Wichita and Kansas City, Kansas; Oklahoma City, Enid, Tulsa, and

Stillwater, Oklahoma; Lexington and Louisville, Kentucky; Miami, Florida; Charleston, West Virginia; Sumter, South Carolina; East St. Louis, Illinois; Nashville, Tennessee; Atlanta, Georgia; and Durham, North Carolina. The Greensboro sit-ins are important as a unique link in a long chain of sit-ins. Although this book will concentrate on the uniqueness of the Greensboro link, there were important similarities in the entire chain. Previous studies have presented accounts of most of the earlier sit-ins, but without due appreciation of their scope, connections, and extensive organizational base.[51]

The early sit-ins were initiated by direct action organizations. From interviews with participants in the early sit-ins and from published works, I found that civil rights organizations initiated sit-ins in fifteen of the sixteen cities I have identified.[52] The NAACP, primarily its Youth Councils, either initiated or co-initiated sit-ins in nine of the fifteen cities. CORE, usually working with the NAACP, played an important initiating role in seven. The SCLC initiated one case and was involved in another with CORE and FOR. Finally, the Durham Committee on Negro Affairs, working with the NAACP, initiated sit-ins in Durham. From these data we can conclude that the early sit-ins were a result of a multifaceted organizational effort.

Those sit-ins received substantial backing from their respective communities. The black church was the chief institutional force behind the sit-ins; nearly all of the direct action organizations that initiated them were closely associated with the church. The church supplied those organizations with not only an established communication network but also leaders and organized masses, finances, and a safe environment in which to hold political meetings. Direct action organizations clung to the church because their survival depended on it.

Not all black churches supported the sit-ins, and many tried to keep their support "invisible." Clara Luper, the organizer of the 1958 Oklahoma City sit-ins, wrote that the black church did not want to get involved, but church leaders told organizers "we could meet in their churches. They would take up a collection for us and make announcements concerning our worthwhile activities."[53] Interviewed activists revealed that clusters of churches were usually directly involved with the sit-ins. In addition to community support generated through the churches, the activists also received support from parents of those participating in demonstrations.

The early sit-ins were organized by established leaders of the black community. The leaders did not spontaneously emerge in response to a crisis but were organizational actors in the fullest sense. Some sit-in leaders were also church leaders, taught school, and headed the local direct action organization; their extensive organizational linkages gave them access to a pool of individuals to serve as demonstrators. Clara Luper wrote, "The fact that I was teaching American History at Dungee High School in Spencer, Oklahoma, and was a member of the First Street Baptist Church furnished me with an ample number of young people who would become the nucleus of the Youth Council."[54] Mrs. Luper's case is not isolated. Leaders of the early sit-ins were enmeshed in organizational networks and were integral members of the black community.

Rational planning was evident in this early wave of sit-ins. As we have seen, during the late 1950s the Reverends James Lawson and Kelly Miller Smith, both leaders of Nashville Christian Leadership Council, formed what they called a "nonviolent workshop." In them Lawson meticulously taught local college students the philosophy and tactics of nonviolent protest. In 1959 those students held "test" sit-ins in two department stores. Earlier, in 1957, members of the Oklahoma City NAACP Youth Council created what they called their "project," whose aim was to eliminate segregation in public accommodations.[55] The project comprised various committees and groups that planned sit-in strategies. After a year of planning, the project group walked into the local Katz Drug Store and initiated a sit-in. In 1955 William Clay organized an NAACP Youth Council in St. Louis. Through careful planning and twelve months of demonstrations, its members were able to desegregate dining facilities at department stores.[56] In Durham, North Carolina, in 1958 black activists of the Durham Committee on Negro Affairs conducted a survey of "five-and-dime" stores in Durham.[57] It revealed that such stores were heavily dependent on black trade. Clearly, the sit-ins in Durham were based on rational planning.

Rational planning was evident in CORE's sit-ins during the late 1950s. CORE prepared for more direct action, including sit-ins, by conducting interracial workshops in Miami in September 1959 and January 1960. Dr. King assisted in the training of young people in one of the CORE workshops. In April 1959 a newly formed Miami CORE group began conducting sit-ins at downtown variety store lunch counters.[58] In July 1959 James Robinson, writing to affiliated CORE groups and others, stated: "You have probably read in the newspaper about the dramatic all-day sit-ins which Miami CORE has conducted at a number of lunch counters. Up to 50 people have participated at many of these sit-ins."[59] In early September 1959 CORE conducted a sixteen-day workshop on direct action in Miami, called the September Action Institute. Robinson wrote of it: "The discussion of the theory and techniques of nonviolent direct action will become understandable to all Institute members precisely because their actual participation in action projects will illuminate what otherwise might remain intangible."[60] While the institute was in session, sit-ins were conducted at the lunch counters of Jackson's–Byrons Department Store. According to

Gordon Carey of CORE, "Six days of continuous sit-ins caused the owners of the lunch counter concession to close temporarily while considering a change of policy."[61] Immediately following that store's closing,
CORE activists began sitting in at Grant's Department Store. Carey
wrote: "We sat at the lunch counter from three to six hours daily until
the 2-week Institute ended on September 20."[62] On September 19, 1959,
officials of the Jackson's-Byrons Store informed CORE that Negroes
would be served as of September 21. Four black CORE members went
to the store on September 21 but were refused service. Carey's account
continues:

> *Miami CORE determined to return to Jackson's–Byrons every day.*
> *The lunch counter has about 40 seats: On September 23 we had 40*
> *persons sitting-in. It is not easy to get 40 persons on a weekday to sit-*
> *in from 10 A.M. till 3 P.M.,* but we maintained the demonstrations
> throughout the week. One woman who sat with us daily, works
> nights from 10 P.M. to 6 A.M. Cab drivers and off-duty Negro police-
> men joined us at the counter.[63]

On September 25, 1959, city officials in Miami began arresting CORE
members, and local whites physically attacked the protesters. Carey was
told to be "out of Miami by Monday." Yet, Carey reports, "That day
we had 80 persons sitting-in—half of them at Grant's."[64] The Grant's
store closed rather than serve blacks. On November 12, 1959, CORE
made plans to sit in at the "white" waiting room of the Greenville, South
Carolina, airport. The action was planned to protest the fact that the
black baseball star Jackie Robinson had been ordered to leave the
"white" waiting room a few days earlier. On January 23, just ten days
before the famous sit-in at Greensboro, North Carolina, the CORE organization in Sumter, South Carolina, reported that its teenage group
was "testing counter service at dime store: manager says he plans to
make a change."[65] Again, the action in Sumter had long-range planning
behind it: A year earlier, at CORE's National meeting of 1959, the Sumter group had reported that students were involved in its activities. The
Sumter CORE organization also had expressed the opinion that "emphasis should be on students and children. In future projects [we] hope
to attack employment in 10¢ stores, food stores and chain stores."[66]

In the summer of 1959 the SCLC, CORE, and FOR jointly held a
nonviolent workshop on the campus of Spelman College in Atlanta.
When the conference ended, James Robinson, Executive Secretary of
CORE, along with the Reverend Wyatt Walker, James McCain, Professor Guy Hershberger, and Elmer Newfield, headed for Dabbs, a segregated restaurant in Atlanta. This interracial group shocked everyone
by sitting down and eating. In a CORE news release, James Robinson
humorously wrote: "We all had agreed that it was the best coffee we

had ever had—the extra tang of drinking your coffee interracially across the Georgia color bar is highly recommended!"[67] Besides providing an example for the other workshop participants, these acts of defiance showed everyone how to protest. Marvin Rich of CORE explained: "They were being demonstrated in a public form, so people would just walk by and see it. And people who didn't think things were possible saw that they were possible, and six months later, in their own home town, they may try it out."[68]

Finally, the early sit-ins were sponsored by indigenous resources of the black community; the leadership was black, the bulk of the demonstrators were black, the strategies and tactics were formulated by blacks, the finances came out of the pockets of blacks, and the psychological and spiritual support came from the black churches.

Most of the organizers of the early sit-ins knew each other and were well aware of each other's strategies of confrontation. Many of the activists belonged to the direct action wing of the NAACP. That group included such activists as Floyd McKissick, Daisy Bates, Ronald Walters, Hosea Williams, Barbara Posey, and Clara Luper, who thought of themselves as a distinct group because the national NAACP was usually disapproving or at best ambivalent about their direct action approach.

The NAACP activists built networks that bypassed the conservative channels and organizational positions of their superiors. At NAACP meetings and conferences they sought out situations where they could freely present their plans and desires to engage in confrontational politics and exchange information about strategies. Once acquainted, the activists remained in touch by phone and mail.

Thus it is no accident that sit-ins occurred between 1957 and 1960. Other instances of "direct action" also occurred during this period. Daisy Bates led black students affiliated with her NAACP Youth Council into the all-white Little Rock Central High School and forced President Eisenhower to send in federal troops. CORE, beginning to gain a foothold in the South, had the explicit goal of initiating direct action projects. We have already noted that CORE activists were in close contact with other activists of the period. Although the early sit-ins and related activities were not part of a grandiose scheme, they were tied together through organizational and personal networks.

The Sit-in Cluster of the late 1950s

Organizational and personal networks produced the first cluster of sit-ins in Oklahoma in 1958. In August 1958 the NAACP Youth Council of Wichita, Kansas, headed by Ronald Walters, initiated sit-ins at the lunch counters of a local drug store.[69] At the same time Clara Luper and the young people in her NAACP Youth Council were training to conduct sit-ins in Oklahoma City. The adult leaders of the two groups knew each other: They worked for the same organization, so several members of the two groups traded numerous phone calls to exchange information and discuss mutual support. Direct contact was important, because the local press often refused to cover the sit-ins. Less than a week after Wichita, Clara Luper's group in Oklahoma City initiated its planned sit-ins.

Shortly thereafter sit-ins were conducted in Tulsa, Enid, and Still-water, Oklahoma. Working through CORE and the local NAACP Youth Council, Clara Luper's friend Shirley Scaggins organized the sit-ins in Tulsa.[70] Mrs. Scaggins had recently lived in Oklahoma City and knew the details of Mrs. Luper's sit-in project. The two leaders worked in concert. At the same time the NAACP Youth Council in Enid began to conduct sit-ins. Mr. Mitchell, who led that group, knew Mrs. Luper well.[71] He had visited the Oklahoma Youth Council at the outset of its sit-in and had discussed sit-in tactics and mutual support. The Still-water sit-ins appear to have been conducted independently by black college students.

The network that operated in Wichita and several Oklahoma communities reached as far as East St. Louis, Illinois. Homer Randolph, who in late 1958 organized the East St. Louis sit-ins, had previously lived in Oklahoma City, knew Mrs. Luper well, and had young relatives who participated in the Oklahoma City sit-ins.

In short, the first sit-in cluster occurred in Oklahoma in 1958 and spread to cities within a 100-mile radius through established organizational and personal networks. The majority of these early sit-ins were (1) connected rather than isolated, (2) initiated through organizations and personal ties, (3) rationally planned and led by established leaders, and (4) supported by indigenous resources. Thus, the Greensboro sit-ins of February 1960 did not mark the movement's beginning but were a critical link in the chain, triggering sit-ins across the South at an incredible pace. What happened in the black community between the late 1950s and the early 1960s to produce such a movement?

In my view the early sit-ins did not give rise to a massive sit-in movement before 1960 because CORE and the NAACP Youth Council did not have a mass base. The SCLC, which did have a mass base, had not developed fully. Besides, direct action was just emerging as the dominant strategy during the late 1950s.

As the SCLC developed into a Southwide direct action organization between 1957 and 1960, it provided the mass base capable of sustaining a heavy volume of collective action. It augmented the activities of CORE and the NAACP Youth Councils, because they were closely tied to the church. Thus the SCLC, closely interlocked with NAACP Youth Councils and CORE chapters, had developed solid movement centers by late 1959. The centers usually had the following seven characteristics:

1. A cadre of social change–oriented ministers and their congregations. Often one minister would become the local leader of a given center, and his church would serve as the coordinating unit.

2. Direct action organizations of varied complexity. In many cities local churches served as quasi-direct action organizations, while in others ministers built complex church-related organizations (e.g. United Defense League of Baton Rouge, Montgomery Improvement Association, Alabama Christian Movement for Human Rights of Birmingham, Petersburg Improvement Association). NAACP Youth Councils and CORE affiliates also were components of the local centers.

3. Indigenous financing coordinated through the church.

4. Weekly mass meetings, which served as forums where local residents were informed of relevant information and strategies regarding the movement. These meetings also built solidarity among the participants.

5. Dissemination of nonviolent tactics and strategies. The leaders articulated to the black community the message that social change would occur only through nonviolent direct action carried out by masses.

6. Adaptation of a rich church culture to political purposes. The black spirituals, sermons, and prayers were used to deepen the participants' commitment to the struggle.

7. A mass-based orientation, rooted in the black community, through the church.

From the perspective of this study, the period between the 1950s bus boycotts and the 1960 sit-ins provided pivotal resources for the emerging civil rights movement. My analysis emphasizes that the organizational foundation of the civil rights movement was built during this period, and active local movement centers were created in numerous Southern black communities. The next chapter will demonstrate that those movement centers were the new force enabling the 1960 sit-ins to become a mass movement and a tactical innovation within the movement.

1960: ORIGINS OF A DECADE OF DISRUPTION

Nineteen sixty was the year when thousands of Southern black students at black colleges joined forces with "old movement warriors" and tremendously increased the power of the developing civil rights movement. Between February 1 and April 1, 1960, students were involved in lunch counter sit-in demonstrations in approximately seventy Southern cities. It is significant that by 1960 Dr. King was only thirty-one years of age, and the average age of the top SCLC leaders was close to that. The youthfulness of those leaders suggested to black college students that they themselves should become more directly involved in the fight for their own liberation. Moreover, it was widely known in college circles that the courageous protesters in the Little Rock crisis of 1957 were high school students. From the privileged position of hindsight, it is clear that the student sit-ins of 1960 were the introduction to a decade of political turbulence.

This chapter will explore how the student sit-ins of 1960 rapidly evolved into a mass protest that strengthened the civil rights movement and its organizational base; gave rise to the Student Non-violent Coordinating Committee (SNCC), a major student civil rights organization; and gave rise to the modern white student movement of the early 1960s. The first step in explaining this complex set of phenomena is to investigate why black educational institutions and students were ideal candidates for involvement in the movement.

BLACK EDUCATIONAL INSTITUTIONS
AND THE MOVEMENT

The term "black educational institutions" rather than "black colleges" is more fitting here, because elementary and high school, college, seminary, and university students were involved in the movement. Most of the analysis will focus on black colleges, however, because they were responsible for the bulk of the protest activities, but high school students also played an important role.

Black educational institutions were important to the movement because they, like the church, comprised organized groups with developed communication networks and skilled student leaders. Indeed, student governments, fraternities, sororities, kinship and friendship networks, and theological seminaries linked students, making the schools ideal organizations for rapid mobilization to occur. Several studies have shown that students who participated in the movement were more likely than nonparticipants to belong to these networks.[1]

There was, however, an important difference between the schools and the churches. Most of the schools relied on financial support supplied by the white power structure. This meant that if the schools' administrations supported the movement their funds could be withdrawn. Dr. Mays, former president of Morehouse College stated the situation succinctly: "If you knew that the legislature, with no Negroes in at all, have got to decide on what you get, how you expect a bunch of radicalism coming out of that?"[2] Rather than support the movement, therefore many of the teachers and administrators attempted to block it from taking root on the campuses.

Nevertheless, the schools housed a group relatively free of those pressures—the students. Students are ideal candidates for protest activities. Usually they do not have families to support, employers' rules and dictates to follow, or crystallized notions of what is "impossible" and "unrealistic." Students have free time and boundless energy to pursue causes they consider worthwhile and imperative.[3] But most of all, students were available for protest because, like the ministers, they were an organized group within the black community who were relatively independent of white economic control.

STUDENTS AND MOVEMENT CENTERS

Most scholars of the 1960 sit-ins have consistently argued that they were a product of an independent student-initiated movement. But many of the students were in fact deeply involved with the movement centers already discussed here. This was inevitable given the historical close ties of black educational institutions with the churches. Indeed, many of the colleges were established by black churches. In many cases the churches that made up the movement centers had large student memberships and were referred to as college churches. We have already seen that students were closely tied to the centers in Nashville, Shreveport, Petersburg, Sumter, and elsewhere.

In this analysis of the sit-in movement it will be demonstrated that the student sit-ins were rapidly spread by student leaders and leaders of the movement centers working in concert. It will be shown that in many instances it was the leaders of the movement centers who organized the student protesters. The tie between the students and the centers is crucial because of the atmosphere of intense repression in which the sit-ins spread. Without the mobilization of the black community by the centers, it is doubtful that the spread of the sit-ins could have been sustained.

THE 1960 STUDENT SIT-INS

In the South during the 1950s segregation laws prohibited blacks and whites from eating together.[4] In stores such as Woolworth's and Kresge's Southern blacks could shop but could not eat at the segregated lunch counters. On February 1, 1960, four black freshmen students at North Carolina Agricultural and Technical College in Greensboro violated the law by taking seats at the segregated lunch counter of the local Woolworth store and asked to be served. Within weeks similar sit-ins were rapidly spreading across the South. Between February 1 and March 1, 1960, sit-in protests had occurred at segregated lunch counters in eleven cities in North Carolina; seven in Virginia; four in South Carolina; three in Florida; two in Tennessee; two in Alabama; one in Kentucky; and one in Maryland. In the month of March sit-ins continued to spread within these states, and by the end of the month they had spread to cities in Georgia, Texas, Ohio, West Virginia, Louisiana, and Arkansas. This chapter will analyze the first two months of the sit-ins, which provide a good sense of the underlying social dynamics.

The Greensboro Connection

On February 1, 1960, Ezell Blair, Jr., Franklin McCain, Joe McNeil, and David Richmond, all students at North Carolina A. and T., sat in at the Woolworth's lunch counter in Greensboro. Many commentators, as noted, mark this as the first sit-in, the four protesters knew that they were not the first to sit in in the state of North Carolina. Sit-in activity in the state had begun in the late 1950s, when a young black attorney named Floyd McKissick; a young Board member of the SCLC, the Reverend Douglas Moore; and a small group of other young people, including a few whites from Duke University, began conducting sit-ins in Durham.[5]

The early Durham sit-ins were part of the network of sit-ins that occurred between 1957 and 1960. The activists involved in the early sit-ins belonged to the NAACP Youth Division, which McKissick headed, and to their own organization, the Durham Committee on Negro Affairs. During the late 1950s McKissick and Moore's group conducted sit-ins in local bus station waiting rooms, parks, hotels, and other places. In 1957 Reverend Moore and others were arrested for sitting in at a local ice cream parlor. The subsequent legal case became known as the "Royal Ice Cream Case." McKissick, who also headed the local Boy Scout organization, periodically took the young "all-American" scouts into segregated restaurants and ordered food.

The four students who sat in at Greensboro and sparked the widespread sit-in movements had been members of the NAACP Youth Council headed by McKissick and had ties with Dr. George Simpkins, who headed the local NAACP chapter in Greensboro.[6] McKissick recalls that he knew them all well, and they knew all about the Durham activities. Martin Oppenheimer, an early sociologist-historian of the sit-ins, concurs: "All of the boys were, or at some time had been, members of an NAACP Youth Council."[7] Indeed, the four students had participated in numerous meetings in social action–oriented churches in Durham. The Durham churches that constituted the movement centers included Union Baptist, pastored by the Reverend Grady Davis; Ashbury Temple, pastored by the Reverend Douglas Moore; Mount Zion, pastored by Reverend Fuller; St. Mark's, pastored by Reverend Speaks; and St. Josephs, pastored by the Reverend Melvin Swann. Involvement with the NAACP Youth Council meant that the four students not only were informed about the Durham sit-ins but also knew about many of the other sit-ins conducted before 1960. Thus, the myth that four college students got up one day and on impulse went to sit in at Woolworth's— and sparked a movement—is not supported by the evidence.

The national office of the NAACP and many conservative ministers refused to back the Greensboro sit-ins.[8] The NAACP's renowned team of lawyers did not defend the "Greensboro Four." Nevertheless, on the same day they sat in, the students got in touch with a lawyer whom they considered their friend, and Floyd McKissick became the counsel for the "Greensboro Four." The network of college students and adult activists was in business.

Well-forged networks existed between and among black churches and colleges in North Carolina, facilitated by the large number of colleges concentrated in the state. Indeed, ten black colleges existed within a ten-mile radius of Greensboro.[9] Interactions between colleges and churches were frequent and intense. A number of North Carolina churches were referred to as "college churches" because they had large student memberships. These two sets of social organizations were also linked through college seminaries, where black ministers received their theological training.

The church–student networks enabled activist-oriented students to become familiar with the emerging civil rights movements through local movement centers and enabled adult activists to tap the organizational resources of the colleges. In North Carolina leaders of student governments and other campus groups facilitated student mobilization because they, like the ministers, had organizing skills and access to numbers of people. The concentration of colleges in the state provided an extensive network of contacts. Fraternity and sorority chapters linked students within and between campuses, as did dating patterns and cultural and athletic events. Finally, intercollegiate kinship and friendship networks were widespread.

Of course, black communities across North Carolina also could be rapidly mobilized through the churches, which were linked through ministerial alliances and other networks. By 1960 these diverse and interlocking networks were capable of being politicized and coordinated through existing movement centers, making North Carolina a logical setting for the rapid statewide diffusion of collective action.

Beyond Greensboro

Shortly after the sit-ins started in Greensboro, the network of movement centers was activated. In the first week of February 1960 students continued to sit in daily at the local Woolworth's, and the protest population began to grow. The original four protesters were joined by hundreds of students from North Carolina A. and T. and several other local black colleges. Black high school students and a few white college students also joined the protest. Influential local whites decided to close the Woolworth's in Greensboro, hoping to take the steam out of the developing mass movement. It was too late.

Floyd McKissick, the Reverend Douglas Moore, and others who had conducted previous sit-ins formulated plans to spread the movement across the state. They were joined by CORE's white field secretary, Gordon Carey, whose services had been requested by the local NAACP president, Dr. George Simpkins. Carey, with his knowledge of nonviolent resistance and his earlier contact with movement centers in Southern black communities, was a sound choice. He arrived in Durham from New York on February 7 and went directly to McKissick's home, where the sit-ins were being planned.

On February 8—exactly one week after the Greensboro sit-ins—the demonstrations spread to nearby Durham and Winston-Salem. McKissick, Moore, Carey, and others helped organize those protests by bringing students from local colleges to churches, where they were trained to conduct sit-ins. The Durham students were trained at the same churches through which McKissick and Moore had planned direct action in the late 1950s. Following training and strategy sessions, the students went to the local lunch counters and sat in.

The organizing effort was not confined to the two nearby cities. Within the first week of the Greensboro sit-ins McKissick, Carey, and Reverend Moore made contact with activists in movement centers throughout North Carolina, South Carolina, and Virginia, urging them to train students for sit-ins. They not only phoned these activists but traveled to various cities to provide assistance. Upon arrival they often found sit-in planning sessions already under way. According to Carey, "when we reached these cities we went directly to the movement-oriented churches," because "that's where the protest activities were being planned and organized."[10] So sit-ins were largely organized at the movement churches rather than on the campuses. To understand the sit-in movement, one must abandon the assumption that it was a college phenomenon. As Reverend Moore said early in the campaign, "If Woolworth and other stores think this is just another panty raid, they haven't had their sociologists in the field recently."[11] The sit-ins grew out of a context of organized movement centers.

As anticipated, the SCLC was essential to the rise of the 1960 sit-in movement. When Reverend Moore and other organizers visited churches in the Carolinas and Virginia, they found church leaders already training students for sit-ins. Regarding the ministers who headed those movement churches, Carey said, "All of these ministers were active in the Southern Christian Leadership Conference. At least 75 percent were getting inspiration from King."[12] The same ministers also had contacts with and often were leaders of both CORE and the activist wing of the NAACP.

The movement centers, already in place, served as both receiving and transmitting "antennas" for the sit-ins. As receivers they gathered information on the sit-ins, and as transmitters they rebroadcast information throughout the networks. Because this internal network already existed, information was rapidly channeled to groups prepared to engage in nonviolent collective action.

During the second week of February 1960 plans were formulated to conduct sit-ins in a number of Southern cities. Communication and co-ordination among cities was intensified. Early in the second week of February, for example, the Reverend B. Elton Cox of High Point, North Carolina, and the Reverend C. A. Ivory of Rock Hill, South Carolina, informed McKissick and other leaders by telephone that their groups were "ready to go."[13] Cox's group sat in on February 11 and Ivory's on February 12. Reverend Ivory organized and directed the Rock Hill sit-ins from a wheelchair. Moreover, during February and March 1960 James McCain of CORE traveled across South Carolina organizing students to conduct sit-ins. McCain recalled, "Right after the Greensboro sit-ins I visited Claflin College [Orangeburg], Morris College [Sumter], and Friendship College [Rock Hill] and helped organize the sit-ins."[14] McCain emphasized that in each locale he worked closely with the cadre of ministers associated with direct action and the SCLC.[15] Within the week, sit-ins were being conducted in several cities in Virginia, most of them organized through the dense network of SCLC movement centers in the state.[16] For example, the Petersburg sit-ins were organized at the Reverend Wyatt Walker's Gillfield Baptist Church, and the demonstrations occurred at the same public library that Walker had attempted to desegregate in 1959.[17]

The movement hot lines reached far beyond the seaboard states of North Carolina, South Carolina, and Virginia. The Reverend Fred Shuttlesworth, an active leader of the Birmingham movement center, happened to be in North Carolina when the first wave of sit-ins occurred, fulfilling a speaking engagement for Reverend Cox, the leader of the High Point sit-ins. According to Shuttlesworth, Cox "carried me by where these people were going to sit-in. . . . I called back to Atlanta and told Ella [Baker] what was going on. I said, 'this is the thing. You must tell Martin [King] that we must get with this, and really this can shake up the world.' "[18] Baker, the Executive Director of the SCLC, immediately began calling her numerous contacts at various colleges to ask, "What are you all going to do? It is time to move."[19] In Montgomery student leaders from Alabama State College met at the home of the MIA president, Ralph Abernathy, and together they planned and organized the Montgomery's sit-ins.[20] Dr. C. O. Simpkins, who headed the local SCLC affiliate in Shreveport, traveled to Bishop and Wyler Colleges in Marshall, Texas, and organized sit-ins. In Simpkins's words, "We went to Wyler College and got students involved there and Bishop College. We got them involved in the sit-ins."[21] In Birmingham students met at Shuttlesworth's home to plan the sit-ins.[22] In Little Rock Daisy Bates, who headed the local NAACP Youth Council, sent cars to Philander Smith College to pick up students, whom she then trained to conduct sit-ins.[23] In Tallahassee the sit-ins were organized by Patricia Due, who headed the local CORE chapter and was a student at Florida A. and M. University. The CORE chapter worked closely with the Reverend C. K. Steele and the Inter Civic Council (ICC). In fact, the ICC served as the headquarters when the sit-ins were organized. Three of Reverend Steele's children participated in the original Tallahassee sit-ins.[24]

Carey and Reverend Moore phoned the movement center in Nashville to ask Reverend Lawson if his people were ready to move. The student and church communities coordinated by the Nashville Christian Leadership Conference answered in the affirmative. Lawson has recalled:

> Of course there was organizing because after the sit-ins, the first one in February, people like Doug Moore, Ella Baker, myself, did call around to places that we knew and said, "Can you start? Are you ready? Can you go? And how can we help you?" So there was some of that too that went on. Even there the sit-in movement did not just spread spontaneously. I mean there was a readiness. And then there were . . . phone calls that went out to various communities where we knew people and where we knew student groups and where we knew minister groups, and said, you know, "This is it, let's go."[25]

Reverend Lawson offered his thoughts on why the sit-in movement occurred:

> Because King and the Montgomery boycott and the whole development of that leadership that clustered around King had emerged and was ready and was preaching and teaching direct action, nonviolent action and was clearly ready to act, ready to seed any movement that needed sustenance and growth. So there was . . . in other words the soil had been prepared.[26]

The facts and recollections assembled here provide insight into how a political movement can rapidly spread between geographically distant communities. The sit-ins spread across the South in a short period because activists, working through local movement centers, planned, coordinated, and sustained them. They spread despite the swinging billy clubs of policemen, despite Ku Klux Klansmen, white mobs, murderers, tear gas, and economic reprisals.[27] The preexisting movement centers provided the resources and organization required to sustain the sit-ins in the face of opposition.

This analysis of the sit-ins breaks with previous research. As noted in Chapter Eight, previous studies maintain that the sit-ins were either student-initiated without assistance from previously established organizations, or else that the preexisting organizations simply responded by jumping on the student bandwagon.[28] The argument put forth here is that adult activists—Ella Baker, Martin Luther King Jr., Douglas Moore, Floyd McKissick, Wyatt Walker, Ralph Abernathy, Fred Shuttlesworth, James McCain, Gordon Carey, C. O. Simpkins, Daisy Bates, James Lawson, C. T. Vivian, C. K. Steele, and many others—were directly engaged in planning, executing, and sustaining the 1960 sit-ins. Many of them went directly to local colleges and organized sit-ins; others phoned preexisting activist groups within and across state borders, encouraging them to initiate sit-ins. These activists were affiliated with existing civil rights organizations and were integral members of movement centers.

The historical record, as examined in the present study, does not support the dominant view that the SCLC was a symbolic, amorphous, and nonfunctional organization. The SCLC, assisted by CORE and the NAACP Youth Councils, spearheaded the organization of movement centers that enabled the sit-ins to take hold as a tactical innovation. Adam Fairclough's study of the SCLC also reached the conclusion that the SCLC's affiliates were crucial to the 1960 sit-ins.[29] In support of his conclusion he quotes William H. Peace, a student leader in the Raleigh sit-ins, who stated that the SCLC affiliates, "working in close conjunction with the Negro church, became the backbone of the student movement."[30] Thus during the 1960 sit-ins the movement centers of the South were accomplishing the goals for which they were created—generating and sustaining collective action.

The Sit-in Clusters of 1960

The organizational and personal networks that produced the first cluster of sit-ins in Oklahoma in 1958 have already been described. The cluster concept can be applied to the entire set of sit-ins of February and March 1960. Many of the sit-ins that occurred can be grouped by geographic and temporal proximity. A cluster can be defined as two or more cities within a 75-mile radius where sit-in activity took place within a span of fourteen days. Indeed, forty-one of the sixty-nine cities having sit-ins during this two-month period meet these criteria. In February 76 percent of the cities having sit-ins were part of clusters, whereas for March the percentage dropped to 44 percent; for the two month period overall, it was 59 percent.

The clustering differentials between the two months can be explained by taking region into account. In February 85 percent of the cities experiencing sit-ins were located in Southeastern, Seaboard, and border states. This pattern had been established earlier, when most of the pre-1960 sit-ins occurred in border states. The reason in both cases was that repression against blacks was not as severe in border and sea-board states as in the deep South, which made it possible for activists outside the deep South to build dense networks of movement centers. We have already seen that North Carolina, South Carolina, and Virginia had numerous social action churches and direct action organizations. By the time the sit-ins occurred in Virginia, the SCLC had affiliates throughout the state, and the Reverend Wyatt Walker, who was the leader of Virginia's movement centers, was also the state director of CORE and president of the local NAACP. Similar patterns existed in the other states. Small wonder that in the month of February 73 percent of cities having sit-ins were in Virginia, North Carolina, and South Carolina. Those cities produced 88 percent of the February clusters. This clustering reflected both the great density of movement centers and a system of domination less stringent than that of the deep South.

In March a change took place: The majority of the sit-ins occurred in cities of the deep South. With a few exceptions, the sit-ins in the deep South did not occur in clusters. They occurred almost exclusively in cities where movement centers were already established: Montgomery, Birmingham, Baton Rouge, New Orleans, Tallahassee, Nashville, Memphis, Atlanta, and Savannah. Repression would have been too great on student protesters operating outside the protection of such centers in the deep South. On March 9, 1960, King sent a telegram to President Eisenhower describing the repression:

> A reign of terror has broken out in Montgomery, Alabama. Gestapo-like methods are being used by police and city authorities to intimidate Negroes who have been pursuing peaceful and non-violent techniques. . . . While students of Alabama State College were convened in an orderly protest on this campus, city officials and police launched an incredible assault, and infiltrated the college campus with police armed with rifles, shotguns, and tear gas. . . . Telephones are being tapped and telephones of Negro leaders are left disconnected so that they cannot make or receive calls.[31]

Pointing to the centrality of movement centers in this repressive environment, the Reverend Bernard Lee, a leading student organizer of the Montgomery sit-ins, recalled:

> We were very fortunate to have an organization [MIA] committed to nonviolence, committed to some discipline, and a tactic for social change, that could give guidance to babes out there facing wolves. . . . In some other areas where there were attempts at sit-ins [but no] adult black organization in the community . . . the students

ultimately had to quickly disband the activities, and many of them never got off the ground, simply because of that reason.[32]

Thus, the decrease in clustering in the deep South reflected both the high level of repression and the absence of dense networks of movement centers. Focusing on the internal movement centers enables us to explain both the clustering phenomenon and its absence.

The large proportion of sit-ins occurring in clusters invites the conclusion that they did not spread randomly. The clusters represented the social and temporal space in which sit-ins were organized, coordinated, spread, and financed by the black community. Within these clusters, cars filled with organizers from the SCLC, the NAACP, and CORE raced between sit-in points relaying valuable information. Telephone lines and the community "grapevine" sent forth protest instructions and plans. These clusters were the sites of numerous midday and late night meetings, where the black community assembled in the churches, planned mass boycotts of downtown merchants, filled the collection plates, and vowed to mortgage their homes to raise the necessary bail money in case the protesting students were jailed. The work force of the mass-based black church mobilized the resources necessary for collective action. Black lawyers pledged their legal services to the movement, and black physicians made treatment available to injured demonstrators. Amid these exciting scenes black spirituals that had grown out of slavery reinforced the participants' poise and deepened their commitment to black liberation. A detailed view of the Nashville sit-ins provides an example of these dynamics, because the Nashville movement epitomized the sit-ins, whether they occurred singly or in clusters.

The Nashville Sit-in Movement

As discussed in the previous chapter, a well-developed, church-based movement center headed by the Reverend Kelly Miller Smith was organized in Nashville during the late 1950s. The Reverend James Lawson, an expert tactician of nonviolent protest, was in charge of the NCLC's direct action committee. Lawson received a call from the Reverend Douglas Moore about two days after the Greensboro sit-ins began. The Nashville group was ready to act, as a cadre of students had already received training in nonviolent direct action and had conducted "test sit-ins" in two large department stores in downtown Nashville before the 1959 Christmas holidays. Moreover, the group had already made plans in late 1959 to begin continuous sit-ins in 1960 with the stated intention of desegregating Nashville.[33] Thus Greensboro provided the impetus for the Nashville group to carry out its preexisting strategy.

Reverend Smith's First Baptist Church became the coordinating unit of the Nashville sit-in movement. A decision to sit in at local lunch counters on Saturday, February 13, 1960, was reached after much debate. The adults (mostly ministers) of the NCLC met with the students at movement headquarters and tried to persuade them to postpone the demonstrations for a couple of days until money could be raised. According to Reverend Smith, the "NCLC had $87.50 in the treasury. We had no lawyers, and we felt kind of parental responsibility for those college kids. And we knew they were gonna be put in jail, and we didn't know what else would happen. And so some of us said, 'we need to wait until we get a lawyer, until we raise some funds.' "[34]

NCLC leaders told the students that the money could be collected through the churches within a week. Then, according to Reverend Smith,

> James Bevel, then a student at American Baptist Theological Seminary, said that, "I'm sick and tired of waiting," which was a strange thing to come from a kid who was only about nineteen years old. You see, the rest of us were older. [Bevel said], "If you asked us to wait until next week, then next week something would come up and you'd say wait until the next week and maybe we never will get our freedom." He said this, "I believe that something will happen in the situation that will make for the solution to some of these problems we're talking about." So we decided to go on.[35]

Here we see the students playing a catalytic role in the organization of sit-ins, for in some instances they were willing to take risks sooner than the adults. By the same token, we see adult activists quickly agreeing with the students and committing their organizational skills and resources to the effort.

The proximity of four black institutions in Nashville facilitated the mobilization of large numbers of students. In its extensive ties between students and churches, Nashville resembled the State of North Carolina. Indeed, John Lewis, James Bevel, and Bernard Lafayette, who became sit-in leaders, were students at the American Baptist Theological Seminary, where they took courses from Reverend Smith. Furthermore, they were student leaders:

> John Lewis, Bernard and myself were the major participants in the seminary. All of us were like the top student leaders in our schools. I think John at the time was the president of the Student Council. I was

a member of the Student Council. I was one of the editors of the year-book. So all of us were like the top leaders in our school.[36]

The student leaders could rapidly mobilize other students, because they already had access to organized groups. Other writers have pointed out that college networks were critical to sit-in mobilization.[37] However, the sit-in movement cannot be explained without also noting the crucial interaction between black college students and local movement centers. Speaking of Reverend Smith and his church, Bevel recalled that "the First Baptist basically had the Baptist people who went to Fisk and Meharry and Tennessee State, and the Seminary were basically members of his church."[38] The students had been introduced to the civil rights movement when they attended church.

On the first day of the sit-ins in Nashville, students gathered in front of their respective campuses. The NCLC sent cars to each college to transport the students to Reverend Smith's church. Again, the main organizational tasks were performed in the church, which served as the coordinating unit of the local movement center, rather than on the campuses. Coordination of sit-in activity between the college community and the churches was simplified by the fact that many of the students (especially student leaders) were already immersed in the local movement centers prior to the sit-ins. The pattern of close connection between student demonstrators and adult leaders had already shown itself in such places as Greensboro and even Oklahoma City in 1958; indeed, this pattern undergirded the entire movement. The Baton Rouge sit-in demonstrators "were schooled right over there at our church; they were sent out from here to go to the lunch counters," Reverend Jemison recalled. "The student leaders attended church here. We had close ties because they were worshipping with us while we were working together."[39]

At the movement headquarters the Nashville students participated in workshops, where they learned the strategies of nonviolent confrontation from experts like Reverend Lawson, the Reverend Metz Rollins, the Reverend C. T. Vivian, and the core group of students that Lawson had already trained. This pool of trained leaders was a preexisting resource harbored by the NCLC. After the workshops the students were organized into groups with specific protest responsibilities, each having a spokesperson who had been trained by Lawson during the late 1950s. They then marched off to confront Nashville's segregated lunch counters and agents of social control.

High school students were involved in the Nashville sit-ins, as they had been in those in High Point and Chapel Hill, North Carolina, where no black colleges existed. In Nashville the high schoolers swelled the ranks of the hundreds of college demonstrators. Cordell Reagon, a high

school organizer in 1960, explained the high school students' participation in the Nashville sit-ins:

> Well, demonstrations were going on in Nashville. There were some
> high school students who wanted to participate and wanted to do
> something, 'cause we thought it would be fun if for no other reason.
> We didn't have any politics, but we wanted to do something.[40]

Reagon recalled that college students did not want the high school students involved in their sit-ins. College students argued that high school
students were too undisciplined to participate in carefully orchestrated
demonstrations. But, according to Reagon:

> In order for [college students] to go downtown they would have to
> come right by our school. So they went on their march and when they
> went by our school we just turned school out and went on the dem-
> onstration anyhow. They didn't try to stop us this time, because the
> demonstration was already in progress.[41]

Even high school students did not demonstrate spontaneously. When
asked, "How did all these students get involved?", Reagon, speaking of
himself and other organizers replied: "Oh, we went to the lunch room,
we went from table to table . . . and some people talked it up in their
classes through whispering and everything. And when time came forth,
we just knocked on doors and said it was time."[42]

The adult black community immediately mobilized to support the
students. Shortly after the demonstrations began, large numbers of students were arrested. Reverend Smith describes what happened:

> We just launched out on something that looked perfectly crazy and
> scores of people were being arrested, and paddy wagons were full and
> the people out in downtown couldn't understand what was going on,
> people just welcoming being arrested, that ran against everything they
> had ever seen. . . . I've forgotten how much we needed that day, and
> we got everything we needed. [That particular day?] Yes, sir. About
> $40,000. We needed something like $40,000 in fives. And we had all
> the money. Not in fives, but in bail. Every bit of it came up. You
> know—property and this kind of thing . . . and there were fourteen
> black lawyers in this town. Every black lawyer made himself available
> to us.[43]

So basic preexisting resources in the dominated community were used
to accomplish political goals. It was suggested to Reverend Smith that

a massive movement such as that in Nashville would need outside resources. He replied:

> *Now let me quickly say to you that in early 1960, when we were really out there on the line, the community stood up. We stood together. This community had proven that this stereotyped notion of black folk can't work together is just false. We worked together a lot better than the white organizations. So those people fell in line.*[44]

Reverend Smith's comments are applicable beyond Nashville. For example, in Orangeburg, South Carolina, after hundreds of students were arrested and brutalized, the adult black community came solidly to their aid. Bond was set at $200 per student, and 388 students were arrested. More than $75,000 was needed, and adults came forth to put up their homes and property in order to get students out of jail. Reverend McCollom, the leader of the Orangeburg movement center, remarked that "there was no schism between the student community and the adult community in Orangeburg."[45] Jim McCain of CORE, who played a central role in organizing sit-ins across South Carolina and in Florida, confirms that community support was widespread.[46] According to Julian Bond, a student leader of Atlanta's sit-ins, "black property owners put up bond which probably amounted to $100,000" to get sit-in demonstrators released from jail.[47]

These patterns were repeated across the South. The community support should not be surprising, considering the number of ministers and congregations involved before and during the movement. Yet Howard Zinn, an analyst of these events, has written: "Spontaneity and self-sufficiency were the hallmarks on the sit-ins; without adult advice or consent, the students planned and carried them through."[48] This erroneous conclusion illustrates the inadequacies of analyses that neglect or ignore the internal structure of oppressed communities and protest movements.

The continuing development of the Nashville sit-ins sheds further light on the interdependence of the movement and the black community. A formal structure called the Nashville Nonviolent Movement was developed to direct sit-in activities. Its two substructures, the Student Central Committee and the Nashville Christian Leadership Council, worked closely together and had overlapping membership (Reverends Lawson and Vivian were members of both groups). The Student Central Committee usually consisted of twenty-five to thirty students drawn from all the local colleges. The NCLC represented adult ministers and the black community. The two groups established committees to accomplish specific tasks, including a finance committee; a telephone, publicity, and news committee; and a work committee. The work committee had subgroups responsible for painting protest signs and providing food and transportation. The city's black lawyers became the movement's defense team, and students from Meharry Medical School were the medical team.

This intricate structure propelled and guided the sit-in movement of Nashville. A clear-cut division of labor developed between the Central Committee and the NCLC. The Central Committee's chief responsibilities were to train, organize, and coordinate the demonstration. The NCLC developed the movement's financial structure and coordinated relations between the community and the student movement. Diane Nash Bevel, a prominent student leader of the Nashville sit-ins, was asked why the students did not take care of their own finances and build their own relationships with the larger community. She replied:

> We didn't want to be bothered keeping track of money that was collected at the rallies and stuff. We were just pleased that NCLC would do that, and would handle the bookkeeping and all that trouble that went along with having money. . . . Besides, we were much too busy sitting in and going to jail and that kind of thing. There wasn't really the stability of a bookkeeper, for instance. We didn't want to be bothered with developing that kind of stability. . . . We were very pleased to form this alliance with NCLC who would sponsor the rallies and coordinate the community support among the adults and keep track of the money, while we sat in and . . . well, it took all our time, and we were really totally immersed in it. My day would sometimes start . . . well, we'd have meetings in the morning at six o'clock, before classes, and work steady to extremely late at night, organizing sit-ins, getting publicity out to the students that we were having a sit-in, and where and what time we would meet. Convincing people and talking to people, calming people's fears, going to class, at the same time. It was a really busy, busy time for all of the people on the Central Committee. We were trying to teach nonviolence, maintain order among a large, large number of people. That was about all we could handle.[49]

Although black students were able to engage in protest activities continuously because of their student status, a one- sided focus on them diverts attention from the larger community, which had undergone considerable radicalization. Speaking of the adults, James Bevel, a student organizer of the Nashville sit-ins, remarked, "But when you talk to each individual, they talked just like we talked—the students. They had jobs and they were adults. But basically, their position would be just like ours. They played different roles because they . . . had to relate based on where they were in the community."[50]

The adults of the NCLC organized the black community to support the student sit-in movement. Once the movement began, the NCLC instituted weekly and sometimes daily mass meetings in the churches. Reverend Smith recalled:

> Sometimes we had them more than once a week if we needed to. When things were really hot we called a meeting at eight o'clock in the morning. We'd call one for twelve that day, twelve noon, and the place would be full. We had what we called our wire service. People got on telephones, that was our wire service, and they would fill that building. They'd fill that building in just a matter of relatively short time.[51]

At these mass meetings ministers from across the city turned over the money that their respective churches had donated to the movement. Thousands of dollars were collected at the mass meetings, while black adults, ministers, and students sang such lyrics as, "Before I'd be a slave, I'd rather be buried in my grave." Then, too, bundles of leaflets were given to adults at mass meetings, who then distributed them throughout the black community. This shows how the movement built communication channels through which vital information, strategies, and plans were disseminated.

During the Nashville sit-ins word went out to the black community not to shop downtown. Reverend Smith recounted:

> We didn't organize the boycott. We did not organize the boycott. The boycott came about. We don't know how it happened. I tell you there are a lot of little mystical elements in there, little spots that defy rational explanation. . . . Now, we promoted it. We adopted it. But we did not sit down one day and organize a boycott . . . ninety-nine percent of the black people in this community stayed away from downtown during the boycott. It was a fantastic thing—successful. It was fantastically successful.[52]

Yet the boycott was largely organized by the NCLC. James Bevel has reported that Dr. Vivian Henderson, who was head of Fisk University's economics department and a member of the NCLC, was instrumental in the boycott:

> Vivian Henderson was basically responsible for calling the boycott. He got up at a mass meeting and said, "At least what we could do to support students, if we've got any decency, we can just stop paying bills and just don't shop until this thing is resolved." A very indignant type of speech he made. It just caught on. All the bourgeois women would come to the meeting, and they just got on the phone and called

up everybody, all the doctors' wives and things. They just got on the phone and called 300 or 400 people and told them don't shop downtown. Finally there was just a total boycott downtown. There would be no black people downtown at all.[53]

Activists were stationed downtown to ensure that blacks received the word not to shop. According to Reverend Smith, shortly after the boycott was initiated, merchants began coming to his home wanting to talk. Diane Nash Bevel attributed the boycott's effectiveness to reduced profits during the Easter shopping season. It also changed the merchants' attitude toward the sit-ins:

> It was interesting the difference that [boycott] made in terms of how the managers were willing to talk with us, because, see, we had talked with the managers of the stores. We had a meeting at the very beginning and they had kind of listened to us politely, and said, "Well, we just can't do it. We can't desegregate the counters because we will lose money and that's the end of it." So, after the economic withdrawal, they were eager to talk with us, and try to work up some solution.[54]

In early 1960 the white power structure of Nashville was forced to desegregate a number of private establishments and public transportation facilities. SNCC's Student Voice reported that in Nashville, "A long series of negotiations followed the demonstrations, and on May 10, 6 downtown stores integrated their lunch counters. Since this time others have followed suit, and some stores have hired Negroes in positions other than those of menial workers for the first time."[55] Daily demonstrations by hundreds of students, who when arrested refused to accept bond and instead remained to crowd the jails, coupled with the boycott, gave blacks the upper hand in the conflict situation. Careful organization and planning was the hallmark of the Nashville sit-in movement.

By the summer of 1960 numerous cities had desegregated their lunch counters. It was clear by then that student groups were a unique and powerful social force capable of winning victories against a seemingly entrenched establishment. Three principal reasons explain why the sit-in movement developed and was sustained. First, the sit-ins grew out of preexisting social structures, including activists groups, churches, formal movement organizations, colleges, high schools, and overlapping personal networks. Second, the data strongly suggest that the Greensboro protest generated sit-ins across the South because of the presence of a well-developed and widespread internal organization that emerged between the 1955–56 Montgomery bus boycott and the 1960 sit-ins. In short sit-ins arose as a tactical innovation within the movement in 1960 because students and seasoned activists were anchored to the same internal organization, hence able to coordinate them and spread them rapidly.

Third, the sit-ins became an important tactical innovation of the period because they were well suited to the existing internal organization of the civil rights movement. The internal organization that gave rise to the sit-ins specialized in what was called nonviolent direct action, which included mass marches, negotiations, and boycotts as well as sit-ins. Thus the resources necessary for the sit-ins to spread rapidly were already in place.

The "sit-in" movement, it should be noted, usually included other nonviolent tactics, especially the boycott. Indeed, the boycott of local businesses by the black community, coupled with sit-ins, was often critical in influencing local elites to desegregate the lunch counters.[56] Generally, the use of sit-ins in combination with other tactics of direct action to force concessions from the white power structure was made possible by the internal organization, which enabled the supporting tactics to go into action simultaneously with the sit-ins. In short, the characteristics of the internal organizations determine the types of tactical innovations that can occur.

Sit-ins and Organizational Base of the Movement

The sit-ins pumped new life into the civil rights movement. They demonstrated that organized disruptive politics could bring about change much faster than the legal approach. In addition, the 1960 sit-ins pulled many people, often entire communities, directly into the movement, making civil rights a towering issue throughout the nation. Consequently, the sit-ins produced more experienced activists and provided the movement with more funds, because blacks as well as sympathetic whites sent money to the movement following the dramatic sit-ins. CORE and the SCLC benefited directly from the sit-ins, which led to conflict between the students and existing civil rights organizations, especially the SCLC.

CORE had been seeking to become a large-scale organization since it entered the South in 1957. The sit-ins gave it a chance to become just that. CORE's field secretary, Gordon Carey, became involved with the North Carolina sit-ins in February 1960. By April he was back at the national office in New York with the title of field director. According to Carey, in the midst of the early sit-ins CORE immediately hired as field secretaries a "number of bright young college kids who were being kicked out of school and who were totally committed to the movement."[57] As a result of the sit-ins CORE was able to become a large organization, reflected in the fact that during April of 1960 it added three full-time staff members.[58]

The SCLC's growth during 1960 was related to the sit-ins. Like CORE, it added new staff members and raised far more money following the sit-ins. In fact King, the attorney Levison, and others raised funds around the sit-in movement. That is where the SCLC ran into conflict with student activists, who were in the process of organizing their own independent direct action organization called the Student Non-violent Coordinating Committee (SNCC). Some students charged that the SCLC used the sit-in movement to raise large sums of money, which it did not share with the students. An SCLC document shows that this charge was not unfounded: The SCLC contributed only 2.8 percent of its income to SNCC during the first six months of SNCC's existence.[59]

Reverend Walker, who became the SCLC's executive director in 1960, was asked about the tensions generated over money following the sit-ins. He maintained:

> The SNCC people felt that the money that came to SCLC should have come to them. First of all, at that time, they didn't have an organization, so where was it gonna go? The students who got in jail, we went around the South bailing them out, and, you know, I never bit my tongue, but we had a right to the money. And, it was the people who made up the constituency of SCLC who were the back-up source . . . the kids didn't have nothing to lose but their time in school. They had no mortgage to pay, no car payments, no nothing, they'd just go out and get arrested.[60]

In reply to a suggestion that the SCLC could have funneled more money to student activists who were attempting to build their own organization because the SCLC had raised money specifically around the sit-ins, Walker said:

> We raised money around the issue of sit-ins for which we were paying bail bonds and getting kids out of jail and transporting them and so on. . . . When [student demonstrators] were having a rally or something, who did they want to come and speak? Martin Luther King, all back and forth across the country, see? So if we got money from the sit-in movement, well, we deserved it! We didn't take the money and send it to Switzerland. We put on more staff and opened offices and sent people out to work and keep this flame going.[61]

On the other hand, some of the student leaders felt that SCLC leaders raised funds around student protest and then used it to further their

own organizational interest rather than for the good of the entire movement. Thus a basic tension related to fundraising emerged between the
SCLC and SNCC following the sit-ins and endured throughout the early
1960s.

At times the tension between the SCLC and SNCC proved counterproductive, though some scholars of the movement claim that conflict
between civil rights organizations was beneficial in forcing the organizations to be more productive.[62] In some cases this may be true, but
in others the conflict seemed to have gone far in strengthening the opposition. This issue will be confronted when the Albany, Georgia,
movement is examined. Overall, the 1960 sit-ins strengthened the organizational base of the movement and gave rise to an effective new
student organization, SNCC.

THE BIRTH OF SNCC

The Student Nonviolent Coordinating Committee grew out of almost
the same circumstances as did the SCLC.[63] SNCC was created to coordinate the local movements in which students were already immersed. As with the SCLC, it was people outside the immediate battles
who saw the need to create structure and coordination among the various sit-in centers. Ella Baker, one of the SCLC's founders, made arrangements to bring the students together. Baker felt that for the student
movement to continue, the various student groups organized around
the sit-ins had to be put in contact with each other so that they could
share ideas and resources. In 1957 Baker and others had called together
the "Southern Negro Leaders Conference on Transportation and Nonviolent Integration," from which the SCLC was organized. In 1960
Baker called a "Southwide Student Leadership Conference on Nonviolent Resistance to Segregation," out of which SNCC was organized.

With $800 secured from the SCLC and space made available by Shaw
University in Raleigh, North Carolina, where Baker had graduated as
valedictorian years before, she laid the plans for the first student conference, held on April 15–17, 1960. In order to understand what happened at Raleigh that Easter weekend, one must remember that Baker's
tenure as the SCLC's Executive Director was being terminated and that
she had fundamental disagreements with the SCLC's perspective on
leadership. Most analysts of this conference have concluded that the
principle protest organizations—the NAACP, CORE, and the SCLC—
were all out to co-opt the students and that the students simply made
a decision to remain independent. Because of the close relationship
between the students and SCLC leaders, however, it seems chances

were good that the students would have become a part of the SCLC, had not Baker and her concept of leadership prevailed. In this sense Baker had an important role in the emergence of the new student organization.

It has been shown that the SCLC's church leadership was closely involved in the rise and development of the sit-in movement. The same held true of those NAACP leaders who advocated direct action and of CORE. It was unlikely that the students would have been drawn to the NAACP because of its almost exclusive belief in the legal method. Indeed, the students were well aware that the national leaders of the NAACP were making public pronouncements in support of the sit-ins but usually refusing to back them in practice.[64] Furthermore, the students were also aware that the NAACP leaders who had cooperated with the student movement had been those who challenged the law-oriented NAACP. The students would not have been drawn into CORE, because CORE was a white Northern organization they knew little about and was a secular organization with no institutional base among Southern blacks.

The SCLC represented the black church. Most Southern black students grew up in the church and had great respect for it. Furthermore, King was a hero to most of the young demonstrators, as were such SCLC officials as Reverends Lawson, Walker, McCollum, Shuttlesworth, Williams, Vivian, and Smith; Miss Baker; and a host of others. James Forman, who later became the Executive Secretary of SNCC, has written that at the Raleigh conference the SCLC's ministers thought they could attract the students: "King was sure he could deliver the students from Georgia, headed by Lonnie King. Abernathy felt the Alabama delegation headed by Bernard Lee would automatically follow his lead. And Walker knew he could deliver the Virginia delegation."[65] What Forman did not mention is that the SCLC ministers thought along these lines because they had worked very closely with the students in planning and carrying through the sit-ins.

It is true that the SCLC's leaders wanted the students to become a wing of the SCLC. But by the time of the Raleigh Conference the students had begun to experience themselves as a potent independent social force. According to Myles Horton, they "had begun to feel their oats."[66] Then, too, many adults (parents, teachers, college administrators, and ministers) had attempted to slow down the young protesters because of their own fears and vested interests. The students simply worked past what they considered the "hang-ups" of the adults. In many cases the students generalized their perceptions regarding conservative adults to adult activists. Given these factors, it is hard to judge whether the students would have joined any adult group.

There are activists who argue, along with Reverend Lawson, that

Dr. King could have persuaded the students to become a wing of the SCLC if he had made a strong appeal to them. "I personally did not try to take over the student movement," Lawson recalls. "I did not see Dr. King trying to take it over. And there's no doubt in my mind that we could have, had we wanted to. . . . Because we were the symbols of the students."[67] Lawson attested that he and King decided beforehand not to impose their views on the students:

> We made an explicit decision that the students—the Conference would proceed as they wanted to proceed, and that we would encourage them in . . . the democratic process and in an open process. That we would not try to impose upon them our own analysis or our own determination of how they should go. . . . But it should be said that if he and I decided we should establish an SCLC student arm—boom!—it could have been done. I have no doubt that we had the votes from the students to do that.[68]

Bernard Lee, the student leader from Montgomery, maintains that King definitely had enough student votes to bring about the formal affiliation. Asked why King did not pursue the affiliation, Lee replied:

> I recommended it, I talked to Dr. King about that. I talked to him before he arrived at Raleigh, at Shaw University. . . . Apparently Martin Luther King, Jr., did not want to leave that conference with the press, the New York Times and other leading papers in this country, and blacks who had succumbed to the notion [convinced] that here was Martin Luther King trying to co-opt students for his own good. The Montgomery Advertiser, and all of the papers, anyway, were forecasting that was to be the outcome of that Conference. They were predicting that Martin Luther King, Jr., would co-opt these poor, innocent students, now, and take them over.[69]

James Bevel was asked if the SCLC could have attracted the students. He answered:

> They probably could, because the people had more natural affinity to King. You have got to remember now, King was about 31 at the time. . . . He was himself like a student. But I don't think he was after that. The emphasis was on nonviolent movements. You had guys like Lawson there and as I said, the emphasis was on how do you make a nonviolent movement be a nonviolent movement, rather than on organizations. So there was organizational interests, but the dominant concept of a nonviolent movement was the most dominant thing in the whole process.[70]

Two of the most important opponents of the students' entry into the SCLC were Ella Baker and members of the Nashville student movement. Baker, who believed in strong decentralized local leadership, forcefully argued that adult groups would attempt to dominate the student movement if the young activists affiliated with the SCLC. Forman wrote:

> Miss Baker stated that she felt it was too early for the students to structure their movement, that nothing more should come out of this Conference than a continuation committee to explore what kind of structure they might eventually have. She felt the students had a right to determine their own structure—if they wanted one at all at that point; that it was their right to explore all possibilities and make their own decisions, since thus far it was they who had propelled the sit-in movement to national and international importance.[71]

Baker was asked why she opposed structuring the student movement, when she had pleaded for certain forms of structure in the SCLC. She explained that the student sit-in movement "needed some structure but not restrictive structure."[72] The adults thought they knew what was best for the young people, she said. Had the students affiliated with an adult organization, therefore, their elders would have dictated their actions.

Baker's thinking found concurrence from at least some students at the conference. Members of the Nashville group were accustomed to reaching decisions by what they called the "Quaker model," which required that debate occur among a group until a majority arrived at the same conclusion. Once a majority decision was reached, the entire group endorsed it. Such a decision-making process was impossible for a large group of people spread across the South. Consequently, members of the Nashville group, including Diane Nash and James Bevel, argued at the Raleigh conference in favor of strong local organization as opposed to strong central organization.

A smaller group of sit-in participants had met at Highlander Folk School two weeks before the Raleigh meeting and had addressed many of the issues discussed at Raleigh. The meeting reflects the importance of Highlander as a movement halfway house and the importance of certain issues confronting the student sit-in movement. According to a Highlander report prepared by Septima Clark, eighty-two participants—forty-seven Negroes and thirty-five whites—from nineteen states met at Highlander on April 1–3, 1960, and discussed the sit-in movement. Most of the participants were students who were actively participating in sit-in demonstrations. The following recommendation emerged:

The workshop participants recommend that the student movement should not affiliate with any other movement or organization, but should welcome cooperation from all agencies and in turn cooperate with the agencies in their special programs. It was also recommended that a Southwide organization for promoting the student movement be considered, following the pattern of the already existing organization of college students in South Carolina.[73]

Similar recommendations were implemented at the Raleigh conference and other meetings that immediately followed.

The large turnout at the Raleigh conference reflected Baker's exceptional organizing skills and the social conditions of the times. According to Forman, only a hundred students were expected, but three hundred attended. After the politics of the conference ended, Forman reports, "the students decided on April 17, 1960, not to become a wing of anything or a permanent organization of any kind, but to set up a temporary Student Nonviolent Coordinating Committee to continue the dialogue established at Raleigh."[74] At follow-up meetings in May and October 1960 the temporary Student Nonviolent Coordinating Committee, composed of delegates from about ten states, decided that SNCC should become a permanent organization. The success of the sit-in victory in Nashville contributed to the election of a Fisk student, Marion Barry, as SNCC's first chairman. Various committees were set up to carry out administrative functions (e.g. communication, finance, and coordination). The close relationship between Baker, the SCLC, and SNCC was reflected in the fact that SNCC's first office was housed in a corner of the SCLC's headquarters. Within a couple of months SNCC moved its headquarters directly across the street from the SCLC. Even though Baker remained with the SCLC until June 1960, it is safe to say that her allegiances, time, and influence shifted to the student movement shortly after the first sit-ins.

In its early years SNCC, like the SCLC, is best understood by focusing on the local protest movements that created the conditions leading to its formation in the first place. However, an important difference existed between the SCLC and SNCC. Although the SCLC comprised protest leaders, it nevertheless had a formal, centralized decision-making group headed by King. SNCC, on the other hand, began as a very loosely structured coordinating committee with little power or control over local groups. Moreover, following Baker's lead, the students of SNCC counseled against a strong, centralized organization on the grounds that it would impede both the democratic process and the initiation of mass-based movements. SNCC's central office provided important resources for the student movement, but not centralized leadership. It created a SNCC newspaper that informed the various local groups of the many protest activities and accomplishments of the entire movement. The central office also arranged conferences for the new organization. For example, a conference on "Nonviolence and the Achievement of Desegregation" was held on October 14–16, 1960. Adult advisers, including Dr. King, Lawson, and Walker, were on hand to conduct nonviolent workshops. So were CORE officials and personnel of such movement halfway houses as Fellowship of Reconciliation and the American Friends Service Committee.

Baker urged SNCC students to be concerned with all the problems that resulted from racial domination. She stressed that the student sit-in movement was about "more than a hamburger." Julian Bond, a student leader in the Atlanta sit-ins, said that Baker told the students "that we ought to be interested in more than integrating lunch counters, that there was a whole social structure to be changed here."[75] But here again, Baker insisted that change would emerge from group-centered indigenous leadership rather than a formal organization. Baker's influence is evident in SNCC's early literature. In a document explaining the purpose of the nonviolence conference of October 1960, we find the following statement:

> If we forget the importance of means, then we shall not obtain the goals. If we use the movement as an abstract cause, as a way to quick glory, as a dramatic device to manipulate—then we cheat. If our concern is that we, as chairman of such and such a group, be re-elected chairman, be given publicity, be asked to speak all over the nation— then we, too, are victims of the same kind of fear that has built segregation. The Conference must not discuss this generally. The using of the movement for personal security is a very present danger. This must not happen—not because it would make us look bad, but because it would kill the movement and forever prevent the reaching of being and the redemptive community.[76]

The document is signed "The Student Nonviolent Coordinating Committee," but it clearly reflects Baker's view of leadership and movements, which was adopted by SNCC. Thus SNCC emerged as a loosely structured organization with an ideology that counseled against strong central leadership and pervasive bureaucratic procedures.

Finally, the SCLC gave SNCC important help in establishing itself. As pointed out earlier, SNCC headquarters was first housed in the SCLC's offices. Then, shortly after the headquarters moved across the street, Jane Stembridge, SNCC's first office secretary, wrote Dr. King:

> When the Coordinating Committee wishes to thank SCLC, Ella Baker, and you . . . it is rather difficult to know where to begin. Certainly the

Coordinating Committee owes its very existence to SCLC. We could never have opened an office or functioned in any way without your guidance and financial assistance. On July 8, 1960, we received $250 from you. This will enable us to continue our efforts toward building of real communication. We are deeply grateful, again, for this help.[77]

The Southern Conference Educational Fund also figured importantly in SNCC's early development. According to Anne Braden, in early October 1960 SNCC hotly debated whether to grant the SCEF observer status, because it had been labeled communist. Many adult friends of SNCC advised the students not to have anything to do with SCEF. Braden said that Rev. Walker

. . . got up and spoke and told [SNCC] that this was ridiculous not to have SCEF there, and that SCEF was doing this, that, and the other, and they shouldn't be listening to people telling them not to associate with somebody at this point . . . that's how I started going to the SNCC meetings, because they voted that we should be one of the observers. [Walker] was always very friendly to SCEF, and he was opposed to that idea of dividing the movement that way or giving in to the "Red" scare.[78]

In the November 1960 issue of SNCC's *Student Voice,* we find the following statement:

This issue of "The Student Voice" owes much to the encouragement of Carl and Anne Braden, field secretaries for the Southern Conference Educational Fund. . . . Readers of this paper know how much help the Bradens have given SNCC and the student movement by their calls for support, articles, and news items.[79]

Thus the SCEF's assistance to SNCC in becoming an established organization was similar to the help it had given the local movements of the late 1950s.

Sit-ins, SNCC, and the White Student Movement

The dramatic sit-ins and the emergence of SNCC had an immediate national impact.[80] Activist-oriented students at predominantly white Northern campuses were instantly struck by the sit-ins' rapid spread across the South and by the fact that most of the black demonstrators were college students. Kirkpatrick Sale captured the response of these students to the sit-ins:

[B]y the end of that spring students at perhaps a hundred Northern colleges had been mobilized in support, and over the next year civil-rights activity touched almost every campus in the country: support groups formed, fund raising committees were established, local sit-ins and pickets took place, campus civil-rights clubs began, students from around the country traveled to the South.[81]

No previous actions of the Southern civil rights movement had generated this kind of widespread activism among whites across the nation. In effect, the 1960 sit-ins generated the activist stage of the modern white student movement. The central question is, Why did the sit-ins have this effect?

To get at the answer, it is instructive to know what type of white students usually became involved in the movement during the sit-ins. Studies have shown that the typical student was affluent, excelled in scholarly pursuits, usually majored in the social sciences, and had liberal-to-radical political values.[82] Thus the students were not marginal to universities, but they were dissatisfied with the huge gap between America's democratic rhetoric and its actual practices. But prior to the sit-ins these students were likely to engage in academic analysis of social problems and debate them at student government meetings rather than attempt to change them through overt protest and demonstrations. The black student sit-ins challenged that approach. In the words of one activist of the period, "the sit-ins demonstrated that white students could act on their beliefs rather than sitting on them."[83]

We can begin to answer the question of why that discontented group of affluent white students became involved in the politics of protest. That group entered into the politics of protest because the sit-ins by dominated black students provided them with a visible protest model, which demonstrated how they could proceed tactically and organizationally. It was an especially attractive model because the white student shared two important characteristics with the sit-in demonstrators: Both groups were students, and both were young.

Direct action became the tactic of the emerging white student movement, and SNCC supplied the organizational blueprint. There was no denying that the sit-ins were direct action. They demonstrated to white students that youth could enter the political process directly and force older generations to yield to their demands. White student leaders quickly realized that the methods of direct action allowed them to take the initiative away from adult authorities and to formulate their own policy.[84] Direct action techniques, according to one activist and scholar of the period, "were seen by white intellectual students as ways of living one's values and simultaneously changing the world."[85] Beginning in early 1960, such pioneering white student leaders as Robert Haber and Tom Hayden of the University of Michigan adopted the method of nonviolent direct action and spent considerable time at civil rights conferences and workshops with black activists, who taught them how to apply it.

Students for a Democratic Society (SDS), the chief white student movement organization of the 1960s, was modeled after SNCC. White student activists were impressed that black students involved in the sit-ins organized their own independent organization. In January 1960 SDS was a small student organization with little visibility. Following the sit-ins representatives of SDS went south and observed the meetings from which SNCC was organized. Ella Baker's philosophy on leadership and organizational structure was adopted by leaders of SDS. Obviously influenced by SNCC, Robert Haber, the most central figure in organizing SDS, contended:

> SDS should play down the . . . idea of establishing its own little chapters for its own little purposes at various campuses and concentrate instead on forming alliances with the existing campus groups that had already come into being in response to their own local needs. . . . Second . . . SDS could play its most valuable role by trying to coordinate these groups and service their needs on a national scale. . . . Third, SDS should involve itself as much as possible with direct social action.[86]

Clearly, these were the same ideas articulated by Baker, which shaped and molded SNCC. Haber attended some of the early SNCC meetings, and he acknowledges that they had an important impact on him.[87] Shortly after SNCC was organized, Haber served as liaison between SNCC and SDS. That function allowed him to attend top-level meetings of SNCC. During this period, Haber recalls, Ella Baker provided a bridge between the black student movement and the emerging white student movement.[88] SDS, like SNCC, emerged as a loosely structured organization that emphasized local autonomy and direct action rather than strong centralized leadership. In this sense Ella Baker was the "mother" of both SNCC and the activist phase of SDS.

Overall I have argued that the activist stage of the modern white student movement was generated by the 1960 sit-ins, because they provided these students with a protest model with both a tactical and an organizational blueprint. In short, from an indigenous perspective it is expected that dissatisfied members of affluent groups will enter into protest following a suitable tactical innovation made possible by well-developed movement centers of a dominated group. The sit-ins also provided a favorable climate for the further development of the SCLC.

The Reverend Wyatt Walker's Administration of SCLC

The sit-in movement occurred precisely at the time when the SCLC's staff decided to make basic changes at the Atlanta headquarters. In early 1960 it was decided that the Reverend Wyatt Walker of the movement center in Petersburg, Virginia, would be hired as the new Executive Director of the SCLC. Walker's accomplishments in building the SCLC state unit across Virginia, his successful Prayer Pilgrimage in protest of the closing of Virginia schools, and his role in the Virginia sit-ins had won him great respect among SCLC leaders as an outstanding organizer and administrator. In this regard Louis Lomax wrote that "Walker was master of all he surveyed in Petersburg, his home-grown protest movement was one of the best in the nation."[89] Furthermore, the SCLC wanted Walker because he was a minister. They thought he could relate to the clergy-oriented SCLC and function effectively among black ministers across the nation.

Moreover, Walker shared King's view of leadership. They were both Baptist ministers who believed that the leader should have the last word, because that is the way they ran their churches. In Baker's writing very little reference to the role of the church in the movement is found, whereas in Walker's statements like the following are numerous:

> The Negro church, more than any other institution, has dominated every facet of the life of the Southern Negro. Its role as it relates to the Negro Community is perhaps a unique sociological phenomenon. The Civil Rights struggle of the Negro community has directly paralleled the activity and development of the Negro church. The Negro church is his only forum, owned, operated and controlled by him; it affords him the broadest opportunity for social intercourse; it is generally the headquarters of the Negro's struggle for full citizenship; the pastor is the community leader and champion of the Negro's civil liberties. Most of the protest centers in the South are clergy-led.[90]

When Walker attempted to bring the church and clergy into the movement, he never ceased to remind them that they had to become involved, because

1. Churches are located in practically every community.
2. The church membership meets regularly, usually each Sunday, and often several members meet during the week.
3. Churches are committed to the idea of serving or meeting the basic needs of people and having genuine concern for their problems.
4. Church membership cuts across all age, economic, educational, class, and geographic lines in a community.

5. Churches have the resources and techniques for motivating people to voluntary and altruistic service.

6. The schedules of pastors can be adjusted more naturally and easily than those of persons in most other professions.

7. Churches remain free from narrow partisan and divisive handicaps more easily than other types of organizations.[91]

Walker was accorded administrative freedom immediately. As a precondition of accepting the directorship, the SCLC allowed Walker to bring two of his top staff members from the Petersburg Improvement Association. On August 1, 1960, Walker came in as Executive Director, James Wood as Director of Public Relations, and Mrs. Dorothy Cotton as Secretary to the Executive Director. They joined two SCLC secretaries, a bookkeeper, and a field secretary. Thus, in the fall of 1960 the number of salaried employees of SCLC increased from four to seven. This meant the SCLC was faced with problems of increasing its income to meet the new operating expenses and problems of supervising the new staff.

Walker introduced a more clearly defined structure in the SCLC shortly after his arrival. With Walker came monthly budget control sheets, anticipated versus actual earning data, stable secretarial services, 501–C4 tax status, established personnel procedures, systematic press releases and press relations, and organizational discipline on the staff level. According to the Reverend C. T. Vivian:

> He made everybody snap to attention. You were going to produce when Wyatt was around. You might not like the form in which he put it, but he saw himself very much as the executive putting a corporation together. His guidelines may have seemed too corporate for a movement, but nobody was going to overrule him.[92]

In addition to supervising the SCLC's staff, Walker usually took to the road with King and Abernathy. He insisted on ordering the activities on the road. As Walker recalled, "My job was to book the airplane reservations, book us into the hotel, filter the calls, arrange the schedule of who we were going to see in the city, keep on time with the appointment. That was my job."[93] Most people familiar with the SCLC during Walker's administration agree on two things: Walker was a "workaholic," and he introduced definite structure into the SCLC's Atlanta headquarters.

After the outbreak of the 1960 sit-ins Southern white power structures attempted to destroy King's leadership. In May 1960 the State of Alabama took King to court on a charge of having filed fraudulent tax returns for 1957 and 1958. Such tactics on the part of the opposition forced SCLC leaders to make sure that their organization was in compliance with the tax laws.

Chauncey Eskridge, a young black Chicago attorney who specialized in tax law, came to Atlanta and assisted King's lawyers during the tax trial. After the favorable verdict, Eskridge became the SCLC's tax counsel free of charge. After the tax trial, Eskridge explained,

> . . . it became perfectly apparent to [King] and all the members of the Board that the way to get at him and the movement, was for his enemies to use the taxing laws. They [the SCLC] had to have all their records, and all of the things that they did, kept in a fashion that they would not be vulnerable to the tax authorities' laws. Because [the SCLC's leaders] knew nothing when it came to tax laws.[94]

In 1960 Eskridge obtained a 501–C4 tax status for the SCLC, which enabled the organization to generate tax-free income but stipulated that money donated to the SCLC was not deductible. Tax laws covering protest organizations were complicated. There were special rules regarding money that passed between 501–C3 organizations (foundations) and 501–C4 activist organizations. Eskridge worked out arrangements whereby donors made their donations tax deductible by first sending it to a 501–C3 organization (a church), which turned it over to the SCLC. The point is that by 1960 the opposition forced the SCLC to systematize its financial activities, and Reverend Walker, assisted by specialists like Eskridge, worked diligently to protect the organization from external attacks.

Walker and SCLC Finances

Reverend Walker takes credit for the fact that the SCLC's income more than doubled in the first year of his administration. Shortly after Walker arrived at SCLC headquarters, he drew up a proposed budget covering the fiscal year, November 1, 1960, to October 30, 1961. Under the budget the SCLC needed an annual income of $63,000 to pay salaries and operating costs. Between November 1, 1960, and April 30, 1961, the SCLC's income was $62,611.98[95] That six-month period contrasts sharply with the $54,755.64 that SCLC earned over the entire fiscal year ending on October 31, 1960.[96] Within a six-month period the SCLC under Walker had earned what the organization had hoped to earn in a year. According to Louis Lomax, "During the fiscal year September 1, 1960–August 31, 1961, the SCLC raised over $193 thousand; its expenditures exceeded $179 thousand."[97] The SCLC's annual income rose continually during Walker's years as Executive Director.

For that six-month period ending on April 30, 1961, nearly half of the SCLC's income came from donations sent through the mail. Without detailed financial data it is difficult to determine what proportion of the money came from Northern black communities and white liberal communities. The Reverend Thomas Kilgore, an SCLC fundraiser in New York, stated that black churches of the North were seriously engaged in sending money south:

> The largest amount of money that came from blacks for the King movement came out of the North, came out of cities like New York, Philadelphia, Detroit, Chicago, Los Angeles, Cleveland, and so on. The largest amount of money raised by blacks came out of the cities, simply because the big cities had more money to offer than the cities in the South.[98]

Kilgore noted that white liberals also contributed heavily to the movement: "We went to the *New York Times* with a four-page ad that cost at that time over $6,000, but we reaped from that ad $362,000 and that was coming from white liberals, some blacks and all, but most of them white people."[99] By the early 1960s the SCLC had established the "Hollywood connection." A number of celebrities, including Nat "King" Cole, Harry Belafonte, Sammy Davis, Jr., Floyd Patterson, Marlon Brando, and others contributed considerable sums of money to the SCLC. They also organized concerts and benefits for the specific purpose of supporting the movement.[100] According to Reverend Kilgore, "the people in television and movies were tremendously concerned about the movement."[101] Thus, following the sit-ins two communities of the North—blacks and liberal whites—contributed to the movement. Wyatt Walker maintains that during his tenure (1960–63) as Executive Director of the SCLC 90 percent of SCLC funds came from King's personal appearances. Asked how much of that came from black people, Walker responded:

> With me, you can just ask me a straight-out question—I'm gonna give you the straight answer. People try to say that Martin was funded by Eastern liberals; that's not true. Most of Martin's money came from ordinary folks like in this [Walker's] church right here . . . and that's why the Board of SCLC and more especially why Martin Luther King was free to make any kind of decision he wanted to make. You see, 'cause he was not beholden to no Eastern money sources.[102]

There were a number of reasons for the SCLC's financial success. The financial base of the SCLC's Atlanta headquarters was built on King's ability to raise money as a speaker. This was the main reason King traveled six to eight months out of a year. When Walker came in, he carefully arranged King's calendar with the help of the Harry Walker Agency of New York so that the most money could be made in the least amount of time. The Harry Walker Agency specialized in arranging speaking engagements.

Reverend Walker revealed that King's speaking engagements were arranged in such a way that he could reach diverse audiences:

> We felt that there were some critical platforms [King] needed to occupy. . . . You can't just speak to black people all the time, you've got to speak in those places where there were people who mold influence. So we wanted him to speak at Princeton, Harvard, and Yale, and Marquette University.[103]

In a similar vein Stanley Levison, the New York lawyer, said that part of his job was to advise King on lecture engagements and to learn about the background of various interested organizations.[104] According to Walker, the SCLC made the maximum amount of money from these speaking engagements, because

> . . . I worked out something like [King] would come in there [a given city] and speak at noon on Monday, Monday night, and Tuesday morning. So, it would take the least amount of his time, and I'd get a minimum of $1,000 an appearance. So I had $3,000 for a day and a half of Martin Luther King's time.[105]

The careful husbanding of King's time certainly increased the SCLC's income during the early 1960s. It should be pointed out, however that it was easier for the movement to raise money following the sit-ins, because they made civil rights the main issue during the early 1960s. Following the dramatic sit-ins, contributions from white and black sympathizers increased. Thus, the SCLC moved into the 1960s with increased income, enlarged staff, centralized administrative structure, a compatible president and Executive Director, and a vibrant constituency fueled by the student movement. It is important to point out that this discussion of the SCLC's finances has been concerned only with the Atlanta headquarters. But as we have seen, the SCLC was rooted in local movement centers, which were usually financed by indigenous blacks.[106] From 1961 to 1963 the movement continued to become a major social force. The confrontation of this period became highly refined and wide-reaching in scope. The next chapter will focus on those developments.

10

BIRMINGHAM: A PLANNED EXERCISE IN MASS DISRUPTION

The aim of this chapter is to explain the Birmingham confrontation of 1963 within the framework of this study. Significant movements that led to the Birmingham confrontation, however, must be discussed first. The student sit-in movement gave birth to SNCC and increased the protest activities and influence of the SCLC, the NAACP, and CORE. Massive sit-in demonstrations, like the Montgomery bus boycott, were proof that organized collective action produced gains for blacks. These demonstrations made it clear to blacks, to their immediate opposition, and to societal elites that masses of people could force social change by participating in organized disruptive protest activities. The protest organizations and their leaders came to be perceived as the levers that switched on the collective power of masses and the attendant social uncertainties.

Beyond mere perceptions, the SCLC, SNCC, CORE and the NAACP did acquire social power in the context of the movement. The relative degree of power of those organizations varied with their ability to generate mass disruption. James Robinson, former Executive Director of CORE, said that immediately after the sit-ins leaders of CORE definitely experienced a sense of power. Asked to define that power, he stated: "Well, it isn't money. It is a sense of power and certainly we got ahold of something. It gave us a great sense of power, because what we did was making a difference to society."[1]

Robinson provided an example of how CORE was making a difference:

I was astonished. Woolworth's [the chain] eventually caved in. I thought we were just doing a lot of demonstrations in the North and that we were doing quite a lot of sitting in in the South, but when you added it all together, it wasn't enough to make a big corporation change its policy. But it did. When I first got interested in racial equality, I had no idea that it could make that amount of difference in that amount of time.[2]

Once a protest organization generates power, its internal operation and its status vis-à-vis the larger society changes. As Robinson stated:

We got our names in the paper too, you know. There certainly was a sense of power about it. You also, you were living inside this machine, and there were periods when we were in the office or out doing something seven days a week. You lose your perspective of where you fit into the broad range of society. The only thing you're thinking about is how you're going to make the next project work, and how you're going to publicize it, how you're going to raise the funds for it, and can you make it successful.[3]

All the protest organizations of this period underwent changes similar to CORE. And they all attempted to maintain their position of power and influence within the society.

CORE's top leaders, who were all white, decided that the National Director had to be removed from office; it was to the organization's disadvantage, they reasoned, for a white man to lead the black revolt. Thus, James Farmer, a CORE founder and a charismatic black leader, became the National Director of CORE in February 1961. This organizational move by CORE's top officials was aimed at keeping CORE in a powerful position within the black movement. Indeed, it seems that some of CORE's white leaders attempted to relegate Farmer to figurehead status while reaping the advantages of having a charismatic black leader. Jim Peck, an influential white leader in the organization, has said Farmer was brought in as National Director because CORE "didn't have a black person of stature that could appear on National television and play that role. [Farmer] played the front man. The real leader of CORE was Marvin Rich," the white Director of Community Relations.[4] Farmer agreed that some whites in CORE attempted to make him a figurehead:

I was in effect hired by my staff, by the people who were going to work under me. . . . The tendency would be for me to be, or for others to seek for me to be a figurehead. [Marvin Rich] tended to take things on and do things himself on his own, and tried to make decisions on his own when I thought that those decisions had to come to me. And so we had some tense moments.[5]

Farmer's refusal to accept the figurehead role generated internal conflict for CORE. Beyond that, while CORE's white leaders made organizational mileage from moving a black man into the top post, they would pay a big price for it several years later, when blacks in the organization began to advocate black power.

In late 1961 James Forman became the Executive Secretary of SNCC. It was hoped that Forman would introduce stability into the fluid structure of the student organization. That was a formidable task, because SNCC activists had adopted an antileadership and an antistructure ideology at the outset. That ideology rested in part on Ella Baker's insistence that SNCC avoid becoming leader-centered like the SCLC, but it also grew out of the desire of students to maintain their local autonomy. On one hand SNCC's students sensed that some leadership and coordination were needed, while on the other hand they attempted to avoid leadership and structure. Often SNCC's staff attempted to solve the resulting ambivalence with the slogan, "We are all leaders."

Despite the claims of SNCC's staff, by late 1961 SNCC had become an organization with leaders and with organizational interests. Anne Braden recalls that Forman told her, "Just because you don't have a structure and you don't have leaders doesn't mean that nobody is running things. It just means you don't know who is running it."[6] James Bevel, a former student leader, said that SNCC activists always argued, "Let the people decide, let the people decide! And, what he means is his people, that agree with him."[7] At any rate, by 1961 SNCC had become an organization and, therefore, functioned as an organizational actor, just as did the other protest organizations, despite differences in approach and structure.

THE FREEDOM RIDES

It was CORE that initiated the project which gripped the attention of protest organizations, Southern segregationists, and the society in general during 1961.[8] The project was called the Freedom Rides. It was decided that on May 4, 1961, two small integrated groups would ride a Greyhound bus and a Trailways bus from Washington, D.C., to New Orleans to test whether buses and terminal facilities were desegregated. The Freedom Ride was tailor-made for CORE—which lacked a mass base in the black community—because such a project did not require mass participation. In fact, only thirteen persons were on the original

Freedom Ride. Also, the probability was high that such a ride would provoke dramatic responses, especially in the states of the deep South. There was virtually no chance that white segregationists were going to permit the "Freedom Riders" to journey peacefully through the states of Alabama, Mississippi, and Louisiana. Confrontations were inevitable. In 1961 CORE leaders were looking for just such a dramatic project to produce publicity and support for the organization.[9]

The Freedom Riders were severely attacked after entering the State of Alabama. The Reverend Fred Shuttlesworth and his organization, the Alabama Christian Movement for Human Rights, had to rescue them. They had been so badly beaten that CORE leaders were forced to discontinue the ride. The movement center in Nashville, which included both SNCC and the SCLC's affiliate, the NCLC, was responsible for continuing the Freedom Rides even in the face of great danger.

Diane Nash, a SNCC leader in Nashville and a salaried staff member of the NCLC, called Shuttlesworth in Birmingham to express determination that the Freedom Ride not be called off and to tell him that some Nashville activists were prepared to continue it. Reverend Shuttlesworth asked, "Young lady, do you know that the Freedom Riders were almost killed here?" Diane said, "Yes, and this is exactly why the Ride must not be stopped."[10] Shuttlesworth agreed and assisted Nash in working out the details for continuing the Ride. They devised secret codes, because Eugene "Bull" Connor had Shuttlesworth's phones tapped. (Shuttlesworth recalls that when he answered his phone, he could hear people at the fire station and at the police department saying, "Hello, hello, hello!") Shuttlesworth, in a language understood by the Southern black community but not by Connor, told Nash to send the speckled chickens (integrated group), who included pullets (women) and roosters (men), on to Birmingham, and the Ride would continue.[11]

SNCC, working in harmony with the NCLC, had a tight organization in Nashville. At the founding meeting of SNCC it had been decided that students across the South would stage massive demonstrations at segregated theaters on February 1, 1961, to celebrate the reputed birthday of the sit-in movement on February 1, 1960. According to James Bevel,

> . . . Nashville was the only group to follow through on that. And we opened up the theaters. So that's why when CORE, for instance, called off the Freedom Ride, we already had our army standing. 'Cause we had been demonstrating from the first of February to Good Friday. There's a lot of discipline, a lot of organizational development.[12]

Thus it was tight organization that solved the mobilization problem of the Freedom Ride at a critical moment. The Nashville students dispatched members of their "standing army" to Birmingham.

The Freedom Riders finally made it out of Birmingham but ran into trouble in Montgomery, where they were attacked and beaten by mobs. Reverend Abernathy, Dr. King, and the MIA came to the rescue. The Riders and hundreds of supporters were forced to spend the night at Ralph Abernathy's First Baptist Church, while mobs outside the church were held in check by the National Guard. Reverend Abernathy explained that it was fitting for the demonstrators to be penned up in his church: Historically the First Baptist Church of Montgomery had been a haven where blacks pursued by lynch mobs and bloodhounds were hidden.

Without federal intervention, it is almost certain that the angry mobs of whites would have attacked the people inside First Baptist. Abernathy's church study became the movement's end of a hot line to the White House. Robert Kennedy and other top White House officials stayed in contact with King and Abernathy through the night.

The mob was restrained by U.S. marshals, enabling the Freedom Riders to leave the following morning for Mississippi. Howard Zinn wrote:

> At seven-thirty in the morning on Wednesday, May 24, with National Guardsman lining both sides of the street near the bus terminal twelve Freedom Riders (eleven Negro, one White), accompanied by six Guardsman and sixteen newspapermen, left Montgomery for Jackson. Before leaving, they tasted victory by eating in the "white" cafeteria at the Trailways terminal. On the road, a convoy of three airplanes, two helicopters, and seven patrol cars accompanied the bus while, inside, James Lawson held a workshop on nonviolence.[13]

From then on the Freedom Rides assumed the character of a mass movement. Zinn wrote: "Through June, July, and August, the pilgrimage continued, with students, ministers, and many others, white and Negro, coming into Jackson."[14] William Kunstler, a white lawyer from New York who defended civil rights activists, reported that by late August at least four hundred Freedom Riders had been arrested in Mississippi.[15] Most of those arrested were charged with breach of the peace, and many of them received long jail sentences in Mississippi, including James Farmer, the new director of CORE. The Kennedy Administration provided the Riders with protection after they had been attacked by mobs but did not prevent local authorities from arresting demonstrators in large numbers, because Kennedy did not want to jeopardize his political support in the South.[16] The Freedom Rides, like the sit-ins, generated movement activity and music, helping to educate and galvanize the black community for protest. SNCC played key roles in the

Freedom Rides, and the NAACP was heavily involved in providing legal services and financing.

After the Freedom Rides small teams of SNCC activists were sent to organize nonviolent projects in specific communities in Mississippi and Georgia.[17] Communities such as McComb, Mississippi, and Albany, Georgia, were extremely dangerous places in which to organize protest movements. Poverty and the white man made sure that blacks stayed "in their place." Young SNCC workers were instructed to live in these communities, get to know the people, and mobilize the community for protest. James Bevel described how this process operated:

> We decided to use the nonviolent approach in Selma and in Albany and in Mississippi. We called it the SNCC approach, where you get the people involved in doing it, rather than sitting back waiting till the field secretaries of an organization or a lawyer does it. You get the people themselves involved in it.[18]

SNCC had very little money when it began organizing these controversial direct action projects in 1961. SNCC activists risked their lives daily while receiving only $10 subsistence wages per week.[19] SNCC's financial situation improved in the summer of 1962, when it received some funds from the Taconic Foundation, the Field Foundation, and the Stern Family Fund.[20] Those foundations worked in close conjunction with the Kennedy Administration and shared the Administration's view that black activists should channel their energies into efforts aimed at acquiring the vote for Southern blacks. With these funds and money raised by SNCC itself the organization expanded its direct action projects in the South during 1962 and 1963.[21]

Following the tumultuous Freedom Rides, the Kennedy Administration made overt attempts to funnel the efforts of all the civil rights organizations into voter registration activities rather than disruptive protest movements. Indeed, the Kennedy Administration was adamant in opposing wide-scale civil disobedience. President Kennedy thought that low-key voting activities would result in peaceful change and provide additional votes for the Democratic party.[22]

James Farmer, who at that time was in jail for the Freedom Rides, explained how the Kennedy Administration attempted to "cool out" the demonstrations:

> I was in jail in Mississippi. Bobby Kennedy called a meeting of CORE and SNCC, in his office. I could not be there, of course. I was in the clink. But several people from CORE went. And several people from SNCC went, just those two because these were the activist groups in the Freedom Rides. This was in the summer of '61. And at that meet-

ing, what Bobby said to them according to the reports, he said, "Why don't you guys cut out all that shit, Freedom Riding and sitting-in shit, and concentrate on voter education." Says, "If you do that I'll get you a tax exemption." That cold- blooded. This was Bobby Kennedy. Says, "Cut out this sitting-in and Freedom Riding shit and work on voter registration. If you do that I'll get you tax exemption."[23]

Farmer's account continued:

The SNCC guy almost hit him [Bobby Kennedy]. One of the SNCC guys and Bobby Kennedy were standing in the middle of the floor, in the middle of the office, they tell me, forehead to forehead, shouting at each other. It looked like they were going to start throwing punches some time. And one of the CORE people stepped in between them, had to pull them apart. SNCC was outraged, you know. "Tell us that we concentrate on voter registration when we're fighting a tiger down there in Mississippi and Alabama. You're trying to buy us off."[24]

Bevel adds that Robert Kennedy promised the activists money and exemption from the draft if they turned to voter registration.

Arthur M. Schlesinger, Jr., makes it clear that the Kennedy Administration attempted "to keep the turbulence of Civil Rights in the ordered channels of due process,"[25] and President Kennedy's means of doing so was to give first priority to voting rights. Schlesinger further shows Kennedy's pursuit of the electoral strategy to be a desperate effort to satisfy Southern whites as best he could:

Negro voting did not incite social and sexual anxieties; and white Southerners could not argue against suffrage for their Negro fellow citizens with quite the same moral fervor they applied to the mingling of races in schools. Concentration on the right to vote, in short, seemed the best available means of carrying the mind of the white South.[26]

Robert Kennedy, in accord with the President's wishes, moved to shift the power and disruption of the civil rights movement onto the "safe" electoral ground:

In a behind-the-scenes effort reminiscent of the campaign to save the Bay of Pigs prisoners, the administration, with helpful assistance from the Taconic Foundation and collaboration from the Southern Regional Council, persuaded the leading Negro organizations to undertake a drive which in 1963 registered a considerable number of Negro voters across the South.[27]

While the Attorney General attempted to contain the movement, his brother continued appointing Southern racist federal judges, who used their power to impede the movement. William Kunstler, who as a lawyer dealt with these judges, wrote:

> It is tragically ironic that Kennedy's Judicial appointments in the deep South included so many outright racists. The political necessity of clearing appointments to the federal bench with such Democratic stalwarts as Eastland, Russell, and Byrd has resulted in a surfeit of district judges devoted to the continuation of segregation.[28]

Time and again these judges issued injunctions, set high bail bond, and ordered jail sentences to help the movement's opposition toward victory in conflict situations.

But, as Schlesinger pointed out, by 1961 the movement could not be directed into orderly channels. The Kennedys seem to have misunderstood that even Southern blacks who attempted to vote were in fact engaging in movement activity. Nothing less than massive disruptions, generated by a social movement, would help blacks to seize voting rights in the South. So the Kennedy plan backfired. SNCC, the SCLC, CORE, and the NAACP received money from the liberal foundations associated with the Kennedy Administration. In many cases they used these resources to organize movements or develop programs that quietly vigorized the movement.

THE SCLC AND THE CITIZENSHIP SCHOOLS

The SCLC's Citizenship Education Program was important to the development of the civil rights movement, although most outsiders knew nothing about it. The few who did thought it was a poor attempt to get Southern blacks registered to vote.

In 1961 SCLC officials were seeking a program through which the black masses could be reached, educated, and mobilized. Dr. King asked Myles Horton of Highlander Folk School to work out such a program for the SCLC. Horton recommended that the SCLC take over the Citizenship Education Program that he, Septima Clark, Esau Jenkins, and Bernice Robinson had developed. As noted in Chapter Eight, it was a highly successful program, and Horton was trying to have it administered elsewhere because it had outgrown HFS's capacities. Andrew Young entered the civil rights movement as a result of Horton's effort to transplant the administration of the Citizenship Schools into the black community. Horton had been informed that Young, who was employed by the National Council of Churches in New York, would be an excellent choice for the job of transplanting the program to responsible black organizations. Horton went to New York in search of Young. He recalled:

> I went up to see him and Andy wasn't too interested. I never will forget, I said, "Andy, you're too good a man just to be a token black for white people, running around speaking to white religious groups. . . . " I said, "that's all you doing, isn't it?" Andy said, "Well yes, I guess so." I said, "Things are happening in the South that are important." Finally we persuaded Andy to give up that job and come down.[29]

When Young arrived at Highlander, the movement halfway house was being closed down by the State of Tennessee on trumped-up charges.

At that time Dr. King was consulting with Horton about acquiring the Citizenship Schools. Some critics of King say he lacked administrative skills. The way in which he dealt with the Citizenship Program suggests otherwise. Horton recalls that after he informed King and Wyatt Walker about the program in detail,

> . . . Martin said, "I want to think it over and I want some more information." I sent information and I made an appointment to go down and see him, and he spent about four hours going over the costs and every detail . . . just little details that I had never handled. . . . He was very meticulous about the whole program, everything. He didn't jump at it at all.[30]

King accepted the Citizenship School after being convinced that it was a solid program.

The SCLC acquired the Citizenship Schools in late 1961 and financed them with a grant from the Marshall Field Foundation. Movement halfway houses often provide movement organizations with skilled staff members. Septima Clark, considered the mother of the program, and Andrew Young joined the SCLC staff to administer the Citizenship Schools. Bernice Robinson, the first Citizenship School teacher, eventually left Highlander and joined the SCLC. Dorothy Cotton, who came to the SCLC with Wyatt Walker, also was prominent in administrating the Citizenship Schools. It was pointed out earlier that the singing of spirituals was an important technique used by citizenship instructors to teach blacks to read and write. Dorothy Cotton was a great church singer who used her musical skills to train Citizenship School teachers.

The SCLC used the Citizenship Schools to prepare blacks for the

movement. Clark, Cotton, and Young traveled throughout the South recruiting the future teachers of grassroots Citizenship Schools. The recruits were brought to the SCLC's Dorchester training center in
McIntosh, Georgia. At Dorchester blacks from the farms, plantations,
and Southern cities were taught how to teach others to read, write, and
protest. Mrs. Cotton said people were taught to raise questions about
power distribution in their communities and about domination: "So
they started to get involved, you know, in their own minds and realizing that, hey, I don't have to leave the running of the town and that
of the education system to the white folks downtown, that I can raise
questions, I can be involved."[31] She recalled further:

> The men folk had never been in the courthouse. The courthouse was
> synonymous with the place where black folk got beat up and just
> abused, you know. And so at the end of hearing all of the problems
> in the teaching session where you're really trying to turn people on to
> thinking new ways about themselves and their own functioning, we
> started to ask questions like, "Why aren't you that clerk?" It blew their
> minds.[32]

Clark further highlighted the political role of the Citizenship Schools:

> You see, people having been living on plantations for so many years,
> had a feeling that they were afraid to let white people know that they
> wanted to be a part of the governing body. They were afraid to do
> that. So, we used to put up a regular form on our blackboard with the
> government at the head and all the people who would come under.
> Then on down to the masses, and show how you too can become a
> part of this great governing body, if you will register and vote. In that
> way, they learned that in a country like the United States they had
> the right to be a part.[33]

Citizenship teachers returned to local communities and taught the
masses about their rights in a democracy. The schools were so effective, Cotton recalled, that Andrew Young thought the training program
was the base upon which the whole civil rights movement was built.
For several reasons, there was some truth in that conclusion. First, the
SCLC affiliate structure was closely linked with the Citizenship Schools.
According to Cotton, people who attended the Citizenship Schools
"definitely knew they were a part of SCLC. Many SCLC chapters often
grew out of, you know, sprung from people's participation there. They
knew they were part of something—a big network."[34]

Second, people trained by the Citizenship Schools' staff often became directly involved in demonstrations. James Bevel, who sent peo-

ple to the Citizenship Schools from Mississippi, explained: "See, that's how we developed a momentum. So when you start talking about all those folks in Mississippi, that's how you train local leadership. Take them off to the Citizenship Schools, they start organizing their own communities."[35] Dorothy Cotton told about the relationship of the Citizenship Schools program to protest demonstrations:

> It was just a quiet building base of community by community across the South. People were going back saying they're not gonna take segregation and discrimination anymore. And they'd go back and just act differently which meant very often sitting in, demonstrating, registering and voting, running for public office. It meant just a whole new way of life and functioning.[36]

A number of great civil rights leaders, including Mrs. Fannie Lou Hamer, attended the SCLC's Citizenship Schools.

Third, in Mrs. Clark's words, Citizenship recruits "had a special job of going into the community and getting the community ready to accept Dr. King with his way of speaking. Ready to accept Andrew Young, Dr. Abernathy, and the others."[37] Mrs. Clark explained that by the time the movement organizations moved into a community, Citizenship School personnel had made sure that the local people "were already prepared to listen to a black man and to know that the government of that state can be handled by blacks as well as whites. They didn't know it before. We used to think everything white was right. We found out differently, though."[38] Movement activists of various persuasions stated repeatedly that the Citizenship Schools were one of the most effective organizing tools of the movement. The "less militant" aspects of the movement like the Citizenship Schools were a significant mobilizing factor throughout the movement, often serving as "quiet structures" behind what appeared to be spontaneous uprisings.

ALBANY, GEORGIA

In 1961 SNCC activists were divided over whether to engage in direct action demonstrations or the voter registration activities favored by the Kennedy Administration. When SNCC came close to falling apart over the issues of direct action versus voter registration, Ella Baker intervened. She instructed SNCC's staff to develop a wing of direct action and one of voter registration. She further counseled that once they got down to the "nitty gritty," they would discover that there was no substantive difference between the two. By late 1961 SNCC was heavily involved in organizing activities in several deep South states, where they attempted to register blacks to vote. These movements were organized by such important leaders as Robert Moses, James and Diane Bevel, Bernard Lafayette, and Marion Barry. It was in Albany, Georgia, that SNCC organized an imposing mass movement.[39]

In the fall of 1961 Charles Sherrod and Cordell Reagon, two field secretaries of SNCC, arrived in Albany, Georgia, with the explicit goals of registering blacks to vote and helping them protest against segregation. The SCLC usually attempted to mobilize a community by recruiting the ministers first. The SCLC staff reasoned that once the ministers were recruited, then members of the various congregations would follow. SNCC usually started from the opposite end. Being young activists, SNCC organizers focused attention on college and high school students first. They reasoned that if they mobilized the young people, who were usually less conservative, then the adult community and the ministers would get involved to protect their children and to hold their respect. Yet the church was essential to both groups. Thus, while SNCC activists in Albany were organizing in the high schools and at Albany State College, they simultaneously held continuous discussions with the ministers, urging them to join in.[40] The efforts to recruit the ministers in Albany were helped by the fact that Sherrod was trained as a minister.

Cordell Reagon explained how he and Sherrod entered the community and began their organizing efforts:

> We slept in abandoned cars, and eventually we started going out on the college campus. We would sit in the student union building on the college campus all day long, drinking soda, talking with the students, trying to convince them to test the public accommodations at the bus station.[41]

Reagon and Sherrod made strong organizing efforts at the high schools. Reagon told how:

> We spent many days in the playgrounds at high schools. We went to football games, and went to programs at the school. We talked to the students. We'd go to their homes. You know, we'd hang out and play ball with 'em, whatever . . . we did a little bit of everything. We became a part of that community. And after people got over their initial fears of us, I mean we were taken in as sons of the community. I mean, it got to the point where people didn't see us as being out of town.[42]

Within a short time SNCC organizers had persuaded and trained students from Albany State College to sit in at the "white" bus terminal.

The black community of Albany immediately mobilized around the efforts of the students. In November 1961 the Ministerial Alliance, the Federation of Women's Clubs, the Negro Voters' League, the Criterion Club, the NAACP and its Youth Council, and SNCC formed an organization of organizations, which they named the Albany Movement. William Anderson, a thirty-year-old black doctor, was elected president of the Albany Movement. Here again, the "newcomer" status was critical in the choice of the official leader of a movement. Dr. Anderson, who came to Albany in 1957, told the author: "I hadn't been there long enough to make enemies, had not been closely affiliated or allied with any factions in the community. I guess I was the least objectionable."[43] C. B. King, a local black attorney in Albany who was prominent in the movement, remembers that Dr. Anderson "was the kind of personality or figure who everybody could rally around" because "he represented a new figure in the black community."[44] Thus the Albany Movement was guided by an organization of organizations with a newcomer as its leader. By the time the Albany movement formed, many of the churches had opened their facilities to the movement. Organizers used the church and its familiar culture to mobilize the masses. Black spirituals became so important to the process that Albany came to be known as the "singing movement."[45]

The goals of the Albany movement differed drastically from those of previous movements: This movement, it was decided, would end all forms of racial domination in Albany. Demonstrations were to be held against segregated buses, libraries, bowling alleys, restaurants, swimming pools, and other facilities. In early December 1961 large numbers of blacks from every walk of life, including several hundred high school students, were arrested for demonstrating. High school students were so important in the Albany movement because only one black college was located there, and SNCC activists had concentrated much of their organizing activities at the high schools. Never before had such a large number of people been arrested in a single city as in Albany. The SNCC activists had provided the exemplary behavior that made these mass arrests possible. Dr. Anderson recalls that "going to jail was about the worst thing that could happen to a Negro in Albany, Georgia, prior to the civil rights movement. . . . They thought that for you to go to jail and risk losing your job was about as bad a thing as you could do."[46] Anderson pointed out that SNCC organizers changed that attitude because "they came down and went to jail like they were going to a Sunday school picnic. That was a dramatic difference from anything these people had been taught to do."[47] Thus another striking difference between the Albany movement and others was the large number of community people who decided to demonstrate despite the certainty of arrest.

In response Laurie Pritchett, sometimes referred to as the "nonviolent police chief," immediately arrested demonstrators in large numbers. Pritchett's method was to arrest quickly and to refrain from using overt violence against the protesters. The South had not seen a total community mobilized on such a wide scale since the Montgomery bus boycott. The usual activities of the city were severely disrupted by continuous demonstrations. The jails were full, and merchants were filled with anxiety. The collective power of masses generated by the movement was significant. According to Anderson, "Albany was literally paralyzed for about a month. Nobody would go into town to shop— black or white. They never knew when there was going to be another mass demonstration and nobody knew when there was going to be a shooting war."[48]

As a result, on December 15, 1961, after large numbers of people had been arrested, "the city agreed to hold unofficial talks."[49] Before the movement, as the Reverend Bernard Lee pointed out, the white power structure and its police chief, Laurie Pritchett, had never considered "niggers" worthy of negotiations. Lee said of Pritchett: "The only experience he had ever had with blacks, either was to kick their behinds, to beat them, to throw them in jail, that kind of thing. . . . 'I am the boss, you are the niggers.' That had been the relationship prior to that time. This was a new for him."[50] As will be shown, the Albany movement made substantial contributions to the larger civil rights movement. However, the movement was not able to force Albany's power structure to desegregate the city. Several factors contributed to the failure: (1) organizational rivalry between the SCLC and the SNCC faction of the Albany movement; (2) King's conservatism; (3) poor planning; and (4) tactical maneuvers of Albany's white power structure.

The December 15 negotiations between members of Albany's white power structure and representatives of the movement collapsed the same day. With approximately five hundred people in jail, meager resources, and a recalcitrant white power structure, the movement reached a critical impasse. Anderson summed up the problems:

> We were in a situation where we had several hundred people in jail, no bond money, people wanted to come out of jail and people had been fired off their jobs. We were initiating a bus boycott that none of us had any experience at, including SNCC. . . . We did not have money, did not have a legal staff, did not have any experienced civil rights workers.[51]

SNCC, according to Anderson, had "provided what was needed—a stimulus—but once the movement got going they did not have the resources to manage this massive movement."[52]

At this point Anderson decided to call in Martin Luther King and the SCLC. Anderson was close friends with both King and Abernathy. In the mid-1940s he and King had attended school together in Atlanta, where they had organized one of that city's first NAACP Youth Councils.[53] Anderson and Abernathy had also been classmates at Alabama State College in Montgomery during the late 1940s.[54] Anderson asked the board of the movement to authorize him to extend a formal invitation to Dr. King, which it did. This decision, however, immediately fanned the simmering conflict between the SCLC and SNCC. James Forman, Executive Secretary of SNCC, vehemently opposed bringing in King. "I opposed the move," he said later "pointing out that it was most important to keep the Albany movement a people's movement—the presence of Dr. King would detract from, rather than intensify this focus."[55] Charles Sherrod and Cordell Reagon, along with other local people sympathetic to SNCC, also had difficulties with the decision to bring King and the SCLC to Albany.[56] When Reagon was asked about King's entry into the movement, he replied: "Well—he didn't come there by our request, that's the first thing. He came there by Dr. Anderson's request, who was president of the Albany movement . . . we were not even consulted on that, by the way. . . . There was no necessity for King to come to town."[57]

The decision to bring in King threatened SNCC's organizational interests as the dominant organization in the vanguard of the Albany movement. According to the attorney C. B. King, who shared some of SNCC's reservations about the decision:

> SNCC looked upon itself as really being the yeomen of the movement but having received little credit, receiving little recognition. [It] viewed [King's presence] as an ominous threat. Here again we [SNCC] have aided in ferment and now Martin will be able, as the great Roman Emperors, to make his triumphant march into the city.[58]

The organizational stakes were significant in Albany, because this was the greatest mass movement of 1961 across the entire South. SNCC's staff had labored long and intensely to build the movement. It was SNCC field secretaries who had risked their lives while organizing the movement when it was most dangerous to do so. Once the movement was rolling with full steam, they had come to see it as a successful SNCC project. Moreover, it was clear that the organization receiving credit for the movement would be in a good position. According to Anderson, SNCC "was concerned as to who, then, would get the credit for whatever happens in Albany and who would have then gained in terms of being able to recruit more people to its organization and raise more money."[59]

For all the organizational conflict, most members of the Albany movement were not opposed to King's coming to Albany. After Forman raised his first objection, by his account, "I had received no support for my position at the meeting, not even from Charles Jones [a SNCC organizer] and was accused . . . of introducing 'factionalism.' I dropped the argument, for it was obvious that it would not prevail."[60] In presenting the case to call King, Anderson convinced the board that a positive decision would mean Albany could serve as a proving ground. With King's assistance, that is, this mass movement against all forms of segregation could force the system of racial domination across the South to crumble. According to Anderson, the intention was to send a message to both the racist white power structures and blacks: "if you don't settle by peaceful means this is what you are going to be confronted with, and the encouragement for black people was that if they don't yield, if they don't capitulate, if they don't do it by peaceful means, here is what you can do to get the results."[61] King consented to come, setting the stage for mass confrontation and internal conflict.

King's arrival in Albany on December 15, 1961, instantly caused big changes. Anderson recalls that "when Martin Luther King came to town there was worldwide press immediately present in Albany." And that was not all:

> More money came in. Martin Luther King touched a number of his sources in major cities that put on fundraising for the Albany Movement. I know this to be a fact cause I spoke at a number of those in Los Angeles, several in New York, in Philadelphia. These were all arranged through Martin Luther King's organization. . . . He had the people in place, he had the organization. The SCLC chapters were nationwide, his organization had the capacity of getting on the phone and say "Albany Movement need some help would you put on a fund raiser," and a Maurice Dawkins in Los Angeles would do it, a Percy Sutton in New York would do it. . . . He had that kind of capacity and it in fact happened.[62]

The effect of King's presence on the local community was that a larger number of people were mobilized to protest and fill up the jails. "They viewed him as a leader," Reagon has said. "I mean it was clear that they loved him. It was clear that they respected him as a leader and it was clear that they would follow him to the end if he wanted 'em to, you know."[63] Within two days King, Abernathy, Anderson, and about two hundred protesters were jailed, bringing the number of people in jail to more than seven hundred. Speaking of the local response, Anderson recalled that King's presence "bolstered the morale of those people who might have sensed that the movement was really shaky.

There was a certain amount of confidence that exuded throughout the community, you could feel it. Well let's face it, a lot of our people thought that Martin Luther King walked on water."[64] When King was arrested, he announced that he would remain in jail until the white power structure agreed to desegregate the city.

With the jails filled, the merchants losing money, and worldwide attention focused on Albany, the white power structure decided to negotiate with representatives of the movement. However, the white power structure was aware of internal problems within the movement, because SNCC's resentment toward the SCLC was escalating. From SNCC's perspective, the SCLC leaders moved quickly to make the Albany movement look like an SCLC project. With King in the city the attention had shifted to him, and SNCC activists charged that SCLC leaders often excluded them from strategy meetings and press conferences. In fact, the SCLC's staff often viewed SNCC activists as young "hotheads." SNCC people, including Reagon, detested this label and, even more, the action that followed from it.

> We resented all of that. . . . —sure we resented that. They would hold press conferences, and we wouldn't be invited to the press conferences. If we were invited, we weren't allowed to speak. This kind of stuff went on all the time, you know. And—look here, call it ego, call it what you like. I don't think anybody appreciates going to jail, getting their balls busted day in and day out, and then you don't even get to speak on it. I'm sure we resented all of that.[65]

SNCC's hostilities were especially directed at the SCLC's Executive Director, Wyatt Walker, because he was in charge of the SCLC's day-to-day logistics and because his personal style was arrogant, often causing him not to pay attention to delicate relationships. Anderson described Walker as a "dominating personality, a brilliant individual, a brilliant tactician. . . . His primary role as Executive Director of SCLC [was] to keep SCLC up front, and he did that quite well . . . even if it meant going around somebody or getting out in front of somebody.[66] The attorney C. B. King agreed that Walker "was a hell of a guy. He was very astute, he was a politician and somewhat Machiavellian."[67] Walker himself admitted that he was "too 'flint-faced' in those days but that he was a 'take-charge' type of person whose goal was to get the ball across the goal line for King."[68]

The environment was not conducive to in-depth cooperation between SNCC and the SCLC. Reagon recalls that the friction between the two became so intense that "There were times when me and Sherrod and Charlie were getting ready to say, 'fuck it. We going to get out of here and let them have it,' you know. Because sure, they became all-powering to an extent."[69] Instead of leaving, SNCC activists entertained ideas of maneuvering King and the SCLC out of the city. Reagon was asked about SNCC thinking at the time. "I'm not going to sit here and tell you that we certainly didn't have discussions on how to get them the hell out of town," he replied. "I said before, I wish they had never come."[70] C. B. King confirmed Reagon's recollection: "I do think that Cordell is accurate in his revelation that there were contrived efforts on the part of SNCC to have the Albany community divested of King's presence. There is no question in my mind regarding the validity of that assertion."[71] This conflict between the organizations, far from benefiting the movement, gave the opposition valuable political leverage.

In the belief that the movement could be defeated—being aware of its internal conflict—and in response to mounting pressure, members of Albany's white power structure decided to maneuver King out of the city by agreeing to a "truce," which they had no intention of honoring. City officials agreed (1) to return all bond money, (2) to release all the jailed protesters on their own recognizance, (3) to postpone trials of protesters indefinitely, (4) to desegregate the buses immediately, and (5) to establish a permanent biracial committee to work out details for desegregating the city.[72] This "truce" was presented orally to representatives of the movement, including the attorney C. B. King, Donald Hollowell, and Marion Page. Some members of the movement's negotiating team felt that the oral agreement was suspect. According to Anderson, Dr. King was distrustful of the verbal agreement and repeatedly asked whether these "white folk could be trusted."[73] Anderson and several other leaders assured King that the city officials could be trusted. Reluctantly King, who had promised to remain in jail until the demands were met, allowed himself to be released from jail. He and Abernathy immediately left Albany.

Within days city officials began systematically reneging on each point of the agreement. The white power structure openly declared that it had defeated the movement. Robert Kennedy contacted the mayor to express satisfaction that a compromise had been reached. However, confrontations between the Albany movement and the white power structure continued after King and Abernathy departed. For example, in January 1962 the Albany movement intensified its boycott of the city buses after a young black woman, Ola Mae Quarterman, was arrested for sitting in the front of a bus. The boycott was so effective that the bus company went out of business a few weeks later.[74] Moreover, between January and July 1962 local activists and SNCC leaders continued to engage in lunch counter demonstrations and picketing of downtown stores.[75] In response, the Albany white power structure refused to negotiate with movement leaders and usually arrested the demonstrators. Members of the white power structure, flaunting their victory, summoned Dr. King and other demonstrators to appear in court in July 1962 for their earlier participation in protest activities. National pressure began mounting against city officials after King was jailed again. In reaction to the arrests, the black community of Albany became solidified once more. The community prepared to generate the collective power of masses through demonstrations after King announced that he and Abernathy would stay in jail until the expiration of the forty-five-day sentence.

Within a couple of days Dr. King was mysteriously bailed out of jail, supposedly by a well-dressed black man. The attorney C. B. King reported discovering recently that it was untrue that a black man bailed King out: A member of a prestigious local white law firm told him he was present at a meeting in Washington with J. Edgar Hoover and Robert Kennedy at the time: "Bobby Kennedy expressed a desire of greatest urgency that he wanted King out of Albany. And it was conceived in that meeting that [the Albany lawyer] would bond him out. . . . It was he who paid . . . about $200 to the city. . . . That is how Martin was released."[76]

After leaving jail, King immediately decided to step up the demonstration. However, on July 20, 1962, Federal District Judge J. Robert Elliot issued a sweeping injunction, "which barred Albany's Negroes from unlawful picketing, congregating or marching in the streets, and from any act designed to provoke breaches of the peace."[77]

Showing his conservative streak, which SNCC activists often viewed as a serious failing, King chose to follow the dictates of Judge Elliott's injunction rather than the will of a black community prepared to generate civil disobedience. William Kunstler wrote that King's position was, "I don't mind violating an unjust state injunction, but I won't violate a federal one."[78] The conservatism of King's posture was made conspicuous by the facts that the blacks of Albany were ready to continue demonstrations and that Elliott was an integral part of the Georgia white power structure bent on defeating the movement. Judge Elliott, appointed by President Kennedy, worked closely with the chief of police, the mayor, and other officials of Albany as well as with racist U.S. Senators of Georgia to defeat the movement.

King decided not to violate the injunction because he considered the federal courts an ally of the movement. Some of King's lawyers advised him that the injunction was illegal. Kunstler wrote:

I constantly stressed the fact that I considered the injunction illegal. While I did not advise King to violate it, I made it quite clear that I

did not think he was bound by it. But he was adamant. Since the re-
straining order bore a federal imprimatur, he was determined not to
flout it.[79]

Kunstler concluded, "It was obvious that Dr. King was extremely troubled over the passive role forced upon him by the injunction."[80] Indeed,
in this situation King took the NAACP legal approach. He instructed
his lawyers to go to court and have the injunction overturned. In the
meantime he refused to lead demonstrations.

That is precisely the kind of behavior that led Miss Baker to write
that often "the prophetic leader turns out to have heavy feet of clay."[81]
Some local Albany leaders decided to conduct demonstrations in spite
of the injunction. A local Baptist minister told a church audience:

I've heard about an injunction but I haven't seen one. I've heard a
few names but my name hasn't been called. But I do know where my
name is being called. My name is being called on the road to Freedom.
I can hear the blood of Emmett Till as it calls from the
ground. . . . When shall we go? Not tomorrow! Not at high noon!
Now![82]

Demonstrators marched out of the church singing "I Ain't Gonna Let
Nobody Turn Me Round." Kunstler recalls that when the demonstrators marched out of the church, Dr. King was jubilant. King remarked,
"They can stop the leaders, but they can't stop the people."[83] At a critical moment in the Albany movement, King had capitulated to the white
power structure. It is almost certain that he could have united the community and possibly the various protest organizations behind him if he
had defied the federal injunction. When he instead obeyed the injunction, however, the internal strife within the movement increased, while
the morale and determination of the masses decreased. One night during the ten-day injunction period some of the Albany demonstrators
rioted out of frustration. King's decision to abide by the directives of
the injunction contributed to the movement's defeat at Albany and further exacerbated the conflict between SNCC and the SCLC. SNCC activists felt that SCLC leaders merely wanted to take credit for a quick
victory without having to pay the necessary costs, which in this case
would have meant violating the federal injunction.

Poor planning also was evident in the defeat of the Albany movement. Members of the several local organizations never completely
transcended their own narrow interests, adding intraorganizational
problems to the conflict between the SCLC and SNCC. The friction between the SCLC and SNCC was especially costly because the two groups
had spent valuable time at meetings attempting to iron out differences

rather than concentrating on the moves of the opposition. Considering that the internal fighting was over "turf" and money, a plan of equal sharing in the proceeds might have diminished some of the conflict. Furthermore, movement tactics were never clearly and meticulously planned. With its aim to eradicate all forms of segregation and discrimination, the community directed its energies and protests at all aspects of domination. The efforts became so diffuse that they lost their effectiveness.

Speaking of the poor planning, Anderson said that when King, Abernathy, and he went to jail the first time, they "left no instructions, we left nobody in charge . . . we had no plans. We had not even planned another mass meeting."[84] Following the sit-ins and Freedom Rides large numbers of white students in the North organized in support of the civil rights movement. Anderson acknowledged that failing to leave instructions was a glaring error also because "there were students . . . from colleges in the East who had committed themselves to come and march. All we had to do was say, come on. All we had to do was put out the word, and we would have filled up every jail in Georgia."[85] The movement made another critical mistake by accepting an oral "truce" from white racist leaders who had demonstrated that they were committed to maintaining racial domination. Again, Anderson admits, "we should never have ccme out of jail with that kind of flimsy agreement. It should have been concrete, in writing, or we should be in jail till today."[86]

As I have pointed out earlier, the economic boycott was a central weapon wielded throughout the civil rights movement. Albany was no exception. During the Albany movement blacks put the local bus company out of business with a boycott, and they also boycotted downtown department stores. Yet it seems that poor planning decreased the effectiveness of the economic boycott as well. David Lewis wrote:

> The boycott of department stores received the support of between 50 and 75 percent of the black community. The boycott worried the business community but not enough to cause it openly to brave the coalition of proletarian and politically potent whites. Incredibly, the SCLC strategists appear not to have ascertained what portion of white business trade was held by blacks. In fact, the general poverty of the blacks limited their buying power so that a boycott by them pained but did not seriously cripple the merchants.[87]

The successful boycotts of the civil rights movement divided different factions of the white power structure. However, such a result required careful and precise planning. In spite of the boycotts, Albany's whites remained united against the blacks.

Indeed, the white power structure made few mistakes in Albany. It exploited the internal division within the movement and King's conservatism by issuing a timely federal injunction. Importantly, the chief of police, Laurie Pritchett, abstained from using open violence on the demonstrators. "No clubs, hoses, or dogs were ever used in Albany."[88] Pritchett's refusal to use violence in public enabled the federal government to remain relatively aloof from the confrontations.

The Albany defeat was particularly disappointing because the entire black community had been mobilized. Although Albany remained segregated in 1962, the confrontation was nevertheless crucial in the development of the larger civil rights movement. The Albany movement (1) demonstrated that an entire community could be mobilized to engage in mass civil disobedience; (2) became a model for other black communities in Georgia, such as Americus and Waycross, where movements were organized concurrently or shortly after the Albany confrontation, and finally (3) revealed to movement leaders that careful planning and organizing was essential in large mass movements. Bernard Lee put it aptly: "This was the university. This was one of the colleges in the university of the movement, that we were doing some work in, and we learned some bitter things."[89]

BIRMINGHAM

The 1963 Birmingham confrontation was successful because the movement that the SCLC organized there divided Birmingham's white political and economic power structures. The division resulted from the collective power of masses generated by the movement. The economic elites of Birmingham capitulated to the demands of the SCLC because of an effective economic boycott and massive demonstrations that disrupted the city at its core. These strategies were so effective that the economic elites yielded to the demands of the movement in spite of tremendous pressure placed on them to resist, applied by the political elites. In Birmingham King and the SCLC's staff corrected the mistakes made in Albany. The Birmingham movement was marked by careful planning and internal cohesion.

Dr. King and the SCLC wanted to accomplish two main goals through a confrontation with Birmingham's white power structure.[90] First, they wanted the Birmingham white power structure to yield to a set of specific demands:

1. The desegregation of lunch counters and other public facilities in downtown department stores
2. The establishment of fair hiring procedures in retail stores and

city departments, with Negroes given an equal opportunity to qualify for other than menial jobs

3. The dropping of all charges against arrested demonstrators

4. The reopening of the parks and playground that the city had closed rather than comply with a federal court order that they be operated on an integrated basis

5. The appointment of a biracial commission to set up a timetable for the desegregation of the public schools[91]

Their second objective was to score a victory that would serve as a pivotal example to be used by other black communities and would force the federal government to take a firm stand against racial domination.

Most writers fail to emphasize the latter objective. Yet in the minds of those who planned the confrontation, it was critical. King wrote:

> We believed that while a campaign in Birmingham would surely be the toughest fight of our civil-rights careers, it could, if successful, break the back of segregation all over the nation. This city had been the country's chief symbol of racial intolerance. A victory there might well set forces in motion to change the entire course of the drive for freedom and justice. Because we were convinced of the significance of the job to be done in Birmingham, we decided that the most thorough planning and prayerful preparation must go into the effort.[92]

In a similar vein, the Reverend Fred Shuttlesworth, who was the SCLC's local leader in Birmingham, stated:

> We wanted confrontation, nonviolent confrontation, to see if it would work on a massive scale. Not just for Birmingham—for the nation. We were trying to launch a systematic, wholehearted battle against segregation which would set the pace for the nation.[93]

Therefore, when the Birmingham confrontation is assessed, it must be judged in terms of both its specific and its long-range objectives.

It will be argued here that to a considerable extent the SCLC accomplished its goals in Birmingham. The movement in Birmingham succeeded because of internal cohesion within the SCLC and within the Birmingham black community. Cultural forces, including music, religious oratory, prayers, and shared symbols, operated to produce the cohesion. The movement was successful also because the SCLC leaders systematically implemented a planned strategy throughout the confrontation. Finally, the Birmingham effort brought all the available power to bear by being a mass movement. It will be shown that Birmingham's white business elites acceded to the SCLC's demands because of these factors.

In many respects Birmingham was an ideal place for the SCLC to organize a movement. Recently a number of social scientists have contended that King chose Birmingham in 1963 because of the presence of "Bull" Connor.[94] The movement's only chance of winning, they say, was to trigger unprovoked white violence against the demonstrators so that the federal government would have no choice but to force local segregationists to meet the demands of the movement. So King chose Birmingham in 1963 supposedly because his main strategy was to provoke its unsophisticated redneck commissioner of public safety, Eugene "Bull" Connor, to use violence. This is a simplistic explanation. It fails to mention that Birmingham's strong SCLC affiliate, led by Reverend Shuttlesworth, made it a logical choice.

As demonstrated in Chapter Four, Shuttlesworth and the Alabama Christian Movement for Human Rights (ACMHR) had built an ongoing mass movement center in Birmingham dating back to 1956. Because it was one of the SCLC's best-organized centers, capable of engaging in sustained collective action, the SCLC leaders decided shortly after their experience in Albany in 1961–62 that a dramatic confrontation with the white power structure would be carefully planned and executed in Birmingham in 1963. With the choice of Birmingham, King was assured that many of the organizational forces needed to engage in social protest were already in place. Indeed, the spirit of protest was very much alive in segments of Birmingham's black community in 1963. For example, in the early part of 1962 some black students from Miles College and leaders of the ACMHR had organized an economic boycott against downtown stores because of their practices of economic and racial exploitation. During the boycott the profits of the merchants decreased by 40 percent.[95]

Birmingham was well suited for a mass protest movement also because it was clearly SCLC territory. The NAACP had been driven out of existence in Alabama by Southern courts in 1956. Neither CORE nor SNCC was strong in Birmingham. From a protest standpoint, Fred Shuttlesworth and the ACMHR dominated. After the Albany experience, SCLC activists decided that in order for them to win a large-scale confrontation they would have to be in control from beginning to end. Walker stated: "We said we need one place where we're going to be in charge from the bottom up, and we built Birmingham from the bottom up, brick by brick. And that's why it went the way it went because we were completely in charge."[96] And, of course, Birmingham was ideal because it was considered one of the most racist cities in the South. "Bull" Connor, the police commissioner of Birmingham, personified the racist sentiments of the South. He was known to hate "niggers" and would not hesitate to whip their heads. Thus SCLC leaders reasoned that if racism could be defeated in Birmingham it could be defeated throughout the South. In short, Birmingham was chosen because the SCLC had a strong organization there and because the city symbolically stood as the racist capital of America.

By 1963 the SCLC had become a powerful organization. According to Reverend Walker, in 1963 the SCLC had a budget of about a million dollars. The staff consisted of about one hundred full-time people. Walker's assessment of SCLC in 1963 is revealing: "At this point in Birmingham, it is my opinion that proportionally we had a front-line staff equal to any corporate giant in America. You take the size of SCLC and General Motors, and our top line leadership was equal to anything that General Motors had."[97] One may quibble with Walker's assessment, yet it reflects the degree to which the SCLC had become an organization with depth. The organization was arranged by departments. The Citizenship Education Department has already been discussed; then there was the Department of Operation Breadbasket, which specialized in implementing economic boycotts against firms that were discriminating against blacks; and there was a Department of Direct Action that planned confrontations such as the one in Birmingham. Those departments were run by specialists who had proved their abilities in the field and amassed substantial movement experiences. Speaking of the SCLC's staff in 1963, the Reverend C. T. Vivian stated: "There wasn't anything around that had as many strong horses as SCLC brought together in one place. When you put all that talent and experience together and flowed it into a town where there was an issue, there was no way of stopping something like that."[98]

Each staff person or team had specific responsibilities in Birmingham and was accountable for them. For example, James Lawson was in charge of teaching nonviolence, James Bevel and Diane Nash Bevel were in charge of organizing the student wing of the movement, and so on. The SCLC's affiliates in other states, such as Virginia and California, were assigned to specific duties such as fundraising. The SCLC's affiliate structure was capable of handling these demands, because by late 1961 the SCLC had at least eighty local and state affiliate organizations.[99] As Wyatt Walker pointed out, "Birmingham was a tremendous organizational operation."[100]

Several months before the confrontation in Birmingham the SCLC held strategy meetings and retreats. These gatherings served to iron out internal conflict as well as to plan strategy. It was emphasized repeatedly that the activities of the SCLC in Birmingham had to be synchronized and harmoniously linked. In part, the SCLC solved its internal problem by bringing on staff some of the best people the movement had produced. One of SNCC's greatest contributions to the civil rights movement stemmed from its genius in organizing college and high school students. In Albany SNCC activists had been quite successful in organizing the entire community and especially the young people. However the unity it achieved was undermined when organizational conflict arose between SNCC and the SCLC. Assessing the organizational conflict in Albany, James Bevel maintained:

> Where there's an authentic trust and an authentic respect, then authentic thoughts can be exchanged. But, where there's hidden attitudes and hoping you fail . . . you have resentment. . . . If you spend thirty minutes with kids, and you're negatively talking about other people, you can't inspire them to do any work. They'll go back home and go to a ball game.[101]

SCLC leaders were determined not to produce the same interorganizational conflict in Birmingham that had plagued the Albany movement.

In the Birmingham movement the SCLC eliminated the organizational conflict but maintained the SNCC dynamic. Shortly after the Albany movement formed, the SCLC hired James Bevel from SNCC. Bevel says he was hired to smooth out the conflict that developed between SNCC and the SCLC. Bevel and his new wife, Diane Nash, were placed in charge of organizing the student wing of the movement in Birmingham. Hosea Williams recalls: "James Bevel was one of the most brilliant men I ever met. Bevel was our youth person. Bevel could do more with young people than any human being on the face of the earth."[102] The Bevels were experienced activists, having been student leaders in the Nashville movement center. They had been well schooled by James Lawson, C. T. Vivian, Kelly Miller Smith, and others. They had acquired most of their experience directly through participation in movement activities. By hiring Bevel and Nash, the SCLC acquired two leaders who understood how to organize high school and college students. Thus, in Birmingham the SCLC incorporated an important SNCC dynamic without bringing in SNCC, the organization. This strategy preserved internal cohesion within the SCLC and within the larger Birmingham movement. All staff people knew their roles, and they agreed to keep working to reach the specified objectives even if disagreement arose.

In Chapter Four it was pointed out that the ACMHR had a difficult time uniting all segments of Birmingham's black community behind the organization. Disunity between black leaders was still a problem in 1963. In fact, before the Birmingham movement could be successful, the SCLC had to create and build internal cohesion within the black community. In 1963 a large number of Birmingham black leaders shared the view of the *New York Times, Newsweek,* the *Washington Post,* the White House, and Southern racists that the planned demonstrations of SCLC were badly timed because a coming mayoral election might throw Commissioner Connor out of office. Connor was one of several candidates for the mayor's office. Both white and black leaders thought race relations in the city might improve with the election of Connor's opponent, Albert Boutwell, who was considered a moderate. Shuttlesworth and King did not share the view that Boutwell's election would substantively change race relations. Boutwell had previously been a leader in the White Citizens' Council, it was pointed out, and had courted the segregationist vote when campaigning for Lieutenant Governor in 1958.[103] Nevertheless, the SCLC did allow the elections to delay the demonstrations, because some felt that they would work to the disadvantage of the moderate candidate. After the election the SCLC had to delay its planned demonstrations again because of a runoff between Boutwell and Connor. After the runoff in early April the SCLC decided to go ahead with its planned demonstrations, but once again King and his associates encountered widespread opposition among Birmingham's black leaders. Some leaders contended that the new administration deserved a chance to bring about change without the pressure of demonstrations, especially as the SCLC had not given sufficient notification about the planned demonstrations.

King, realizing that the success of the demonstrations depended on black unity, decided that he had to move quickly to unite Birmingham's black leaders behind the movement. King wrote:

> I spoke to 125 business and professional people at a call meeting in the Gaston Building. I talked to a gathering of two hundred ministers. I met with many small groups, during a hectic one-week schedule. In most cases, the atmosphere when I entered was tense and chilly, and I was aware that there was a great deal of work to be done.[104]

Andrew Young amplified: "It was necessary to go to Birmingham and get together everybody that thought he was a leader. Anyone who thought of himself as a leader had to be contacted."[105]

Dr. King's stature as a charismatic leader helped to bring about internal cohesion in Birmingham. William Kunstler, who accompanied King to one of the community meetings, explained that King listened patiently and, after the leaders had finished raising their objections, went to the heart of the matter. Kunstler reported what King told the apprehensive blacks:

> "This is the most segregated city in America," he said, "and we have to stick together if we ever hope to change its ways. I and my Asso-

ciates in the Southern Christian Leadership Conference have come to help you break down the walls. With God's help, we cannot fail."[106]

Kunstler went on to relate the results of the meeting:

Although there was a brief flurry of questions after he had finished talking, it was clear that he could now count on his audience. Those who hadn't been won over were at least neutralized and the rest seemed eager to help in the work that lay ahead. I didn't know quite when the turning point was reached, but I was very much aware that it had.[107]

Young, Kunstler, and Walker pointed out that in these community meetings, it was just as important for Dr. King to neutralize blacks who were antagonistic to the movement as it was to win over others. Young said it was important to neutralize people "so that you didn't have anyone working actively against you."[108] This is obviously a lesson that the SCLC activists learned from the Albany experience. Speaking of King's success, Young wrote, "I don't think anyone but a person of Martin's international leadership stature could have done it, and even then he didn't quite make it."[109]

In the Birmingham movement the invocation of black church culture also served to build internal cohesion within the SCLC and the larger black community. SCLC strategists knew that a successful confrontation with "Bull" Connor and the rest of Birmingham's white power structure would require total emotional commitment on the part of movement participants. Reverend Shuttlesworth and the ACMHR were prepared; the preaching was trenchant and captivating.

The ACMHR's choir specialized in the art of organizing blacks through songs. This group, the Birmingham Movement Choir, comprised sixty fine voices. One of the songs written for the Birmingham struggle became renowned for its ability to garner total commitment from participants. The song was "Ninety-nine and a Half Won't Do." The choir would begin this song in a packed mass meeting by rhythmically proclaiming: "Five, ten, fifteen, won't do, twenty, twenty-five, thirty won't do." With a quickening tempo, the choir would continue all the way to "Ninety-nine and a half won't do." Then the crescendo would be reached when the choir and the audience would shout, "A hundred percent will do." Writing of this song, Bernice Reagon pointed out: "The lyrics of this song articulated a commitment to completing a task and an awareness that nothing less than total involvement in the struggle was required."[110] Summing up the role of music in the confrontation, Reagon added, "The music of the Birmingham movement reflected its top-drawer level of organization and strategy."[111]

During the Birmingham confrontation the SCLC held sixty-five consecutive nightly mass meetings. These meetings rotated from church to church in order to maximize community solidarity. King discussed the role of music in the meetings:

> An important part of the mass meetings was the freedom songs. In a sense the freedom songs are the soul of the movement. . . . I have stood in a meeting with hundreds of youngsters and joined in while they sang, "Ain't Gonna Let Nobody Turn Me Round." It is not just a song; it is a resolve. A few minutes later, I have seen those same youngsters refuse to turn around before a pugnacious Bull Connor in command of men armed with power hoses. These songs bind us together, give us courage together, help us to march together.[112]

Through strategy meetings and retreats, hiring procedures, assigning of tasks, community meetings, and mass meetings where commitment was solidified, the SCLC built internal cohesion both within the SCLC and within the larger black community of Birmingham.

Project "C"

Project "C" was the code name of the planned movement that the SCLC prepared for Birmingham. The "C" stood for confrontation, which was to be with Birmingham's white power structure. That power structure was three-pronged. The first prong comprised the business and industrial elites, which ran the city's economy. The second prong was the political elites in charge of maintaining the status quo and the traditional patterns of race relations. The job of the political elites was to ensure that Birmingham's blacks remained exploited economically, politically, and personally. The political elites included such notables as Governor George C. Wallace; Colonel Albert Lingo, the State Director of Public Safety; Birmingham's Mayor Arthur Hanes; and Eugene "Bull" Connor, the avowed racist who had tremendous power as Birmingham's commissioner of public safety. At Connor's beck and call were the police force, the fire department, and the state militia under Governor Wallace's office.

The third prong of Birmingham's white power structure comprised the white extremist organizations and the general white population of Birmingham. The political elites relied on such organizations as the White Citizens' Councils and the Ku Klux Klan to do the dirty work. The roles of these organizations were to fan the flames of racial hatred through propaganda and to keep blacks in line by beating and bombing them. There was overlapping membership between the political elites and the white extremist organizations.[113] They often worked hand in hand to maintain the status quo. Finally, members of Birmingham's white power structure relied on the general white population to condone their practices of racial discrimination and exploitation. Indeed, the practice of racism was so intricately woven and structured into the institutions and minds of local whites that the power structure operated with the knowledge that under pressure it could count on the majority of white Birminghamians. Members of the white power structure had few problems in proclaiming that they governed in the "best interest of the people."

The three-pronged white power structure was the formidable beast that Project "C" was designed to confront. SCLC strategists had to design effective ways of dividing this three-pronged power structure so that it would have no choice but to meet its demands. That was a difficult assignment. The problem was to find a way to gain leverage on Birmingham's white power structure. In the repertoire of tactics of the civil rights movement, the economic boycott, supplemented by disruptive demonstrations, was the combination that would force racist white power structures across the South to yield to the demands of the movement.

The SCLC leaders decided that if the movement were to be successful in Birmingham it would have to paralyze the business community through an economic boycott. It was determined also that massive daily demonstrations were needed to dramatize the racist nature of Birmingham and to prevent the city from operating normally. Again, Garrow and others are incorrect when they say that the SCLC's main strategy in Birmingham was to have the demonstrators beaten by "Bull" Connor and his police force, thereby to elicit federal intervention and the nation's outrage and sympathy.[114] To the contrary, the Birmingham movement was designed to generate the necessary power needed to defeat local segregationists by using the economic boycott and mass demonstrations.

The Birmingham movement was scheduled to start at the beginning of the Easter shopping period, when the boycott would have the greatest effect. SCLC activists were aware that the effective economic boycott in Nashville during the sit-ins occurred during the Easter period. The main strategy planned for Project "C" was an effective boycott of Birmingham's business community. Reverend Walker, who was an architect of Project "C," stated:

> In Birmingham we decided we would concentrate on the ebb and flow of the money downtown, see? So all of our concentration was on effecting the ebb and flow of the commerce and industry of the South's

*largest and baddest city. . . . Not only did we concentrate on down-
town but we said that if we couldn't get into the downtown area, that
we'd go to the federal installations. . . . If we couldn't get the federal
installations, then we'd concentrate on some outlying suburban shopping centers.*[115]

Similarly Dr. King, another architect of Project "C", wrote:

*We concluded that in hard-core communities a more effective battle
would be waged if it was concentrated against one aspect of the evil
and intricate system of segregation. We decided, therefore, to center
the Birmingham struggle on the business community, for we knew
that the Negro population had sufficient buying power so that its withdrawal could make the difference between profit and loss for many
businesses.*[116]

King pointed out that this lesson had been learned in Albany a few
months earlier from the unsuccessful attempt to attack all aspects of
domination simultaneously. Clearly, if the main strategy was to get federal help by provoking white racists to beat blacks, then no economic
boycott was needed.

Moreover, the SCLC leaders had reason to believe that an economic
boycott would be effective because of the outcome of the 1962 boycott.
In reaction to that boycott and a threat by Shuttlesworth to bring King
and the SCLC to Birmingham, merchants had begun to make modest
changes. However, Connor and the political officials of the city had
halted those modest changes and in fact had reversed them by turning
their power against the economic elites. "Bull" Connor had the last
word on race relations, because the merchants were afraid to challenge
him. To get the merchants back in line after the 1962 boycott, Connor
threatened to close stores for alleged code infractions, forcing some
proprietors to pay large repair costs, urged numerous whites to cancel
their charge accounts at stores that capitulated to blacks, and used other
pressure tactics.[117] Consequently, the merchants gave in to the "Bull"
and the political officials and returned to doing segregated business as
usual.

The SCLC planned the boycott and demonstrations well in advance.
It was critical for the SCLC that the boycott and demands be thought
out carefully, because the intent of the boycott was to force businessmen to grant specific concessions, which they had the power to do.[118]
Wyatt Walker designed the boycott and demonstrations down to the
smallest detail. Lerone Bennett wrote: "All through the early months
of 1963 . . . SCLC aides worked. Information on the ownership of busi-

ness and industrial concerns in Birmingham was compiled."[119] King wrote:

> *Wyatt familiarized himself with downtown Birmingham, not only plotting the main streets and landmarks (target stores, city hall, post office, etc.), but meticulously surveying each store's eating facilities, and sketching the entrances and possible paths of ingress and egress. In fact, Walker detailed the number of stools, tables and chairs to determine how many demonstrators should go to each store. His survey of the downtown area also included suggested secondary targets in the event we were blocked from reaching our primary targets.*[120]

Also, in contrast to Albany, the SCLC did its homework to determine what would constitute a successful boycott. This came through clearly in Walker's recollection:

> *We know that in most businesses 6 percent is the margin of profit. Black folks made up 35–40 percent of the consumer population [in Birmingham]. So all we felt we had to do was get a 50 percent response from the black community. We didn't think that all blacks would go along with it.*[121]

SCLC strategists decided that the Birmingham movement should be a drama. That is, it would start out slow and low-keyed and then continue to build up, step by step, until it reached a crisis point, where the opposition would be forced to yield. In Bevel's words, "Every nonviolent movement is a dialogue between two forces, and you have to develop a drama to dramatize the dialogue to reveal the contradictions in the guys you're dialoguing with within the social context. That's called a socio-drama."[122] Bevel explains that as the drama unfolds it is important that movement participants refuse to compromise or sacrifice at any point.

All the principal architects of Project "C" (e.g. King, Walker, Bevel, and Young) emphasized that the SCLC had anticipated that Birmingham would be a long struggle. Project "C" was prepared according to a precise timetable designed to produce maximum drama. Phase I would kick off "B" (Birmingham) Day and last for several days. During this period the economic boycott would be implemented, and small groups of demonstrators were to sit in and picket at downtown stores. The Phase II plan called for mass marches on City Hall by waves of demonstrators. "D" Day would signal the beginning of Phase III, when grammar school, high school, and college students would begin going to jail in staggering numbers. Through all phases the economic boycott was to be maintained. Such were the plans of Project "C". As Walker stated, "it was just a matter of unfolding our plan, progressively and we were in charge of the timetable."[123]

Dr. King and his associates were aware, however, that a court injunction against demonstrations would impede their plans if they obeyed it. King and his strategists made plans for the court injunction that was sure to come. Prior to the movement the SCLC's staff and lawyers carefully explored the legal and social implications of violating both a state injunction and a federal one. King decided that he would violate either, but he hoped for a state injunction. King had learned from the Albany experience. On the subject of an injunction in Birmingham he wrote:

> Planned, deliberate civil disobedience had been discussed as far back as the meeting at Harry Belafonte's apartment in March. There, in consultation with some of the closest friends of the movement, we had decided that if an injunction was issued to thwart our demonstrations, it would be our duty to violate it. . . . The injunction method has now become the leading instrument of the South to break the direct-action civil-rights drive and to prevent Negro citizens and their white allies from engaging in peaceful assembly, a right guaranteed by the First Amendment. . . . We had anticipated that this procedure would be used in Birmingham.[124]

Thus King decided it made more political sense to take action that would enhance the movement rather than impede it. The injunction had to be violated.

Movement strategists knew that a "planned deliberate" confrontation on paper was one thing, while actually executing it was quite another. Indeed, to crack the three-pronged white power structure of Birmingham would require precise coordination and organization of massive human effort. Fortunately for the SCLC, the basic organizational outline already existed in Birmingham. The Citizenship Schools had been quietly preparing some people for the confrontation. Moreover, as pointed out earlier, it was the Reverend Fred Shuttlesworth and the Alabama Christian Movement for Human Rights that served as the SCLC's launching pad in Birmingham. Hence an organization and a nucleus of people already existed for protest purposes.

Still, the black churches were the power centers through which the Birmingham confrontation was organized and coordinated. As Young stated:

> We often talk about the "hand of God" in the leadership. There were four young men in Birmingham, in churches, that had come there within a year, that happened to be pastors of the largest churches in

the city. John Cross at 16th Street Baptist Church, A. D. King [Dr. King's brother] had just gone to First Baptist in Ensley which was a very influential church, Nelson Smith at New Pilgrim, and John Porter who had been Martin's assistant in Montgomery at Dexter, was at Sixth Avenue Baptist. The members of those four Baptist Churches gave the movement a constituency of close to 5,000—to start with. When you add that constituency to the 500 or 600 that Fred Shuttlesworth had organized, we had the basis of a movement.[125]

Throughout the confrontation the Sixteenth Street Baptist Church served as Walker's organizational headquarters.

From the Sixteenth Street Baptist Church blacks were recruited, trained, and exposed to challenging movement songs, prayers, and oratory. A few blocks away, in the heart of the black community, King and Abernathy set up their headquarters in the A. G. Gaston Motel. With "B" Day fast approaching, Ralph Abernathy shouted out, "Tell 'em we're going to rock this town like it has never been rocked before."[126] King made a promise. He said he would lead demonstrations in the city until "Pharaoh lets God's people go."[127]

On the other side of the political fence "Bull" Connor "predicted that 'blood would run in the streets' of Birmingham before it would be integrated."[128] However, a crack had already appeared in the "Bull's" armor. Connor had been defeated in the runoff election for mayor, although he was refusing to leave office on the basis of a legal technicality. He had filed a suit to prevent the new mayor, Albert Boutwell, from taking office. During the confrontation "Birmingham was treated to the spectacle of both administrations serving simultaneously".[129] Connor was still in power in spite of having been voted out. It was he who still exercised power over the police force, the fire department, and, through them, the economic elite, who were interested in making a profit whatever the system of race relations. Connor had the direct ear of Governor Wallace, who had pledged, "Segregation now, segregation tomorrow, segregation forever!" It was Connor and his associates who still wielded heavy influence with the White Citizens' Council and the Ku Klux Klan. It was from Connor that many white Birminghamians received their action cues.

"B" Day

April 3, 1963, was "B" Day. Project "C" swung into action, and the planned confrontation was under way. Between the third and the sixth, limited sit-ins and picketing at segregated lunch counters in several department stores and drugstores were carried out. No mass arrests or marches were to occur during that first phase. In addition to the sit-ins, SCLC leaders attempted to start negotiations with Birmingham economic elites, while simultaneously mobilizing the black community and implementing the economic boycott.

Shortly after the sit-ins began, thirty-five of the demonstrators were quietly arrested on trespassing charges. This was the low-keyed but important beginning. At the end of the first day of sit-ins the mass meetings began. "After the first day we held a mass meeting," King wrote, "the first of sixty-five nightly meetings conducted at various churches in the Negro community. Through these meetings we were able to generate the power and depth which finally galvanized the entire Negro community."[130] At those meetings people were recruited and trained in the techniques of nonviolent protest. They were informed also that demonstrations were needed because all previous methods had failed.

Many of the activities of Phase I were directed at persuading blacks to support the movement. Indeed, massive cooperation was essential for the success of the economic boycott. During "B" Day word was disseminated throughout the black community, mainly through the churches not to shop downtown. Andrew Young explained:

The preachers who were afraid of demonstrations and who didn't want to be a part of the demonstrations in the beginning would at least announce the boycott in their churches. We produced about 50,000 handbills every week and over the weekend, through the churches and door-to-door leafletting, we kept the community informed and encouraged the boycott.[131]

Realizing the need for church support, King directly challenged the ministers to back the movement during the first phase of the project: "I'm tired of preachers riding around in big cars, living in fine homes, but not willing to take their part in the fight. . . . If you can't stand up with your own people, you are not fit to be a leader!"[132] Many ministers made the decision to support the movement after this "tough" talk had put them on trial before an oppressed black community. The movement was beginning to gain momentum.

During "B" Day representatives of the movement approached the economic elites asking that they yield to the demands so as to prevent a crisis. Vincent Harding, a black Mennonite minister who became one of the negotiators between the movement and Birmingham's business leaders, reported: "At the outset of the demonstrations it was not easy to find whites of stature and influence who were eager to discuss the city's difficulties. Most of the businessmen said that they would not negotiate while the demonstrations were in process."[133] It was clear that this group would negotiate only if put under pressure. At that point it was decided to introduce Phase II of Project "C," which called for the intensification of demonstrations and the introduction of mass marches.

Phase II

SCLC strategists methodically intensified the drama when they implemented Phase II of Project "C" on April 6. On that day forty-five demonstrators attempted to march to City Hall and hold a prayer session. Connor's police force blocked that attempt by arresting the forty-five demonstrators. Each day demonstrators attempted to march to City Hall to pray but were arrested by Connor's police. Walker said of the marches: "We just made that the focal point and had those marches every day. Day after day. Week after week."[134] David Lewis indicated the persistency of the marchers: "They were the vanguard of the marching army of singing demonstrators that would advance each day, for the next thirty-four days."[135] The number of arrests began to grow, and so did the effectiveness of the downtown boycott, as well as the drama.

The black community began to gather solidly behind the movement once Phase II was initiated. Large numbers of blacks began filing into 16th Street Baptist Church, making it known that their services were available to the movement. Reverend Walker remarked: "There's two kinds of people. People who are committed to the movement and people who get committed by the movement. And the largest proportion of the people in Birmingham including most of the black pastors, they got committed by the movement."[136] Reverend Lawson and other experts took the "converted" to the back of the church, "where the Leadership Training Committee made an appointment with them to come to our office the following day for screening and intensive training."[137]

"Bull" Connor, recognizing that the jails were beginning to fill and that the movement was gaining momentum, acquired an injunction. King and the SCLC's staff was pleased to learn that it was a state rather than a federal injunction. The state injunction was issued on April 10 at 9:00 P.M. Through the injunction the white power structure of Birmingham ordered that all demonstrations cease. Dr. King immediately directed Walker to call a news conference at 1:00 A.M. on April 11. King, Shuttlesworth, and Abernathy appeared before reporters and television cameras to receive the injunction. After answering questions, King announced, "Regardless of what's in this injunction, we've got an injunction from heaven."[138] It was clear now that not only was

King going to violate the injunction, but he was going to get all the mileage he could out of it.

King instructed Walker to arrange for another news conference the following day for a formal reply to the injunction. Walker was pleased at the course King had chosen, for to obey the injunction would mean that "all of our planning and organizing, a year's effort, would have been in vain, and that was exactly what the city was trying to accomplish by going to court."[139] By the time of the press conference members of the black community were gathered around the A. G. Gaston Motel to hear what the movement leaders would say about the injunction. King, Shuttlesworth, and Abernathy took their places at a table jammed with microphones. They had on their marching clothes. The table was on a balcony overlooking the crowd. King informed his supporters and the nation that the movement leadership would disobey the injunction and lead a march on Good Friday. The black audience immediately broke into ringing applause. King then stated, "The direct action will continue today, tomorrow, Saturday, Sunday, and on through."[140] The drama heightened.

Before the injunction King had purposely avoided jail by not participating in street demonstrations. He had stayed out of jail to complete "the job of unifying the Negro community".[141] Strategically, King decided that he would go to jail on Good Friday while violating the injunction. King could choose the exact time he would be arrested, because the injunction had been handed down two days prior to Good Friday, and the moment he participated in a demonstration he would be arrested for defying it. Again, King was getting maximum mileage out of the injunction, because Good Friday was a symbolic day to religious Southern blacks. Jesus had made the ultimate sacrifice on that day, and now King, his servant, was following in his footsteps to free the dominated in the "Egypt Land" of the Southern United States. NAACP lawyers went to court to have the injunction overturned while King and Abernathy marched toward the waiting handcuffs and the paddy wagons that would take them to jail. Meanwhile Harry Belafonte raised $50,000 dollars to bail demonstrators out of jail after the city heavily increased bond. James Bevel, Dorothy Cotton, and Bernard Lee were visiting the grammar schools, high schools, and colleges, busily organizing the young.

The number of people jailed began to climb toward a thousand. King wrote his famous letter from the Birmingham jail. It was a movement halfway house—the American Friends Service Committee—that distributed the letter to the public. Andrew Young wrote later:

As soon as the "Letter from a Birmingham Jail" was issued, the Friends Service Committee printed and distributed 50,000 copies. This appeal had a circulation of close to a million before Martin got out of jail. It was re-printed everywhere, and it pulled supporters together. . . . It was the kind of document that spoke so much to the conditions of Birmingham that it was nationally distributed. . . . It was an important feature in making the movement work.[142]

Being an established movement halfway house, the American Friends Service Committee had the organizational resources necessary to assist the movement at that point.

Following King's and Abernathy's arrest business leaders began to meet with leaders of the movement. Harding wrote:

For the next two weeks semi-secret meetings were called, usually early in the morning or late at night. . . . Yet the merchants were hesitant to move without broader support from the business community or from an established city government.[143]

The fact that these businessmen had to meet in secrecy reflects the degree to which the political leaders dominated the business community in issues concerning race relations. The uncertainty as to which city administration would eventually take power further contributed to the indecisiveness of the economic elites.

The economic elites of Birmingham were vulnerable to outside pressure, because Northern capitalists owned most of the businesses they managed. But pressure from Northern capitalists to change racial exploitation in Birmingham was nonexistent as long as the profits kept rolling northward. Northern capitalists became concerned with racial problems in the South only after the movement began choking off their profits. Birmingham had been rocked by racial confrontations since 1956, usually organized by Shuttlesworth and his Alabama Christian Movement for Human Rights, and well-publicized lawsuits had been fought out in the courts. An article describing Birmingham's racial tensions had been published in 1960.[144] None of that had stirred the Northern financial centers to use their influence over the economic enterprises they owned in Birmingham to change their policies. It took Project "C" to generate the power to force the Northern capitalists to take action.

"D" Day: Separation of Economic and Political Elites

King and Abernathy returned to their movement headquarters after spending eight days in jail. They found that some members of the business community were meeting with movement negotiators but doing very little negotiating. The decision was made to turn up the drama to a high pitch by moving to Phase III of Project "C."

On May 2, 1963, "D" Day went into effect. The organized student section of the movement took its place on the stage. Under the leadership of James Bevel, more than a thousand children went to jail. In Kunstler's words, "On the appointed day, hundreds of teenagers met in the Sixteenth Street Baptist Church. As fast as they arrived, they were sent downtown in successive waves, each larger than the last. Before nightfall, more than a thousand were behind bars."[145] What was happening in Birmingham at that moment was quite similar to what had happened in Nashville during the successful student sit-in movement. Young pointed out the similarity:

> The student movement, primarily in Nashville, began to develop tactics of community organization that were different from the tactics of community organization that had emerged in Montgomery. . . . [W]hen we got to Birmingham, basically we had effected that merger between students and preachers, between community organizers and charismatic leaders.[146]

Harding reported that the business elite began to feel pressure to bring about changes at the close of "D" Day number one. Bull Connor and his political officials also felt pressure, because the jails were filling up. The movement was generating collective power by the masses, which King referred to as "creative tensions." By any name, Birmingham was experiencing a crisis.

On May 3 thousands of students gathered at movement headquarters prepared to protest. "Bull" Connor ordered out the fire hoses, the billy clubs, and the dogs. The students were attacked as they attempted to leave Sixteenth Street Baptist Church. Pictures that captured the cruelty were distributed around the world. The crisis in Birmingham became the top priority of the nation and of the government. On the fourth and fifth of May, violence broke out between some members of the black community and the police. President Kennedy sent Burke Marshall, head of the Justice Department's Civil Rights Division, to Birmingham. His assignment was to press the economic elites to reach a settlement. Kennedy's office made contact with the Northern capitalists who owned most of Birmingham's businesses, and urged them to use their influence over the local business leaders of Birmingham. Yet by May 5 Birmingham's business elites were not capitulating.

Demonstrations were stepped up. On May 5 the black church culture weighed heavily in the power struggle taking place in the streets, and many consider that day the turning point in the movement. The Reverend Charles Billups led a group of marchers to city hall to pray, as they had attempted to do since April 6. However, by May 5 Connor's men were using fire hoses and dogs to contain the demonstrators. When Connor ordered the marchers to turn back and they refused, he directed the firemen to turn the hoses on the protesters. According to King, Connor shouted, "Dammit. Turn on the hoses!" King's account went on:

> What happened in the next thirty seconds was one of the most fantastic events of the Birmingham story. Bull Connor's men, their deadly hoses poised for action, stood facing the marchers. The marchers, many of them on their knees, stared back, unafraid and unmoving. Slowly the Negroes stood up and began to advance. Connor's men, as though hypotized, fell back, their hoses sagging uselessly in their hands while several hundred Negroes marched past them, without further interference, and held their prayer meeting as planned.[147]

This was the first time Connor ordered the water hoses turned on the group of marchers headed for City Hall. Reverend Billups, who led the group, sensed the immediate danger and gave the signal for the anxiety-filled marchers to drop to their knees and pray, rather than get excited.

The outcome of this event can be explained by examining the church culture. The instant the serious prayer was uttered, the determination of the demonstrators escalated. They had sung in the church over and over that ninety-nine and a half percent would not do. In this tense situation blacks asked God to give them strength, just as they had during services in the black church down through the centuries. When confronted by high-power water hoses, blacks reached deep down into their psyches or souls and summoned up that "something extra." It was that same "something extra" they prayed for at church services when they were not sure they could bear the humiliation they had to face every Monday morning when they had to "meet the man." After prayer, Reverend Billups and the protesters rose from their knees. Billups told "Bull" Connor and members of the fire department, "Turn on your water, turn loose your dogs, we will stand here till we die."[148]

Andrew Young described what happened next. An old woman rose from her knees and said, "The Lord is with this movement and we're going on to the jail." Young continued:

> And everybody got up and started walking. We walked right on through. "Bull" Connor was standing there screaming: "Stop them, stop them!" The men with the fire hoses had evidently been caught in all this, and they just dropped them, and the dogs were just as quiet. Walking through the red fire trucks, folks started preaching about the Lord parting the Red Sea again.[149]

Lewis reported that the marchers interpreted the event as a "providential sign."[150] Kunstler was moved to write of the incident: "Then, in one of those rare moments in human affairs, morality proved irresistible."[151] For the purposes at hand, this event suggests that the black church culture enabled the demonstrators to win an important victory in the heat of battle.

SCLC officials intensified the drama. On May 6 one thousand demonstrators, including four hundred juveniles, were arrested while attempting to demonstrate. The economic boycott was being felt by the business community, and Burke Marshall was bringing pressure on the economic elites to negotiate. Walker told how the boycott was working:

> Black folk in cooperation or out of fear stayed out of downtown. The boost we got was that white husbands told their wives, "Don't go downtown. The niggers are down there. Too much trouble going on." So that doubled the effect of our boycott . . . that's what made [the merchants] decide they need to sit down and get some amelioration of this stranglehold we had on the downtown area.[152]

Young also praised the boycott effort:

> We really began to use the muscle in nonviolence when we began the economic withdrawal. . . . [T]he real power was that 250,000 black citizens were not buying anything but food and medicine. Out of a population of about 600,000, you can understand how that would cripple the economy, and it didn't take long for that to happen. Black citizens didn't buy anything but food and medicine. Three times a day we would check downtown, and anytime we saw more than five black people in a store, we got concerned that the boycott was slipping. It was really tight.[153]

Recalling the period around May 5, King wrote: "We were advised, in the utmost confidence, that the white business structure was weakening under the adverse publicity, the pressure of our boycott, and a parallel falling-off of white buying."[154] The business community held fast to its position until May 7. However, it was becoming clear that economic and social pressures were squeezing it away from the political powers.

On May 7, around the lunch hour, literally thousands of demonstrators, mostly young people, invaded Birmingham's downtown business district. Michael Dorman, a *Newsday* reporter on the scene, wrote:

> At this point thousands of Negroes—some demonstrators, other former bystanders—surged through yards and back alleys leading to the

*business section. They formed ranks again in front of downtown de-
partment stores. For about a half-hour they turned the busy noon rush
hour into a complete state of confusion on downtown streets. Some
knelt to pray on the sidewalks. Other marched along the streets, singing freedom songs. Some crowded whites off the sidewalks. "We're
marching for freedom!" they shouted.*[155]

It is clear that these disruptive tactics by the black masses were aimed
primarily at the economic elites. Some of the demonstrators, Harding
wrote, "marched into several downtown stores, and in one—owned by
the most recalcitrant merchant—they sat on the floor and sang freedom
songs."[156]

The drama of confrontation reached its zenith on May 7. The jails
were already filled with more than two thousand blacks. Business as
usual in downtown Birmingham was brought to a definite halt. No
longer could capitalists make rational profit predictions or lament their
losses in quiet isolation. The demonstrators were shouting to the merchants, "The police can't stop us now. Even Bull Connor can't stop us
now."[157] The political leaders, with their attack dogs and high-pressure
water hoses, disagreed. They invaded downtown and physically attacked the demonstrators, because the jails were too full to make arrests. Because it was extremely hot in Birmingham, many of the young
people enjoyed bathing and wading in the water sprayed at them by
the political elites. The protesters shouted to the firemen, "We'll be back
tomorrow, with soap."[158] The "Bull" was being maneuvered into a
"steer." Yet, being a great fighter, he refused to budge an inch.

The business community began to see the handwriting on the wall.
King explained that only hours before the noon confrontation, the economic elites had met and "were so intransigent that Burke Marshall
despaired of a pact".[159] Harding, one of the black negotiators, wrote,
"On Tuesday morning, May 7, Marshall urged the merchants, and other
businessmen as well, to meet the demands of the Negroes. There was
still hesitancy, and several thought the National Guard should be
brought in to stop all protest activity."[160] But as the merchants headed
out for lunch, they were confronted with the noonday crisis. King wrote:

*Astounded, those businessmen, key figures in a great city, suddenly
realized that the movement could not be stopped. When they returned—from the lunch they were unable to get—one of the men who
had been in the most determined opposition cleared his throat and
said: "You know, I've been thinking this through. We ought to be able
to work something out."*[161]

At that point the Kennedy Administration increased its pressure on
the economic elites. The Kennedy response meant that the SCLC had

successfully created an economic and political crisis in Birmingham. To be sure, the nation was being treated to the spectacle of an American city practicing totalitarian behavior against some of its own citizens. The world, including countries that had long maintained that the United States' rhetoric about democracy was in fact a lie, watched "American justice" being displayed in Birmingham by television and satellite. At home many citizens were shocked by the oppression existing in Birmingham and looked to a President whose image epitomized liberalism and fair play. Kennedy had little choice but to act. Northern capitalists who owned businesses in Birmingham were also forced to act, because the boycott and political crisis ensured that profits would cease until a solution was reached. Rich and powerful Northerners in Kennedy's Administration began calling their colleagues in industry who owned most of Birmingham's businesses and telling them to apply pressure on Birmingham's elites. The impact of the collective power of masses had reached the White House.

Harding reports that on the afternoon of May 7 the businessmen began serious negotiations:

> As a group they came as close to representing the economic power structure as any group could. Included were merchants, industrialists, corporation and bank presidents, prominent insurance and real-estate men. . . . Together, they represented—by their own estimate—more than eighty percent of the hiring power of the Birmingham area.[162]

It was this group that had the resources required to meet the demands of the dominated. The united white power structure of Birmingham began to fracture once the business leaders began seriously considering capitulating to the collective power of masses. Birmingham's economic elites began to realize what black masses had discovered in Baton Rouge back in 1953: that there is power in organized collective action. To some degree the business owners felt liberated by the power of the movement. "There was also a certain sense of self satisfaction," Harding wrote, "for these men had finally decided to stand together in defiance of the racist sentiment that had so long ruled the city."[163]

Late in the evening on May 7, 1963, the businessmen and movement negotiators reached an agreement on the demands. Albert Boutwell, the candidate who had won the election against Connor, had been secretly sending representatives to the negotiations. Boutwell's representative was present when the settlement was reached. The businessmen agreed that (1) lunch counters, rest rooms, fitting rooms, and drinking fountains would be desegregated within a specified time period; (2) Negroes would be hired and upgraded on a nondiscriminatory basis throughout the industrial community of Birmingham; (3) demonstrators who had been jailed were to be released without having to post bond; and (4) a biracial committee would be established to keep communications open between the white and black communities. Boutwell was afraid to take sides publicly, because he wanted to head the city's government irrespective of whether the collective power of masses or institutional power triumphed in Birmingham. But the mere existence of the split between "Bull" Connor and Boutwell increased the chances that the movement would win. The presence of Boutwell's representative at the negotiations suggested that if he succeeded in taking office, the economic elite would not be punished for yielding to the demands of the movement. To be sure, the business leaders felt they could count on Boutwell's acquiescence as they yielded to movement demands.

Meanwhile "Bull" Connor and the political leaders of Birmingham moved quickly to snatch away from the movement the power that had been apparent at noon. On the evening of May 7 the mayor and Connor asked Governor Wallace to send state police to Birmingham. Wallace agreed and pledged, "We shall fight the agitators, meddlers and enemies of constitutional government."[164] Dorman reported: "By late Tuesday, about 575 troopers, virtually the entire manpower of the state police, were swarming into the city under the personal direction of State Public Safety Director Albert J. Lingo."[165] Lewis's assessment of the situation was that the political elites were preparing to terrorize the black community on May 8, when they thought demonstrations would continue. "The Connor forces had every intention of engineering a slaughter," he wrote.[166]

When word reached the political elites that the business leaders had yielded to the demands, Connor and his associates attempted to destroy the agreement. On May 9 differences over an issue in the agreement emerged between movement leaders and economic elites. The political leaders moved swiftly to exploit the disagreement and plead for the white power structure to reunite. Birmingham's mayor sounded the appeal. Dorman wrote:

> Hanes [the mayor] said that segregationist forces had King "whipped" and "on the run." He said it "breaks my heart" to see whites negotiating with the Negro minister. "If they would stand firm, we would run King and that bunch of race agitators out of town," Hanes said.[167]

To demonstrate to the economic elites that they were serious, the political officials arrested King and Abernathy on an old charge, setting their bond at $2,500 each. Mr. Gaston, a black millionaire, bailed them out in order to preserve the agreement.

In the same appeal the political elites attempted to reach the third component of the three-pronged white power structure, the white masses. First, Hanes attacked the white business negotiators:

"If this committee is doing such a grand thing for the white people of Birmingham, why are they ashamed to release the names of those on the negotiating committee? It is because they're ashamed of the fact that they are selling the white folks down the river? . . . They call themselves negotiators. I call them a bunch of quisling, gutless traitors."[168]

The economic leaders refused to be intimidated and made the settlement public on May 10.

At that juncture the political elites appealed to the extremist prong of the white power structure, the Ku Klux Klan and the White Citizens' Council. Connor made it known that the agreement did not mean anything to him. Hanes, the mayor, was more direct in his appeal to the extremists:

"King is greatly encouraged by these easy victories and by the Attorney General's office, and is becoming so power mad that he feels that he is truly the King of the United States. He should be put out of circulation because if any group, organization or person can divide a country, then it is wrong and should be stopped."[169]

The next night the Klan assembled. Clearly, "Bull" Connor intended to honor his promise that before integration came to Birmingham "blood would flow in the street." That night King's brother's home and Dr. King's headquarters at the Gaston Motel were bombed. However, King had left town. The bombings caused a riot. Movement leaders hit the streets at once in order to persuade members of the black community not to engage in violence. President Kennedy alerted the military to be ready to move in if necessary. The President was clearly acting on behalf of the movement to save the agreement. Kennedy recognized that if the agreement fell through, the demonstrations and boycott would continue, forcing his Administration to become preoccupied with the Birmingham crisis. Thus he wasted little time in bringing the power of his office to bear so that the agreement could be saved. When Kennedy mobilized the National Guard, Connor and the political leaders were deprived of the riot they so desperately wanted. In short, the political elites and the extremists had been defeated.

The agreement stood, and the planned exercise of "people power" had been successful. Andrew Young summed it up:

Bull Connor made the impact greater, but the dynamics would have taken effect without Bull Connor and the dogs. . . . When the demonstrators were so massive and the economic withdrawal program was so tight, literally, the town was paralyzed.[170]

Indeed, the combination of the demonstrations and the boycott forced the economic elites to separate from the political elites. Once the separation occurred, the business leaders capitulated for the sake of their own interests—profits. Thus, the SCLC's leadership was able to force them to concede to all the principal demands put forth at the outset of the confrontation. In Birmingham the SCLC was successful because of (1) internal cohesion within the SCLC and the black community, (2) careful planning, (3) the solidifying effect of church culture, and (4) the economic boycott, coupled with demonstrations. Together they generated the "people power" needed to win the conflict in Birmingham.

Not only did the SCLC accomplish its specific goals in Birmingham, but it also accomplished its long-range goal by setting in motion hundreds of movements designed to destroy segregation and forced the national government to pass the 1964 Civil Rights Act, which legally prohibited racial segregation. Indeed, within ten weeks following the Birmingham confrontation 758 demonstrations occurred in 186 cities across the South and at least 14, 733 persons were arrested.[171] As Fred Shuttlesworth put it in his 1963 annual address to the ACMHR:

> Yes, my friends, the New Frontier is trying to catch up with the Negro frontier. Unless the President moves with dispatch, vigor and with a degree of dedication . . . Negroes will be demonstrating in every nook and cranny of the nation—north, east and west.[172]

The Birmingham confrontation also revived the Northern white student movement. "Martin Luther King's Birmingham march woke up the campuses again," Kirpatrick Sale wrote, because large numbers of students organized in support of the civil rights movement.[173] In short, the Birmingham movement was successful because it was a carefully planned exercise in mass disruption. It generated unprecedented movement activity in both the black community and segments of the white community. It became clear to many people in 1963 that there is power in organized collective action. The 1963 Birmingham movement was the climax of a decade of political turbulence that had taken root in Baton Rouge in 1953.

11

THEORETICAL OVERVIEW AND CONCLUSIONS

SOCIAL MOVEMENT THEORY AND THE INDIGENOUS APPROACH

The present analysis of the civil rights movement is informed by three important sociological theories of social movements and collective action: classical collective behavior theory, Weber's theory of charismatic movements, and the resource mobilization theory. Insights have been drawn from those theories when appropriate, and they have served as a point of departure for further theorizing. I shall briefly present the main points of these theories and assess them in light of my findings on the civil rights movement. I shall then present the outlines of an indigenous approach to movements of the dominated.

Classical collective behavior theory has come out of a diverse collection of writings by a number of sociologists.[1] Two major theoretical premises link these writings, although the various authors often differ on important issues. The *first premise* shared by all the principal formulators of collective behavior theory is that collective behavior differs from everyday organizational and institutional behavior in that it arises in response to unusual situations. More precisely, collective behavior occurs during periods of rapid social change or crises, including urbanization, modernization, industrialization, and national disasters. In such conditions it is postulated that behavior ceases to be guided by traditional norms, customs, communication systems, and institutions. In short, collective behavior is that activity in which people engage when attempting to repair and reconstitute a ruptured social structure.

275

Because collective behavior is said to be discontinuous with preexisting social structure, its theorists usually perceive it as relatively spontaneous rather than planned; largely unstructured rather than organized; emotional rather than reasoned; nonrational rather than rational; and spread by crude, elementary forms of communication such as circular reaction, rumor, imitation, social contagion, and generalized beliefs rather than preestablished formal and informal communication networks.[2] Collective behavior theorists recognize that organizations and planning occur in social movements, but it is argued that these are by-products of movements emerging only in their later stages.

The *second premise* central to collective behavior theory is that such behavior comprises a family of behaviors ranging from primitive forms to more sophisticated forms that resemble ordinary behavior. For example, milling, panics, mobs, cults, fads, crusades, revivals, social movements, and revolutions are all viewed as collective behavior forms. Even though writers make various distinctions among these forms, they nevertheless maintain that they share the same inner logic. That is, these forms can be contrasted with everyday behavior in that they are relatively spontaneous, unorganized, nonrational, and emotional, and break from preexisting social structures. In summary, collective behavior theories share the premises that collective behavior is discontinuous with prior social structure and that an inner logic binds the various forms into a coherent family of behaviors.

Collective behavior approaches have generally been grouped and criticized by various writers as if they constituted an internally consistent body of theory. In my view those approaches can be criticized from the standpoint of the two premises they share. So far, however, they have drawn indiscriminate criticism for their ideological biases. A close reading of collective behavior theories suggests that the writings of Park and Burgess, Blumer, Lang and Lang, and Smelser have tended to discredit movement participants by characterizing their activities as crude and elementary and as tension-releasing devices for pent-up frustrations.[3] This view was often pushed even while the theorists maintained that collective behavior often leads to meaningful social change.

However, Ralph Turner and Lewis Killian, both prominent formulators of collective behavior theory, explicitly rejected the assumption that collective behavior is irrational and emotional.[4] They also cautioned against basing theoretical generalizations on the notion that the activities of collective behavior participants are responses to psychological tensions and frustrations.[5] In his later writings Turner even raised serious doubts as to whether collective behavior was discontinuous with preexisting social structures.[6] These departures from the classical collective behavior model have become central components of the resource mobilization model to be considered shortly. Nevertheless, after taking these caveats into account, Turner's and Killian's basic analysis is consistent with the overall collective behavior model.[7]

There are several convergences between my analysis and the collective behavior model. First, this study supports the important idea found in most collective behavior writings that social movements are efforts geared toward social change. Indeed, I agree with Killian that social movements are "deliberate, conscious efforts of men to change their societies."[8] Second, my analysis is in agreement with the implicit notions found in many of the collective behavior writings that creativity and innovations are central to the efforts of people engaged in movement activities aimed at establishing a new social order.[9]

Still, the present analysis of the civil rights movement does not fit the basic thrust of the collective behavior model. In the investigation of numerous local movements it was demonstrated that organizing and planning were central to all of them. What is more, those movements spread through sophisticated, preexisting formal and informal communication networks. Although emotionalism and excitement were important in those movements, they were far from being their defining characteristics, and they usually occurred within organized settings. Neither can the behavior of the various movements be accurately characterized as nonrational. Of course, institutionalized behavior is not totally rational. In situations where choices must be made, social actors select what appears to be the best choice at the time. In social movements, as in other forms of organized behavior, individuals settle for acceptable alternatives rather than the optimum one when making choices.[10] In short, the findings of this study suggest that movement participants, as well as their actions, were as rational as the actions of individuals and groups in other contexts.

Moreover, it is hard to see how the civil rights movement could be conceptualized as belonging to the same family of behaviors as fads, panics, mobs, cults, and the like. Rather, in my view the civil rights movement was essentially a political phenomenon in that blacks were engaging in struggles for power against whites. In this context movement centers, strategic planning, organizing, charisma, and preexisting institutions were central to the civil rights movement in that they enabled the black community effectively to confront an entrenched opposition dedicated to keeping them subserviant. Grouping the civil rights movement with the other forms obscures the political nature of the civil rights confrontations, their defining characteristic.

Finally, in contrast to collective behavior theory, it was demonstrated that preexisting institutions, leaders, and organizations were critically involved in all phases of the movement and were especially important in the beginning stages, when the action was planned and resources mobilized. Even the new organizations that were formed (e.g. the MIA, the SCLC, the Albany Movement) grew out of a configuration of preexisting organizations. Piven and Cloward, in their sophisticated collective behavior analysis of the civil rights movement, were confronted with the empirical problem of explaining the obvious prominence of organizational processes in a movement they conceptualized as a spontaneous phenomenon. The authors attempted to escape this dilemma by arguing that SNCC, CORE, and the SCLC were not complex organizations but small, committed cadre groups.[11] Their approach does not begin to capture the centrality of those organizations in the origins of the movement or the mass base and dynamism supplied to them by the church and the black colleges. In short, my analysis does not fit the thrust of classical collective behavior theory because I have found that rational planning, well-developed preexisting communication networks, and established leaders, institutions, and organizations, rather than psychic strain, spontaneity, and emotionalism, were the driving forces behind the movement.

Similar to but distinct from collective behavior theory is the theory of charismatic movements, initially articulated by Max Weber. He argued that at certain periods in history a charismatic leader and followers are able to intervene in the otherwise routine and bureaucratic functioning of modern society and produce revolutionary changes. In Weber's view such leaders arose because they possessed extraordinary personalities and the ability to preach, create, and demand new obligations from followers.[12] For Weber, such leaders were charismatic only to the extent that they convinced followers, by successfully performing exemplary acts, that as leaders they possessed supernatural or superhuman qualities. Weber resembled the collective behavior theorists in that he argued that charismatic authority occurs during periods of stress and crises and is therefore devoid of formal rules. In the sense that charisma theoretically operates outside of everyday routine, it is irrational.[13]

Therefore, people follow charismatic leaders not because of their organizations or organizing abilities but because followers identify closely with their visions, missions, and magnetic personalities. Weber argued, however, that pure charismatic processes are present only in the early stages of a movement. If the movement is to endure over time, it must acquire formal organization and become routinized. As that happens, charismatic movements lose their distinctiveness and become subject to the same rationalized processes prevalent throughout society.

Weber's theory of charismatic movements is relevant to the present analysis of the civil rights movement. Indeed, it was found that Dr.

King's affiliation and presence were very important to local movements. Moreover, King had precisely the type of personality that Weber conceptualized as charismatic: He was viewed as extraordinary by large numbers of people; he was competent at his tasks; many people identified with his visions of a "beloved community" devoid of racism; and King had the talent to articulate this view forcefully through powerful oratory. However, as Charles Tilly has pointed out, Weber provided no explanation for why charismatic movements arise or how they are mobilized.[14] It is in this regard that Weber's analysis has limited power to account for the dynamics of the civil rights movement.

My analysis indicates that King and other charismatic leaders facilitated the mobilization of the movement because they had both organizational backing and charisma. Furthermore, it was demonstrated that in the civil rights movement charisma and organization were conjoined from the very beginning and were mutually reinforcing. Specifically, churches, colleges, and movement organizations, reinforced by charismatic leadership, provided the resources essential to the development of the movement. It was found also that the movement did not create charismatic leaders out of a vacuum; charisma as a social form already existed within an enduring institution of the black community—the church—long before the movement. The movement provided a larger stage for the further development of preexisting charismatic relationships. In summary, Weber's theory is important to understanding the civil rights movement because it maintains that charisma has an independent effect on movements rather than being peripheral. However, Weber failed to link charisma with such other key factors as organization and the mobilization of resources, which operated in the civil rights movement. The recently formulated resource mobilization theory goes far in filling the gaps left by Weber.

Resource mobilization theory emphasizes the resources necessary for the initiation and development of movements. They include formal and informal organizations, leaders, money, people, and communication networks. The climate of the larger political environment is also accorded importance in facilitating or inhibiting the development of collective action. Grievances, psychic strain, and other psychological states of participants are not central to the analysis. It is the ability of groups to organize, mobilize, and manage valuable resources that determines whether they will be able to engage in social protest.

Collective action from this view is rational and grows out of preexisting social structures and political processes. Resource mobilization theory predicts that social actors who have access to resources and who are well integrated within the institutions of a community are more likely to engage in protest than individuals who are marginal and uprooted. The more developed those institutions and resources, the greater the probability a particular group will engage in social movement activity. Moreover, groups in possession of these resources but excluded from the political structures and processes of a society are likely to engage in nontraditional political behavior characteristic of social movements.[15]

The resource mobilization model holds that third parties can have an important effect in social protest. One version of the theory says that dominated groups rarely possess the skills and resources needed for social protest and are unable to organize and sustain movements by themselves unless they receive assistance from outside elites. Outside resources are said to be crucial in determining the outcomes of movements. Outside elites include governmental leaders, courts, affluent liberals, and philanthropic foundations. It is these groups, the theory holds, that are able to provide the dominated with the necessary skills and resources required for protest. Finally, the resource mobilization approach is a structural theory in that it downplays the importance of culture, charisma, and belief systems while emphasizing "hard, measurable" factors such as organization and money.

The resource mobilization model fits my analysis of the civil rights movement at several crucial points. First, as resource mobilization theory predicts, it was found that participants acted rationally under the circumstances, and they tended to be well integrated into black society through churches and other forms of social organization. Second, in agreement with resource mobilization theory, it was found that preexisting social organization and communication networks were crucial to the movement's development. It was these forms of social organization that made widespread mobilization possible. Finally, it was found that urbanization of the Southern black population during the first half of the twentieth century created the conditions that generated the resources needed to support a sustained movement against racial domination. Thus resource mobilization theory goes far in providing an explanation for this movement. But there are serious limitations to this approach in accounting for the dynamics of the civil rights movement.

Existing resource mobilization analyses of the civil rights movement have assigned heavy weight to the role played by outside elites and events. Theorists of resource mobilization are not alone in claiming that the civil rights movement was heavily dependent on elites and resources outside the movement. This view had been offered by such political scientists as Michael Lipsky, Howard Hubbard, and David Garrow[16] and articulated by such sociologists writing outside the resource mobilization perspective such as Gary Marx and Michael Useem.[17] Michael Lipsky provides a clear statement of this thesis:

The "problem of the powerless" in protest activity is to activate "third parties" to enter the implicit or explicit bargaining arena in ways favorable to the protesters. . . . I have argued that the essence of political protest consists of activating third parties to participate in controversy in ways favorable to protest goals . . . relatively powerless groups cannot use protest with a high probability of success. They lack organizational resources by definition.[18]

The approaches and analytical sophistication of these writers differ substantially, but they do agree that protest groups are dependent on outside resources because they lack organizational resources and skills. I contend that this view of the civil rights movement assigns undue weight to the role of outside elites and events. An examination of Anthony Oberschall's resource mobilization approach to the civil rights movement suggests that theories which overemphasize the importance of outside factors can unnecessarily restrict the scope of analysis of social movements.

Oberschall begins his analysis of the movement with the statement that "one must realize that a negatively privileged minority is in a poor position to initiate a social protest movement through its own efforts alone."[19] He argues that outside support is especially important in the early phases of such a movement. Thus Oberschall maintains that the emergence of the civil rights movement during the 1950s and 1960s was heavily dependent on the outside support it received from Northern white liberals, the federal government, courts, mass media, philanthropic foundations, and white college students.[20] Without presenting evidence he asserts that "the bulk of the financing of the Southern Christian Leadership Conference was white liberal."[21] Oberschall correctly notes that the black community, and especially the church, provided an important preexisting mobilization and resource base for the movement. However, because his approach assigns heavy weight to outside elites and events, it does not reveal the scope or the capacity of the movement's indigenous base. In contrast, my research demonstrates that the overwhelming majority of local movements were indigenously organized and financed. Furthermore, Oberschall argues that Northern white money was essential to the movement but seems not to have investigated whether a substantial proportion of this money actually came from Northern black communities. Thus Oberschall's analysis provides new insight into the organizational and mobilization base of the movement, but the insight is not fully developed because in my view the analysis attributes inordinate causal weight to outside elites and resources.

There is, besides, a more general problem with the resource mobilization perspective when applied to the civil rights movement. The present study found that such cultural factors as religious beliefs, music, and sermons, although refocused by activists, were important to the development of the movement. Similarly, it was found that charisma had an independent effect on the mobilization and organizational dynamics of the movement. The centrality of these factors is not captured by existing formulations of resource mobilization theory, because those formulations treat these fluid qualities as a residual category rather than a central component of the theory.

This study of the civil rights movement has employed an indigenous perspective. That perspective draws heavily from resource mobilization theory, adopting its emphasis on resources, organization, and rationality. It also draws from Weber by reconceptualizing his theory of charisma. The indigenous perspective supplies additional concepts and analytical statements relevant to mass-based movements of dominated groups. As the present study is confined to a single movement, the generalizability of its findings is still to be established. It is believed. however, that a number of the findings are broad in scope and relevant to understanding other movements by dominated groups.

The indigenous perspective is concerned with movements by dominated groups. A dominated group is defined as one that is excluded from one or more of the decision-making processes that determine the quantity and quality of social, economic, and political rewards that groups receive from a society.[22] Because of this exclusion, dominated groups at different times attempt to change their situation of powerlessness by engaging in nontraditional and usually nonlegitimized struggles with power holders. The task of the indigenous perspective is to examine how dominated groups take advantage of and create the social conditions that allow them to engage in overt power struggles with dominant groups.

The indigenous approach maintains that the emergence of a sustained movement within a particular dominated community depends on whether that community possesses (1) certain basic resources, (2) social activists with strong ties to mass-based indigenous institutions, and (3) tactics and strategies that can be effectively employed against a system of domination.

The basic resources enabling a dominated group to engage in sustained protest are well-developed internal social institutions and organizations that provide the community with encompassing communication networks, organized groups, experienced leaders, and social resources, including money, labor, and charisma, that can be mobilized to attain collective goals. These indigenous resources are especially important in the early phases of a movement because it is at this time that such an effort requires stable, predictable sources of funding, organization, communications, and leadership. From this perspective, indigenous resources are far more likely to be crucial in the early phases of movements, because outside resources tend to be sporadic and highly conditional, in most cases coming in response to pressure from indigenous movements already under way.[23] The significance of outside resources, in this view, lies in the help they can give in sustaining movements. However, our evidence suggests that they are not a causal determinant, because they are triggered by the strength and force of indigenous movements. The same holds true for the larger political climate, because the force of indigenous movements affects that environment, causing outside groups to act to protect or enhance their interests.

The presence of indigenous resources within a dominated community does not ensure that a movement will emerge. Rather, movements are deliberately organized and developed by activists who seize and create opportunities for protest. Social activists, in this view, play creative roles in organizing and developing movements; they must redirect and transform indigenous resources in such a manner that they can be used to develop and sustain social protest. For example, black church congregations have historically provided the money needed to sustain the church and its diverse activities. During the movement, however, activist clergymen and other church leaders had to redefine fundraising activities in such a way that additional funds could be raised to support protest activities. In some cases this even meant redefining the role of religion by broadening its scope to include supporting those efforts aimed at changing the social order. In order for activists to mobilize indigenous resources they must have access to them. Therefore, activists who have strong ties to mass-based indigenous institutions are in an advantageous position to mobilize a community for collective protest. Mass-based institutions provide activists with groups of people who are accustomed to accomplishing goals in an organized manner and with much of the money and labor force capable of being harnessed for political goals.

The availability of resources and strategically placed activists will not crystallize into a protest movement if a dominated group has not developed tactics and strategies that can be effectively used in confrontations with a system of domination. Effective tactics and strategies are those that can be employed by masses of people to generate widespread disruption of a social order. It is the widespread disruption of a society that generates the collective power of masses used by dominated groups in their struggle to redistribute power.

When a dominated group has assembled the required resources, strategically placed activists, and effective tactics and strategies for protest purposes, it has developed a local movement center. More specifically, a movement center has been established in a dominated community when that community has developed an interrelated set of protest leaders, organizations, and followers who collectively define the common ends of the group, devise necessary tactics and strategies along with training for their implementation, and engage in protest actions designed to attain the goals of the group. A local movement center is thus a distinctive form of social organization specifically developed by members of a dominated group to produce, organize, coordinate, finance, and sustain social protest. The ability of a given community to engage in a sustained protest movement depends on that community's development of a local movement center. An important sociological task is to identify and analyze the social mechanism(s) that enable protest to spread between dominated communities, broadening the scope and influence of a movement. From the indigenous perspective, sustained social movements will spread between communities that develop local movement centers. The pace, location, and volume of protest in various communities are directly dependent on the quality and distribution of local movement centers.

The term "local movement center" refers to a dynamic form of social organization. Movement centers vary in their degree of organization, hence in their capacity to produce and sustain protest. Moreover, the distribution and quality of local movement centers vary over time. An important task of social movement theory is to explicate the conditions that produce tactical innovations within movements, and to account for the timing and forms of such innovations. From the indigenous perspective tactical innovations within movements are likely to occur and succeed when local movement centers are extensive and well developed across dominated communities. Such conditions provide the internal social organization that enables activists to spread rapidly and sustain the innovations in the context of active opposition.

In addition, social movement theory must account for the specific forms of tactical innovations that can occur within movements. From the indigenous perspective, the type of preexisting internal organization limits the innovations that can occur within movements. Local movement centers are developed to initiate and sustain certain types of protest activities. A specific type of protest can develop into a tactical innovation if it corresponds to the resource capability and ideological framework of a movement's preexisting internal organization. Thus, both the extent and type of preexisting internal organization determine the scope and types of innovations that can occur within movements.

Formal organization is an important property of local movement centers. Existing movement literature is unclear as to whether mobilization of social protest is facilitated more by formal bureaucratic organizations or loosely organized groups. The present study suggests that an intermediate form of organization can be crucial in mobilizing and coordinating protest by large numbers of people. The key organizations of the civil rights movement usually were not highly bureaucratic or loosely organized; rather, they were nonbureaucratic formal organizations such as the Montgomery Improvement Association, the Southern Christian Leadership Conference, and the Student Nonviolent Coordinating Committee. From the indigenous perspective, nonbureaucratic but formal organizations are often the most appropriate for wide-scale social protest because they facilitate mass participation, tactical innovations, and rapid decision-making. That conclusion leads to two corollaries. One, bureaucratic protest organizations of a dominated group may prevent wide-scale disruptive protest, because they inhibit mass participation, rapid decision-making, and the development of innovative tactics. Two, attacks on bureaucratic protest organizations by ruling groups during periods of political tension can precipitate new forms of mass protest by forcing activists to develop and use nonbureaucratic formal organizations, which, as noted, are more appropriately structured for mass mobilization and wide-scale protest.

Leadership is an important property of local movement centers. Protest leaders are not by-products of movements, nor is their behavior totally determined by structural imperatives. The behavior of leaders is voluntary to the extent that they engage in organization-building, mobilizing, formulation of tactics and strategies, and articulation of a movement's purpose and goals to participants and the larger society. However, I do not take a purely voluntaristic view of movement leadership. This study suggests that if most leaders are not created by their movements, they were usually leaders in other spheres of the community before the outset of the movement. It was from preexisting leadership groups that individuals were chosen as movement leaders. Furthermore, leadership in dominated communities is often characterized by conflict and disunity prior to a movement. The central question becomes: How are movement leaders chosen in those communities where deep leadership divisions exist? The present study found that this problem was solved in various black communities by choosing preexisting leaders who were well integrated into the community but were still relative newcomers not identified with conflicting factions. Finally, our data show that charismatic leadership can be an important property of movement centers in that it facilitates the mobilizing and organizing processes of movements. However, charisma is conceptualized here as a preexisting institutional process of a dominated group. This charisma is able to operate best in movements characterized by nonbureaucratic formal organizations, where bureaucratic procedures are relaxed and the more fluid and personalized qualities of charisma are freed.

Movement halfway houses help the development of movement centers by providing valuable resources that otherwise would prove costly and time-consuming to acquire. By the same token, indigenous movements provide halfway houses with opportunities to effect social change on a wider scale than they can attain alone. This mutual need increases the likelihood that halfway houses and indigenous movements will establish cooperative relationships.

The indigenous perspective takes into account that resources and the activities of individuals and groups outside a dominated community can assist in sustaining and shaping the outcome of indigenous movements. A distinction must be made, however, between resources voluntarily supplied by individuals and groups who identify with the goals of the movement and those supplied by political actors (e.g. heads of state, courts, national guards) in response to political crises created by the movement. Resources and activities by political actors, I argue, should be conceptualized as part of the social change activity sought and politically established by the movement. Hence those resources nonvoluntarily supplied by political actors are outcomes of movements rather than assistance to them. On the other hand, when groups and individuals outside of an indigenous movement voluntarily provide that movement with resources, they facilitate the social change efforts of the dominated community. What is similar about the two kinds of outside response is that both depend on the strength of an indigenous movement and the scope of change it seeks.

Finally, well-entrenched indigenous movements can generate collective action by other groups in the larger society, because a strong indigenous movement develops visible organizational structures and tactics that can be adopted by other discontented groups. In this sense, the presence of an indigenous movement serves as a resource for other groups and provides outside activists with a training ground, enabling them to learn the intricacies of social protest.

IMPACT OF THE CIVIL RIGHTS MOVEMENT

The Southern civil rights movement had a profound impact on American society. First, it significantly altered the tripartite system of domination, largely dismantling those components which severely restricted the personal freedom of blacks and disfranchised them in the formal political sense. Second, the movement altered and expanded American politics by providing other oppressed groups with organizational and tactical models, allowing them to enter directly into the political arena through the politics of protest.

Prior to the movement the system of segregation forced blacks to live in a separate and limited world characterized by poverty, racial discrimination, powerlessness, symbolic subordination, and imperative acts of deference to white supremacy. The South is a different place today. Most of the "white" schools, washrooms, theaters, swimming pools, parks, bus seats and other facilities are either integrated or at least not segregated by law. This does not mean that the races are thoroughly integrated in the South, because economic and residential segregation, which lead to segregation in other spheres of life, is widespread nationally. Nevertheless, with many symbols of white supremacy dismantled and many facilities formally desegregated, Southern blacks now live in a world where they can function with fewer restrictions and one that does not automatically strip them of human dignity. In a recent speech Stokely Carmichael told a young questioner who doubted that the civil rights movement had made a difference that "blacks in Montgomery will never go to the back of the bus again."[24] That is the essence of the change. The battles of the movement, culminating in the passage of the 1964 Civil Rights Act, made this significant change possible.

Before the movement most Southern blacks were politically disfranchised and had no chance to elect black officials. Twenty years later Birmingham and Atlanta have black mayors. Most Southern blacks are able to vote and have proceeded to elect a significant number of black officeholders. For example, in 1982 there were 5,160 black elected officials nationally, and the South accounted for 61 percent of that total.[25] This is remarkable, given that as late as 1965 there were only seventy-eight black officeholders in the South.[26] The Joint Center for Political Studies places this "political progress" in perspective by pointing out that in 1982 black elected officials accounted for only 1.1 percent of the elected officials in the country "while blacks made up approximately 12 percent of the total population of the United States."[27] Nevertheless, some significant progress has been made, and it was the movement with its citizenship schools, freedom houses, and political confrontations such as Selma in 1965 that was primarily responsible for the passage of the 1965 Voting Rights Acts and the political enfranchisement of blacks. Only time will establish whether these social and political changes are permanent.

The impact of the civil rights movement penetrated far beyond the black community. During the civil rights movement a number of other groups in the United States, including American Indians, women, farm workers, and college students shared an experience somewhat similar to the blacks': They were excluded from one or more of the main centers of power and decision-making in American society. To be sure, the extent of the exclusion varied and had different impacts on these groups. But nevertheless they were all disadvantaged, because their interests were not routinely taken into account by the powerful. In the years immediately preceding the civil rights movement these groups attempted to change their position through traditional routes or quietly bore their hardships. The civil rights movement transformed those tame and relatively ineffective approaches.

In a loud and clear voice the civil rights movement demonstrated to those groups that organized nontraditional politics was a viable method of social change, capable of bringing about the desired results far faster than traditional methods. Moreover, the civil rights movement provided excluded groups with concrete organizational (e.g. the SCLC, SNCC, the NAACP) and tactical (e.g. sit-ins, marches, boycotts) models they could follow in their struggles against oppression. Furthermore, the civil rights movement served as a training ground for many of the activists who later organized movements within their own communities. Indeed, the modern women's movement, student movement, farm workers' movement, and others of the period were triggered by the unprecedented scale of nontraditional politics in the civil rights movement.[28] Following the civil rights movement it has become commonplace for groups traditionally excluded from power to pursue their interests through demonstrations and protest.

The impact of the civil rights movement is not confined to the United States. Its influence can be seen in the antinuclear movement in Europe. Karl-Dieter Opp, a German scholar, recently wrote that participants in the antinuclear movement often maintain that the movement should be nonviolent and should employ tactics of civil disobedience, including boycotts, "sit-ins," and "go-ins."[29] Bernadette Devlin-Mc-Alishey, a leader of the Irish Catholics in Northern Ireland, maintains that "there is a strong affinity between the black civil rights movement in this country and the civil rights movement in our country."[30] Thus the civil rights movement has transformed the American national political community to a considerable degree and has had an impact on international politics.

However, the civil rights movement was unable to change significantly one of the components of the tripartite system of domination—economic exploitation—which still severely limits the rights won by the movement. Before the movement Southern blacks fared worse economically than blacks in other sections of the country. For example, throughout the 1950s and early 1960s the median family income of Southern blacks remained considerably less than 50 percent of Southern white income. In contrast, the median family income for blacks in other sections of the country for the same period was better than 60 percent of that for whites.[31] Following the peak years of the movement the median family income of Southern blacks began slowly rising so that by 1979 it was about 55 percent of Southern whites'. The civil rights movement facilitated this small economic change by demanding the upgrading of black employment and making it possible for some blacks to attend the better-equipped white schools and hold political office. Despite this small increase, it is clear that Southern blacks are severely dominated economically. Even more striking is the fact that the median family income of blacks in other sections of the country compared to whites has been steadily declining, so that the regional differentials between blacks are beginning to disappear. As of 1979, the national median family income for blacks was only 56 percent of that for whites, and the regional differences were becoming insignificant.[32] In contrast to the decades preceding the civil rights movement, this means that there are no great differences today between the types of oppression blacks endure in the South and in the rest of the nation. Economic exploitation of blacks throughout America is now the severe and critical problem plaguing the national black community.

By the mid 1960s movement participants were well aware that neither the Southern civil rights movement nor the Northern urban disorders of the late 1960s had been effective in changing the economic conditions of American blacks. This awareness comes through in an SCLC document prepared prior to the 1968 Poor People's March on Washington:

> The American blackman, after centuries of suppression, achieved, finally, his basic social and political rights. He fought non-violently, along with many white freedom fighters, in Montgomery, Birmingham, and Selma, to be able to assert those rights that most other Americans take for granted.
>
> We fought hard those years, some of us died, all of us were psychologically and spiritually resurrected. And, as a result, we are now more sophisticated; of necessity, we have recreated our vision, placed it in its proper perspective. WE CAN NOW SEE OURSELVES AS THE POWERLESS POOR TRAPPED WITHIN AN ECONOMICALLY ORIENTED POWER STRUCTURE. . . .
>
> Our insight into the structure of American society teaches us that the right to vote or to eat in any restaurant, while important, does not penetrate the "power plant" and therefore does not actually effect conditions of living. We have learned that fruitful existence in America requires money, for the society offers no degree of mobility, creativity, or power to those without it.[33]

A critical question confronting the black community today is whether the organizations, leadership, tactics, and philosophies of the civil rights movement are appropriate for bringing about basic economic change, or whether a whole new set of structures and tactics is needed. The civil rights movement suggests some basic lessons regarding the prospects for economic change: First, economic changes are likely to occur not through traditional politics but through creative social protest and disruption; second, if a successful struggle for economic justice is to occur, it will require a high level of internal organization that uses all of the resources of the black community; finally, indigenous black leadership will have to devise creative tactics and strategies appropriate for bringing about economic changes. Past struggles have proved Frederick Douglass was correct when he concluded that without struggle there is no progress.

NOTES

Introduction

1. Many of the works on the slave revolts do not explicitly discuss the organizational infrastructure of those revolts. However, particular students of slave revolts do discuss the elaborate planning and organizational dimensions of particular revolts. See John Hope Franklin, *From Slavery to Freedom* (New York: Alfred A. Knopf, 1968), pp. 210–13, and Herbert Aptheker, *American Negro Slave Revolts* (New York: International Publishers, 1943), pp. 80, 88, 220, 269. See also Leslie Owens, *This Species of Property*, (Oxford: Oxford University Press, 1976), pp. 70–105, for a useful discussion suggesting that a high level of organization and planning undergirded slave resistance. For an excellent discussion of the organizational basis of the Garvey movement, see Tony Martin, *Race First* (Westport, Conn.: Greenwood Press, 1976), pp. 3–21. For an excellent discussion of the organizational foundations of the March on Washington Movement, see Herbert Garfinkel, *When Negroes March* (Glencoe: Free Press, 1959), pp. 53–177, and Lerone Bennett, Jr., *Confrontation: Black and White* (Baltimore: Penguin Books, 1965), pp. 147–61.

2. A number of writers have noted the central role that black religious institutions played in slave revolts. John Hope Franklin, in *From Slavery to Freedom*, wrote, "In most states Negro preachers were outlawed between 1830 and 1835. It was believed that too many of the conspiracies had been planned in religious gatherings." (p. 200). For a good discussion of black religion and slave protest, see Gary T. Marx, *Protest and Prejudice* (New York: Harper & Row, 1969), p. 96. For a superb discussion of the link between black religion and the Garvey movement, see Martin, *Race First*, pp. 67–80. For a succinct discussion of the role of the black church in the March on Washington Movement see Bennett, *Confrontation*, pp. 162–63.

3. Bennett, *Confrontation*, p. 159.

4. Martin, *Race First*, pp. 16–17.

5. Charles Flint Kellogg, *NAACP: History of the National Association for the Advancement of Colored People* (Baltimore: Johns Hopkins University Press, 1967), p. 135.

6. See Appendix A for a detailed discussion of the data and methods of this study.

Chapter 1: Domination, Church, and the NAACP

1. U.S. Bureau of the Census, *Seventeenth Decenniel Census of the United States: Census of Population, 1950* (Washington, D.C.: U.S. Government Printing Office, 1952).

2. U.S. Bureau of the Census, *Income of Families and Persons in the United States*, Current Population Reports, series P–60 (Washington, D.C.: U.S. Government Printing Office, 1950).

3. The concept "tripartite system of domination" does not imply that all Southern blacks were unable to vote, that there were no Southern black policemen, or that no blacks held occupations usually restricted to whites. Numerous studies, including August Meier and Elliott Rudwick, *Along the Color Line* (Urbana: University of Illinois Press, 1976), p. 363; William H. Chafe, *Civilities and Civil Rights* (New York: Oxford University Press, 1980), pp. 32–37; J. Mills Thornton III, "Challenge and Response in the Montgomery Bus Boycott of 1955–1956," *Alabama Review: A Quarterly Journal of Alabama History*, 32–33 (1979–80): 171–72, have pointed out that after the Supreme Court ruling abolishing the all-white primary in 1944, blacks began voting in the South in relatively small numbers. Even more striking were the large numbers of black voter organizations formed across the South in the mid-1940s aimed at registering black voters. Similarly, Robert G. Corley, "The Quest for Racial Harmony: Race Relations in Birmingham, Alabama, 1947–1963," Ph.D. dissertation, University of Virginia, 1979, p. 75; Charles U. Smith and Lewis M. Killian, "The Tallahassee Bus Protest" (New York: Anti-Defamation League of B'nai B'rith, 1958), p. 5; Thornton, "Challenge and Response," pp. 174–75, and other studies have shown that in the early to mid-1950s some Southern cities hired small numbers (usually two or three) of black policemen. These policemen were usually hired in response to black pressure, and their activities were restricted to the black community. Thus, the concept "tripartite system of domination" means that overall whites were able to dominate blacks politically, economically, and personally and that exceptions occurred within the framework of racial segregation and highlighted the general rule.

4. Louis E. Lomax, *The Negro Revolt* (New York: New American Library, 1962), pp. 80–81.

5. E. Franklin Frazier, *The Negro in the United States* (New York: Macmillan, 1949), p. 242.

6. For an informative account of the institutional growth of black colleges and churches during this period, see Doug McAdam, "Political Process and

the Black Protest Movement, 1948–1970," Ph.D. dissertation, State University of New York at Stony Brook, 1979.

7. This theme is central in the following works: W. E. B. DuBois, *The Philadelphia Negro* (New York: Schocken Books, 1967 [first published in 1899]), pp. 197–207; Benjamin Mays and Joseph Nicholson, *The Negro Church* (New York: Arno Press, New York Times, 1933); E. Franklin Frazier, *The Negro Church in America* (New York: Schocken Books, 1963); Gunnar Myrdal, *An American Dilemma* (New York: Harper & Brothers, 1944), p. 858–78; and Joseph R. Washington, Jr., "Black Politics" in Hart M. Nelsen, Roytha L. Yokley, and Anne K. Nelsen (eds.), *The Black Church in America* (New York: Basic Books, 1971), pp. 299–315.

8. Mays and Nicholson, *The Negro Church*.

9. *Ibid.*, pp. 209–13.

10. Percentage increases calculated from United States Bureau of the Census, data for Alabama, Florida, and Louisiana between 1940, and 1960.

11. DuBois, *The Philadelphia Negro*, p. 204.

12. For example, see Lomax, *The Negro Revolt*, where he maintains that "the Negro Baptist Church is a nonorganization," p. 97. The theme of emotionalism in the black church has also been popularized in such novels as James Baldwin, *Go Tell It on the Mountain* (New York: Dial Press, 1963). The point here is not that emotionalism is absent from the black church but rather that such accounts usually ignore the organizational reality and capacity of the church.

13. DuBois, *The Philadelphia Negro*, p. 206.

14. Max Weber, *The Theory of Social and Economic Organization* (New York: Free Press, 1947), esp. pp. 360–63.

15. Charles Steele interview, October 12, 1978, Tallahassee.

16. Southern Conference Educational Fund, "They Challenged Segregation at Its Core," undated, p. 3.

17. C. T. Vivian interview, December 7, 1978, Philadelphia.

18. *Ibid.*

19. *Ibid.*

20. Martin Luther King, *Stride Toward Freedom* (New York: Harper & Row, 1958), p. 17.

21. Mays and Nicholson, *The Negro Church* (note 7 above), p. 158.

22. Dr. DuBois, that most sensitive analyst of the black experience, wrote in *The Philadelphia Negro*, first published in 1899, that "all movements for social betterment are apt to centre in the churches . . . the race problem in all its phases is continually being discussed, and, indeed, from this forum many a youth goes forth inspired to work" (p. 207).

23. Myrdal, *An American Dilemma* (note 7 above), p. 873.

24. For accounts of the origin of the NAACP, see B. Joyce Ross, *J. E. Spingarn and the Rise of NAACP, 1911–1939* (New York: Atheneum, 1972); Charles Flint Kellogg, *NAACP: A History of the National Association for the Advancement of Colored People, Vol. I, 1909–1920.* (Baltimore: Johns Hopkins University Press, 1967); and Langston Hughes, *Fight for Freedom* (New York: W. W. Norton, 1962).

25. Ross, *J. E. Spingarn and the Rise of NAACP*, pp. 48–59.

26. In her historical account of the NAACP Ross wrote that "by the end of the 1920's, successive branch constitutions (which were formulated by the Board of Directors) had firmly established the National office's prerogative to determine the most minute details of branch operation including for example, the number of individuals who were to comprise a branch's local governing body, and the proper and acceptable procedure for conducting programs and governing members." *Ibid.*, p. 58.

27. Hughes, *Fight for Freedom*, p. 24.

28. In 1910 the State of Oklahoma passed an amendment stating that no illiterate person could register to vote. The amendment came to be known as the "grandfather clause" because it did not apply to persons whose ancestors were eligible to vote prior to 1866. The intent of the amendment was to enfranchise illiterate whites while disfranchising blacks, for the ancestors of most blacks were slaves. In the 1915 case (*Guinn* v. *United States*) the Supreme Court ruled the amendment invalid in Oklahoma and any other state where it was in effect. Before 1927 it was illegal for blacks to vote in the Democratic primary in the state of Texas. In the 1927 case (*Nixon* v. *Herndon*) the Supreme Court ruled that Texas could not bar blacks from the Democratic primary. Southern states immediately began employing legal measures designed to circumvent the 1927 ruling. It was not until a 1944 case (*Smith* v. *Allwright*) that the all-white primary was finally defeated. In that case the Supreme Court ruled that all citizens regardless of race had a right to participate in choice of elected officials. The NAACP fought legal segregation in public education as tenaciously as it fought for the franchise. In a 1938 case (*Gaines* v. *University of Missouri*) the Supreme Court ruled that the state of Missouri had to either admit Gaines to its all-white law school or provide equal facilities for blacks. In a 1950 case (*Sweatt* v. *Painter*) the Supreme Court ruled that the all-white University of Texas Law School had to admit Sweatt because its resources were superior to any black school in the state. Information pertaining to these and similar cases pursued by the NAACP can be found in Harry A. Ploski and Ernest Kaiser (eds.), *Afro USA* (New York: Bellwether, 1971), pp. 242–73).

29. Kellogg, *NAACP*, p. 134.

30. *Ibid.*, p. 135.

31. *Ibid.*, p. 137.

32. *Ibid.*, p. 136.

33. For discussions of the close relationship among the Southern NAACP, the church, and black ministers, see August Meier, "Negro Protest Movements and Organizations," *The Journal of Negro Education*, Fall 1963, p. 445, and NAACP *Annual Report*, 1947, 1948, and 1953.

Chapter 2: Beginnings and Confrontations

1. T. J. Jemison interview, October 16, 1978, Baton Rouge.

2. *New York Times*, June 20, 1953.

3. For another account of the 1953 Baton Rouge bus boycott, see August Meier and Elliott Rudwick, *Along the Color Line* (Urbana: University of Illinois Press, 1976), pp. 365–66.

4. Jemison interview.

5. *New York Times,* June 20, 1953.

6. Jemison interview.

7. *Ibid.*

8. *Ibid.*

9. *Ibid.*

10. *Ibid.*

11. Meier and Rudwick, *Along the Color Line,* p. 366.

12. *State Times,* June 26, 1953. I thank Jeff Selbin, Eric Selbin, and Helen Cordes for providing me with additional information on the Baton Rouge boycott.

13. *Ibid.*

14. *Ibid.*

15. Jemison interview.

16. This position differs from that of Meier and Rudwick, who argue, "The Baton Rouge boycott did not inspire similar demonstrations in other cities." *Ibid.,* p. 366. Our data indicate that a high level of awareness and sharing of knowledge occurred between Jemison of Baton Rouge and other leaders of the early bus boycotts. This is not to say that the Baton Rouge movement caused the later movements, but that it did play a role in their subsequent development.

17. Jemison interview.

18. Martin Luther King, in his book *Stride Toward Freedom* (New York: Harper & Row, 1958), pp. 75–76, discusses the cooperation between Jemison and the Montgomery boycott leaders.

19. Interviews with the Reverend C. K. Steele, October 12, 1978, Tallahassee, and Reverend Jemison revealed that these two leaders exchanged information about the boycotts in the two cities.

20. Jemison interview.

21. Langston Hughes, *Fight for Freedom* (New York: W. W. Norton, 1962), p. 138.

22. Benjamin Muse, *Ten Years of Prelude* (New York: Viking Press, 1964), pp. 8–15.

23. *Ibid.*

24. *Ibid.*

25. Anthony Lewis, *Portrait of a Decade* (New York: Random House, 1964), p. 108.

26. Muse, *Ten Years of Prelude,* p. 76.

27. *Ibid.,* p. 75.

28. John Hope Franklin and Isidore Starr, *The Negro in 20th Century America* (New York: Vintage, 1967), p. 282.

29. *Ibid.,* p. 283.

30. For discussions of these organizations and the massive movement against desegregation, see Reed Sarratt, *The Ordeal of Desegregation* (New York: Harper & Row, 1966); Numan V. Bartley, *The Rise of Massive Resistance* (Baton Rouge: Louisiana State University Press, 1969); Neil R. McMillen, *The Citizens' Council* (Urbana: University of Illinois Press, 1971); and Francis M. Wilhoit, *The Politics of Massive Resistance* (New York: George Braziller, 1973).

31. For example, the White Citizens' Council was originally organized in Indianola, Mississippi, in 1954 and in attendance at one of the early organizing

meetings were prominent white bankers, lawyers, businessmen, and Indianola's mayor and city attorney. Mississippi's Governor Hugh L. White intensified the organization of Citizens' Councils when he called a special session of the legislature "to consider ways of preserving segregated education." See McMillen, *The Citizens' Council*, pp. 15–19.

32. American Friends Service Committee (High Point, N.C.), National Council of Churches of Christ (New York, N.Y.), and Southern Regional Council, "Intimidation, Reprisal, and Violence in the South's Racial Crisis," Atlanta, Georgia, 1960.

33. NAACP *Annual Report*, 1955, p. 21.

34. For an excellent discussion of the tactics employed by Southern segregationists between 1956 and 1960 to prevent racial integration and cripple the NAACP, see Wilhoit, *The Politics of Massive Resistance*, pp. 135–58.

35. NAACP *Annual Report*, 1957.

36. Muse, *Ten Years of Prelude*, p. 162.

37. NAACP *Annual Report*, 1958.

38. NAACP *Annual Report*, 1959.

39. Albert Blaustein and Robert Zangrando, *Civil Rights and the American Negro* (New York: Washington Square Press, 1968), p. 488.

40. Gunnar Myrdal, *An American Dilemma* (New York: Harper & Brothers, 1944), p. 810.

41. NAACP *Annual Report*, 1955 and 1957.

42. NAACP *Annual Report*, 1957.

43. NAACP *Annual Report*, 1955, 1956, 1957, 1958, and 1959.

44. Hughes, *Fight for Freedom*, (note 17 above), p. 146.

45. NAACP *Annual Report*, 1957, p. 12.

46. Frances F. Piven and Richard A. Cloward, in *Poor People's Movements* (New York: Vintage Books, 1979), esp. pp. ix–37, reach a somewhat similar conclusion that bureaucratic organizations are incapable of generating and sustaining mass collective action because of the very nature of their structure and operating procedures. However, their position differs substantially from the one put forth in the present study in that they argue that formal organizations in general, along with the process of organization-building, prevent mass insurgency. Thus on page 26 they conclude that "disruption itself is not necessarily spontaneous, but lower class disruptions often are, in the sense that they are not planned and executed by formal organizations."

47. For discussions of the bureaucratic nature of NAACP, see B. Joyce Ross, *J. E. Spingarn and the Rise of NAACP, 1911–1939* (New York: Atheneum, 1972), and Elliott Rudwick and August Meier, "Organizational Structure and Goal Succession: A Comparative Analysis of the NAACP and CORE, 1964–1968," in James Geschwender (ed.), *Black Revolt* (Englewood Cliffs, N.J.: Prentice-Hall, 1971).

48. Wyatt Walker interview, September 29, 1978, New York.

49. Benjamin E. Mays interview, September 20, 1978, Atlanta.

50. Tillman Cothran and William Phillips, Jr., "Negro Leadership in a Crisis Situation," *Phylon*, 22, no. 2 (1961): 107–18.

51. David C. Thompson, *The Negro Leadership Class* (Englewood Cliffs, N.J.: Prentice-Hall, 1963).

52. Fred Shuttlesworth interview, September 12, 1978, Cincinnati.

Chapter 3: Movement Centers: MIA, ICC, and ACMHR

1. U.S. Bureau of the Census, Seventeenth Decennial Census of the United States, *Census of Population: 1950* (Washington, D.C.: U.S. Government Printing Office, 1952).

2. E. Franklin Frazier, *The Negro in the United States* (New York: Macmillan, 1949), p. 190.

3. U.S. Bureau of the Census, *Census of Population: 1950.* The census data do not provide a breakdown of the percentage of whites within a given occupational category. It is possible, however, to calculate the percentage of whites within an occupational category. Here, this percentage is obtained by (1) subtracting the number of nonwhite workers in an occupation from the total number of workers in that occupation; (2) subtracting the number of nonwhite workers from the total number of workers; and (3) dividing the number of white workers in an occupation by the total number of white workers.

4. Martin Luther King, Jr., *Stride Toward Freedom* (New York: Harper & Row, 1958), p. 34.

5. Daniel Speed interview, October 11, 1978, Tallahassee.

6. Fred Shuttlesworth interview, September 12, 1978, Cincinnati.

7. King, *Stride Toward Freedom*, pp. 34–35.

8. E. D. Nixon, interviewed in Howell Raines, *My Soul Is Rested* (New York: Bantam Books, 1977), p. 40.

9. Speed interview.

10. Shuttlesworth interview. For an account of the schisms between the ACMHR and other community organizations, see Robert G. Corley, "The Quest for Racial Harmony: Race Relations in Birmingham, Alabama, 1947–1963," Ph.D. dissertation, University of Virginia, 1979, pp. 128–29. Corley's study also documents occasions when these same community groups supported the ACMHR. See pp. 144–223.

11. Writing about the ACMHR during the 1950s, Shuttlesworth stated that "a friendly relationship appears to exist between members of the Executive Board of the ACMHR and former members of the NAACP for the most part. . . . Our assistant secretary . . . our treasurer, and three of the ministers on the Executive Board were members of the NAACP." Fred Shuttlesworth, cited in Jacquelyne J. Clarke, "Goals and Techniques in Three Negro Civil Rights Organizations in Alabama," Ph.D. dissertation, Ohio State University, 1960, p. 147.

12. E. D. Nixon interview, August 19, 1979, Montgomery.

13. King, *Stride Toward Freedom*, p. 61.

14. Lerone Bennett, Jr., "When the Man and the Hour Are Met," in C. Eric Lincoln (ed.), *Martin Luther King, Jr.* (New York: Hill & Wang, 1970), pp. 7–39.

15. August Meier and Elliott Rudwick, "The Boycott Movement Against Jim Crow Streetcars in the South, 1900–1906," *Journal of American History*, Vol. 51, March 1967.

16. Benjamin Muse, *Ten Years of Prelude* (New York: Viking Press, 1964), p. 84.

17. Preston Valien, "The Montgomery Bus Protest as a Social Movement," in Jitsuichi Masuoka and Preston Valien (eds.), *Race Relations: Problem and Theory* (Chapel Hill: University of North Carolina Press, 1961), pp. 112–27.

18. *Ibid.*

19. Shuttlesworth interview.

20. Rosa Parks interview, October 14, 1981, Detroit.

21. *Ibid.*

22. E. D. Nixon interview.

23. See J. Mills Thornton III, "Challenge and Response in the Montgomery Bus Boycott of 1955–1956." *Alabama Review: A Quarterly Journal of Alabama History*, 32–33 (1979–80): 173–74.

24. *Ibid.*, pp. 174–77.

25. *Ibid.*

26. See Eugene P. Walker, "A History of the Southern Christian Leadership Conference, 1955–1956: The Evolution of a Southern Strategy for Social Change," Ph.D. dissertation, Duke University, 1978, p. 11.

27. E. D. Nixon interview.

28. *Ibid.*

29. *Ibid.*

30. King, *Stride Toward Freedom*, p. 45.

31. *Ibid.*, p. 46.

32. *Ibid.*, p. 47.

33. See Thomas J. Gilliam, "The Montgomery Bus Boycott of 1955–1956," M. A. thesis, Auburn University, 1968, p. 58.

34. Two previous studies of the Montgomery bus boycott have concluded that during the early months it was financed by the black community of Montgomery. See Gilliam, "The Montgomery Bus Boycott of 1955–1956," p. 58, and Lamont H. Yeakey, "The Montgomery Alabama Bus Boycott," Ph.D. dissertation, Columbia University, 1979, p. 372. Yeakey, in his definitive study of the boycott, maintains that more than a quarter of a million dollars was raised from within the black community of Montgomery during the first months of the boycott.

35. For an account of money sent from outside the South by black people, see Gilliam, "The Montgomery Bus Boycott of 1955–1956," pp. 59–60.

36. Information regarding $4,027.36 sent to the MIA by the collaborative body is contained in a letter written by Dr. King on June 1, 1956, to John Morsell of the NAACP; information regarding $3,000 sent to the MIA by the Brooklyn Branch of the NAACP is contained in a telegram of December 10, 1956, sent by that branch; information regarding $2,227.18 sent to the MIA by the Pittsburg Branch of NAACP is contained in a letter written by King on May 4, 1956, to that branch; finally, information regarding $4,500 sent to the MIA by the national NAACP is contained in a letter written by Roy Wilkins on May 8, 1956, to King. All materials located in Martin Luther King, Jr., Collection, Special Collections, Mugar Memorial Library, Boston University. Hereafter, all documents from this collection will be identified with the initials *MLK:BU.*

37. King, *Stride Toward Freedom*, p. 80.

38. E. D. Nixon interview.

39. This information is found in letters written by Bayard Rustin on May 9, 1956, and September 12, 1956, to M. L. King, *MLK:BU.*

40. Letter from Dr. King, September 20, 1956, to Bayard Rustin, *MLK:BU.*

41. Letter from Warren Bunn on August 6, 1956, to M. L. King, *MLK:BU.*

42. King, *Stride Toward Freedom*, p. 75.

43. *Ibid.*, p. 77.

44. *Ibid.*

45. For in-depth biographies of Dr. King that discuss various aspects of his life, see Lawrence D. Reddick, *Crusader Without Violence: A Biography of Martin Luther King, Jr.* (New York: Harper & Brothers, 1959); and David Lewis, *King: A Critical Biography* (New York: Praeger, 1970).

46. B. J. Simms interview, August 20, 1979, Montgomery.

47. *Ibid.*

48. E. Franklin Frazier, *The Negro Church in America* (New York: Schocken Books, 1963), p. 43.

49. For an account of the Reverend Martin Luther King, Sr., as a brilliant church politician, see Louis E. Lomax, *The Negro Revolt* (New York: Signet Books, 1962), pp. 97–98.

50. See King, *Stride Toward Freedom*, p. 163.

51. Smiley interview. See also King, *Stride Toward Freedom*, pp. 62–63.

52. Charles K. Steele interview, October 12, 1978, Tallahassee.

53. *Ibid.*

54. *Ibid.* This account fails to mention the fact that some of Florida A & M's faculty did play roles in the Tallahassee boycott. See Charles U. Smith, "Student Activism, Benign Racism and Scholarly Irresponsibility," *Florida A & M Research Bulletin*, 20, no. 1 (September, 1974): p. 66.

55. The account here on the role of Florida A. and M. students in initiating the boycott relies heavily on the exhaustive report on this boycott by Charles U. Smith and Lewis M. Killian, "The Tallahassee Bus Protest," a pamphlet issued by the Anti-Defamation League of B'nai B'rith, New York, 1958, pp. 7–8.

56. Steele interview.

57. *Ibid.*

58. Speed interview.

59. Steele interview

60. Speed interview.

61. *Ibid.*

62. Steele interview.

63. Southern Regional Council, "Bus Integration Spreads," *New South*, January 1957, p. 14.

64. Alan Westin and Barry Mahoney, *The Trial of Martin Luther King* (New York: Thomas Y. Crowell, 1974), p. 15.

65. Shuttlesworth interview.

66. Southern Conference Educational Fund, "They Challenged Segregation at Its Core," undated, p. 4.

67. Quoted in Clarke, "Goals and Technique in Three Negro Civil Rights Organizations in Alabama" (note 11 above), pp. 144–53.

68. Shuttlesworth interview.

69. Southern Conference Educational Fund, "They Challenged Segregation," p. 3.

70. Shuttlesworth interview.

71. *Ibid.*

72. For a discussion of this interracial committee and its activities regarding the hiring of black policemen in Birmingham, see Corley, "The Quest for Racial Harmony" (note 10 above) pp. 73–77.

73. See Jacquelyne J. Clarke, *These Rights They Seek: A Comparison of the Goals and Techniques of Local Civil Rights Organizations* (Washington D.C.: Public Affairs Press, 1962), p. 54.

74. Shuttlesworth interview.

75. Ibid.

76. Glenn Smiley interview, October 1, 1978, Los Angeles.

77. Steele interview.

78. Lewis M. Killian and Charles U. Smith, "Negro Protest Leaders in a Southern Community," *Social Forces*, 38, no. 3 (March 1960): 257.

79. Smith and Killian, "The Tallahassee Bus Protest," p. 6.

80. Clarke, *These Rights They Seek*, p. 76.

81. *Ibid.*, p. 77.

82. *Ibid.*, p. 37

83. *Ibid.*, p. 36.

84. *Ibid.*, p. 58.

85. *Ibid.*

86. For example, see Anthony Oberschall, *Social Conflict and Social Movements* (Englewood Cliffs, N.J.: Prentice-Hall, 1973), p. 223.

87. Frances F. Piven and Richard A. Cloward, *Poor People's Movements: Why They Succeed, How They Fail* (New York: Vintage Books, 1979), pp. xv, 223–24.

88. For example, Clarke pointed out that the MIA and the ACMHR faced "a major problem of gaining support from Negroes involved in social action programs designed to attain full citizenship rights for Negroes." Clarke, *These Rights They Seek*, p. 75. When these remarks are placed in the context of Clarke's overall study, however, it is clear that they do not refer to the several hundred people who weekly attended the mass meeting, and she supplies data that suggest otherwise. For example, on page 57 she points out that more than 50 percent of the MIA's membership was favorably disposed toward mass marches and that the MIA had been directly involved "in two mass marches—the 1957 Prayer Pilgrimage and the 1959 Youth Pilgrimage." Robert White, in a study of the Tallahassee movement and its protest organizations, conveys the notion throughout that the NAACP–ICC office was ineffective until CORE entered Tallahassee and began initiating direct action projects. Robert M. White, "The Tallahassee Sit-Ins and CORE: A Non-violent Revolutionary Submovement," Ph. D. Dissertation, Florida State University, 1964. What he himself points out, but fails to emphasize, is that the NAACP–ICC movement center had developed an organizational base for social protest. Indeed, it served as CORE's headquarters, and White continuously refers to the ways in which this center was directly involved in these protest activities. See pp. 102–3, 110–11, 115–17, 122–23, 129, and 137. A key claim by White is that the NAACP–ICC (what I refer to as the movement center of Tallahassee) was weak and uninterested in aggressive action. See pp. 190–91. For him it was the Congress of Racial Equality that was responsible for direct action projects in Tallahassee during the late 1950s. But White fails to say why CORE established its headquarters in the

NAACP–ICC office if activists associated with these organizations were conservative. Furthermore, he fails to explain why these "conservative" activists mobilized the community behind CORE's direct action projects. Indeed, the response of people such as Steele, Speed, and others to CORE suggest that these activists firmly believed in direct action. For this study I interviewed James McCain and Gordon Carey, both CORE leaders who played important roles in organizing the CORE group in Tallahassee. They both maintained that the movement center in Tallahassee was a key resource that enabled CORE to accomplish what it did in Tallahassee. Indeed, CORE joined forces with the established center in Tallahassee and thereby increased the overall strength of this center, making it more capable of engaging in protest activities.

89. I am indebted to Professor Gary Marx of the Massachusetts Institute of Technology, who read an earlier draft of this manuscript and urged me to tease out the connections between the projected image of spontaneity by activists and collective behavior theories emphasizing spontaneity and disorganization as key properties of social movements.

90. Smith and Killian, "The Tallahassee Bus Protest," p. 11.

91. *Ibid.*

92. *Ibid.*

93. See Piven and Cloward, *Poor People's Movements*, p. 26, where they argue that the paucity of stable organizational resources among the poor lead to spontaneous disruptions, and Oberschall, *Social Conflict and Social Movements*, p. 214, where he argues that blacks were unable to initiate protest through their own efforts and therefore had to depend heavily on the assistance of outside groups.

Chapter 4: The SCLC: The Decentralized Political Arm of the Black Church

1. Bayard Rustin, *Strategies for Freedom* (New York: Columbia University Press, 1976), pp. 40–41.

2. Doug McAdam, *Political Process and the Development of Black Insurgency 1930–1970* (Chicago: University of Chicago Press, 1982), pp. 108–16, provides an excellent discussion of how blacks experienced "cognitive liberation" between 1931 and 1954.

3. This is not to say that there were no organized struggles by blacks in rural areas to gain their liberation. Professor Vincent Harding has written a brilliant book detailing the many struggles blacks waged against domination from the moment they were seized and put on slave ships up to the Civil War. See Vincent Harding, *There Is a River: The Black Struggle for Freedom in America* (New York: Vintage Books, 1983). The point, however, is that such struggles were isolated and relatively short-lived, mainly because oppression in those times was so thorough.

4. E. Franklin Frazier, *The Negro in the United States* (New York: Macmillan, 1949), p. 204.

5. For a discussion of the violence and terror used to keep Southern rural blacks under control, see McAdam, *Political Process*, pp. 87–90.

6. Frazier, *The Negro in the United States*, p. 230.

7. For a discussion of how urban blacks fared better economically than their rural counterparts, see Francis F. Piven and Richard A. Cloward, *Poor People's Movements: Why They Succeed, How They Fail* (New York: Vintage Books, 1979), p. 204.

8. For discussions of institution-building in urban black communities following the great migration, see *ibid.*, pp. 204, and McAdam, *Political Process*, 1982, pp. 93–112.

9. *New York Times*, November 28, 1953.

10. Benjamin Mays interview, September 20, 1978, Atlanta.

11. *Ibid.*

12. Benjamin E. Mays, "We Are Unnecessarily Excited," *New South*, Vol. 9, no. 2, February 1954.

13. Mays interview.

14. In *Poor People's Movements*, p. 183, Piven and Cloward argue that economic and political modernization were the fundamental causes that "created mounting unrest among masses of blacks eventually culminating in a black struggle against the Southern caste system." Commenting on changes in black–white relations following the civil rights movement Piven and Cloward state, "The civil rights movement was not, then, the fundamental cause of this political transformation; the fundamental cause was economic change, and the political forces set in motion by economic change" (p. 252). Piven and Cloward do acknowledge "that the civil rights movement was a vital force in this process because of the impact of its disruptive tactics on the electoral system" (p. 183). In my view civil rights organizing and the civil rights movement were also causal variables in producing both unrest and social change.

15. *New York Times*, March 20, 1956.

16. *Ibid.*

17. Joseph Lowery interview, September 21, 1978, Atlanta.

18. For a discussion of the "In Friendship" group, see Eugene P. Walker, "A History of the Southern Christian Leadership Conference, 1955–1965: The Evolution of a Southern Strategy for Social Change," Ph.D. dissertation, Duke University, 1978.

19. Charles Steele interview, October 12, 1978, Tallahassee.

20. Ella Baker interview, August 28, 1978, New York.

21. Stanley Levison, letter to Aldon Morris, March 21, 1979.

22. According to Walker, "A History of the Southern Christian Leadership Conference, 1955–1965," p. 32, only one white person, the Reverend Robert Graetz of Montgomery, attended the SCLC's first organizing meeting. Graetz had been active in the Montgomery bus boycott. For another account of the origin and development of the SCLC, see Adam Fairclough, "A Study of the Southern Christian Leadership Conference and the Rise and Fall of the Nonviolent Civil Rights Movement," Ph.D. dissertation, University of Keele, 1977.

23. Glenn Smiley interview, October 1, 1978, Los Angeles.

24. SCLC, "Southern Negro Leaders Conference on Transportation and

Non-Violent Integration," *Working Papers*, 1–7, January 10–11, 1957, Atlanta, Georgia, *MLK:BU*.

25. SCLC, *Working Paper 1*: "The Meaning of the Bus Protest in Southern Struggle for Total Integration," January 10–11, 1957, *MLK:BU*. Emphasis in original.

26. *Ibid.* Emphasis in original.

27. SCLC, *Working Paper 7*: "The Role of Law in Our Struggle: Its Advantages and Limitations," January 10–11, 1957, *MLK:BU*. Emphasis in original.

28. SCLC, *Working Paper 1*, 1957, *MLK:BU*.

29. *Ibid.* Emphasis in original.

30. *Ibid.*

31. SCLC, *Working Paper 4*: "The Relationship of Community Economic Power Groups to the Struggle," January 10–11, 1957, *MLK:BU*.

32. T. J. Jemison interview, October 16, 1978, Baton Rouge.

33. Lowery interview.

34. Fred Shuttlesworth interview, September 12, 1978, Cincinnati.

35. Ralph Abernathy, "Our Lives Were Filled with Action," in C. Eric Lincoln (ed.), *Martin Luther King, Jr.* (New York: Hill & Wang, 1970), pp. 219–27.

36. The view that the SCLC *was* Martin Luther King, Jr., is entrenched in most studies on the subject. An accompanying view is that King was in essence a symbolic leader. For example, Kenneth B. Clark, "The Civil Rights Movement: Momentum and Organizations," *Daedalus*, 95 (Winter 1966): 612, argues: "One cannot understand SCLC solely in terms of its organization, which is amorphous and more symbolic than functional, even though the National Headquarters in Atlanta, Georgia, has sixty-five affiliates throughout the South. To understand this organization one has to understand King because SCLC is Martin Luther King, Jr., King is a national hero, a charismatic leader." Eugene Walker argues in his dissertation that the SCLC was "but the lengthened shadow of a man." Walker, "A History of the SCLC, 1955–1965," p. 63. August Meier, "The Conservative Militant," in Lincoln (ed.), *Martin Luther King, Jr.*, p. 152, argues that "despite his charisma and international reputation, King thus far has been more a symbol than a power in the civil rights movement. Indeed his strength in the movement has derived less from an organizational base than from his symbolic role." Similarly, Adam Fairclough says in his dissertation that during the first five years of SCLC's existence it functioned as a paper organization. Fairclough, "A Study of the Southern Christian Leadership Conference," p. 38. All of these studies suffer from two shortcomings: They fail to investigate SCLC affiliates in depth, and they implicitly accept Weber's view that charisma and organizational dynamics are antithetical. In-depth investigation of the SCLC's affiliates reveals that the SCLC was not simply King. It was also Fred Shuttlesworth, Kelly Miller Smith, Ella Baker, C. K. Steele, C. O. Simpkins, Wyatt Walker, and many others. Such an investigation reveals further that the SCLC was numerous churches, local direct action organizations, and large numbers of black folk. By accepting Weber's view of charismatic leadership, these studies fail to link the charismatic leader to his organizational base and therefore arrive at the erroneous conclusion that King was merely a symbolic leader without a functional base. My argument is that

the SCLC's real power stemmed from its ability effectively to combine organizational dynamics (movement centers) with charismatic leadership.

37. Anthony Oberschall, *Social Conflict and Social Movements* (Englewood Cliffs, N.J.: 1973), p. 223.

38. Jacquelyne J. Clarke, *These Rights They Seek* (Washington, D.C.: Public Affairs Press, 1962) p. 37.

39. *Ibid.*

40. *Ibid.*, p. 27.

41. *Ibid.*, pp. 65–66.

42. Simpkins interview.

43. See Kenneth B. Clark, "The Civil Rights Movement: Momentum and Organization," *Daedalus*, vol. 95, Winter 1966.

44. Piven and Cloward, *Poor People's Movements*, p. 224.

45. SCLC, *Constitution and By-Laws of the Southern Christian Leadership Conference*, Atlanta, undated, *MLK:BU*.

46. Kelly Miller Smith interview, October 13, 1978, Nashville.

47. For example, in 1959 the SCLC held a meeting in Columbia, South Carolina. At that time a number of churches there, including Ebenezer Baptist, Case Methodist, Second Nazareth Baptist, and Sidney Park C.M.E., became affiliates. Churches in nearby cities, such as Mt. Zion in Winsboro, also became affiliates. This information is contained in the SCLC's Office of Financial Secretary-Treasurer's "Report of Finance Received at SCLC Meeting in Columbia South Carolina, October 8, 1959," *MLK:BU*.

48. Wyatt Walker interview, September 29, 1978, New York.

49. *Ibid.*

50. Baker interview.

51. James Lawson interview, October 2 and 6, 1978, Los Angeles.

52. Smith interview.

53. Steele interview.

54. Lowery interview.

55. Baker interview.

56. Diane Nash Bevel interview, December 14, 1978, Chicago.

57. Shuttlesworth interview.

58. Lerone Bennett, Jr., "When the Man and the Hour Are Met," in Lincoln (ed.), *Martin Luther King, Jr.*, p. 33.

59. Ralph Abernathy interview, November 16, 1978, Atlanta.

60. *Ibid.*

61. *Ibid.*

62. Jemison interview.

63. C. T. Vivian interview, December 7, 1978, Philadelphia.

64. C. O. Simpkins interview, October 25, 1978, Merrick, N.Y.

65. Shuttlesworth interview.

66. Lowery interview.

67. Steele interview.

68. Smith interview.

69. For a discussion of the conservative role that "otherworldly" philosophies and ideologies of black religion played in keeping blacks subservient,

see Benjamin Mays and Joseph W. Nicholson, *The Negro's Church* (New York: Arno Press, New York Times Press, 1969) p. 7.

70. Martin Luther King, *Stride Toward Freedom* (New York: Harper & Row, 1958) p. 36.

71. Mays interview.

72. Lerone Bennett, Jr., *Confrontation: Black and White* (Baltimore: Penguin Books, 1965), pp. 196–97.

73. Walker interview.

74. Septima Clark interview, November 17, 1978, Charleston, S.C.

75. Daniel Speed interview, October 11, 1978, Tallahassee.

76. C. B. King interview, August 7, 1981, Albany, Ga.

77. Shuttlesworth interview.

Chapter 5: The SCLC's Crusade for Citizenship

1. SCLC, "Southern Negro Leaders Conference on Transportation and Non-Violent Integration," *Working Paper* 1: "The Meaning of the Bus Protest in the Southern Struggle for Total Integration," Atlanta, Georgia, January 10–11, 1957, *MLK:BU*.

2. SCLC, *Working Paper* 2: "The Next Stop for Mass Action in the Struggle for Equality," Atlanta, Georgia, January 10–11, 1957, *MLK:BU*.

3. Martin Luther King, Jr., letter to Dr. Benjamin E. Mays, December 12, 1957, *MLK:BU*.

4. SCLC, *Working Paper* 2, *MLK:BU*.

5. *Ibid.*

6. For Ella Baker's account of her role in organizing the SCLC central office in the late 1950s, see Ella Baker interview, 1968, Civil Rights Documentation Project, Moorland Spingarn Research Center, Howard University, Washington, D.C., pp. 10–37.

7. NAACP, *Annual Report*, 1941, 1942.

8. See Howard Zinn, *SNCC: The New Abolitionists* (Boston: Beacon Press, 1964), p. 32, and Coretta King, *My Life with Martin Luther King, Jr.* (New York: Holt, Rinehart & Winston, 1969), p. 153.

9. See Ella Baker interview, pp. 10–37.

10. James Forman, *The Making of Black Revolutionaries* (New York: Macmillan, 1972), p. 215.

11. Ella J. Baker interview, August 28, 1978, New York.

12. Forman, *The Making of Black Revolutionaries*, p. 218.

13. Fred Shuttlesworth interview, September 12, 1978, Cincinnati.

14. Forman, *The Making of Black Revolutionaries*, p. 218.

15. Southern Conference Educational Fund, "The Color Line in Voting," October, 1959.

16. *Ibid.*

17. Martin Luther King, Jr., address delivered at 2nd Anniversary of the NAACP Legal Defense and Educational Fund, May 17, 1956, *MLK:BU*.

18. John Tilley, "Report of Executive Director of SCLC for the Executive Board," December 10, 1958, *MLK:BU.*

19. SCLC, *Plan of Action for Southwide, Year-round Voter Registration Program,* February, 1959, *MLK:BU.*

20. SCLC, "Aims and Purposes," *Crusade for Citizenship,* 1957, *MLK:BU.*

21. Ibid.

22. SCLC, *Crusade for Citizenship,* 1957, *MLK:BU.*

23. Ibid.

24. Ibid.

25. Ibid.

26. Ibid.

27. SCLC, "A Brief Digest of the Clarksdale, Mississippi, Meetings," May 29, 1958, *MLK:BU.*

28. SCLC, *Crusade for Citizenship, MLK:BU.*

29. SCLC, "Work in Washington," *Crusade for Citizenship,* 1957, *MLK:BU.*

30. SCLC, *Crusader,* February, 1959, *MLK:BU.*

31. Civic leagues were to be found in most Southern cities during the late 1950s. They were known by such names as Progressive Voters League of Mississippi, Palmetto State Voters League of South Carolina, Tuskegee Civic Association in Alabama, and so on.

32. SCLC, "Public Relations Prospectus," *Crusade for Citizenship,* 1957, *MLK:BU.*

33. SCLC, Letter to Pastors of Churches, June 30, 1958, *MLK:BU.*

34. SCLC, *Crusade for Citizenship, MLK:BU.*

35. SCLC, "Report of Activities in Local Communities Since February 12 Meetings," April 3, 1958, p. 1, *MLK:BU.*

36. Ibid., p. 2.

37. Ella Baker, "Report of Executive Director, May 16–September 29, 1959," p. 2, *MLK:BU.*

38. Montgomery Improvement Association, "Report from the Registration and Voting Committee," July 1, 1958, p. 3, *MLK:BU.*

39. C. O. Simpkins interview, October 25, 1978, Merrick, N.Y.

40. Ella Baker, "Report of the Director to the Executive Board," May 15, 1959, p. 2, *MLK:BU.*

41. Ella Baker, "Report of Executive Director, May 16–September 29, 1959," p. 2, *MLK:BU.*

42. Loren Miller, *The Petitioners* (New York: Pantheon Books, 1966), p. 301.

43. Ella Baker, memo to SCLC's Committee on Administration, October 23, 1959, *MLK:BU.*

44. Joseph Lowery interview, September 21, 1978, Atlanta.

45. Shuttlesworth interview.

46. Baker interview.

47. Simpkins interview.

48. Baker, memo to SCLC Committee on Administration, October 23, 1959, *MLK:BU.*

49. Baker, "Report of the Director to the Executive Board," May 15, 1959, *MLK:BU.*

50. SCLC *Crusader,* November 1959, *MLK:BU.*

51. Ella Baker, letter to Martin Luther King, Jr., May 28, 1959, *MLK:BU*.

52. Wyatt Walker interview, September 29, 1978, New York.

53. *Ibid.*

54. King, "Recommendations to the Board," October 1, 1959, *MLK:BU*.

55. *Ibid.*

56. Martin Luther King, "Recommendations to Committee on Future Programs," October 27, 1959, *MLK:BU*.

57. *Ibid.*

58. It is important here to emphasize that the present discussion refers to SCLC finances between 1957 and early 1960. The pattern of funding shifted somewhat after the February 1960 sit-ins, for it was then that the civil rights movement became highly visible and generated contributions from individuals who identified with the new surge of protest activity.

59. SCLC, undated document written in 1957, *MLK:BU*.

60. For discussions of King's central role as fundraiser for the SCLC, see Anthony Oberschall, *Social Conflict and Social Movements* (Englewood Cliffs, N.J.: Prentice-Hall, 1973), p. 218, and Eugene P. Walker, "A History of the SCLC, 1955–1965," Ph.D. dissertation, Duke University, 1978, p. 86.

61. The regional, organizational, and individual breakdowns were derived from Ralph Abernathy's "Financial Secretary–Treasurer Report" of September 29, 1959, to the Executive Board of the SCLC, *MLK:BU*. The report covers the financial transactions of SCLC from May 13, 1959, to September 25, 1959.

62. Martin Luther King, Jr., letter to the Reverend Wilbert B. Miller, September 4, 1959, *MLK:BU*.

63. Abernathy, "Financial Secretary–Treasurer Report," September 29, 1959, *MLK:BU*.

64. Coretta King, *My Life with Martin Luther King, Jr.*, 1969, p. 160.

65. Martin Luther King, Jr., letter to Dr. Fey, May 5, 1959, *MLK:BU*.

66. SCLC, *Constitution and By-Laws*, p. 5, *MLK:BU*.

Chapter 6: Organizational Relationships: The SCLC, the NAACP, and CORE

1. James Weldon Johnson, *Negro Americans, What Now?* (New York: Viking Press, 1934), pp. 36–37.

2. James Farmer interview, November 9, 1978, Washington, D.C.

3. Joseph Lowery interview, September 21, 1978, Atlanta.

4. *Pittsburgh Courier*, August 24, 1957.

5. Herbert H. Lehman, letter to Martin Luther King, Jr., December 20, 1957, and Ralph Bunche, letter to Martin Luther King, Jr., December 31, 1957, *MLK:BU*.

6. James Lawson interview, October 2 and 6, 1978, Los Angeles.

7. Farmer interview.

8. NAACP, *Annual Report*, 1957, p. 68.

9. Farmer interview.

10. Martin Luther King, quoted in Adam Fairclough, "A Study of the South-

ern Christian Leadership Conference and the Rise and Fall of the Non-Violent Civil Rights Movement," Ph.D. dissertation, University of Keele, 1977, p. 14.

11. Farmer interview.

12. Lawson interview.

13. Clara Luper, *Behold the Walls* (Jim Wire, 1979), p. 7.

14. *Ibid.*, pp. 10–11.

15. Benjamin Mays interview, September 20, 1978, Atlanta.

16. Lawson interview.

17. Martin Luther King, Jr., speech, May 17, 1957, Washington, D.C. *MLK:BU.*

18. Martin Luther King, Jr., letter to Thurgood Marshall, February 6, 1958, *MLK:BU.*

19. SCLC, Constitution and By-Laws, *MLK:BU.*

20. Ella Baker, memorandum to the Reverend Martin Luther King, Jr.; the Reverend Ralph D. Abernathy; the Reverend Samuel W. Williams; the Reverend J. E. Lowery; and Dr. L. D. Reddick, July 2, 1959, p. 3, *MLK:BU.*

21. Martin Luther King was so successful at fundraising that top NAACP officials attempted to persuade him to become an officer or board member of the NAACP. On the NAACP's attempt to persuade King to accept an official position with the NAACP, see the extensive correspondence between Kivie Kaplan and Martin Luther King in *MLK:BU.*

22. Arthur L. Johnson, letter to Martin Luther King, Jr., March 6, 1958, *MLK:BU.*

23. SCLC, "Crusade for Citizenship," 1957, *MLK:BU.*

24. King, letter to Thurgood Marshall, 1958, *MLK:BU.*

25. King, speech, 1957, *MLK:BU.*

26. Stanley Levison, letter to Aldon Morris, March 21, 1979.

27. James McCain interview, November 18, 1978, Sumter, S.C.

28. For a discussion of the problems that Southern interracial CORE groups encountered, see Inge P. Bell, *CORE and the Strategy of Non-violence* (New York: Random House, 1968), pp. 150–60.

29. Gordon Carey interview, November 18, 1978, Soul City, N.C.

30. Farmer interview.

31. James Robinson interview, October 26, 1978, New York.

32. Farmer interview.

33. Robinson interview.

34. Carey interview.

35. Farmer interview.

36. *Ibid.*

37. Floyd McKissick interview, November 18, 1978, Soul City, N.C.

38. Carey interview.

39. McCain interview.

40. *Ibid.*

41. *Ibid.*

42. August Meier and Elliott Rudwick, *CORE: A Study in the Civil Rights Movement 1942–1968* (New York: Oxford University Press, 1973), p. 295.

43. McCain interview.

44. *Ibid.*

45. *Ibid.*

46. *Ibid.*

47. *Ibid.*

48. *Ibid.*

49. Robinson interview.

50. Farmer interview.

51. Robinson interview.

52. *Ibid.*

53. Meier and Rudwick, *CORE*, p. 78.

54. *Ibid.*

55. See *ibid.*, p. 81.

56. Robinson interview.

57. *Ibid.*

58. Marvin Rich interview, October 24, 1978, New York.

59. *Ibid.*

60. James Robinson, letter to Martin Luther King, Jr., July 12, 1959, *MLK:BU.*

61. Robinson interview.

62. McCain interview.

63. For information on the black clergy functioning as CORE leaders in these cities, see Meier and Rudwick, *CORE*, pp. 88–90.

64. CORE, Contact List, September 15, 1960, pp. 1–9, *MLK:BU.*

Chapter 7: Movement Halfway Houses

1. Septima Clark, *Biographic Sketch* (n.p., n.d.). For background information on Mrs. Clark and her role at Highlander, see Septima P. Clark and LeGette Blythe, *Echo in My Soul* (New York: E. P. Dutton, 1962).

2. Anne Braden interview, December 11, 1978, New York.

3. For a good historical account of the Highlander Folk School and its Director, Myles Horton, see Frank Adams, *Unearthing Seed of Fire: The Idea of Highlander* (Charlotte, N.C.: John F. Blair, 1975).

4. Myles Horton interview, December 5, 1978, Knoxville, Tenn.

5. Frank Adams, "Highlander Folk School: Getting Information, Going Back and Teaching It," *Harvard Educational Review*, 42, no. 4 (1972): 497–520.

6. Horton interview.

7. *Ibid.*

8. *Ibid.*

9. *Ibid.*

10. *Ibid.*

11. *Ibid.*

12. Adams, "Highlander Folk School," p. 508.

13. Horton interview.

14. *Ibid.*

15. *Ibid.*

16. *Ibid.*

17. *Ibid.*
18. *Ibid.*
19. Septima Clark, "Report of the 7th Annual Highlander Folk School College Workshop," April 1–3, 1959, *MLK:BU.*
20. James Bevel interview, December 27, 1978, New York.
21. Horton interview.
22. Septima Clark interview, November 17, 1978, Charleston, S.C.
23. *Ibid.*
24. *Ibid.*
25. Horton interview.
26. Adams, "Highlander Folk School," p. 512.
27. Horton interview.
28. *Ibid.*
29. *Ibid.*
30. Clark interview.
31. *Ibid.*
32. Horton interview.
33. *Ibid.*
34. Adams, "Highlander Folk School," p. 512.
35. Horton interview.
36. Clark interview.
37. Horton interview.
38. *Ibid.*
39. Hosea Williams interview, September 22, 1978, Atlanta.
40. Adams, "Highlander Folk School," p. 513.
41. *Ibid.*
42. Myles Horton, letter to Martin Luther King, Jr., October 31, 1959, *MLK:BU.*
43. Martin Luther King, Jr., letter to Myles Horton, October 13, 1959, *MLK:BU.*
44. Septima Clark, *Biographical Sketch.*
45. Ella Baker, Report of the Executive Director, May 16–September 29, 1959, *MLK:BU.*
46. *Ibid.*
47. Horton interview.
48. Glenn Smiley interview, October 1, 1978, Los Angeles.
49. August Meier and Elliott Rudwick, *CORE: A Study in the Civil Rights Movement 1942–1968* (Urbana: University of Illinois Press, 1975), p. 4.
50. Williams interview.
51. Smiley interview.
52. *Ibid.*
53. Richard Gregg, *The Power of Nonviolence* (Philadelphia: J. B. Lippincott, 1959), p. 150. Gregg's book became popular reading for the early participants of the civil rights movement. A new edition of the book was published in 1958 with a chapter on the Montgomery movement, and Dr. King wrote the introduction. For information on the valuable role this book played in disseminating information to black leaders, see William R. Miller, *Martin Luther King,*

Jr.: His Life, Martyrdom and Meaning for the World (New York: Weybright & Talley, 1968), pp. 91, 297.

54. Smiley interview.

55. Ralph Abernathy interview, November 16, 1978, Atlanta.

56. Smiley interview.

57. *Ibid.*

58. Martin Luther King, Jr., *Stride Toward Freedom* (New York: Harper & Row, 1958), p. 214.

59. *Ibid.*, p. 163.

60. Smiley interview.

61. King, *Stride Toward Freedom*, p. 163.

62. *Ibid.*

63. *Ibid.*, p. 173.

64. Smiley interview.

65. *Ibid.*

66. James Lawson interview, October 2 and 6, Los Angeles.

67. *Ibid.*

68. Smiley interview.

69. Daniel Speed interview, October 11, 1978, Tallahassee.

70. Fred Shuttlesworth interview, September 12, 1978, Cincinnati.

71. King, *Stride Toward Freedom*, p. 217.

72. Glenn Smiley, letter to Martin Luther King, Jr., November 18, 1958, *MLK:BU.*

73. James Lawson, memo to Martin Luther King, Jr., October 30, 1958, *MLK:BU.*

74. *Ibid.*

75. Smiley interview.

76. Miller, *Martin Luther King, Jr.*, p. 6.

77. *Ibid.*, p. 86.

78. Smiley interview.

79. *Ibid.*

80. Ralph Abernathy, "Our Lives Were Filled with Action," in C. Eric Lincoln (ed.), *Martin Luther King, Jr.* (New York: Hill & Wang, 1970), pp. 219–27.

81. Thomas A. Krueger, *And Promises to Keep* (Nashville: Vanderbilt University Press, 1967), p. 26.

82. *Ibid.*

83. *Ibid.*, p. 36.

84. Braden interview (note 2 above).

85. *Ibid.*

86. *Ibid.*

87. Anne Braden, *The Wall Between* (New York: Monthly Review Press, 1958), p. 28.

88. Braden interview.

89. Shuttlesworth interview.

90. Braden interview.

91. *Southern Patriot*, January 1957.

92. *Southern Patriot*, March 1959.

93. Braden interview.

94. *Ibid.*

Chapter 8: Internal Organization and Direct Action

1. Professor Clayborne Carson has written an interesting and detailed book on the history of SNCC. See Clayborne Carson, *In Struggle: SNCC and the Black Awakening of the 1960s* (Cambridge: Harvard University Press, 1981). He points out that Nashville produced a disproportionate share of the original leaders of SNCC (pp. 21–25) and mentions the importance of two ministers associated with the Nashville Christian Leadership Conference (the local SCLC affiliate) to these students' development.

2. Kelly Miller Smith interview, October 13, 1978, Nashville.

3. John Lewis interview, November 8, 1978, Washington, D.C.

4. James Bevel interview, December 27, 1978, New York.

5. Smith interview.

6. C. T. Vivian interview, December 7, 1978, Philadelphia, and Dr. Benjamin Alexander interview, March 18, 1983, Washington, D.C.

7. Diane Nash Bevel interview, December 14, 1978, Chicago.

8. Smith interview.

9. *Ibid.*

10. NAACP, *Annual Report*, 1956.

11. *Ibid.*

12. C. O. Simpkins interview, October 25, 1978, Merrick, N.Y.

13. *Ibid.*

14. *Ibid.*

15. Louis E. Lomax, *The Negro Revolt* (New York: New American Library, 1962), p. 104. For a general discussion of protest leaders as political entrepreneurs, see Anthony Oberschall, *Social Conflict and Social Movements* (Englewood Cliffs, N.J.: Prentice-Hall, 1973), pp. 157–72.

16. Joseph Lowery interview, September 21, 1978, Atlanta.

17. Simpkins interview.

18. *Ibid.*

19. *Ibid.* In the late 1950s Bishop College was in Marshall, Texas. It is now located in Dallas.

20. *Ibid.*

21. *Ibid.*

22. *Ibid.*

23. *Ibid.*

24. *Ibid.*

25. *Ibid.*

26. *Ibid.*

27. *Ibid.*

28. *Ibid.*

29. *Ibid.*

30. *Ibid.*

31. *Ibid.*

32. *Ibid.*

33. *Ibid.*

34. *Ibid.*

35. Ella Baker, "Salute to Youth," *SCLC Newsletter*, 1959, *MLK:BU.*

36. Wyatt Walker interview, September 29, 1978, New York.

37. Marvin Rich interview, October 24, 1978, New York.

38. Walker interview.

39. Dorothy Cotton interview, November 13, 1978, New York.

40. Ralph Abernathy, "Dear Friend of Freedom." undated letter written in 1959, *MLK:BU.*

41. Wyatt Walker, letter to M. L. King, Jr., November 6, 1958, *MLK:BU.* Dr. King's name was originally Michael, later changed to Martin.

42. Wyatt Walker, "Brethren in Christ," draft letter enclosed in Walker's letter to M. L. King, Jr., November 6, 1958, *MLK:BU.*

43. *Ibid.*

44. Wyatt Walker, letter to M. L. King, Jr., January 16, 1959, *MLK:BU.*

45. *Ibid.*

46. *Ibid.*

47. Walker interview.

48. *Ibid.*

49. *Ibid.*

50. The student sit-in movement of early 1960, the watershed that produced a heavy volume of collective action, will be discussed in detail in the next chapter. At this point I intend only to document that some studies have called the sit-ins a break from previous activity. Howard Zinn, *SNCC: The New Abolitionists* (Boston: Beacon Press, 1964) p. 29: The "sit-in took the established Negro Organizations by surprise" and without adult advice or consent, the students planned and carried them through." Carson, *In Struggle* (note 1 above) pp. 17–18: "The southern sit-in movement had demonstrated that black students could initiate a social struggle without the guidance of older black leaders and existing organizations." A similar view is that previous organizations supported the sit-in movement but had little to do with the planning and execution of sit-ins. Meier and Rudwick, *CORE: A Study in the Civil Rights Movement, 1942–1968* (New York: Oxford University Press, 1973), pp. 105–6: "Both CORE and SCLC, despite their past contributions in the use of non-violent direct action, like the NAACP, found themselves in the position of attempting to get on the student bandwagon." Francis F. Piven and Richard A. Cloward, *Poor Peoples Movements* (New York: Vintage Books, 1979), p. 222: "Quick to see the significance of the student-initiated sit-in movement, SCLC officials offered moral and financial support." In the next chapter I shall document the central roles that movement centers played in the initiation and planning of the 1960 sit-ins.

51. See Southern Regional Council, "The Student Protest Movement, Winter 1960," SRC–13, April 1, 1960; Martin Oppenheimer, "Genesis of the Southern Negro Student Movement," Ph.D. dissertation, University of Pennsylvania, 1963; Donald Matthews and James Prothro. *Negroes and the New Southern Politics* (New York: Harcourt, Brace & World, 1966); and Meier and Rudwick, *CORE.*

52. The interviews were with Douglas Moore, November 1, 1978, Washington, D.C.; James McCain, November 18, 1978, Sumter, S.C.; James Lawson, October 2 and 6, 1978, Los Angeles: Kelly Miller Smith, October 13, 1978, Nashville; Floyd McKissick, November 18, 1978, Soul City, N.C.; Homer Randolph, 1981, East St. Louis, Ill.; Clara Luper, January, 1981, Oklahoma City; and Chester Lewis, February 3, 1981, Wichita. Published sources included Southern Regional Council, "The Student Protest Movement," and Meier and Rudwick, *CORE*.

53. Clara Luper, *Behold the Walls* (N.p.: Jim Wire, 1979), p. 3.

54. *Ibid.*, p. 1.

55. *Ibid.*, p. 3.

56. Meier and Rudwick, *CORE*, p. 93.

57. Southern Regional Council, "The Student Protest Movement."

58. Meier and Rudwick, *CORE*, p. 91.

59. James Robinson, "Memo to Affiliated CORE Groups, National Advisory Committee, and National Officers," July 10, 1959, *MLK:BU*.

60. *Ibid.*

61. CORE, *Core-Lator*, Fall 1959, *MLK:BU*.

62. *Ibid.*

63. *Ibid.*

64. *Ibid.*

65. CORE, *Minutes of National Council Meeting*, January 23–24, 1960, *MLK:BU*.

66. CORE, *Minutes of National Council of CORE*, February 21–22, 1959, *MLK:BU*.

67. CORE, news release, July 24, 1959, *MLK:BU*.

68. Rich interview (note 37 above).

69. Chester Lewis interview, February 3, 1981, Wichita.

70. Luper interview.

71. *Ibid.*

Chapter 9: 1960: Origins of a Decade of Disruption

1. Donald Von Eschen, Jerome Kirk, and Maurice Pinard, "The Organizational Substructure of Disorderly Politics," *Social Forces*, 49 (1971): 529–44, and Doug McAdam, "Political Process and the Civil Rights Movement 1948–1970," Ph.D. dissertation, State University of New York at Stony Brook, 1979.

2. Benjamin Mays interview, September 20, 1978, Atlanta.

3. See Seymour Martin Lipset and Sheldon S. Wolin, *The Berkeley Student Revolt* (Garden City, N.Y.: Doubleday, 1965), p. 3, and J. D. McCarthy and Mayer N. Zald, *The Trend of Social Movements in America: Professionalism and Resource Mobilization* (Morristown, N.J.: General Learning Press, 1973), p. 10.

4. The author published an earlier version of this section on the sit-ins as Aldon Morris, "Black Southern Student Sit-in Movement: An Analysis of Internal Organization," *American Sociological Review*, 46 (December 1981): 744–67. Used by permission of the American Sociological Association.

5. For a good account of the background of the four black students in Greensboro, see William H. Chafe, *Civilities and Civil Rights* (New York: Oxford University Press, 1980), pp. 109–16. It is curious that Chafe never mentions the earlier sit-ins that occurred in Durham, approximately twenty miles from Greensboro, during the late 1950s. Nor does he mention McKissick and Moore as participants in early sit-ins or for their part in the 1960 sit-ins. For an account of the early Durham sit-ins and the Durham Committee on Negro Affairs, see Southern Regional Council, "The Student Protest Movement," *SRC–13* (April 1, 1960), pp. iv and viii.

6. For a discussion of Dr. Simpkins's desegregation activities in Greensboro prior to February 1, 1960, see Chafe, *Civilities and Civil Rights*, pp. 110–11.

7. Martin Oppenheimer, "The Southern Student Movement: Year I," *Journal of Negro Education*, 33 (1964): 396–403.

8. Chafe, *Civilities and Civil Rights*, p. 117, points out that when the Greensboro sit-ins occurred, "the national NAACP criticized the sit-in tactic and refused legal or moral support for some time."

9. Miles Wolff, *Lunch at the Five and Ten* (New York: Stein & Day, 1970), p. 590.

10. Gordon Carey interview, November 18, 1978, Soul City, N.C.

11. Douglas Moore, "New Trespass Laws Strongly Protested," *Journal and Guide*, Vol. LX, March 5, 1960.

12. Carey interview.

13. Floyd McKissick interview, November 18, 1978, Soul City, N.C.

14. James McCain interview, November 18, 1978, Sumter, S.C. For an account of McCain's activities during the sit-ins, see August Meier and Elliot Rudwick, *CORE: A Study in the Civil Rights Movement 1942–1968* (New York: Oxford University Press, 1973), pp. 104–5.

15. McCain interview.

16. Southern Regional Council, "The Student Protest Movement, Winter 1960," *SRC–13*, April 1, 1960, and Wyatt Walker interview, September 29, 1978, New York.

17. Walker interview.

18. Fred Shuttlesworth interview, September 12, 1975, Cincinnati.

19. Ella Baker interview, August 28, 1978, New York.

20. Bernard Lee interview, November 10, 1978, Washington, D.C.

21. C. O. Simpkins interview, October 25, 1978, Merrick, N.Y.

22. Shuttlesworth interview.

23. Daisy Bates interview, February 2, 1981, Little Rock.

24. Patricia Due interview, November 5, 1982, Miami, and Henry Steele interview, November 5, 1982, Tallahassee.

25. James Lawson interview, October 2 and 6, 1978, Los Angeles.

26. *Ibid.*

27. Southern Regional Council, "The Student Protest Movement;" Donald Matthews and James Prothro, *Negroes and the New Southern Politics* (New York: Harcourt, Brace & World, 1966); and Anthony Oberschall, *Social Conflict and Social Movements* (Englewood Cliffs, N.J.: Prentice-Hall, 1973).

28. For the view that the sit-ins were student-initiated and independent of existing civil rights organizations, see Howard Zinn, *SNCC: The New Aboli-*

tionists (Boston: Beacon Press, 1964) p. 29, and Clayborne Carson, *In Struggle: SNCC and the Black Awakening of the 1960's* (Cambridge: Harvard University Press, 1981), pp. 17–18. For the view that existing organizations simply responded to the sit-ins and had little to do with planning and generating them, see Meier and Rudwick, *CORE*, pp. 105–6, and Francis F. Piven and Richard A. Cloward, *Poor People's Movements* (New York: Vintage Book, 1979), p. 222. Although Chafe, *Civilities and Civil Rights*, p. 136, does find that the "sit-in demonstrations represented a dramatic extension of, rather than a departure from, traditional patterns of black activism in Greensboro," in the spread of the sit-ins across the state, he concludes, "there was no conspiracy or collective planning involved. Rather each group acted upon its own impulse" (p. 120).

29. Adam Fairclough, "A Study of the Southern Christian Leadership Conference and the Rise and Fall of the Nonviolent Civil Rights Movement," Ph.D. dissertation, University of Keele, 1977, pp. 32–33.

30. William H. Peace, quoted in *ibid.*, p. 32.

31. Martin Luther King, Jr., telegram to President Dwight Eisenhower, March 9, 1960, *MLK:BU*.

32. Lee interview.

33. Kelly Miller Smith interview, October 13, 1978, Nashville, and Diane Nash Bevel interview, December 14, 1978, Chicago.

34. Smith interview.

35. *Ibid.*

36. James Bevel interview, December 27, 1978, New York.

37. Von Eschen et al., "The Organizational Substructure of Disorderly Politics" (note 1 above) and McAdam, "Political Process and the Civil Rights Movement 1948–1970" (note 1 above).

38. Bevel interview.

39. T. J. Jemison interview, October 16, 1978, Baton Rouge.

40. Cordell Reagon interview, January 3, 1979, New York.

41. *Ibid.*

42. *Ibid.*

43. Smith interview.

44. *Ibid.*

45. Matthew McCollom interview, October 31, 1979, Orangeburg, S.C.

46. James McCain interview, November 18, 1978, Sumter, S.C.

47. Julian Bond interview, October 19, 1980, Ann Arbor, Mich.

48. Howard Zinn, *SNCC: The New Abolitionists* (Boston: Beacon Press, 1964), p. 29.

49. D. Bevel interview.

50. J. Bevel interview.

51. Smith interview.

52. *Ibid.*

53. J. Bevel interview.

54. D. Bevel interview.

55. Student Nonviolent Coordinating Committee, *The Student Voice*, August, 1960.

56. Southern Regional Council, "The Student Protest Movement: A Recapitulation" *SRC–21*, September 29, 1961, and Morris, "Black Southern Student Sit-in Movement" (note 4 above).

57. Carey interview.

58. Meier and Rudwick, *CORE*, p. 113.

59. This percentage was derived from Ralph Abernathy, "Financial Secretary–Treasurer Report to the Executive Board of Southern Christian Leadership Conference," October 11, 1960, *MLK:BU*.

60. Walker interview.

61. *Ibid.*

62. See August Meier, "On the Role of Martin Luther King," *New Politics*, 4 no. 1 (1965): 56–58, and Oberschall, *Social Conflict and Social Movements*, p. 230.

63. For a study of the early years of SNCC, see Zinn, *SNCC*; for a study covering the entire history of SNCC, see Carson, *In Struggle*, 1981.

64. For example, in the early stages of the 1960 sit-ins the NAACP's *Crisis* magazine, March 1960, pp. 162–63, stated, "Those Americans who genuinely believe in democracy for all should support these young people in every way possible. The NAACP has already called upon its branches to support them. And the Association has notified all branch leaders that these young people 'have the cooperation and support of the NAACP, for they are legitimate expressions of citizens in a democracy.' " On the other hand, the NAACP often conveyed a different message privately regarding the sit-ins. C. T. Vivian recalls that when the sit-ins began in Nashville, "Thurgood Marshall came to Nashville and we were in a back room talking around the table, and he looked at me and said, 'You're a dangerous man.' He pointed his finger at me and said, 'You're a dangerous man.' " When Vivian was asked why Marshall took such an attitude, he stated, "Because he saw no action outside the courtroom. He did not understand direct action. As far as he was concerned, it was all going to be settled in the courtroom." C. T. Vivian interview, December 7, 1978, Philadelphia.

65. James Forman, *The Making of Black Revolutionaries* (New York: Macmillan, 1972), p. 217.

66. Myles Horton interview, December 5, 1978, Knoxville, Tenn.

67. Lawson interview.

68. *Ibid.*

69. Lee interview.

70. J. Bevel interview.

71. Forman, *The Making of Black Revolutionaries*, p. 217.

72. Baker interview.

73. Septima Clark, "Report of the 7th Annual Highlander Folk School College Workshop," April 1–3, 1960, *MLK:BU*.

74. Forman, *The Making of Black Revolutionaries*, p. 217.

75. Julian Bond interview, in Howell Raines, *My Soul Is Rested* (New York: Bantam Books, 1977), p. 106.

76. SNCC, "Special Note to Workshop Leaders and Speakers," issued sometime shortly before the October 1960 conference.

77. Jane Stembridge, letter to Martin Luther King, Jr., July 13, 1960, *MLK:BU*.

78. Anne Braden interview, December 11, 1978, New York.

79. SNCC, *The Student Voice*, November 10, 1960.

80. The intent here is to provide an account of the link between the civil

rights movement and the white student movement. For analyses of the white student movement proper, see Todd Gitlin, *The Whole World is Watching* (Berkeley: University of California Press, 1980); David L. Westby, *The Clouded Vision: The Student Movement in the United States in the 1960s* (London: Associated University Press, 1976); Kirkpatrick Sale, SDS (New York: Vintage, 1973); Max Heirich, *The Spiral of Conflict: Berkeley, 1964* (New York: Columbia University Press, 1971); Julian Foster and Durward Lang (eds.), *Protest: Student Activism in America* (New York: William Morrow, 1970); and Seymour Martin Lipset and Sheldon S. Wolin, *The Berkeley Student Revolt* (New York: Doubleday, 1965).

81. Sale, SDS, p. 23.

82. Richard Flacks, "Who Protests: The Social Bases of the Student Movement," in Julian Foster and Durward Long (eds.), *Protest! Student Activism in America* (New York: William Morrow, 1970), pp. 134–57.

83. Mark Chesler, lecture, University of Michigan, winter 1981.

84. Robert A. Haber, "From Protest to Radicalism: An Appraisal of the Student Movement 1960," in Mitchell Cohen and Dennis Hale (eds.), *The New Student Left* (Boston: Dorsey, 1966), pp. 41–49.

85. Richard Flacks, *Youth and Social Change* (Chicago: Rand-McNally College Publishing, 1973), p. 76.

86. Sale, SDS, pp. 24–25.

87. Robert Alan Haber interview, April 24, 1982, Berkeley, Calif.

88. Ibid.

89. Louis E. Lomax, *The Negro Revolt* (New York: New American Library, 1962), p. 106.

90. SCLC, "Southwide Voter Registration Prospectus," prepared by M. L. King, Jr., and Wyatt Walker during 1961, MLK:BU.

91. Ibid.

92. Vivian interview.

93. Walker interview.

94. Chauncey Eskridge interview, December 15, 1978, Chicago.

95. SCLC, Report of the Treasurer, November 1, 1960–April 30, 1961, MLK:BU.

96. SCLC, "Statement of Receipts and Expenditures for the Fiscal Year ending October 31, 1960," MLK:BU.

97. Lomax, *The Negro Revolt*, pp. 104–5.

98. Thomas Kilgore interview, October 5, 1978, Los Angeles.

99. Ibid.

100. Kilgore interview. For an account of the role that entertainers played in raising funds for the SCLC, see Eugene Walker, "A History of the Southern Christian Leadership Conference, 1955–1965: The Evaluation of a Southern Strategy for Social Change," Ph.D. dissertation, Duke University, 1978, pp. 86–87.

101. Kilgore interview.

102. Walker interview.

103. Ibid.

104. Stanley Levison, letter to Aldon Morris, March 21, 1979.

105. Walker interview.

106. For an example of how a local movement center raised funds for a particular project, see Appendix D.

Chapter 10: Birmingham: A Planned Exercise in Mass Disruption

1. James Robinson interview, October 26, 1978, New York.
2. *Ibid.*
3. *Ibid.*
4. James Peck interview, October 26, 1978, New York.
5. James Farmer interview, November 9, 1978, Washington, D.C.
6. Anne Braden interview, December 11, 1978, New York.
7. James Bevel interview, December 27, 1978, New York.
8. For accounts of the Freedom Rides, see James Peck, *Freedom Ride* (New York: Simon & Schuster, 1962); Howard Zinn, *SNCC: The New Abolitionists* (Boston: Beacon Press, 1964), pp. 40–61; August Meier and Elliott Rudwick, *CORE: A Study in the Civil Rights Movement 1942–1968* (New York: Oxford University Press, 1973), pp. 135–58; and Clayborne Carson, *In Struggle: SNCC and the Black Awakening of the 1960s* (Cambridge: Harvard University Press, 1981), pp. 31–44.
9. See Meier and Rudwick, *CORE*, p. 135.
10. Fred Shuttlesworth interview, September 12, 1978, Cincinnati.
11. *Ibid.*
12. J. Bevel interview.
13. Zinn, *SNCC*, p. 51.
14. *Ibid.*, pp. 53–54.
15. William Kunstler, *Deep in My Heart* (New York: William Morrow, 1966), p. 33.
16. Meier and Rudwick, *CORE*, p. 143.
17. For accounts of SNCC activities in the South following the Freedom Rides, see Zinn, *SNCC*, pp. 62–146, and Carson, *In Struggle*, pp. 45–82.
18. J. Bevel interview.
19. Carson, *In Struggle*, p. 71.
20. *Ibid.*, p. 70.
21. *Ibid.*, p. 71.
22. For an account of President Kennedy's views on the black vote, see Steven F. Lawson, *Black Ballots: Voting Rights in the South, 1944–1969* (New York: Columbia University Press, 1976) pp. 259–61. On page 260 Lawson writes: "According to Theodore Sorensen, his trusted confidant, when Kennedy talked privately about Negroes at all in those days, it was usually about winning Negro votes."
23. Farmer interview. For additional accounts of the meetings between Robert Kennedy and the civil rights organizations regarding voting activities and social protest, see Arthur M. Schlesinger, Jr., *Robert Kennedy and His Times* (Boston: Houghton Mifflin, 1978), pp. 286–316, and Lawson, *Black Ballots*, pp. 260–68.

24. Farmer interview.

25. Arthur M. Schlesinger, Jr., *A Thousand Days* (Boston: Houghton Mifflin, 1965), p. 937.

26. *Ibid.,* p. 935.

27. *Ibid.*

28. Kunstler, *Deep in My Heart,* p. 110.

29. Myles Horton interview, December 5, 1978, Knoxville, Tenn.

30. *Ibid.*

31. Dorothy Cotton interview, November 13, 1978, Atlanta.

32. *Ibid.*

33. Septima Clark interview, November 17, 1978, Charleston, S.C.

34. Cotton interview.

35. J. Bevel interview.

36. Cotton interview.

37. Clark interview.

38. *Ibid.*

39. For discussions of the Albany movement, see Howard Zinn, "Albany," *Southern Regional Council,* 22 (January 8, 1962): 1–30; *idem,* "Albany: A Study in National Responsibility," *Southern Regional Council,* 1962, pp. v–35; *idem, SNCC,* pp. 123–46; David Lewis, *King: A Critical Biography* (New York: Praeger, 1970), pp. 140–70: and Carson, *In Struggle,* pp. 56–65.

40. Charles Sherrod interview, August 7, 1981, Albany, Ga.

41. Cordell Reagon interview, January 3, 1978, New York.

42. *Ibid.*

43. W. G. Anderson interview, August 14, 1981, Detroit.

44. C. B. King interview, August 7, 1981, Albany, Ga.

45. Bernice Reagon, "Songs of the Civil Rights Movement 1955–1965; A Study in Culture History," Ph.D. dissertation, Howard University, 1975, p. 134.

46. Anderson interview.

47. *Ibid.*

48. *Ibid.*

49. Lewis, *King: A Critical Biography,* p. 146.

50. Bernard Lee interview, November 10, 1978, Washington, D.C.

51. Anderson interview.

52. *Ibid.*

53. *Ibid.*

54. *Ibid.*

55. James Forman, *The Making of Black Revolutionaries* (New York: Macmillan, 1972), p. 254.

56. Sherrod says he did not oppose the decision to bring Dr. King to Albany. However, Sherrod pointed out, SNCC's reservations about King's entering Albany had to do with publicity. Sherrod maintains that the SCLC had an excellent media department, which would enable it to garner the attention and credit for the Albany movement. This process was enhanced by the fact that the black masses viewed King as the Messiah. Sherrod interview.

57. Reagon interview.

58. C. B. King interview.

59. Anderson interview.

60. Forman, *The Making of Black Revolutionaries*, pp. 255–56.

61. Anderson interview.

62. *Ibid.*

63. Reagon interview.

64. Anderson interview.

65. Reagon interview.

66. Anderson interview.

67. C. B. King interview.

68. Wyatt Walker interview, September 29, 1978, New York.

69. Reagon interview.

70. *Ibid.*

71. C. B. King interview.

72. Anderson interview.

73. *Ibid.*

74. Zinn, "Albany: A Study in National Responsibility" (note 39 above), p. 5.

75. For an account of the activities between January and July 1962, see *ibid.*, pp. 5–8.

76. C. B. King interview.

77. Kunstler, *Deep in My Heart*, p. 101.

78. *Ibid.*, p. 102.

79. *Ibid.*

80. *Ibid.*, p. 101.

81. Forman, *The Making of Black Revolutionaries*, p. 218.

82. Lewis, *King: A Critical Biography*, p. 161.

83. Kunstler, *Deep in My Heart*, p. 103.

84. Anderson interview.

85. *Ibid.*

86. *Ibid.*

87. Lewis, *King: A Critical Biography*, p. 155.

88. *Ibid.*, p. 150.

89. Lee interview.

90. For valuable accounts of the Birmingham movement, see Lerone Bennett, Jr., *The Negro Mood* (Chicago: Johnson Publishing, 1964); David Lewis, *King: A Critical Biography*, pp. 171–209; David J. Garrow, *Protest At Selma: Martin Luther King, Jr., and the Voting Rights Act of 1965* (New Haven: Yale University Press, 1978) pp. 133–60; and Robert G. Corley, "The Quest for Racial Harmony: Race Relations in Birmingham, Alabama, 1947–1963," Ph.D. dissertation, University of Virginia, 1979, p. 246.

91. Kunstler, *Deep in My Heart*, p. 178.

92. Martin Luther King, Jr., *Why We Can't Wait*, (New York: New American Library, 1963), p. 54.

93. Shuttlesworth interview.

94. See Howard Hubbard, "Five Long Hot Summers and How They Grew," *Public Interest*, 12 (1968): 5; Garrow, *Protest at Selma*, p. 222; and Doug McAdam, *Political Process and the Development of Black Insurgency 1930–1970*

(Chicago: University of Chicago Press, 1982), p. 178. It is curious that these writers put forward the "violent thesis" without giving any attention to the centrality of the economic boycott in the 1963 Birmingham struggle.

95. King, *Why We Can't Wait*, p. 52.

96. Walker interview.

97. *Ibid.*

98. C. T. Vivian interview, December 7, 1978, Philadelphia.

99. Eugene P. Walker, "A History of the Southern Christian Leadership Conference, 1955–1965: The Evolution of a Strategy for Social Change," Ph.D. dissertation, Duke University, 1978, p. 108.

100. Walker interview.

101. J. Bevel interview.

102. Hosea Williams interview, September 22, 1978, Atlanta.

103. Corley, "The Quest for Racial Harmony," p. 246.

104. King, *Why We Can't Wait*, p. 67.

105. Andrew Young, "And Birmingham," *Drum Major*, Southern Christian Leadership Conference, 1971, pp. 21–27.

106. Kunstler, *Deep in My Heart*, p. 183.

107. *Ibid.*, p. 184.

108. Young, "And Birmingham," p. 23.

109. *Ibid.*

110. Reagon, "Songs of the Civil Rights Movement," p. 147.

111. *Ibid.*

112. King, *Why We Can't Wait*, p. 61.

113. In this regard Numan V. Bartley, *The Rise of Massive Resistance* (Baton Rouge: Louisiana State University Press, 1969), p. 88, wrote: "From its inception the Alabama Council Movement was deeply intertwined with much of the black-belt political power structure."

114. The argument by Garrow and others is misleading because it directs attention away from the fact that local merchants were a primary target of the movement. SCLC activists devised tactics that disrupted the businesses of local merchants, causing them to change their stance toward the demands of the movement.

115. Walker interview.

116. King, *Why We Can't Wait*, p. 54.

117. Harding, "A Beginning in Birmingham," p. 14.

118. *Ibid.*

119. Bennett, *The Negro Mood*, p. 6.

120. King, *Why We Can't Wait*, p. 56.

121. Walker interview.

122. J. Bevel interview.

123. Walker interview.

124. King, *Why We Can't Wait*, p. 70.

125. Young, "And Birmingham," p. 23.

126. Lewis, *King: A Critical Biography*, p. 184.

127. Michael Dorman, *We Shall Overcome* (New York: Dial Press, 1964), p. 144.

128. *Ibid.*

129. *Ibid.,* p. 145.

130. King, *Why We Can't Wait,* p. 60.

131. Young, "And Birmingham," p. 23.

132. Lewis, *King: A Critical Biography,* p. 179.

133. Harding, "A Beginning in Birmingham," pp. 13–19.

134. Walker interview.

135. Lewis, *King: A Critical Biography,* p. 181.

136. Walker interview.

137. King, *Why We Can't Wait,* pp. 62–63.

138. Alan F. Westin and Barry Mahoney, *The Trial of Martin Luther King* (New York: Thomas Y. Crowell, 1974), p. 77.

139. *Ibid.,* p. 76.

140. *Ibid.,* p. 79.

141. King, *Why We Can't Wait,* p. 71.

142. Young, "And Birmingham," p. 26.

143. Harding, "A Beginning in Birmingham," p. 15.

144. See Harrison Salisbury, *New York Times,* April 9, 1960. For a discussion of lawsuits in Birmingham prior to 1963, see Westin and Mahoney, *The Trial of Martin Luther King,* pp. 16–20.

145. Kunstler, *Deep in My Heart,* p. 189.

146. Young, "And Birmingham," p. 22.

147. King, *Why We Can't Wait,* p. 101.

148. Lewis, *King: A Critical Biography,* p. 194.

149. Young, "And Birmingham," p. 27.

150. Lewis, *King: A Critical Biography,* p. 194.

151. Kunstler, *Deep in My Heart,* p. 191.

152. Walker interview.

153. Young, "And Birmingham," p. 26.

154. King, *Why We Can't Wait,* p. 100.

155. Dorman, *We Shall Overcome,* p. 153.

156. Harding, "A Beginning in Birmingham," p. 16.

157. Dorman, *We Shall Overcome,* p. 153.

158. Harding, "A Beginning in Birmingham," p. 16.

159. King, *Why We Can't Wait,* p. 104.

160. Harding, "A Beginning in Birmingham," p. 16.

161. King, *Why We Can't Wait,* p. 105.

162. Harding, "A Beginning in Birmingham," p. 16.

163. *Ibid.*

164. Dorman, *We Shall Overcome,* p. 154.

165. *Ibid.*

166. Lewis, *King: A Critical Biography,* p. 197.

167. Dorman, *We Shall Overcome,* p. 161.

168. *Ibid.*

169. *Ibid.,* p. 166.

170. Young, "And Birmingham," p. 26.

171. Thomas Brooks, *Walls Come Tumbling Down: A History of the Civil Rights Movement 1940–1970* (Englewood Cliffs, N.J.: Prentice-Hall, 1974), p. 210.

172. Fred Shuttlesworth, Seventh Annual Address to the ACMHR, June 5, 1963, p. 2.

173. Kirkpatrick Sale, SDS (New York, Vintage Books, 1973), p. 83.

Chapter 11: Theoretical Overview and Conclusions

1. The principal formulations of classical collective behavior theory include Robert E. Park and Ernest W. Burgess, Introduction to the Science of Sociology (Chicago: University of Chicago Press, 1921), pp. 865–952; Herbert Blumer, "Collective Behavior," in A. M. Lee (ed.), New Outlines of the Principles of Sociology (New York: Barnes & Noble, 1946), pp. 165–220; Ralph Turner and Lewis Killian, Collective Behavior (Englewood Cliffs, N.J.: Prentice-Hall, 1957); Kurt Lang and Gladys Lang, Collective Dynamics (New York: Crowell, 1961); and Neil Smelser, Theory of Collective Behavior (New York: Free Press, 1962).

2. Later theorists in the collective behavior tradition—e.g. Clark McPhail and David Miller, "The Assembling Process: A Theoretical and Empirical Examination," American Sociological Review, 38 (December 1973): 721–35; Clark McPhail, "Toward a Theory of Collective Behavior," paper presented at Symposium on Symbolic Interaction, University of South Carolina, 1978; Jack M. Weller and E. L. Quarantelli, "Neglected Characteristics of Collective Behavior," American Journal of Sociology, 79 (November 1973): 665–85; and Gary T. Marx, "Conceptual Problems in the Field of Collective Behavior," paper presented at the American Sociological Association Meetings, Boston, 1979—have either rejected or revised many of the basic tenets of classical collective behavior theory. In general these writers tend to deemphasize the break between institutionalized behavior and collective behavior posited by the classical theorists. In this vein the role of communication processes, norms, and social organization is stressed, along with the emphasis on spontaneity, emotionalism, and psychic strain.

3. For example see, Park and Burgess, Introduction to the Science of Sociology; Blumer, "Collective Behavior," esp. pp. 170–77; Lang and Lang, Collective Dynamics, esp. pp. 31, 43, 209–89; and Smelser, Theory of Collective Behavior, esp. pp. 8, 71–73, 79–130.

4. Turner and Killian, Collective Behavior, pp. 16–17.

5. Ibid., pp. 17–19.

6. Ralph Turner, "Collective Behavior," in Robert E. L. Faris (ed.), Handbook of Modern Sociology (Chicago: Rand McNally, 1964), p. 384.

7. For example, in the second edition of Collective Behavior (Englewood Cliffs, N.J.: Prentice-Hall, 1972), p. 32, Turner and Killian argue that "rumor is the characteristic mode of communication in collective behavior." This argument is based on the notion that rumor is central because preexisting channels of communication have broken down in collective behavior situations.

8. Lewis Killian, "Social Movements," in Robert E. L. Faris (ed.), Handbook of Modern Sociology (Chicago: Rand McNally, 1964), p. 426.

9. For example Park and Burgess, Introduction to the Science of Sociology, p. 925, emphasize that collective behavior represents the processes by which

people reorganize and rearrange their social relationships in ways that give rise to new organizations and new societies. Herbert Blumer, "Collective Behavior," pp. 173–75, also stresses the idea that collective behavior is concerned with reorganization that gives rise to new moral and social orders.

10. The idea that individuals satisfice rather than optimize when making decisions was formulated by James March and Herbert Simon, *Organizations* (New York: John Wiley & Sons, 1958), pp. 136–71. Although March's and Simon's insight that there are cognitive limits on rationality was formulated to explain behavior in formal organizations, it seems equally applicable for social movement behavior. It is particularly so given that activists in movements are forced to make numerous complex decisions, and rapidly. See Michael Schwartz, *Radical Protest and Social Structure* (New York: Academic Press, 1976), esp. pp. 135–45, 177–83, for an excellent discussion of rationality in movements. Schwartz takes a position parallel to the one presented here.

11. Frances Fox Piven and Richard A. Cloward, *Poor People's Movements* (New York: Vintage Books, 1979), pp. 222–24.

12. Max Weber, *The Theory of Social and Economic Organizations*, Talcott Parsons (ed.) (New York: Free Press, 1947), p. 361.

13. *Ibid.*

14. Charles Tilly, *From Mobilization to Revolution* (Reading, Mass.: Addison-Wesley, 1978), pp. 39–40.

15. The resource mobilization model has emerged as the dominant sociological theory of social movements. The chief formulations of this view include Anthony Oberschall, *Social Conflict and Social Movements* (Englewood Cliffs, N.J.: Prentice-Hall, 1973); John D. McCarthy and Mayer Zald, *The Trend of Social Movements in America: Professionalism and Resource Mobilization*" (Morristown, N.J.: General Learning Press, 1973); idem, "Resource Mobilization and Social Movements: A Partial Theory," *American Journal of Sociology* 82, no. 6 (1977): 1212–41; William Gamson, *The Strategy of Social Protest* (Homewood, Ill.: Dorsey Press, 1975); and Charles Tilly, *From Mobilization to Revolution* (Reading, Mass.: Addison-Wesley, 1978).

16. Michael Lipsky, "Protest as a Political Resource," *American Political Science Review*, 62 (1968): 1114–58; Howard Hubbard, "Five Long Hot Summers and How They Grew," *Public Interest*, 12 (1968): 3–24; and David Garrow, *Protest at Selma* (New Haven: Yale University Press, 1978).

17. Gary T. Marx and Michael Useem, "Majority Involvement in Minority Movements: Civil Rights, Abolition, Untouchability," *Journal of Social Issues*, 27 (1971): 81–104.

18. Lipsky, "Protest as a Political Resource," pp. 1145, 1153, and 1157. Emphasis added.

19. Oberschall, *Social Conflict and Social Movements*, p. 214.

20. *Ibid.*, pp. 214–18.

21. *Ibid.*, p. 218.

22. Two key statements on resource mobilization theory—Gamson, *The Strategy of Social Protest*, pp. 140–43, and Tilly, *From Mobilization to Revolution*, pp. 52–55—argue that challenging groups are those excluded from the formal political process of a society, referred to as the polity. The chief aim of challenging groups is to become a part of the polity. My definition of domi-

nated groups differs from this position in that such groups may be excluded not only from the polity but other spheres such as the economic and cultural. Challenging behavior by dominated groups may be aimed at inclusion in the political, economic, or cultural spheres, or it may be aimed at destroying the society.

23. In this connection Doug McAdam, "Political Process and the Black Protest Movement 1948–1970," Ph.D. dissertation, State University of New York at Stony Brook, 1979, pp. 240, 302–6, to date the most comprehensive analysis of the funding patterns of the civil rights movement, concludes that "outside support increases sharply *following, rather than preceding*, the initial period of widespread protest activity" and that "external support, far from triggering insurgency, is actually a product of it." Emphasis added.

24. Stokeley Carmichael (Kwame Ture), speech, October 29, 1981, Washtenaw Community College, Ann Arbor, Michigan.

25. *National Roster of Black Elected Officials,* Vol. 12 (Washington, D.C.: Joint Center for Political Studies, 1982): pp. vii–viii.

26. Harry A. Ploski and Ernest Kaiser, *Afro USA* (New York: Bellwether, 1971), p. 279.

27. *National Roster of Black Elected Officials,* 1982, p. vii.

28. For discussions of the relationships between the civil rights movement and (1) emergence of the modern women's movement, see Jo Freeman, "The Origins of Women's Liberation Movement," *American Journal of Sociology,* 78 (January 1973): 792–811; (2) the rise of the modern white student movement, see Clayborne Carson, *In Struggle* (Cambridge: Harvard University Press, 1981), pp. 175–90; (3) the emergence of the farm workers' movements, see Robert J. Thomas and William H. Friedland, "The United Farmworkers Union: From Mobilization to Mechanization?" Center for Research on Social Organization, Working Paper 269, undated, University of Michigan.

29. Karl-Dieter Opp, "Economics, Sociology, and Political Protest," in W. Raub (ed.), *Theoretical Models and Empirical Analyses: Contributions to the Explanation of Individual Actions and Collective Phenomena* (Utrecht, Netherlands: VOS, 1982).

30. *The Michigan Daily,* November 2, 1982.

31. U.S. Bureau of the Census Current Population Report, Series P–60, No. 129, *Money Incomes of Families and Persons in the United States: 1979* (Washington, D.C.: U.S. Government Printing Office, 1981). Percentages prior to 1967 are only approximate, because the income of blacks is included with that of other "nonwhite" races.

32. *Ibid.*

33. SCLC Program Office, "Statement of Purpose: Poor People's Campaign, Washington, D.C.," SCLC Poor People's Campaign, May 21, 1968.

Appendix A:
Data and Methods

Data

This study covers the first decade of the civil rights movement. The following archives were examined: the King papers at Boston University; portions of the civil rights interviews located in the Moorland Spingarn Research Center at Howard University; portions of the Southern Christian Leadership Conference papers located at the SCLC's headquarters in Atlanta, Georgia; and portions of Reverend Kelly Miller Smith's papers at the First Baptist Church in Nashville, Tennessee. Thousands of original documents (memoranda, letters, field reports, organizational histories and directives, interorganizational correspondences, and so on) generated by movement participants were examined. These sources contained a wealth of information pertaining to key variables—organization, mobilization, finance, rationality, spontaneity—relevant to the study of movements.

Interviews with participants of the movement constituted the second source of data. Detailed interviews with more than fifty civil rights leaders were conducted. Interviews made it possible to followup on many issues raised by the archival data; being fairly open-ended, they revealed unexpected insights into the movement. Whenever statements were heard that seemed novel or promising, the subjects were given freedom to discuss them in detail.

Methods

The strategy for the archival research was straightforward. The author examined every document possible within the time allocated for a particular site. The main objective was to examine the roles played in the civil rights movement by variables associated with Weberian theory and theories of collective behavior and resource mobilization. Following collective behavior theory, I was concerned with the extent to which the civil rights movement was spontaneous and discontinuous with established social structure. From Weberian theory I was interested in whether a charismatic attraction between a leader and followers was sufficient to produce the heavy volume of collective action generated during the movement. Finally, several issues addressed by resource mobilization theory were of interest. I examined archival sources to ascertain the role of social organization and resources in the movement. Also, I was concerned with whether the leadership, money, and skills behind the movement were supplied by outsiders or by the indigenous Southern black community.

Three strategies were employed in the interview process. First, the researcher attempted to learn as much as possible about the movement from extensive library and archival sources before conducting interviews. This prior knowledge enabled the interviewer to ask specific questions and to assist interviewees in placing their memories in the social, temporal, and geographical context of their actions twenty years earlier. Prior knowledge enabled the interviewer to gain the respect of interviewees and increased the likelihood that they would approach the interview in a serious manner.

Second, the interviews were semistructured, usually lasting two or three hours. An extended list of questions structured around the variables used in the archival research were formulated beforehand. The interviewees were instructed to feel free to deviate from the questions and to discuss what they thought to be important. Their "digressions" produced new information.

Third, the interview sample was assembled in two ways. While examining the archival material, the names of leaders associated with various activities turned up constantly. These were the first individuals contacted for interviews. Once the interview process was under way, interviewees would invariably remark, often in response to queries, "you know, you really should speak to [so-and-so] regarding that matter." Subsequent interviews were arranged with many of the named individuals. Thus, the snowball effect was central to the sampling process. Although the activists interviewed came from numerous organizations and represented different, if not conflicting, viewpoints, to our surprise they agreed on many basic issues.

Given that the movement occurred twenty years ago, it is reasonable to wonder whether interview accounts are reliable and valid. Moreover, there is the suspicion that participants might have vested interests in presenting the "facts" in such a way as to enhance their own status. Such problems of recall and vested interest have been minimized in this research because the analysis does not rely on any one source. Rather, it is built on an array of published material, archival sources, and accounts of individuals who participated in and were eyewitnesses to the same events. Furthermore, cross-references were made throughout the data collection process. Follow-up phone calls were made to clarify ambiguity and to obtain a comprehensive view of the civil rights movement. It appears that neither of these potential trouble spots produced fundamental defects in the data.

Appendix B:
List of
Persons Interviewed

The Rev. Ralph Abernathy
Dr. Benjamin Alexander
Dr. W. G. Anderson
Ella Baker
Daisy Bates
Diane Nash Bevel
The Rev. James Bevel
The Rev. Fred J. Boddie, Jr.
The Hon. Julian Bond
Anne Braden
Gordon R. Carey
Septima Clark
Dorothy Cotton
Dr. W. T. Crutcher
Dr. L. T. Daye
Patricia Due
Chauncey Eskridge, attorney
James Farmer
Alan Haber
The Rev. Curtis Harris
Myles Horton
Ruby Hurley
The Rev. T. J. Jemison
Matthew Jones, Jr.
The Rev. Matthew Jones, Sr.
Dr. Thomas Kilgore
C. B. King, attorney
Lonnie King
The Rev. James Lawson

The Rev. Barnard Lee
Chester I. Lewis, attorney
The Rev. John Lewis
Dr. Joseph Lowery
Clara Luper
Dr. Benjamin Mays
James McCain
Matthew McCollom
Floyd McKissick, attorney
The Rev. Douglas Moore
E. D. Nixon
Rosa Parks
James Peck
Homer Randolph
Cordell Reagon
The Rev. Milton Reid
Marvin Rich
James Robinson
The Rev. Charles Sherrod
The Rev. Fred Shuttlesworth
Dr. B. J. Simms
Dr. C. O. Simpkins
The Rev. Glenn Smiley
The Rev. Kelly Miller Smith
The Rev. Daniel Speed
The Rev. Charles K. Steele
Henry Steele
The Rev. C. T. Vivian
The Rev. Wyatt Tee Walker

Hosea Williams

Appendix C:
Sample Interview
Questionnaire

What follows are the actual interview questions asked of The Reverend Ralph Abernathy. Each interviewee was asked questions specifically designed for him/her. However, all of the interviewees had to respond to a number of basic questions and themes. The questions asked of Reverend Abernathy reflect the overall content and flavor of interview questions.

Instructions

"Dr. Abernathy, I am going to ask you some specific questions regarding the origins and development of the civil rights movement. I hope you will be able to answer all of these questions. However, I want to emphasize that you may discuss any aspects of the civil rights movement which you consider important. Please feel free to provide me with any information that you think will help me understand the movement."

Questions

1. Dr. Abernathy, what type of background did you come from?
2. What other organizations and civil rights organization(s) did you belong to before the creation of MIA?

3. In your opinion did the black church prepare ministers to be effective civil rights leaders?

4. Dr. Abernathy, is it correct to say that you had built a community base in Montgomery before the boycott? Please explain—were you in contact with other community bases across the South prior to the creation of the SCLC?

5. Dr. Abernathy what significance did the creation of the MIA have for the entire civil rights struggle?

6. How was the MIA supported financially?

7. Where did the idea of the Southern Christian Leadership Conference come from?

8. Dr. Abernathy, why did you along with many other leaders feel that an organization such as the SCLC should be created?

9. SCLC brought together in one organizational framework such able leaders as Dr. King, Rev. Lowery, Rev. Shuttlesworth, Rev. Steele, Rev. Jemison, Rev. Davis, Rev. Kelly Smith, and yourself. What kind of effect did this coming together in one organization have on these leaders and their local power bases and struggles?

10. Where did the power in the SCLC reside? What role did the Executive Board, the officers, and staff play within the organization?

11. When SCLC was created, how did other organizations in the field such as CORE, the Urban League, and especially the NAACP view the creation and development of the SCLC?

12. Why was it decided that the SCLC would have neither individual memberships nor chapters?

13. How did the SCLC get affiliates, and how well did it relate to these affiliates in terms of helping them grow and develop?

14. Did the various officers and staff people of the SCLC have organizational skills and competences? How effectively did they perform their tasks?

15. Dr. Abernathy, how did the SCLC get its money from 1957 until 1965?

16. What kind of help did white organizations such as FOR, SCEF, SRC, and the Highlander Folk School give to the SCLC and the movement?

17. What kind of relationship did the SCLC have with the federal government, White Citizens' Councils, and Klu Klux Klan?

18. Dr. Abernathy, what is charisma? How did it function within the SCLC and the movement? What leaders within the SCLC and the movement had charisma? What type of strain, competition, and conflict existed between movement administrators and charismatic leaders?

19. What kind of working relationship did the SCLC develop over time with the NAACP, CORE, and the Urban League?

20. What was the role of women and young people in the SCLC and the movement in general?

21. In your opinion, why did the student sit-ins break out in 1960?

22. How did the sit-ins and the student movement affect the SCLC, the NAACP, CORE, and the relationship between these organizations? How did the SCLC view SNCC, and what kinds of relationships developed between them?

23. What impact did the Freedom Rides have on these organizations?

24. What affect did Albany and Birmingham have on the SCLC?

25. Dr. Abernathy, did the masses force the SCLC in certain directions, or did the SCLC train and direct the masses?

26. Can you think of any significant periods between 1957 and 1964 that changed the nature of the SCLC?

27. How important to the civil rights struggles were the years 1957 through 1964?

28. Dr. Abernathy, was the civil rights movement spontaneous? Did leaders and activists often find themselves in unplanned situations which forced them to respond? In your estimation, how much of the activities of the civil rights movement emerged from spontaneous circumstances and how much of it was deliberately planned and organized?

Appendix D:
Sample Fundraising
Statements

In 1960 the Reverend Wyatt Walker of Petersburg, Virginia, along with
the Congress of Racial Equality, sponsored a Prayer Pilgrimage against
the closing of public schools in Prince Edward County to avoid desegregation. Following the successful 1960 pilgrimage, the Virginia State
Unit of the Southern Christian Leadership Conference decided to re-
peat the Pilgrimage in January 1961. Below are the financial statements
that document the sources of funding for the 1961 pilgrimage. These
documents provide evidence of the crucial financial role that indigenous churches, organizations, and individuals played in local movement centers. These documents support evidence compiled throughout
this study that local movement centers were financed by indigenous
blacks, although these particular documents refer only to Virginia and
one of its major projects.

**Financial Report of Contributing Churches and Organizations
to the Pilgrimage for Free Public School Education
in Prince Edward County**

First Baptist Church, 236 Harrison Street, Petersburg, Va....... $51.59
Ever Ready Cleaners, Petersburg, Va., Mr. Holloman.............. 5.00
The Diamond Hill Baptist Church, Lynchburg, Va.................. 75.00
First Baptist Church, Ivory Avenue, Buena Vista, Va 7.05
Shiloh Baptist Church, Norfolk, Va... 36.20

First Baptist Church, Williamsburg, Va., The Rev. D. L.
Collins 45.00
First Baptist Church, 318 Hull St., Franklin, Va.,
Rev. S. F. Daly 10.00
New Site Baptist Church, Fredericksburg, Va.,
Rev. Edward Smith 10.00
Mt. Zion Baptist Church, Triangle, Va., Rev. Austin Booker.... 10.00
Union Baptist Church, Dumpfreye, Va., Rev. Booker................ 10.00
Gravel Run, Dinwiddie, Va., Rev. W. A. Curley........................ 10.00
Bank Street Baptist Church, Norfolk, Va.,
Dr. J. B. Henderson 10.00
First Baptist Church, McKenney, Va., Rev. L. D. Pollard 10.00
Mr. Charles W. Green, 2706 S. 18th St., Arlington, Va 10.00
St. James A.M.E. Church, Prospect, Va., Rev. J. H. Allen......... 1.00
The Rev. M. H. Hopkins, Rfd. Box 68, Rocky Mt., Va 15.00
The Rev. M. J. Hamilton, Parsonage, Rocky Mt., Va................. 1.00
Rev. E. D. Shands, 744 Halifax St., Emporia, Va 20.00
First Baptist Church, Farmville, Va., Rev. L. F. Griffin............. 10.00
Zion Baptist Church, Petersburg, Va., Rev. R. G. Williams....... 10.00
Populas Mount Church, Rev. Winston.. 14.85
Hopewell Improvement Association, Rev. C. W. Harris 10.00
Petersburg Chapter of N.A.A.C.P. 10.00
Mt. Olivet Baptist Church, Petersburg, Va., Dr. L. C. Johnson . 10.00
Olive Branch Church, Haymarket, Va., Rev. L. A. Jackson....... 25.00
Oakrun Baptist Church, Broad Run, Va., Rev. Pointer............. 35.00
Mt. Gilead Baptist Church, Rev. John R. Gray 10.00
Campbell County Civic League.. 10.00
Mr. Tommie Wood, Box 405 Rfd. 3, Lynchburg, Va 10.00
Mrs. E. Loise Murphy, Barbara Scotia College,
Concord, N. C. 10.00
Cumberland County Branch N.A.A.C.P. 25.00
Mt. Sinai Baptist Church, Holland, Va., Rev. G. R. Daughtrey . 42.10
Rev. R. N. Johnson, 2211 Maplewood Ave., Richmond, Va 5.00
Petersburg Branch N.A.A.C.P. 25.00
Dearington Baptist Church, 146 Smith Street, Lynchburg, Va.. 10.00
Dr. Lawrence E. Paxton, 16 Wells Avenue N.W.,
Roanoke, Va 10.00
W. Russell Bowie* 5.00
Rockbridge Branch N.A.A.C.P., c/o Mr. C. Wallace, 219 Taylor
St., Lexington, Va.* 10.00
Arthur H. Bissell, Jr., 13 Fairfax Avenue, Alexandria, Va.*...... 5.00
Jimmy W. Kyle, 1907 Link Rd., Lynchburg, Va.*...................... 5.00
Bethlehem Baptist Church, 1000 Buchanan St., Richmond 25,
Va.*.. 13.69

Alleen Avoria Oakerson* 1.00
Stringfellow Carr, 9 Wilton Street, Princeton, N. J.* 5.00
Council for Colored Women, 307 Madison St., Farmville,
    Va.* 35.00
Concord Baptist Church, Chase City, Va 20.00
St. Paul A.M.E. Church, Danville, Va 15.00
Danville Branch N.A.A.C.P 19.46
Loyal Baptist Church, Rev. D. J. Thomas 22.64
Calvary Baptist Church, Danville, Va., Rev. D. J. Thomas 22.90
Second Calvary Baptist Church, Norfolk, Va., Dr. Walker 10.00
Mt. Pool Baptist Church, Rt. 1 Box 80, Ford, Va.,
    Laura A. Crawley 10.00
Mt. Mariah Baptist Church, Rev. S. M. Thompson 10.12
Rev. J. A. Shelton, 913 Randolph Lane, Lynchburg, Va 10.65
Rev. Doyle J. Thomas, 352 Ross Street, Danville, Va 5.00
Memorial Baptist Church, Rev. T. E. Holes 10.00
First Baptist Church, Norfolk, Va 25.00
Court St. Baptist Church 35.00
Rev. Harold A. Carter, Lynchburg, Va 5.00
Queen St. Baptist Church, 413 E. Brambleton Ave., Norfolk, Va.
    J. Jasper Freeman 26.20
New Central Baptist Church, Norfolk, Va., W. B. Westbrook ... 45.00
Va. Teachers Association, Clay at 4th Sts., Richmond, Va 10.00
Union Christian Sunday School, 1344 Wide St., Norfolk, Va ... 10.00
Mount Olive Baptist Church, Norfolk, Va., Rev. Wise 24.00
First Baptist Church, 700 E. Berkley Ave., Norfolk, Va 27.00
Rev. George Johnson, Franklin, Va 10.00
Mt. Zion Baptist Church, Norfolk, Va., Thelma R. Harty 35.00
Mt. Lebanon Baptist Church, Rev. F. P. Wise 35.00
Beulah Baptist Church, Woodford, Va., Rev. Charles Franklin 15.00
Dr. M. F. Robinson, 110 Cherry St., Covington, Va 5.00
Va. Baptist State Conv., Rev. L. C. Johnson 50.00
First Calvary Baptist Church, 813 Henry Street, Norfolk, Va ... 50.00
Hill St. Baptist Church, 131 Madnald Ave., Roanoke, Va 30.41
Ambassador's Lyceum of Richmond, Rev. M. L. Spencer 5.00
Sweet Union Baptist Church, 521 Madison Ave. N.W.,
    Roanoke, Va 39.00
Besean Baptist Church, Chase City, Va 5.00
Jane C. Belcher, Sweet Briar College, Sweet Briar, Va.* 5.00
Zion Poplar Baptist Church, Deacon Thomas Lomax, Zanona,
    Va 10.06
Union Zion Baptist Church, Mrs. Helen Brown, Ware Neck,
    Va 10.00

Zion Hill Baptist Church, Mrs. Fannie Bran, White Marsh,
  Va 7.15
Mrs. Brown, c/o Mrs. Harriet Watkins, Box 304, Gloucester,
  Va 3.00
Shepherdsville Baptist Church, Mrs. Helen Driver, Ark, Va..... 8.20
Bethel Baptist Church, Miss Helen Booth, Sign Pine, Va 15.30
Ever Blooming Garden Club, Mrs. Susie Brooks, Star Rt.,
  Glouster, Va 6.00
Mrs. Billy Georgery, James Store, Va... 3.35
Beres Baptist Church, Mr. G. M. Garnette, Glouster, Va 5.00
Mildred's Beauty Salon, White Marsh, Va. 5.00
Mr. William Foster's Store, Hayes, Va....................................... 1.06
Mrs. Louise Morris, Ark, Va... 3.00
Grace Institutional Baptist Church, Richmond, Va.,
  Rev. W. T. Barnes... 10.00

Funds Collected and Recorded, January 2–January 16 for
  Pilgrimage for Free Public School Education in
  Prince Edward $1,429.98
Public Offering   607.38

TOTAL RAISED AT PILGRIMAGE $2,037.36

*Monies and checks received from Pilgrimage.

Expenses of Pilgrimage for Free Public School Education

Individual receipts or bills of this itemized account are listed in a separate folder.

Telephone calls, incoming/outgoing, and telegrams .... $ 69.76
Norfolk Journal & Guide paid advertisement............................. 82.32
Photographs (copies may be purchased) 70.00
Secretary to president 75.00
Postage and other mailing costs 69.15
Supplies: Powell & Cole, Inc... 43.55
Additional Office help... 10.00
Car travel expense—including trips to Farmville, Norfolk,
  and Washington, D.C. 57.32
Food for pilgrimage guests 25.00
Installation and supervision of public address system 133.20

Richmond *Afro–American* paid advertisement..........................	67.20
Watkins Florist...	15.00
Programs for pilgrimage	29.00
Honorarium and travel expense of guest speaker....................	200.00

TOTAL TO DATE	$946.50
ESTIMATED COST	$600.00

There may be other expenses unknown to the president, who served as co-ordinator of pilgrimage, incurred by area vice-presidents. If so, it should be made known at this meeting.

Note: These documents are located in the Martin Luther King, Jr. Collection, Special Collections, Mugar Memorial Library, Boston University.

BIBLIOGRAPHY

Abernathy, Ralph. "Our Lives Were Filled with Action." In *Martin Luther King, Jr.* Ed. C. Eric Lincoln. New York: Hill & Wang, 1970. Pp. 219–27.

Adams, Frank. "Highlander Folk School: Getting Information, Going Back and Teaching It." *Harvard Educational Review*, no. 42, 4 (1972): 497–520.

——. *Unearthing Seed of Fire: The Idea of Highlander.* Winston-Salem, N.C.: John F. Blair, 1975.

Allen, Robert L. *Black Awakening in Capitalist America.* Garden City, N.Y.: Doubleday, 1970.

Aptheker, Herbert. *American Negro Slave Revolts.* New York: International Publishers, 1943.

Baldwin, James. *Go Tell It on the Mountain.* New York: Dial Press, 1963.

Banks, Melvin J. "The Pursuit Of Equality: The Movement For First Class Citizenship Among Negroes In Texas, 1920–1950." Ph.D. dissertation, Syracuse University, 1962.

Bartley, Numan V. *The Rise of Massive Resistance.* Baton Rouge: Louisiana State University Press, 1969.

Bell, Inge P. *CORE and the Strategy of Non-Violence.* New York: Random House, 1968.

Bennett, Lerone, Jr. *Confrontation: Black and White.* Baltimore: Penguin Books, 1965.

——. *The Negro Mood.* Chicago: Johnson Publishing Company, 1964.

——. "When the Man and the Hour are Met." In *Martin Luther King, Jr.* Ed. C. Eric Lincoln. New York: Hill & Wang, 1970. Pp. 7–39.

Blaustein, Albert, and Robert Zangrando. *Civil Rights and the American Negro.* New York: Washington Square Press, 1968.

Blumer, Herbert. "Collective Behavior." In *New Outlines of the Principles of Sociology.* Ed. A. M. Lee. New York: Barnes & Noble, 1946. Pp. 165–220.

Braden, Anne. *The Wall Between.* New York: Monthly Review Press, 1958.

Brink, William, and Louis Harris. *The Negro Revolution in America.* New York: Simon & Schuster, 1963.

Brooks, Thomas. *Walls Come Tumbling Down: A History of the Civil Rights Movement 1940–1970.* Englewood Cliffs, N.J.: Prentice-Hall, 1974.

Carson, Clayborne. *In Struggle: SNCC and the Black Awakening of the 1960s.* Cambridge: Harvard University Press, 1981.

Chafe, William H. *Civilities and Civil Rights.* New York: Oxford University Press, 1980.

Clark, Kenneth B. "The Civil Rights Movement: Momentum and Organizations." *Daedalus,* 95 (Winter 1966): pp. 595–625.

Clark, Septima P., and LeGette Blythe. *Echo in My Soul.* New York: E. P. Dutton, 1962.

Clarke, Jacquelyne J. "Goals and Techniques in Three Civil Rights Organizations in Alabama." Ph.D. dissertation, Ohio State University, 1960.

————. *These Rights They Seek: A Comparison of the Goals and Techniques of Local Civil Rights Organizations.* Washington, D.C.: Public Affairs Press, 1962.

Clayton, Edward, ed. *The SCLC Story.* Atlanta: Southern Christian Leadership Conference, 1964.

Corley, Robert G. "The Quest for Racial Harmony: Race Relations in Birmingham, Alabama, 1947–1963." Ph.D. dissertation, University of Virginia, 1979.

Cothran, Tillman, and William Phillips, Jr. "Negro Leadership in a Crisis Situation." *Phylon,* 22, no. 2 (1961): 107–18.

Dorman, Michael. *We Shall Overcome.* New York: Dial Press, 1964.

DuBois, W. E. B. *The Philadelphia Negro.* New York: Schocken Books, 1967.

Eschen, Donald von; Jerome Kirk; and Maurice Pinard. "The Organizational Substructure of Disorderly Politics." *Social Forces,* 49, no. 4 (1971): 529–44.

Fairclough, Adam. "A Study of the Southern Christian Leadership Conference and the Rise and Fall of the Nonviolent Civil Rights Movement." Ph.D. dissertation, University of Keele, 1977.

Flacks, Richard. "The Liberated Generation: An Exploration of the

Roots of Student Protest." *Journal of Social Issues*, 23 (July 1967): 52–75.

———. "Who Protests: The Social Bases of the Student Movement." In *Protest! Student Activism in America*. Ed. Julian Foster and Durward Long. New York: William Morrow, 1970. Pp. 134–57.

———. *Youth and Social Change*. Chicago: Rand McNally College Publishing Company, 1973.

Forman, James. *The Making of Black Revolutionaries*. New York: Macmillan, 1972.

Foster, Julian, and Durward Long, eds. *Protest: Student Activism in America*. New York: William Morrow, 1970.

Franklin, John Hope. *From slavery to Freedom*. New York: Alfred A. Knopf, 1968.

Franklin, John Hope, and Isidore Starr. *The Negro in 20th Century America*. New York: Vintage Book, 1967.

Frazier, E. Franklin. *The Negro Church in America*. New York: Schocken Books, 1963.

———. *The Negro in the United States*. New York: Macmillan, 1949.

Freeman, J. "The Origins of the Women's Liberation Movement." *American Journal of Sociology*, 78, no. 4 (January 1973): 792–811.

Gamson, William. *The Strategy of Social Protest*. Homewood, Ill.: Dorsey Press, 1975.

Garfinkel, Herbert. *When Negroes March*. Glencoe, Ill.: Free Press, 1959.

Garrow, David J. *Protest at Selma: Martin Luther King Jr. and the Voting Rights Act of 1965*. New Haven: Yale University Press, 1978.

Gilliam, Thomas J. "The Montgomery Bus Boycott of 1955–1956." M.A. thesis, Auburn University, 1968.

Gitlin, Todd. *The Whole World Is Watching*. Berkeley: University of California Press, 1980.

Gregg, Richard. *The Power of Nonviolence*. Philadelphia: J. B. Lippincott, 1959.

Haber, Robert A. "From Protest to Radicalism: An Appraisal of the Student Movement 1960." In *The New Student Left*. Ed. Mitchell Cohen and Dennis Hale. Boston: Dorsey, 1966. Pp. 41–49.

Harding, Vincent. "A Beginning in Birmingham." *Reporter*, 28 (June 6, 1963): 13–19.

———. *There Is a River: The Black Struggle for Freedom in America*. New York: Vintage Books, 1983.

Heirich, Max. *The Spiral of Conflict: Berkeley, 1964*. New York: Columbia University Press, 1971.

Himes, Joseph S. *Conflict and Conflict Management*. Athens: University of Georgia Press, 1980.

Hubbard, Howard. "Five Long Hot Summers and How They Grew." *Public Interest*, 12 (1968): 3–24.

Hughes, Langston. *Fight for Freedom*. New York: W. W. Norton, 1962.

Jenkins, J. Craig, and Charles Perrow. "Insurgency of the Powerless: Farm Workers Movements (1946–1972)." *American Sociological Review*, 42: 249–68.

Johnson, James Weldon. *Negro Americans, What Now?* New York: Viking Press, 1934.

Kellogg, Charles Flint. *NAACP: A History of the National Association for the Advancement of Colored People, Vol. I, 1909–1920*. Baltimore: Johns Hopkins University Press, 1967.

Killian, Lewis. *The Impossible Revolution, Phase II: Black Power and the American Dream*. New York: Random House, 1975.

Killian, Lewis, and Charles Grigg. *Racial Crisis in America: Leadership in Conflict*. Englewood Cliffs, N.J.: Prentice-Hall, 1964.

Killian, Lewis M., and Charles U. Smith. "Negro Protest Leaders in a Southern Community." *Social Forces*, 38, no. 3 (March 1960): 253–57.

King, Coretta. *My Life with Martin Luther King, Jr.* New York: Holt, Rinehart & Winston, 1969.

King, Martin Luther, Jr. *Stride Toward Freedom*. New York: Harper & Row, 1958.

——. *Why We Can't Wait*. New York: New American Library, 1963.

Krueger, Thomas A. *And Promises to Keep*. Nashville: Vanderbilt University Press, 1967.

Kunstler, William. *Deep in My Heart*. New York: William Morrow, 1966.

Lang, Kurt, and Gladys Lang. *Collective Dynamics*. New York: Crowell, 1961.

Lawson, Steven F. *Black Ballots: Voting Rights in the South, 1944–1969*. New York: Columbia University Press, 1976.

Lewis, Anthony. *Portrait of a Decade*. New York: Random House, 1964.

Lewis, David. *King: A Critical Biography*. New York: Praeger, 1970.

Lipset, Seymour Martin, and Sheldon S. Wolin. *The Berkeley Student Revolt*. Garden City, N.Y.: Doubleday, 1965.

Lipsky, Michael. "Protest as a Political Resource." *American Political Science Review*, 62 (1968): 1114–58.

Lomax, Louis E. *The Negro Revolt*. New York: New American Library, 1962.

Luper, Clara. *Behold the Walls*. N. P.: Jim Wire, 1979.

March, James, and Herbert Simon. *Organizations*. New York: John Wiley, 1958.

Martin, Tony. *Race First*. Westport, Conn.: Greenwood Press, 1976.

Marx, Gary. "Conceptual Problems in the Field of Collective Behavior." Paper presented at the American Sociological Association Meetings, Boston, 1979.

——. *Protest and Prejudice.* New York: Harper & Row, 1969.

Marx, Gary, and Michael Useem. "Majority Involvement in Minority Movements: Civil Rights, Abolition, Untouchability." *Journal of Social Issues,* 27 (1971): 81–104.

Matthews, Donald, and James Prothro. *Negroes and the New Southern Politics.* New York: Harcourt, Brace & World, 1966.

Mays, Benjamin E. "We Are Unnecessarily Excited." *New South,* 9, no. 2 (February 1954): 1–8.

Mays, Benjamin, and Joseph Nicholson. *The Negro Church.* New York: Arno Press, New York Times, 1933.

McAdam, Doug. "Political Process and the Black Protest Movement, 1948–1970." Ph.D. dissertation, State University of New York at Stony Brook, 1979.

——. *Political Process and the Development of Black Insurgency 1930–1970.* Chicago: University of Chicago Press, 1982.

McCarthy, John D. and Mayer Zald. "Resource Mobilization and Social Movements: A Partial Theory." *American Journal of Sociology,* 82, no. 6 (1977): 1212–41.

——. *The Trend of Social Movements in America: Professionalism and Resource Mobilization.* Morristown, N.J.: General Learning Press, 1973.

McMillen, Neil R. *The Citizens' Council: Organized Resistance to the Second Reconstruction, 1954–1964.* Urbana: University of Illinois Press, 1971.

NcNeil, Genna Rae. *Groundwork: Charles Hamilton Houston and the Struggle for Civil Rights.* Philadelphia: University of Pennsylvania Press, 1983.

McPhail, Clark. "Civil Disorder Participation: A Critical Examination of Recent Research." *American Sociological Review,* 36 (1971): 1058–73.

——. "Toward a Theory of Collective Behavior." Paper presented at Symposium on Symbolic Interaction, University of Southern California, 1978.

McPhail, Clark, and David Miller. "The Assembling Process: A Theoretical and Empirical Examination." *American Sociological Review,* 38 (December 1973): 721–35.

Meier, August. "Negro Protest Movements and Organizations." *The Journal of Negro Education,* Fall 1963, pp. 437–50.

——. "On the Role of Martin Luther King." *New Politics,* 4, no. 1 (1965): 56–58.

——. "The Conservative Militant." In *Martin Luther King, Jr.* Ed. C. Eric Lincoln. New York: Hill & Wang, 1970. Pp. 144–56.

Meier, August, and Elliot Rudwick. *Along the Color Line.* Urbana: University of Illinois Press, 1976.

------. *CORE: A Study in the Civil Rights Movement: 1942–1968.* New York: Oxford University Press, 1973.

------. *From Plantation to Ghetto.* New York: Hill & Wang, 1966.

------. "The Boycott Movement Against Jim Crow Streetcars in the South, 1900–1906." *Journal of American History,* LI (March 1969): 756–75.

Miller, Loren. *The Petitioners.* New York: Pantheon Books, 1966.

Miller, William R. *Martin Luther King, Jr.: His Life, Martyrdom and Meaning for the World.* New York: Weybright & Talley, 1968.

Morris, Aldon. "Black Southern Student Sit-In Movement: An Analysis of Internal Organization." *American Sociological Review,* 46 (December 1981): 755–67.

Muse, Benjamin. *Ten Years of Prelude.* New York: Viking Press, 1964.

Myrdal, Gunnar. *An American Dilemma.* New York: Harper & Brothers, 1944.

Oberschall, Anthony. *Social Conflict and Social Movements.* Englewood Cliffs, N.J.: Prentice-Hall, 1973.

Oppenheimer, Martin. "Genesis of the Southern Negro Student Movement." Ph.D. dissertation, University of Pennsylvania, 1963.

------. "The Southern Student Movement: Year I." *Journal of Negro Education,* 33 (1964): 396–403.

Orum, Anthony, M. "A Reappraisal of the Social and Political Participation of Negroes." *American Journal of Sociology,* 72, no. 1 (1966): 32–46.

------. *Black Students in Protest.* Washington, D.C.: American Sociological Association, 1972.

Owens, Leslie. *This Species of Property.* Oxford: Oxford University Press, 1976.

Park, Robert E., and Ernest W. Burgess. *Introduction to the Science of Sociology.* Chicago: University of Chicago Press, 1921.

Peck, James. *Freedom Ride.* New York: Simon & Schuster, 1962.

Pinard, Maurice; Jerome Kirk; and Donald von Eschen. "Process of Recruitment in the Sit-in Movement." In *The Black Revolt.* Ed. James A. Geschwender. Englewood Cliffs, N.J.: Prentice-Hall, 1971. Pp. 184–97.

Piven, Frances F., and Richard A. Cloward. *Poor People's Movements: How They Succeed, Why Some Fail.* New York: Vintage Books, 1979.

Ploski, Harry A., and Ernest Kaiser, eds. *Afro USA.* New York: Bellwether, 1971.

Proudfoot, Merrill. *Diary of a Sit-in.* New Haven: College and University Press Publishers, 1962.

Quint, Howard H. *Profile in Black and White: A Frank Portrait of South Carolina.* Washington, D.C.: Public Affairs Press, 1958.

Raines, Howell. *My Soul Is Rested.* New York: Bantam Books, 1977.

Reagon, Bernice. "Songs of the Civil Rights Movement 1955–1965: A Study in Culture History." Ph.D. dissertation, Howard University, 1975.

Reddick, Lawrence D. *Crusader Without Violence: A Biography of Martin Luther King, Jr.* New York: Harper & Brothers, 1959.

Ross, Joyce. *J. E. Spingarn and the Rise of NAACP, 1911–1939.* New York: Atheneum, 1972.

Rudwick, Elliott, and August Meier. "Organizational Structure and Goal Succession: A Comparative Analysis of the NAACP and CORE, 1964–1968." In *Black Revolt.* Ed. James Geschwender. Englewood Cliffs, N.J.: Prentice-Hall, 1971. Pp. 64–79.

Rustin, Bayard. *Strategies for Freedom.* New York: Columbia University Press, 1976.

Sale, Kirkpatrick. *SDS.* New York: Vintage, 1973.

St. James, Warren D. *The National Association for the Advancement of Colored People: A Case Study in Pressure Groups.* New York: Exposition Press, 1958.

Sarratt, Reed. *The Ordeal of Desegregation.* New York: Harper & Row, 1966.

Schlesinger, Arthur M., Jr. *A Thousand Days.* Boston: Houghton Mifflin, 1965.

———. *Robert Kennedy and His Times.* Boston: Houghton Mifflin, 1978.

Schwartz, Michael. *Radical Protest and Social Structure.* New York: Academic Press, 1976.

Sitkoff, Harvard. *A New Deal for Blacks.* New York: Oxford University Press, 1978.

Smelser, Neil. *Theory of Collective Behavior.* New York: Free Press, 1962.

Smith, Charles U. "Student Activism, Benign Racism and Scholarly Irresponsibility." *Florida A & M Research Bulletin,* 20, no. 1 (September 1974): 65–75.

Smith, Charles U., and Lewis M. Killian. *The Tallahassee Bus Protest.* New York: Anti-Defamation League of B'nai B'rith, 1958.

Southern Regional Council. "The Student Protest Movement, Winter 1960." *SRC–13,* April 1960.

———. "The Student Protest Movement: A Recapitulation." *SRC–21,* September 1961.

Thomas, Robert J., and William H. Friedland. "The United Farmworkers Union: From Mobilization to Mechanization?" Working Paper #269, Center for Research on Social Organization, University of Michigan.

Thompson, David C. *The Negro Leadership Class.* Englewood Cliffs, N.J.: Prentice-Hall, 1963.

Thornton, J. Mills, III. "Challenge and Response in the Montgomery

Bus Boycott of 1955–1956." *Alabama Review: A Quarterly Journal of Alabama History*, 32–33 (1979–80): 163–235.

Tilly, Charles. *From Mobilization to Revolution*. Reading, Mass.: Addison-Wesley, 1978.

Tilly, Charles; Louise Tilly; and Richard Tilly. *The Rebellious Century 1830–1930*. Cambridge: Harvard University Press, 1975.

Turner, Ralph, and Lewis Lillian. *Collective Behavior*. Englewood Cliffs, N.J.: Prentice-Hall, 1957.

Valien Preston. "The Montgomery Bus Protest as a Social Movement." In *Race Relations: Problem and Theory*. Ed. Jitsuichi Masuoka and Preston Valien. Chapel Hill: University of North Carolina Press, 1961. Pp. 112–27.

Walker, Eugene P. "A History of the Southern Christian Leadership Conference, 1955–56: The Evolution of a Southern Strategy for Social Change." Ph.D. dissertation, Duke University, 1978.

Walker, Jack L. "The Functions of Disunity: Negro Leadership in a Southern City." In *Racial Conflict*. Ed. Gary Marx. Boston: Little, Brown, 1971. Pp. 379–87.

Walton, Norman W. "The Walking City, a History of the Montgomery Boycott." *Negro History Bulletin*, 20 (October–November 1956): 17–20.

Washington, Joseph R., Jr. "Black Politics." In *The Black Church in America*. Ed. Hart M. Nelsen, Roytha L. Yokley, and Anne K. Nelson. New York: Basic Books, 1971. Pp. 299–315.

Washington, Joseph R., Jr. *Black Religion: The Negro and Christianity in the United States*. Boston: Beacon Press, 1964.

Watters, Pat. *Down to Now: Reflections on the Southern Civil Rights Movement*. New York: Pantheon Books, 1971.

Weber, Max. *The Theory of Social and Economic Organizations*. Ed. Talcott Parsons. New York: Free Press, 1947.

Weller, Jack M., and E. L. Quarantelli. "Neglected Characteristics of Collective Behavior." *American Journal of Sociology*, 79 (November 1973): 665–85.

Westby, David L. *The Clouded Vision: The Student Movement in the United States in the 1960s*. London: Associated University Press, 1976.

Westin, Alan, and Barry Mahoney. *The Trial of Martin Luther King*. New York: Thomas Y. Crowell, 1974.

White, Robert M. "The Tallahassee Sit-ins and CORE: A Non-violent Revolutionary Submovement." Ph.D. dissertation, Florida State University, 1964.

Wilhoit, Francis M. *The Politics of Massive Resistance*. New York: George Braziller, 1973.

Wolff, Miles. *Lunch at the Five and Ten*. New York: Stein & Day, 1970.

Yeakey, Lamont H. "The Montgomery Alabama Bus Boycott." Ph.D. dissertation, Columbia University, 1979.

Zald, Mayer N., and Roberta Ash. "Social Movement Organizations: Growth, Decay and Change." *Social Forces*, 44, no. 3 (March 1966): 327–41

Zald, Mayer N., and John D. McCarthy. *The Dynamics of Social Movements*. Cambridge, Mass.: Winthrop Publishers, 1979.

Zinn, Howard. "Albany: A Study in National Responsibility." *Southern Regional Council*, 22 (1962): v–35.

———. "Albany." *Southern Regional Council*, 22 (January 1962): 1–30.

———. *SNCC: The New Abolitionists*. Boston: Beacon Press, 1964.

INDEX